ARISTOCRATS

Stella Tillyard studied English Literature at Oxford, and her PhD on English art of the early 20th century was published as *The Impact of Modernism*. She has taught at Harvard (where she was Knox Fellow) and at UCLA. She lives in London and Florence, and is at present writing a book on militarism and masculinity, to be published by Chatto & Windus.

BY STELLA TILLYARD

The Impact Of Modernism

Aristocrats:
Caroline, Emily, Louisa and Sarah Lennox
1740–1832

Stella Tillyard

ARISTOCRATS
aroline, Emily, Louisa and Sarah Lenn
1740–1832

VINTAGE

Published by Vintage 1995

8 10 9

Copyright © Stella Tillyard 1994

The right of Stella Tillyard to be identified as the author
of this work has been asserted by her in accordance with
the Copyright, Designs and Patents Act, 1988

First published in Great Britain by
Chatto & Windus Ltd, 1994

Vintage
Random House, 20 Vauxhall Bridge Road, London SW1V 2SA

Random House Australia (Pty) Limited
20 Alfred Street, Milsons Point, Sydney
New South Wales 2061, Australia

Random House New Zealand Limited
18 Poland Road, Glenfield,
Auckland 10, New Zealand

Random House South Africa (Pty) Limited
PO Box 337, Bergvlei, South Africa

Random House UK Limited Reg. No. 954009

A CIP catalogue record for this book
is available from the British Library

ISBN 0 09 947711 4

Printed and bound in Great Britain by
The Guernsey Press Co. Ltd., Guernsey, Channel Islands

CONTENTS

For Deborah Colvin and Allen Martens,
who encouraged me

Preface

'Sally's fears for her little one are, thank God, over. The nursing scheme would not do; she had quantities of milk, which makes one regret the more that it would not do, but her nipple could not be drawn out without the greatest difficulty, and the child not being strong could not do it. It was ill from being kept from the breast for so long, but now it has a good clean nurse, sucks, sleeps and thrives.'

This letter, written by Lady Caroline Fox to Emily, Duchess of Leinster about their sister Sarah is, in parts, so blatantly modern that it is hard to believe that it is dated 6 June 1769, and that it is almost 225 years old. It is not just the 'thank God' and the nipples. Its anxiety and relief create a resonant feeling that seems to erase the centuries between its writing and our reading.

Thousands of such letters – between sisters, husbands and wives, servants and employers, parents and children – are the raw material for this book. It tells the story of Caroline, Emily, Louisa and Sarah Lennox, a story of high politics, romance, family life and tragedy that begins in 1744 as the Jacobites were planning their last, desperate assault on the Hanoverian throne and ends in 1832, five years before the beginning of the Victorian age. Nearly a century's worth of letters, and from them time and again we get this sense of intimacy. And it is not just that the Lennox sisters write in a way which makes us feel close to them; they also write about things that are as important to us as they were to them. They discuss love, marriage, food, clothes, political ideas and scandals, war, books, period pains. Everything from conception to death is there, written in voices that we have scarcely ever heard, the voices of eighteenth-century women.

But when we look again, sympathy dissolves into strangeness. Caroline Fox's frank description of breast-feeding problems may be modern, but wet nursing is not. When she worries about a son who is ill, we immediately sympathise, but the doctors' cures – mercury sulphide and ground woodlice – make us recoil. Emily and her husband grumble about their large family, but large means not 4 children or even 7, but 19. Caroline sends Emily news of Sarah's impending marriage and notes with apparent sincerity, 'happily for her she is not the least in love'. These vignettes make us aware of the distance which separates their response to love, marriage, child-rearing and scientific knowledge from ours, and may make us feel they are beyond our reach and understanding.

This sense of distance is heightened because the Lennox sisters' circumstances were extraordinary. They were rich and well educated, speaking French almost as well as English. Their connections gave them access to the newest ideas, the latest books and plays, the most fashionable thinkers, painters, doctors and all the products of the new consumer age. They were the daughters of one Cabinet minister and duke and sisters of another. Caroline Lennox married a man who, if he had played his cards better, might have become prime minister, and she was the mother of the most famous opposition politician of the eighteenth century. Emily Lennox married the senior peer of Ireland, and one of her sons became a prominent republican revolutionary. Louisa married Ireland's richest man. Sarah caught the eye of the young George III and, half resisting, half complying, allowed herself to toy with the idea of being made Queen of England. There is little familiar here, except for the way in which male lives and opinions shaped female ones.

Despite all this – the scores of servants, country houses and ruling families – the intimacy remains; there is a dual sense of closeness and distance. It is this feeling, and the mixture of sympathy and astonishment that it evokes, that I have tried to capture in the pages that follow. I have written the book as a narrative so that commentary intrudes as little as possible on the Lennox sisters' lives and their emotional freshness. But I have framed the narrative with a prologue and an epilogue and broken it with short sections between chapters. I hope these breaks will not only bring readers up short and remind them of the distance between the eighteenth century and our own, but also hint at continuity. These are not, as sections between chapters usually are, discourses on memory, history or war. They are descriptions of things we share, ordinary milestones of innumerable lives: birth, naming, marriage and death.

Finally I have tried to make this book an amalgam of biography and history. The astonishing richness of my sources – thousands of letters, pictures, household accounts and rules, an inventory, library lists, travel journals, prayers, verses, autopsies, maps, parks and buildings – has allowed me to build up a picture of the every day as well as the dramatic in the Lennox sisters' lives. I have tried to merge genres in the belief that biography (especially biography that deals, as this does, with romance and royalty) often gives intimacy without context, and history without biography offers context without the warmth of individual lives. And what lives they were!

Acknowledgements

I would like to thank the staff of the following libraries, record offices and archives, without whom my research would not have been possible: the Bodleian Library, Oxford, the British Library, Cork University Library, the Photographic Survey in the Courtauld Institute, the Greater London Record Office, the Guildhall Library, the London Library, the Mellon Centre for the Study of British Art, the National Library of Ireland, the National Portrait Gallery, the National Register of Archives, Nottingham University Library, the Public Record Office of Northern Ireland, Trinity College Dublin, the West Suffolk Record Office, the Witt Library and the Yale Center for British Art.

Many individuals helped in researching the book and making its writing better and easier. First I must thank Dorothy Porter, whose dramatic rendition of the highlights of Sarah Lennox's life gave me the germ of the book. Roy Porter's steady supply of bibliographies and comments have been invaluable: the enthusiasm of both has been unflagging and accompanied with the bonus of multi-coloured Balkan Sobranies. Brian Moore advised me early on to keep my story firmly focused on the sisters' lives and I have tried to do just that despite the temptations of the lives of Charles James Fox and Lord Edward Fitzgerald that haunted the narrative. Jayne

Lewis read the earliest bits of manuscript and I gratefully absorbed her encouragement. Simon Schama's enthusiasm and optimism has been like a beacon on the horizon, making me feel that the world of infinite words and boundless confidence is possible; he and Ginny Papaiannou have also been friends and co-conspirators in a host of plans. John Brewer has been everything to me and I am tempted to thank him for cooking, child-minding and proof-reading and to add that without him none of this would have been possible.

At various stages along the way I have been grateful for the ideas and advice of Louise Lippincott, with whom I discussed sublime portraiture; Teri Edelstein; Amanda Vickery who has kept me *au courant* with the latest developments in feminist historiography; Susie Steinbach; Robert Illiffe, who told me about Newton's conquest of aristocratic drawing-rooms; and Ann Bermingham. Sally Laird and Charles Jennings asked me useful questions and shared many a gossipy lunch. Rachel Watson asked for (and I hope has got) information about landaus and broughams and other Georgette Heyerish conveyances. Brian Allen helped me with portraits, provenances and the peerage. Peter Mandler, Juliet Gardiner, Claire l'Enfant and Dawn Colvin all read the manuscript; their comments have helped enormously with revisions. Anne McDermid has been unflaggingly supportive of the project. Jenny Uglow has been a marvellous editor.

Many people, on both sides of the Irish Sea, have made the writing of this book possible. First I must thank Guy Strutt, who entertained me at Terling, lent me typescripts and books and introduced me to Eleanor Burgess. By copying Louisa Conolly's letters to Sarah Lennox, Eleanor Burgess has effectively saved them from oblivion. She not only gave them to me, but also gave me meals, information and Irish contacts; I cannot be too grateful to her. The present Duke of Leinster greeted my unexpected appearance with calm and fortitude. He showed me the book of Household Rules which I used to reconstruct life at Carton in the 1760s. Lord Napier and

Ettrick similarly coped with my anxious enquiries about generations of Napiers, Lennox-Napiers and so on. David Legg-Willis, Valerie Griffiths and the staff at Goodwood House generously gave me prints and showed me about the park. The Earl Bathurst and Mrs Charlotte Morrison have been generous with permissions. When I turned up unannounced at Carton the staff who watch over the empty house showed me round and let me take pictures. At Castletown successive curators and staff allowed me to walk about at will, moving carpets and furniture and taking photographs in a way unthinkable in an English country house. In Celbridge Mrs Lena Boylan showed me typescripts of manuscripts salvaged from Castletown, and the staff of St Raphael's, Celbridge, showed me round Sarah's house which is in their grounds. Desmond Guinness showed me his pictures and gave me invaluable contacts and Marianne Faithfull showed me round her house. Desmond FitzGerald, Anne Crookshank, Eleanor Grene and Dennis Fitzgerald gave me references and encouragement. Dick Hill gave me tea and an exhibition of Irish charm that was without parallel.

Picture acknowledgments

Unless otherwise stated, pictures have come from private collections and are reproduced by kind permission of the owners. Copyrights and permissions for the remaining pictures are as follows:

Colour: No. 6. Sir Joshua Reynolds, British, 1723–1792, Lady Sarah Bunbury Sacrificing to the Graces, oil on canvas, 1765, 242 × 151.5 cm, Mr. and Mrs. W. W. Kimball Collection, 1922.4468, photograph © 1993, The Art Institute of Chicago. All Rights Reserved.

Black and white: Nos. 4, 9, 11, 15, 45, 46, 47, 60, Copyright British Museum. Nos. 14, 19, 29, 30, 31, 33, 34, 36, 37, 38, 48, by courtesy of the Trustees of the National Portrait Gallery, London. No. 16, Copyright Guildhall Library, Corporation of London. No. 25, by courtesy of the Fogg Art Museum, Harvard University Art Museums. Bequest of Elizabeth Sears Warren. Nos. 53, 56, 57, 58, 59, by permission of the British Library.

Prologue

On a bleak spring evening in 1741 a crowd gathered in a dark, narrow London street. At its edge well-to-do City merchants on their way westwards through Hatton Garden mingled with the wretched and curious poor, washed up from tenements to the North, East and South, looking for a handout or a meal. In the middle, dozens of women in their best clothes jostled and flowed towards the door of a large double-fronted house like filings drawn towards a magnet. The light filtering out of the house windows sent dim rays over the crowd, illuminating little bundles tied in rags and wrapped in flannel blankets; some sleeping, some gazing about, some sick and crying. All the women gathered round the door carried these small emblems of shame and poverty.

For an hour the crowd ebbed and surged and waited. Then at eight o'clock, in imitation of the mothers' misery and sin, the light in the house's entry way went out. The door opened. The crowd fell silent and a bell rang. A woman sprang forward and plunged with her child into the darkness. The door closed behind her.

Inside the house the woman was ushered into a room on the right of the hall. She gave her name but it was not written down. Then she watched as her child, a boy, was stripped layer by layer of the stain of her folly and poverty. First his clothes were taken off and cast away. Then a little memento she had hoped would stay longer with him than she could was catalogued and set aside. Then Doctor Nesbitt, donating his services for the occasion, inspected the child and pronounced him sound. Finally he was given a number, One, as the first child in the hospital. Distraught and relieved, the mother looked on in silence. A few minutes later she was dismissed, came out of the house and lost herself in the darkness of the crowd. The door closed behind her.

Soon the bell rang again. Another woman darted up with her bundle, entered the house and returned empty-handed. The bell rang, again and again, until thirty women had taken in their children and come out without them and the Foundling Hospital was full.

For four days the house was quiet. The infants slept and sucked, motherless and nameless. Then, on the evening of 29 March, Hatton Garden was crowded and noisy once again. Heavy four-wheeled carriages, with lamps burning and footmen aloft, lumbered across the cobbles. On their sides were tiny emblems with mottoes curling underneath that dignified those inside. By the lighted entrance of number 61, the footmen jumped down and opened the heavy leather-covered doors. Noble men and noble women, physicians, merchants, doctors and Members of Parliament were handed out. Taking care to avoid the mud, they went inside and up the stairs. The state room on the first floor was alive with light. Light twinkled and sparkled from belts and buckles, from necklaces and ornaments. It lay puddled like mercury in the folds of silk gowns and in silver bowls and cups. Servants carrying candles went up and down the stairs and announced the new arrivals: the Duke of Bedford, President of the Hospital; the Earl and Countess of Pembroke; the Duke and Duchess of Richmond with their eldest daughter; William and Anne Hogarth; Lord and Lady Albemarle; Captain Robert Hudson; Mr Lewis Way. Their names rang out over the rustle of gowns, the clink of shoe buckles and the murmur of greetings.

The company sat and the Reverend Samuel Smith read evening prayers. Then the infants, numbered one to thirty, were brought in for christening. Beyond the impromptu font sat not their mothers and fathers but a surrogate family of the finest, wealthiest and worthiest in the land. The Reverend Samuel Smith took the first child from his nurse, approached the font and dabbed the baby's forehead with holy water. The little child, newly clothed in lace and cotton, with a cap jammed tightly on his hairless head, was baptised Thomas Coram, after the hospital's founder. Eunice Coram followed. The aristocracy lent the children their family names. Charlotte Finch was named for the Duchess of Somerset, John Russell for the Duke of Bedford, Charles Lennox for the Duke of Richmond, Sarah Cadogan for his wife. Caroline Lennox was named for the Duke's daughter, an anxious, intelligent girl of eighteen sitting with her parents. Secure in their names, the rich and the mighty bestowed them on little children, sending them forth watered with greatness. Their impoverished, orphaned little doubles would, as long as they lived, reflect the importance of their patrons.

After the baptismal ceremony the company departed, clattering westwards in their carriages out of their namesakes' lives. Lady Caroline Lennox, trundling back to Richmond House in Whitehall, left little Caroline to a life in the shadow. Darkness descends over her as it did over the house in Hatton Garden that night. Perhaps she became a servant, perhaps even a milliner or a mantua maker. But it was just as likely that, like one of Lady Caroline's own children, she would die of a fever before she could understand that she had been orphaned into a life of misery.

CHAPTER
ONE
❖
CAROLINE
AND EMILY

PART ONE
'I know the step I am going to take is a wrong one'.
Caroline to Henry Fox, 28 April 1744.

A t the age of eighteen, Caroline Lennox was a plump,
nervous girl with hurried, wide-open dark-brown eyes,
a small mouth dimpled at the corners and a full, soft chin inherited from her father, the second Duke of Richmond. Her
eyebrows were straight and dark and long. Her nose turned
up slightly at the end.

Caroline was born in Richmond House in Whitehall in
1723, the first of seven children of the Duke and Duchess who
survived to maturity. Richmond House occupied a commanding position in London and Caroline grew up watching
the world go past its windows. Her father had inherited a
dilapidated brick house in Whitehall. In the 1730s a large
chunk of his income was spent building an imposing three-
storeyed pedimented modern residence with gardens on one
side and stables the other. The drawing-room looked north
over the Privy Garden, an open space with shrubs and grass
which had once been part of the Royal Palace of Whitehall.
Members of Parliament, clerks, messenger boys, friends and
lovers met there to gossip, flirt and swap stories. To one side

of the Privy Garden stood the Banqueting House, decorated by Charles I, Caroline Lennox's great-great-grandfather. Beyond that again the clean white spire of St Martin-in-the-Fields rose in front of the theatres in Covent Garden and Drury Lane and the slums of Seven Dials.

To the south and east of Richmond House a lawn sloped down to a balustraded terrace which looked over London's busiest street, the River Thames. On a fine day the occupants of the house could sit on sheltered benches, watch the sun coming up beyond the dome of St Paul's Cathedral, and follow its progress across the river to the slums of Southwark, round past the pavilions and long walks of Vauxhall Pleasure Gardens and see it sink in the west behind the villages of Richmond and Kew.

The Thames carried people and goods up and down and from side to side. Travellers from all over the world, after disembarking down river, continued upstream in smaller boats. From London Basin, where large merchantmen moored, lightermen in skiffs and barges brought the city supplies: flour and grain from East Anglia, fish from the North Sea, wine and cognac from France, fine wool from Spain, silk from China, carpets from Turkey and timber and spices from Madagascar and the East Indies. Occasionally the lighterman brought more durable plunder: paintings from Italy and The Netherlands and crate-loads of Roman statues, some lacking arms, some heads, some legs, that were reassembled and displayed in the halls and libraries of the rich. Snug in their niches, these remade senators and muses guarded public policy and private pleasures, lending the dignity of antiquity to political squabbles and experiments with electromagnetism alike.

Boats also brought more mundane things: wax and tallow to light the houses of London, stone to build them and coal to heat them. The coal barges, disgorging their dusty contents into basements along the riverbank, were of particular importance to Caroline Lennox and her father. For it was in coal that the Richmond family fortunes lay, and it was due to the huge expansion of the coal trade in the eighteenth century that Caroline's father was a man of such immense wealth.

Caroline's grandfather, the first Duke of Richmond, was born in 1672. He was the youngest of Charles II's many illegitimate sons. His mother, Caroline's great-grandmother, was Louise de Kéroualle who, as a young woman of twenty, was sent over to England with Louis XIV's courtiers and diplomats conducting the negotiations for what became the secret and notorious Treaty of Dover. Louise ousted Charles's reigning mistress and, over the years did the King, her country and herself stout service. The Treaty, signed in 1670, bound England and France to peaceful coexistence and held till the revolution of 1688 brought William of Orange to the English throne. Louise was created Duchess of Portsmouth by Charles II. Louis XIV, for his part, recognised her service to his country by granting her the Stuart family lands in France. With the land came two châteaux, Aubigny and La Verrerie. Louise eventually retired to Aubigny and Caroline visited her there in the late 1720s.

In return for royal largesse, Louise gave Charles years of service in the bedchamber and a son, Caroline's grandfather, named Charles Lennox. During his boyhood the child was given a plethora of titles to cover his bastardy. He was created Duke of Richmond, Baron of Settrington and Earl of March in the English peerage, and Baron Methuen of Tarbolton, Earl of Darnley and Duke of Lennox in the Scottish peerage. When his mother died he added the title of Duc d'Aubigny to this list and did homage for it to the French crown.

To this sonorous but worthless panoply Charles II added something more substantial: an annuity of two thousand pounds and a royalty of twelvepence per chauldron on coal dues at Newcastle. In effect the young Duke was given a substantial slice of the crown's tax revenue, which increased in direct proportion to mining and manufacturing.

As manufacturing increased, so did the number of laden barges leaving the Tyne and the wealth of the Dukes of Richmond. At the beginning of the eighteenth century the coal dues already produced five thousand pounds a year, a sum on which an aristocrat, his family, servants and horses could all live in style. By the 1790s the amount had shot up to over twenty thousand pounds annually, prompting the radical Tom Paine to remark 'the Duke of Richmond takes away as much for himself as would maintain two thousand poor and aged persons'. Little of this wealth would come down to Caroline, of course. It was mostly reserved for the male heir, for the continuation of the family line and maintenance of the family properties. But in her childhood Caroline basked in the warm glow of the coal money. She was painted, pampered, richly clothed and well fed. If her own share of the family's dividend from Newcastle, her dowry, was relatively modest, it was backed up by an immense family fortune and enhanced by a great name. With ten thousand pounds and the Lennox name and connections, Caroline was well endowed for the only career open to a woman of her class – marriage into a noble and wealthy family and a job at Court.

When Charles II died in 1685, Louise de Kéroualle took her son back to her château at Aubigny and brought him up as a Catholic and a Frenchman. Duke of Richmond as he was, Charles Lennox was always a Frenchman first and an Englishman second. As a young man he served with the French army against the Prince of Orange. But, like his mother, Richmond had an eye for the main chance. Realising that his titles, his annuity and his coal dues would make him a man of far greater influence and consequence than his French army pay, he renounced his religion (consoling himself with the mysteries of Freemasonry instead), and came to England.

Richmond successfully petitioned William III for his titles, income and property, becoming, by way of payment, a staunch Anglican, a Whig and a supporter of the Hanoverian succession. His children and grandchildren became English subjects and courtiers in their turn. Once he had regained his property and revenues, Caroline's grandfather began to look around for a job at Court and a military commission. But he was conspicuously unsuccessful, partly because he was a new-comer tainted with Frenchness and partly because he was better at holding his drink than any steady employment. So he spent much of his time hunting in Sussex, where he eventually bought the country estate of Goodwood near Chichester, and gambling in London and on the Continent. He was cosmopolitan, charming and feckless, equally at home in Paris and in London. His sense of belonging in France was inherited by his children and grandchildren who always felt that the social and sexual casualness of French aristocratic life chimed better with the family's easy-going informality than the hectic mixture of restraint and intrigue that characterised the English court.

The Lennox children were almost bilingual and read French as easily as English. In Caroline's library and in those of her sisters, French books took up almost as much room as English ones. French was the language of philosophers and the language of romance. Cheap novels, or 'story books', as Caroline called them, books too ephemeral to merit binding and shelving in the library, were very often imported from Paris and stacked in Caroline's dressing-room, and in them, romantic heroines, faced with moral and marital dilemmas, whispered, schemed and (usually) capitulated in the language of love and dalliance. So, for Caroline, dropping into French at amorous or difficult moments had both literary and family sanction.

On his trips to London and to Europe, Caroline's grand-father put off boredom with long bouts of gambling, playing for large stakes with British officers and courtiers who thronged London and the Low Countries during the wars with Louis XIV. In The Hague in 1719, Richmond racked up a large debt to the Irish Earl of Cadogan, one of Marlborough's staff officers and confidants. To pay him off and to seal his friendship, Richmond gave his heir, the Earl of March, as husband for Cadogan's daughter Sarah, accepting a reduction of five thousand pounds in her marriage settlement to make up the difference. The wedding, as Caroline's father was later fond of telling her and her siblings, was very quickly arranged. He was eighteen years old and about to embark on the Grand Tour. His bride to be was only thirteen. They were brought together and told by their fathers that they were going to be married straight away. The little girl was speechless but the horrified young man burst out, 'surely they are not going to marry me to that dowdy!' After this fruitless objection the ceremony was performed. When it was over, the Earl of March, accompanied by his tutor, set off for Italy. His wife went back to the nursery. Thus, in an extreme form, Caroline's parents acted out the powerlessness of aristocratic children, who could become pawns in a parental chess game, who were sacrificed for family alliances or sold for money and prestige.

When he grew up, Caroline's father developed a taste for practical jokes, and came to see his marriage as one of them. He loved to tell its story to his children because it ended happily. When he returned from his continental travels three years later, the Earl was very reluctant to call on and claim his wife. He went to the theatre instead. Like many of those present, he was more occupied in looking at the boxes and stalls than the stage. Noticing one particularly sumptuous young woman, he turned to his neighbour and asked who she was. 'You must be a stranger in London,' came the reply, 'not to know the toast of the town, the beautiful Lady March.'

It was a dénouement as sentimental as Caroline's father could have wished, and he followed it with a well publicised happy marriage. He was never ashamed to demonstrate, in portraits, letters and drawing-rooms his love for his wife and children. Horace Walpole, a voluptuary of gossip who for nearly half a century recorded the scandals of the Whig circle in which the Lennoxes moved, noticed his familial content. At a ball given by a family friend in November 1741, Walpole reported that Caroline's father sat by her mother all night, 'kissing her hand and gazing at his beautiful daughters'. The Duchess returned her husband's feelings. After a quarrel in September 1740 she wrote to him, 'of all the time that I have loved you, I never felt more love and tenderness for you than I did yesterday. I haunted all the places where you had been last. One was to go among your trees where you stood so long on Sunday . . . and as much as I love you I hate myself.'

The second Duke of Richmond's marriage was the most dramatic event of his life. It was involuntarily undertaken, done to him rather than by him, and in it lay the seeds of Caroline's own fascination with the institution of marriage itself. Caroline inherited a good deal of the first Duke of Richmond's recklessness, although it was overlaid with her father's prudence and carefulness, and she believed that love and impulsiveness went together. She championed marriages for love, but at the same time she knew that, although her parents' marriage had been at best a matter of convenience, at worst a cynical sacrifice of youth to pleasure, it was a marriage that worked. She could neither condone nor condemn arranged marriages, and since that was what her parents wanted for her, she solved her dilemma first by remaining unmarried for much longer than most girls and then by making a spectacular choice that flouted her parents' wishes.

After his own marriage Caroline's father continued to take what life had to offer with gratitude and restraint, seeing no reason to become a man who seized the initiative. As a result his career was dignified rather than spectacular. After the accession of George II, the Duke was appointed a Lord of the Bedchamber, while Caroline's mother became Lady of the Bedchamber to Queen Caroline. Once ensconced in his post, Caroline's father pursued his earnest desire to erase any lingering traces of wild roistering, whoring and gambling from his family's reputation. He was a model grandson to Louise de Kéroualle, soaking up without complaint the emotion and expectation she diverted on to him from her unsatisfactory son. When the first Duke died in 1723, Louise shed what she described as 'very bitter' tears. After all, she told the new Duke, it was her son that she had lost. But she recovered quickly, and added that she would survive her bereavement because she knew her grandson loved her. 'I dare flatter myself, my dear boy, that you have a sincere tenderness and affection for a grandmother who has the most lifelong devotion to you; and I shall not consider myself so unhappy, my dear Lord, if you are just a little bit sensible of it.' She felt that to make an adequate demonstration of his love, the second Duke should produce an heir. The Richmond line needed securing and, besides, she said, she wanted another portrait to hang in her château alongside the previous Ducs d'Aubigny. She was pleased enough with the birth of Caroline in 1723, but disappointed with the Duchess of Richmond a year later. Sarah's second child, a boy, lived only a few hours. Louise wrote and, in a perfunctory way, thanked God that Sarah hadn't died too. But, she went on relentlessly, 'She has not kept her promise to me though. For in her last letter she promised me a son, but – the dear child – I'm sure she is very sorry to have failed in her promise! But I hope that her third will be an increase of the right sort in your family.'

The Duke and Duchess worked tirelessly to gratify this hard taskmistress. They had twelve children, seven of whom lived to maturity. After Caroline's birth in 1723 came Emily, in 1731. Charles, who eventually became the third Duke, was born in 1735, too late for Louise de Kéroualle, who battled on in hopes until she was eighty-nine, but had finally died a year before. George, in homage to the King, arrived in 1737, then Louisa in 1743, Sarah in 1745 and Cecilia in 1750.

Throughout her childhood Caroline was continually hustled from place to place as the Court moved about, disbanded and re-formed. If the King was at St James's, the

Lennox family could live in the comfort of Richmond House a mile or so away. But if the King moved to Kensington, Hampton Court or Windsor the whole Lennox family went too. Each move of the Court was like an army decamping: the crush and chaos of wagons piled high with family furniture, silver and clothes chests; the barking of dogs, neighing of horses, crying of children and shouting of courtiers and servants; the noisy rumble through the streets; the undignified scramble for the best lodgings at the other end.

During the social and parliamentary season when the Court was assembled, Caroline might not see her parents for days on end. She lived in their lodgings, chattering in French to her nanny and later doing her lessons with her French governess, while her parents went to work. Caroline's mother waited on the Queen, carrying out tasks whose humbleness was barely mitigated by her salary of £500 a year or the dignity of her office. She ordered meals and clothes, dispatched servants to fetch books, cards, prints, workbags or pastimes, and rationed visitors. Caroline's father performed similar jobs for the King. In compensation for the dullness of their days, Lords and Ladies of the Bedchamber were the monarchs' companions and perhaps their friends.

For a woman at Court, waiting on the Queen was the highest available position. It marked the limit of her possible career. But for men, the Bedchamber was only the beginning: an ambitious courtier used the job as a jumping off point. He saw and perhaps helped determine who was in and who was out of favour and he was ideally placed to lobby the monarch for a better position. Caroline's father, however, was ambitious not for advancement but for sobriety and dignity. He stayed on for seven years, the picture of steadiness but not of success. The King called him an affectionate and sincere friend, and in 1735 rewarded him with the Mastership of the Horse, a step up in rank but sideways into the royal stable. There Richmond managed the monarch's movement from palace to palace and from England to the Continent faithfully until his death. It was his job to accompany the retinue wherever it went in England. When George departed for Hanover at the beginning of each summer, the Duke went as far as Harwich, where he handed the King over to the Royal Navy and to his Hanoverian counterpart and gratefully departed for Goodwood and other pursuits.

Richmond's life was not all courtly business. The Duke inherited his father's interest in Freemasonry, enjoyed practical jokes and revelled in the theatre. When he sat to Philips in the late 1740s, he presented himself as both courtier and collector and a private man. He put on formal but by no means ducal dress, alluding to his station by wearing the royal-blue ribbon of the Order of the Garter. One hand he kept gloved like that of a courtier, the other left bare like that of a man about to greet his onlooker in an intimate and informal way. On the table he put a document referring to himself as Master of the Horse. Behind him, opening out of the formal drawing-room is the library at Richmond House, a secluded room with leather-bound volumes ranged along its shelves. In the doorway stands a draped classical figure, gesturing at once to the Duke's status as a man of learning, his position in the Society of Antiquaries and his love of collecting.

Richmond collected ideas as well as objects. As a follower of Newton and something of a gentleman scientist, he patronised research into marine life in the Solent and built up a collection of exotic plants and animals. He belonged to the Royal Society and often entertained scientists and savants who toured Europe's drawing-rooms explaining the latest theories and discoveries. Medicine was another of his hobbies and he was an eager participant in new operations and cures, believing that the body could be the site of learning as well as the home of the soul.

Objects of all sorts accompanied new ideas into Richmond's houses. He amassed statuary and paintings, and became president of both the Royal Society of Antiquaries and the Society of Arts. But his special passion was for plants and animals. Newton had brought order to the physical universe, so the story ran, and now scores of collectors were trying to do the same for flora and fauna, with menageries and botanical gardens.

In the 1730s scores of animals were brought to Goodwood and many were eventually housed in heated catacombs under the park. In this menagerie were five wolves, two tigers, two lions, three bears, two leopards, a chimpanzee, three racoons, an armadillo and a host of lesser birds and beasts. The Duke was constantly on the look out for rarities and chafed at failure to secure them. His fellow courtier Lord Hervey, who was not an animal lover, joked that the erotic behaviour of Richmond's animals was 'an allegorical epitomy of the whole matrimonial world'. But the Duke's interest in the animal kingdom was more than simply materialistic. He felt that capturing and cataloguing the beasts of the wild brought them out from disordered nature into the ambit of human rationality. By virtue of being studied, animals became almost human, and they certainly became beloved. When a lioness from the menagerie died, Richmond built her a magnificent tomb in the Goodwood grounds where she reposes in marble amongst the trees.

Owning a menagerie, then, involved much more than admiration of animals. Acquisition and taxonomy were forms of conquest, of bringing strange species under man's control. Richmond's collections were part of the explosion in consumption that accompanied industrialisation and the acquisition of foreign territories. The Duke wanted as many animals and plants (he was particularly keen on trees that could fit in with prevailing tastes in landscaping) from all over the world and he paid a lot of money for rare animals and seeds and hired experts to find and look after them. Tigers came from India, lions from Africa, monkeys from the East Indies, vultures and bears from Europe and North America, cedars from Lebanon and maples from New England.

The women of Goodwood also went on this journey of discovery and ownership. In the 1730s naval captains returning to Portsmouth often sailed home with sacks full of shells for the Duchess and her daughters. The Duchess, Caroline and, as soon as she was old enough to help, Emily spent hours arranging the shells into intricate patterns which were built into a grotto in the park. The shell grotto was a tiny, vaulted room where the discarded houses of sea-creatures, flung by the seas on to distant beaches, were carefully sorted and assembled into a rococo caprice that celebrated nature's diversity, man's seafaring prowess and women's artifice. Cornucopias of shells were filled with shell fruits and shell sweetcorn. Shells covered the walls like stuccoed plaster. They were woven into ribbons and bows, twisted into ropes and written in initials: CR for the Duke, EL for Emily Lennox and CL for Caroline.

The shell house was a microcosm of the Lennox family's world, displaying a love for order, rationality and the modernity represented by the natural sciences. But it was also about impersonation and play, plain on the outside, riotous and eccentric within, a place where shells were turned into apples and pears and ribbons. Science and feeling, order and capriciousness mingled together. It was crucial to the family that rationality and sentiment were not exclusive; the Duke and his children always wanted to show both.

Growing up in this world of exalted sense and feeling, Caroline Lennox inherited her parents' belief in rationality and politeness and openly stressed their emphasis on feeling and passion. But she also came to long for a world in which there could be, sometimes, if not privacy, then seclusion and time for private reflection.

From the very beginning, Caroline was an anxious little girl, living her life in what she later called a 'hurry of spirits'. She loved reading and stories and, as a child, developed what became a lifelong taste for Roman history. From her parents she imbibed strong notions of probity, duty and family loyalty, and constantly worried that she might not live up to their expectations of good behaviour. None the less, she was a self-possessed and mature girl, assured in company and schooled in the art of polite conversation. Because her early years were spent without nursery companions, Caroline was the centre of the family world; attention was lavished on her both by her parents and by the ageing Louise de Kéroualle when the Lennox family visited her for the winter season of 1728. She got used to being painted, with her mother, with a pony or acting in Dryden's *Indian Emperor* at the age of nine.

Yet it was not an altogether happy childhood. The Duke and Duchess had little success in producing a son and heir, and Caroline matured in an atmosphere of anxiety about childbirth and sadness about infant sickness and death. Two boys were born, in 1724 and 1730, but neither lived very long. These deaths devastated the household because each swept away the chance to secure the dynasty. Worse still, from Caroline's point of view, her young sister Louisa, born in 1725, died of a fever at the age of three. By that time Caroline was five years old and well able to understand that death was unsparing and inevitable.

This early experience of death left Caroline pessimistic and fearful. She came to feel that any joy she had was bound to be snatched away, and she also became obsessed with the frailty of young children. 'Want of spirits,' she said, was her 'natural disposition' and she believed that because experience had told her that 'joy and happiness' were not to be had, her melancholy was fully justified. If she did feel happy she tended to regard her situation with mistrust and work herself back into a state of unease: 'I can't but always reflect how much more than my share of happiness I have enjoyed already, and that very reflection makes me dread what is to come.'

Caroline tried to temper her habitual sense of foreboding with the consolations of religion. 'For,' she said, 'without religion, the life of man is a wild, fluttering, inconsistent thing without any certain scope or design.' But Caroline's faith was no more than conventional and it never made up for life's sorrows or obliterated her fear of death. It was in fact to men and women rather than God that she turned for understanding. She liked to study the behaviour of the 'human species' as she called it and she read constantly, at home, out of doors in the formal gardens at Goodwood or by the Thames at Richmond House. Histories, geography, philosophy, travels, letters, memoirs of courtly life, plays, novels, scandal sheets, criminal confessions were, in London and the country, her company and her education. Aristocratic girls got no formal schooling: a series of masters and intermittent parental instruction supplemented her own restless enquiry after knowledge. So it was from the word of man rather than of God that Caroline constructed her understanding of the world. 'I love a likeness to a storybook,' she exclaimed, and she found such likenesses in the intrigues and scandals of her parents' circle. And to the inventors of movable type she was proportionately grateful; printing, she declared – along with the great savants of her day – 'has made a more total change in this world than any other thing.' Aphorisms of this sort appealed to Caroline, partly because she had a very good memory and could recall them at will, partly because she enjoyed the display of learning (though not, she always said, of wit) for its own sake.

Books supplied emotion as well as instruction; they made her cry and laugh, and Caroline fervently believed in the importance of passion and its expression. She regarded herself as a woman of strong feelings, 'apt to cry' as she put it, and she intensely disliked people who were even-tempered or reserved. Emotional coldness was akin to bad behaviour in her creed, besides being bad for well-being. Caroline easily lost her temper if she was provoked or neglected and with it her equanimity and tranquillity. Then she demanded both attention and solitude. 'I find when I have anything on my mind I'm much better when I live quietly and sit at home reading or working and have time to reason myself into submitting myself to my affliction. At all times any hurry puts me more out of humour and out of spirits than anything.' Sketching out her ideal kind of life, Caroline laid great stress on a quietness which was almost wholly lacking at Goodwood and at

Richmond House. 'Living alone suits my disposition best, at least passing a good deal of my time so. I love to saunter about the gardens, looking at plants etc by myself or being shut up in my dressing room reading or writing.'

When her sense of oppression lifted, Caroline was the last person to want complete seclusion. She enjoyed company more than she realised and had considerable social poise. From her earliest childhood she had been at home in the drawing-room and, if the company was sufficiently serious to suit her ideas of good taste, she delighted in formal assemblies, where people worked their way around conversational groups. She professed to hate political chat and gossip about people she did not know, but gossip about people she did know was quite another matter. There she was unashamedly curious. Taking her cue from scandal sheets and novels, she used to question servants about their employers. She loved to dig over the gossip of the day with women friends – 'a little nap, a little chat and now and then a little cards' – and regarded herself as a connoisseur of human nature.

There was another side to this intelligent, worried, poised and slightly pedantic young woman – an irresistible pull towards those things she professed to dislike: wit, recklessness, bustle and ambition. 'I don't think wit a necessary ingredient at all,' she said severely. But wit fascinated her, and so did excess, that quality of her grandfather's which her father had worked so hard to suppress in himself and his family. While she wrote peevishly, 'I am apt to grudge people their victuals,' she secretly found appetite – a hunger for women, for power, for food, for cards, for the latest extravagant fashions – overwhelmingly attractive.

This horrified fascination for what she thought of as wickedness was encapsulated in Caroline's attitude towards Voltaire. Voltaire had come into the acquaintance of her family circle during his exile in England between 1726 and 1729, when Caroline was a little girl. As a young woman she read his *Lettres philosophiques*, which appealed to her love of aphorism and of explanations of the human condition. When *Candide* appeared, Caroline couldn't put it down or stop thinking about it. The book was a satire on optimism, and as such in tune with Caroline's own sense that life was fraught with dangers. She felt she shouldn't like it but she did, and therein lay its peculiar fascination. 'Candide is a wicked book to be sure, but infinitely clever in my opinion, and diverts me vastly.' And again, see-sawing backwards and forwards between disgust and delight, 'there is wit in it, but the plan of it is gloomy and wicked to a degree. I think there are some droll things in it; its mighty entertaining.'

Round about 1742, when she was nineteen years old, reckoned a beauty and destined by her parents for a great match, Caroline met a Voltaire of her own, Henry Fox, and fell deeply and passionately in love with him. In 1742 Henry Fox was thirty-seven years old, an ambitious and able Member of Parliament, obsessed with politics and particularly with managing the tricky affairs of the House of Commons.

The Duke and Duchess could not decide whether it was Fox's antecedents or his behaviour that they disapproved of most. Fox's father, Sir Stephen Fox, had been a Tory servant of the Crown who had made his name and fortune as Paymaster General of Charles II's forces at the end of the previous century. At first Fox looked set to follow his father's footsteps. After Eton and Oxford (where he astonished fellow students by reciting reams of Latin verse from memory) he travelled on the Continent. By the 1730s his sights were set on Parliament. But by then to be a Tory was to be condemned to the back benches. After the Jacobite rebellion of 1715, which was supported by a sprinkling of Tories, Toryism was tainted with treachery and disloyalty towards the Hanoverian dynasty; it offered no hope for an ambitious politician. Nothing daunted, Fox changed sides and put himself under the tutelage of the Duke of Richmond's fellow courtier Lord Hervey (who shortly afterwards began a long affair with

Fox's brother Stephen). In 1735 Fox was elected Whig MP for Hindon. He moved quickly up the Whig hierarchy, impressing everyone with his command of detail, ability to manage men and cynical approach to political problems. In 1743 Fox was given a position at the Treasury, the first rung on the ladder to power.

Fox was not a handsome man. He was short, stout and pear shaped, weighing in at over twelve stone. His face was dominated by a double chin, a heavy black jaw and eyebrows that jumped out of his face like rippling caterpillars. But this ungainliness was offset by qualities that Caroline found very attractive. He read widely, wrote verses and had a talent for friendship and domesticity. Even his reputation for atheism, gambling and womanising (made flesh in an illegitimate child of a year and another not yet out of the womb, who was born in 1744) were irresistible to her. Here rolled up in one hirsute form was the personification of the forbidden; and Fox offered it all to her with such persuasive charm that she was overwhelmed.

Caroline and Fox had met at Goodwood in the 1730s and on many occasions since in Whitehall drawing-rooms and at the theatre. By the beginning of the next decade Fox was looking for a way out of his bachelor life. His brother Stephen had recently got married (albeit to the thirteen-year-old daughter of one of Fox's mistresses) and to everyone's surprise had given up Hervey and settled down to an unimpeachable life as a father and country squire. Fox was mildly envious. He fell in love with Caroline, sensing that she could offer him companionship, devotion and a few good contacts besides.

Caroline's parents were happy to entertain Fox as a friend but adamant that he was impossible as a suitor. They recoiled from Fox's naked ambition, his thirst for power and money and his reputation for atheism. They despised his fortune as too little and his presumption as too great. But Fox had made up his mind. Sometime in March 1744 he met Caroline at the theatre and asked her to marry him. Caroline said neither yes nor no. She replied, true to the etiquette of such proposals, that Henry had her permission to approach her father and seek her hand. But it was an acceptance, however demurely given, and from that moment on Henry's confidence rarely faltered. He went straight round to the Richmond family box and asked the Duke for an interview. The next day he went to Richmond House and claimed Caroline's hand. Caroline, he told the Duke, had no objections if he could overcome any scruples her parents might have. And, Fox added triumphantly, 'she wish'd me success', which was as near a declaration of love and intent as propriety would allow a woman in her position.

The Duke and Duchess were horrified and furious. Their own arranged marriage had turned out for the best and they planned to choose a suitable husband for their daughter. A paunchy, ex-Tory career politician, whose learning frightened them and whose brother had carried on a long affair with their friend Lord Hervey, was not their idea of an eligible man. The Duchess refused to entertain Fox's proposal at all, and declared that in six month's time he would thank her for her perspicacity. 'What makes her Grace think so I don't know,' Fox snorted angrily in reply. The Duke, eager for propriety and dignity, decided to treat the affair as an unfortunate episode that would fade away quietly provided good behaviour was maintained by both sides. He wanted, he wrote to Fox after his visit, to retain his friend's good opinion. But something suggested to the Duke that Fox was unlikely to retreat to lick his wounds with gentlemanly dignity. So he added a less than subtle threat as well. Fox, he said, should think no more of the affair. It was over and finished. But if he was foolish enough to persist he would be ruined.

Fox was lashed to fury by the phrase. Hiding his anger under the cloak of his charm, he took up his pen against the Duke on 8 March. He was fairly certain that the contest was going to go his way; he was eloquent, determined and angry.

He knew he had a fair amount to lose. The Duke could not ruin him politically, he was not a powerful enough figure in Court or Parliament for that, but he could make his life uncomfortable by cutting off his access to the monarch. On the other hand, Fox had a lot to gain. If the match came off and he could placate the Duke and Duchess, Fox would instantly rise up the social ladder, and if the Duke accepted the marriage he could smooth his way to lucrative offices with a word in the King's ear. Most of all though, Fox wanted Caroline. It was unfortunate but inevitable that in his tussle with the Duke, Caroline was to be Henry's main weapon. He knew that the worse he was painted to her, the more Caroline would love him, because it was the idea of him as a wicked and excessive man that had overwhelmed her in the first place.

Fox's understanding of the nature of Caroline's love was his strongest card and he played it relentlessly. He knew that the Duke could not understand why Caroline had fallen in love with such an unsuitable man, and in his most bumptious moments he egged the Duke on to denounce him, knowing that it would only make him seem more attractive than ever. He also knew that the Duke was an indulgent father who would never willingly hurt his daughter. 'Serious, considerate, sincere, older far in mind than in years, with a heart as tender but as firm as ever yet was formed, does your Grace think she could take a fancy lightly? Or that she could ever alter?' Fox demanded in his letter of 8 March 1744. 'Indeed, my Lord, she will not, and your Grace is deciding on the happiness or misery of her whole life, not of a few months only.' He suggested that Richmond try to talk Caroline out of her unhappiness, delighting in getting his adversary to do his work for him. 'You only can smooth and help her under this affliction. Pray, my dear Lord, find leisure to speak to her some time.'

Fox had a reply to the Duke's veiled threat of ruin too. Richmond had hinted that Henry was simply too poor to marry Caroline. If Caroline came to him without permission and without a dowry, Fox would never be able to meet her financial expectations. 'Surely *ruin* is too strong a word,' Fox retorted angrily, and folded a statement of his fortune and financial affairs into his letter. The match might not come off, he went on, but 'I beg you . . . cast your eye on the inclosed.' He didn't want to influence the Duke in his favour, he said, only to point out that 'you may think me a little less un-justifiable when you see that, tho' infinitely far from answering her desert or your Grace's expectations, it would not have been quite ruinous.' Fox was stung by the Duke's imputation of his poverty partly because he was by most standards a wealthy man and partly because he longed and schemed to be much wealthier than he was.

The next day, 9 March, Fox went to see the Duke again. The meeting went well; Richmond was polite and said he could return. Fox scented victory, and sent a note to the Duchess on 12 March, saying that because she was still hostile to the match and would not want to see him, he had decided to write rather than visit. Her husband, Fox went on, had asked him two days ago how he could be so sure of Caroline if she had not given him any secret commitment: where did his confidence come from, the bewildered Duke had asked, if everything was above board? The reason was, he told the Duchess, that he knew Caroline's heart better than she did herself. 'Your Grace will perhaps say as the Duke of Rich-mond did – if so unengaged why was I so sure of her? When she found your Graces would not consent she might have re-jected me: and so, indeed, madam, she might with honour; maybe she thought she should. I alone knew she could not; and if this must end unhappily 'tis I have been to blame in taking so much care to hide from herself the impression I had made, lest she alarm'd should give your Grace the alarm too soon. Long and constantly observant of every movement of her heart, the most unaffected and sincere that ever was, I knew (what she knows now but never knew till she was bid to get the better of it) its attachment to be unalterable.' He con-cluded by asking the Duchess how she thought he could press on with his suit if he thought Caroline was going to change her mind.

These tortuous sentences and this tortured reasoning threw the Duchess into a rage. She took Fox's implication that he knew Caroline better than she did very badly. Fox's visits were disagreeable she said, and his letters were more disagreeable still. Both had better stop. She was shocked and offended at his imposition. Fox acknowledged that he had made an error, but he was far from cowed. 'I am in such a situation,' he wrote, 'that I am pretty sure whatever I say it will offend.' He decided on a tactical withdrawal; to all outward appearances there would be no more contact between himself and Caroline, no more visits to the Duke and no more letters. For her part the Duchess declared that the whole affair was over.

For a month there was a stalemate. It was getting near the end of the season; the Duke and Duchess hoped, as April went by, that they could hang on until the beginning of May and then take Caroline down to Goodwood. There, friends could not act as go-betweens, messages were more difficult to deliver and servants to bribe. Caroline would be cut off from Henry for seven or eight months and the tactical victory would be theirs. Secluded in the country, the Duke and Duchess believed, Caroline would come to her senses and remember exactly what she owed her parents. As April passed, the Duke began to hint to the Duke of Newcastle, his neighbour and friend, that Caroline's ardour had cooled. Newcastle passed the message on to his younger brother Henry Pelham who passed it to his good friend Henry Fox. Fox, successful and cool-headed gambler that he was, decided immediately to raise the stakes. He wrote to the Duke on 19 April. It was six weeks since he had spoken one word to Caroline, he said disingenuously, sticking to the letter but not the spirit of the truth, and maybe it was true that Caroline's disposition had altered. 'If it be altered,' he went on, 'if it be ever so little altered, let her tell me so. I shall, unwillingly, but instantly believe her, and never, whatever I may wish, attempt to bring it back again.' By this time Henry could well afford such rhetorical gestures. He wasn't speaking to Caroline, it was true, but he was secretly writing to her, keeping alive the delicious sense of transgression and wickedness that made the misery she was enduring all worth while. Throughout March and April love hardened her resolve and guilt and excitement kept her on tenterhooks.

Henry ended his letter of 19 April with a hint that was mingled with a threat. If Caroline wouldn't back down, wouldn't it be better to accept the situation? 'If she will abide by her unworthy choice – I don't know or presume to think that she will – but if she will, don't make it worse. Perhaps your Grace may have dissuaded her . . . But if she does persist, for God's sake permit it; and that the Duchess and your Grace would see her and own her afterwards is all I should ever hope for.' Here Henry made a blunder that may have given the Duke pause for thought and suggested the need for decisive action. If the wedding was given the Duke's blessing there would be no need for him to see and own his daughter 'afterwards' – he would be there all along. Only if the wedding was secret would Caroline need a separate meeting with her parents. Henry's plans and thoughts were running away with him.

The Duke remained implacable and grew increasingly suspicious. He pressed ahead with his plans to whisk Caroline away to Goodwood the day his duties at Court no longer demanded his presence in London. Fox sensed that time was running out. He sent his friend Henry Pelham to intercede on his behalf with the Duke and gave him instructions to hint that if Richmond continued to be adamant, Caroline might take matters into her own hands.

Towards the end of April, with only a couple of weeks of the season left, Fox decided to act. On the morning of the 27th, he and Caroline met in secret. He was miserable, he told her, and he couldn't bear the thought of not seeing her for seven or eight months. This brief meeting Fox followed with a letter which he urged Caroline to read carefully. In it he reiterated his desperate unhappiness and his dread of being parted from her. The necessary conclusion he left dangling in the April air; the next day he would write again and plead with her to come away with him. For the moment he just wanted her to understand and sympathise with his misery.

Caroline's parents believed that love could blossom within the institution of aristocratic marriage. It had always had a place there. Although children were married against their wishes, treated as elements of the property of a large estate, in most cases fondness and financial and dynastic considerations went hand in hand to the altar. Within certain limits children were allowed to choose and most chose within their family's circle of acquaintance because it was there that opportunity lay. Children only got into trouble if they selected a partner from beyond the agreed boundaries. Caroline's later conduct suggested that as far as others were concerned she was every bit as conventional as her parents and looked for financial and political advantage as well as affection in marriages that she had a hand in. But as far as she herself was concerned she was determined to put love in front of her parents' wishes and interests. Looking in books and plays and at the world around her she saw plenty of examples of successful marriages based on love. Besides she chose to believe that her parents were wrong about Fox's prospects and thus their own interests; although he could never recover from the fact that his father had started life as a humble grammar-school boy, Fox could become a successful politician and a rich man.

It was a moment of crisis: if Caroline made a mistake her gesture would have the double consequence of making her miserable and proving her parents' contention that arranged marriages turned out best. But she did not hesitate. She read Fox's letter, grasped its purport and determined to act decisively. No matter what it cost her, they would elope. Straight away she wrote back a letter which mingled fear, excitement and elation in equal parts. 'I am vastly frightened to think of what I am going to do. I dare not reflect upon it. I fear they will never forgive me, I hope you won't suspect me now of being altered but believe me this is the greatest proof of love it is possible for me to give you. Adieu.'

This letter signalled Caroline's intention to begin a new kind of life, a life in which she and Fox controlled their own emotional destiny. Much as she would have preferred her parents' consent, she recognised that without it her married life would be begun unencumbered by their advice or conventions. She and Henry (who had been orphaned long ago) were free to create their own way of life and their own kind of marriage: there were no manuals of behaviour for eloping couples except those written in story books.

Before Caroline's impassioned letter of commitment could reach him, Henry had already dispatched another laying out his plan. They could be married secretly and quietly at the home of a discreet friend of his, Charles Hanbury Williams. After the ceremony, Caroline could go straight home again and stay there till the day before her parents left for Goodwood. Then she could leave Richmond House and join him. Too much scandal might harm Fox politically; the best outcome he could now hope for was a quiet wedding and an even quieter parting with the Duke and Duchess that would not make him an undesirable political ally. Caroline agreed for her own reasons. She was still terrified about what she was going to do and guilty about her parents' reaction. But any lingering filial piety was quickly being replaced by anger. After all, she wrote to Henry, it was her parents who were actually responsible for her precipitate step. 'Good God. That they should have obliged me to this – you don't know what I have suffered from yesterday.'

At first everything went smoothly. Caroline slipped out of Richmond House on the morning of 2 May 1744. By the Cupola in Whitehall she said goodbye to her twelve-year-old sister, Emily – a parting she still remembered with emotion twenty-five years later – and went to Hanbury Williams's house in Conduit Street. There Henry Fox and Caroline Lennox were married. Hanbury Williams and the Duke of

Marlborough, an old crony of Fox's from the days of his friendship with Lord Hervey, and painted with them by Hogarth, were the only witnesses. The clergyman did not know who he was marrying and was equally ignorant of the scandal about to break about their ears. The party did not linger to savour the moment. Caroline went back to break the news to her parents and Fox sat down to add a letter to her revelations. Now that the victory was his he did not pull his punches. 'My Lord Duke. When there was not the least hope left that the Duchess or your Grace would ever consent, and Lady Caroline was obliged to choose between disobeying you and leaving me for a very great while, probably for ever, she chose what I fear you will never forgive her, and is my wife.' After the triumphant crescendo of this opening sentence Fox came down to more mundane matters and asked the Duke to let Caroline stay in his house till they left for Goodwood. But he was cock-a-hoop and he couldn't hide his joy of victory. Signing off, he declared, with dare-devil irony and consummate rudeness, 'I am with the greatest deference and humility, my Lord, your Grace's most submissive, most respectful and most sincere humble servant.' He meant exactly the opposite and the Duke knew it.

The Duke was insulted and furious at being beaten. He refused to allow Caroline to stay a single night with him, and before the ink was dry on Fox's letter, Caroline was back at Hanbury Williams's house. She had been banished by her mother and father from her childhood homes and the companionship of her siblings. Now she was alone with the man and the marriage she had chosen for love.

PART TWO
'You are always in my thoughts'.
Henry Fox to Caroline, 8 March 1748.

The Duke of Richmond slammed the door on his eldest daughter and hurried back into his library to write to her husband. His worst fears had been realised; the Lennox family was about to be plunged into scandal once again. After a lifetime of probity his name would be on every tongue. And on every tongue he would hear Fox's triumph. He could have kept quiet and slunk off to Goodwood. But he wanted revenge and in the end anger got the better of discretion. So he wrote to Fox, 'I shall make no secret to the world of the injuries done me and my eternal resentment,' and concluded his short note with insult to match insult. 'Write no more to me. For if you do, I shall burn your letters without reading anything more than your name which must ever be disagreeable to me.' Then the Duke sent notes to all the guests invited to a ball he and the Duchess were to have held at Richmond House that evening. He cancelled the ball and told everybody why. Within a matter of hours the story was all over fashionable London. As Fox's friend Hanbury Williams put it, it 'filled the rooms of Kensington' and was hotly debated at White's, Henry's club. Hanbury Williams himself went to Covent Garden on the night of the wedding, and watched as the news went from box to box. It was 'exactly like fire in a train of gunpowder,' he said.

Just as Fox feared, his political enemies tried to make capital out of the scandal by closing ranks against him. Horace Walpole, with his usual combination of exaggeration and drama, summarised the reaction of the Duke's Whig friends. 'The town has been in a great bustle about a private match; but which, by the ingenuity of the ministry has been made politics. Mr. Fox fell in love with Lady Caroline Lennox, asked for her, was refused and stole her. His father was a footman; her great-grandfather was a King; *hinc illae lacri-mae*! All the blood Royal have been up in arms. The Duke of Marlborough, who was a friend of the Richmonds, gave her away. If His Majesty's Princess Caroline had been stolen, there could not have been more noise made. The Pelhams, who are much attached to the Richmonds, but who tried to make Fox and all that set theirs, wisely entered the quarrel, and now don't know how to get out of it.'

The affair rumbled on. Hanbury Williams, glancing again at its political context, wrote to Fox on 15 May: 'Time that overcomes, eats up, or buries all things has not yet made the least impression upon the story of the loves of Henry and Caroline. It still lives, grows and flourishes under the patronage of their Graces of Newcastle and Grafton and Mr. Pelham. But in spite of them the town grows cool and will take the tender lovers' part.' Hanbury Williams remembered what the scandal-mongers tended to forget, that Henry Fox was deeply in love with his bride and that he had married for love. He wrote consolingly to his friend, 'You have made a very *prudent choice*. Your good sense and your good nature (its true) will be well employed for life; you have the properest object for 'em in your arms, who had sense enough to distinguish your merit and love enough to prefer it to all things.' Hanbury Williams set the tone for what the wider world came to understand about the Foxes' marriage. Outsiders saw a well matched and happily united couple. What they saw was much, if not all, of the story. Love, freely chosen and passionately given, flowed around and between Caroline and Mr Fox, as she always called him to friends, charming everybody who met them. Their love was supported on the one hand by intelligence, mutual interests and commitment and on the other by a companionship that Caroline thought was rare amongst married couples.

In the early days, Henry and Caroline were thrown together as co-conspirators. She could not visit her family and she felt betrayed by her parents; his parents were dead and his brother was buried in a rural idyll from which he rarely emerged. Caroline was forbidden to see her sister Emily, on whom she had relied in the heady days of her courtship, and she had few friends of her own whom she knew independently of her family. Her father had refused to see any of his friends who called on his daughter, so Caroline's acquaintance was reduced to a trickle. Fox, on the other hand, was surrounded by cronies and admirers; from the very beginning Caroline thought of him as constantly tempted away from her by company.

Immediately after their wedding there was a quiet period, which corresponded with the end of the London season and the winding down of parliamentary business. In the summer of 1744, Henry and Caroline travelled to Cheltenham, where he entertained her while she drank the mineral water to recover her shattered nerves. Caroline had what she later was bitterly to call a luxury, her husband's company. She immediately began to rely on him to relieve her spirits when they sagged. Slowly she began to identify her happiness with his. Henry became her world. She became fascinated by politicians, especially if they had subtle, legal minds. Henry's successes and failures became her own and she embraced his opinions with unwavering partisanship. So despite her notional and lofty disapproval of politics she began to follow Westminster machinations with avidity. Fox's ambition became her own (although she refused to admit it for twenty years) and the loyalty that she believed was owed to her family was, after the break with her parents, transferred to him.

In the late autumn of 1744, the Foxes returned to London and moved into a house in Conduit Street, close to Henry's Treasury office and a few minutes' walk from Caroline's old home in Whitehall. Willy-nilly, and despite her professed love of solitude, Caroline became something of a political hostess. Fox loved domesticity and encouraged friends, acquaintances and supplicants to call on him at home. Caroline was jealous, complaining that Henry was indiscriminate about company. It was the beginning of a battle which went on as long as their marriage. Henry never budged because he knew that Caroline envied and loved him for his excessive conviviality, and after an outburst of pique, she always apologised abjectly. For his part, Fox had no regrets about leaving his bachelor life behind him. While he still loved gambling, drinking and women, he settled down. Fox's strategy for a happy marriage was very simple but it took time and commitment. In the first place he transferred his club to his house and sat there in domestic comfort while the witty, the friendly and the curious came to call. In the second place he recognised that Caroline was his intellectual equal; if he had the greater learning and better memory, she was a shrewder and more dispassionate judge of character. He often discussed political business with her, and although she professed to despise politics, she was always forthright in her opinions. They read, talked and walked out together in the evenings, chatting over the events of the day and the contents of the newspapers. The 'good nature' that Fox was famous for amongst his friends spread over his home, catching up Caroline and their children, guests and servants. Melancholy and boredom rather than anger and guilt were Fox's nemeses. Provided he had friends to tease and entertain with stories, bad poetry, political news and gossip, he was usually happy. He rarely lost his temper and, if he sank into fatalism, a visit from a friend would usually lift him out of it; he wanted so much to be liked that the effort and pleasure of entertaining made him forget his lethargy.

When Caroline went away he wrote to her constantly. 'I know you love writing so pray let me hear from you three or four times a week,' Caroline ordered when they were parted in the early years of their marriage. Fox's letters to her were portmanteaux for his thoughts: capacious, rambling, sometimes inconsequential and often flirtatious. If a bit of gossip came his way he sent it. He would tease Caroline with stories of beautiful women he had met and charm her with assurances of love and fidelity. He sent books and gossip sheets and wrote wherever he happened to be. Letters came to her from the House of Commons or from the Council Chamber, where once he took up his pen during a lull in the discussion. He wrote from White's or from his office. Sometimes he would scribble notes in his sprawling, octopus-like italic hand between courses at the dinner table.

Apart from one another, Henry and Caroline shared another abiding obsession, their children. When their son Stephen – named for Henry's brother and always called Ste – was born in 1745, they fell in love all over again, with their child and with one another. They thought Ste was the most beautiful, most intelligent, most charming child ever born and they never tired of telling one another so. Henry was proud to have become part of a family. Fatherhood bound him even more closely to his open and freewheeling domestic life. He went on to become famous, even infamous, in the annals of fatherhood, partly because he was so indulgent towards his children and partly because he conspicuously spent so much time with them. Motherhood transformed Caroline's life too. For the first year of her marriage she had sunk herself into Henry's life and personality. Now she added a new love that was almost as great as her love for her husband, although characteristically she added a gloomy caveat to her adoration: 'As for Ste, I don't expect he should love me as well as I do him. That's never the case with a mother and son.' She was devoted to Ste from the moment of his birth. For her second son, Harry, born in 1746, she had little love to spare. She hoped it would come with time. Meanwhile she was merely anxious about him because he did not seem very strong.

Caroline's almost perpetual state of foreboding was both dampened and inflamed by the happiness of marriage and motherhood. On the one hand she felt loved and secure. As she wrote to Henry in 1746, 'indeed, my dear angel, I am often low spirited and vapourish. [But] I can never seriously think myself very unhappy while you love me and are well.' But on the other hand, Caroline's anxieties were heightened precisely because she was so content. Sooner or later all that joy would have to be paid for.

In the early years of her marriage Caroline's anxieties fixed on the health of her older son. Her own memories of two heirs to the Richmond title dying in infancy, as well as her observation of death all around her crystallised into an obsession with Ste's well-being. She was never very well either, constantly plagued with debilitating stomach troubles which made her nauseous and fretful. Immediately after the wedding in 1744, Caroline had gone to Cheltenham to take the waters. In the autumn of 1746 she was ill again. This time she travelled with Ste, who was now getting on for eighteen months old, his nurse and her maid Milward to the fashionable resort of Bath. Henry stayed in London with the baby and a mass of political business.

At the beginning of the eighteenth century Bath was still a small town largely dependent on a moribund wool industry. But it had two natural resources which, combined with the money of speculators and the vagaries of fashion, quickly made its fortune: the local Bath stone, which glowed golden in the damp west-country air, and hot springs of slightly sulphurous mineral water. For two thousand years the sick, the hypochondriac and the valetudinarian had drunk and immersed themselves in the waters. The Roman baths had long since been buried by modern substitutes. In the eighteenth century pride of place went to the Pump Room, where warm mineral water was sold by the glass, and the King's Bath. This giant communal cistern was right under the windows of the Pump Room, open to the gaze of all. Patients sat in the bath with hot water right up to their necks. Men were enveloped in brown linen suits. Women wore petticoats and jackets of the same material. They sat side by side in a hot, faintly sulphurous mist. Limp cotton handkerchiefs caught the sweat which dribbled down the bathers' faces; afterwards they were tucked away in the brims of patients' hats. Lightweight bowls of copper floated perilously on the water. Inside them vials of oil and sweet smelling pomanders bobbed up and down. On a cold morning the bathers in their caps and hats looked to the curious onlookers pressed against the glass above them like perspiring mushrooms rising into the thick gaseous air. A nobleman, flushed and puce in the face lay against the side of the bath chatting to – who knew, perhaps a prosperous butcher or even a well-to-do highwayman who had come to Bath to spend some money and lie low. The brown linen covered a multitude of sores and sins.

By 1735 Bath had become a fashionable resort. Lodgings for patients and their families, for doctors and portrait painters and for servants and coachmen were going up higgledy-piggledy. They were crowded with aristocrats, bored in the summer off season, with sick old people, barren wives, amusement seekers and fortune hunters. Like the theatre, whose spectacle it mirrored, Bath was open to all who could pay. Merchants and peers rubbed shoulders at the card tables and jostled prostitutes, charlatans and quacks in the street. Strange alliances and bad marriages were made in the baths; hot water heated the passions and dissolved social distinctions. Hypochondria and vanity, those old associates, were well catered for. Bath was bursting with apothecaries, quacks and doctors touting the latest cures. In their train came painters in pastel and oil, dancing masters, fencing teachers, mantua makers and milliners. They helped patients, their friends and relatives fill the spare hours between bathing sessions, card parties, concerts and the theatre.

It fell to the Master of Ceremonies to impose some kind of order and some semblance of social distinction on this chaos. Under Beau Nash, who had the job in the early decades of the century, a ritual of greeting and talking, bathing and dancing was instituted. People of high social rank were met by a peal of bells when they first arrived in the town. Once they were settled the Master of Ceremonies called and described the coming social attractions. Music began at eight or nine o'clock in the Pump Room where patients went early for their first dose of the waters, measured out by the pumper in glasses of ascending sizes. At midday, every day except Sundays, there was dancing in the Assembly Rooms, which were built in 1708. Balls were organised twice a week, concerts every other night. Everybody in Bath had time on their hands and anybody could buy tickets to these public entertainments. Despite its mimicry of the London season the social scene at Bath was a mêlée and a scrum.

Architecture too was putting up a façade of order and dignity to hide thieving, quackery, grief and pain. Outside the Pump Room and the Baths the sick spilled out on to the pavement. Paralysed by strokes, swollen with dropsy and blinded by diabetes, patients were wheeled about the streets, their bandaged legs stuck out in front of them, their sightless eyes swivelling giddily about. Lame soldiers hobbled past them. Around these cripples swirled a crowd of nurses and doctors. Anxious relatives passed the time of day with acquaintances and looked for signs of improvement. Healthy hangers-on sneaked into pastry shops or made for the parks. Beside the pavements orderly terraces were rising, their fronts decorated by ranks of tall, upright columns. The regularity, certainty and serenity of the Palladian terraces built in Bath after 1725 contradicted and contained the fear, the sickness and the social chaos they surveyed.

The monumental Palladian building at Bath was the brain-child of the architect John Wood, who moved there in 1727. Wood was a visionary who gradually imposed on the town a fantastic dream of using domestic architecture to re-create what he saw as the mystical harmony embodied in the great buildings of the past. In his vision, Bath was to be re-created, using the medium of Italian-derived Palladianism, as a place where buildings echoed the measured and mystical deliberations of a *mélange* of great leaders of former times, Druids and ancient Britons worshipping at stone circles, Romans in the Forum and the Coliseum, Greeks in the amphitheatre. The new city was to be senatorial and magical at the same time. Dignity and mystical harmony would replace, or at least disguise, the dissolution of gambling and death. Wood planned a Forum, a Circus and an Imperial Gymnasium. Health and activity were the keynotes of Wood's planned city. He described the Circus as a place 'for the exhibition of sport'. Athletes would display their prowess in the gymnasium.

Perhaps these temples of health and ritualised activity were too grotesque ever to be built in a city whose prosperity was founded on the sick and the lame. But some of Wood's schemes did come off, and his son, who built the stately Royal Crescent in the 1760s, inherited his father's notions of grandeur without his eccentric fantasy of a temple to youth and health in the midst of age and illness.

Caroline found lodgings in South Parade, one side of the Forum, which had been completed in 1743. It was a fashionable place to stay, close to open fields but only a short walk from the Pump Room and baths. Caroline was pleased with her lodgings, but she worried about Henry and fretted over Ste. 'You don't expect I suppose to hear I am in vast good spirits yet,' she wrote on her first day there. 'You know I always tense myself with some melancholy apprehensions of what may happen. The two things that hang on my spirits at present are the fear that you should not love me when I return to you and the fear of Ste's catching the small pox.' Caroline was anxious and alone. Without Henry to reassure her about Ste and to reiterate his love, her fear grew bigger and bigger. 'If anything should happen to you or him, or you should grow not to love me I believe I should go mad. He is infinitely dearer to me than anything in the world except you. Do comfort me about it in your letter. Pray, pray, dearest angel, write often to me and believe me tho' I do vex you sometimes I love you with the truest and tenderest affection.'

The next day Caroline left her card with Lady Bell Finch, Lady-in-Waiting to Princess Amelia, George II's unmarried daughter. Her visit was a matter of duty, one of the rituals by which Bath high society tried to hold its head above the mass of humanity thronging the streets. 'I went according to the form here,' Caroline grumbled. 'I did not much care to wait on her as she never visited me in town but was told it was necessary for those who went to court.'

Bath offered Caroline a chance to rest as much as a cure for her stomach trouble. For the first week she couldn't drink the waters because she was menstruating. A month later she had to stop because she thought she was pregnant and was too embarrassed to ask a doctor if pregnancy and the waters went together. 'I can't possibly ask the doctor about drinking the waters (for its so vastly queer to have you come for a week and to be breeding immediately that I will keep it a vast secret for some time if it should prove so) but I know it is not right for Garnier when I came to Bath begged me to be very sure I was not breeding.' Instead she walked about in the fields around the town and played endless dull and soothing games of cards for small stakes. Cards gave Caroline all her life a modest thrill of the forbidden. She disapproved of them in principle but she was easily persuaded to join a table. At Bath she justified herself as an observer of the exotic social mix that thronged assemblies and hung around the games. 'My whist party (for I could not avoid playing a little) were Lady Fitzwilliam . . . Lord Brooke and some other men, of which there are a curious collection here. Lady Bateman and Lady Bell Finch have a highwayman and a tape merchant in their quincy party.' She sat to Hoare, one of the crowd of painters who made a living from the boredom of Bath's wealthier visitors and she read a good deal. Philosophy and history were interspersed with political pamphlets and newspapers. 'I have read le Canapé, couleur de feu. 'Tis the filthiest most disagreeable book I ever read,' she wrote with relish, and she re-read Clarendon's *History of the Rebellion* with more sober enjoyment, siding with its royalist apologia which explained the rebellion as a series of accidents rather than the result of monarchical despotism.

Mostly she was engrossed with Ste. Fears about his catching smallpox subsided when she had a more obvious complaint to worry about. Ste got a cough. At the same time, Henry sent news from London that little Harry had died of a fever. All Caroline's grief was diverted into terror that Ste would die too. 'I'm so frightened about Ste. Do tell me what to do if I should lose him. I could never be happy again. My dear angel, you don't know what I suffer. I think there was too much done for my dear little child in town.'

Caroline hinted that Harry had been killed with kindness and perhaps a surfeit of drugs too. Certainly by the mid-eighteenth century fashionable society was drowning in a tidal wave of potions and syrups. Avalanches of powders and hailstorms of pills engulfed the sick and the well alike. Doctors were setting up offices by the mansions of the rich. They were well connected and well organised, but the opinions and prescriptions they gave for large fees were scarcely distinguishable from the cheaper remedies offered by quacks who toured the streets. Do-it-yourself health manuals poured from the presses into nurseries and libraries. They offered instant consultations with the written word of famous physicians. With them came a new medical language which dressed up seventeenth-century theories of the humours with a new verbal patina that threw a glittering cloak of wisdom and impenetrability over its initiates.

Despite her reservations about Harry's treatment, Caroline was dazzled by doctors and struggled to master this new language. 'Lady Curzon . . . lost a little boy of a year old that had the whooping cough and she says when they opened him up they found he had a twisting of the guts which they attributed to his taking too much of the oxymel of squills and convulsive powder mixed with it. She said it had what she called excoriated his bowels. I don't understand the word but beg your advice about it.' Austere though she professed to be in matters of food or alcohol, medical ingestion called forth in her almost boundless extravagance. Multiple consultations, powders to ward off illness, pills to carry it away, repeated visits from doctors: all were ordered and paid for. Medicine had become a luxury commodity in the new world of goods.

At some point consumption and caring were intermingled. Desperate parents watching beloved children killed in hours by raging fevers or crippled and stunted by disease easily came to believe that doing something was better than inactive, agonising waiting for the workings of God's will. More doctors rattled through the night streets, more pills changed hands, more money, more medical talk and, by and large, no more cures. Doctors had few spectacular successes, although smallpox inoculation was eagerly used and advertised by the aristocracy and demonstrated that cures were possible. But doctors both benefited from and advertised new attitudes towards sickness and the body. Old fatalistic notions about illness were being swept away. Hope and prescriptions were replacing inertia and prayer. That hope was often only a white powder in a screw of paper that had been given the sanction of the regular copperplate of a medical hand. In the apothecary's shop, drugs were like luminous beacons. Syrups lay thickly in crystal vials with cut-glass stoppers. Plum-red, royal-blue and emerald-green decanters twinkled at customers from the windows. Conical mounds of powder, pall-black, earthy-brown and bluey white, squatted on the shelves. All beckoned onlookers with promises of action and cure.

Caroline was soon an ardent believer in the new medicine. Ste was its beneficiary and, in the end, its victim. When he started coughing and twitching in Bath in December 1746, Caroline sent at once for the local apothecary. Later on she brought in two well-known Bath doctors, Pearce and Harrington, who confidently announced that the little boy had worms. Caroline still wanted the opinion of her London doctors. 'I should be easier if I was near Garnier and Truesdale for I have a great opinion of them.' Nevertheless she pressed on with the prescribed cures. Ethiops mineral, a black powder which turned white in the light, was followed by calomel. Calomel was less emollient than it sounded; in fact it was Ethiops mineral under another name and consisted of pure mercury sulphide. Oxymel of squills, a syrup concocted of vinegar, honey and ground up bulbs of the scilla plant, was soon added to the mercury. Ste was learning to talk and take medicine at the same time. He bravely endured blistering and, as a coda, was given mellipidus, a preparation made of ground-up woodlice. Caroline's doctors had some trouble getting this because, they said, live woodlice were hard to find in the country. Ste's illness was the beginning of a long torment for himself and his mother.

All the medicines Ste was given had a similar effect. They brought things out of the body and, the story went, purged it of poisons. There were powders, like mercury sulphide, which made the patient vomit. Others produced diarrhoea, fevers and sweats. Bleeding and cupping drew off excess blood. Blisters and boils gathered pus and poisons to the surface of the skin. Medicines allowed the body to express illness and produce its own graphic account of distress. Caroline and her sisters saw this bodily expression as a close relative of emotion. Emotion was the expression of feeling, pain the expression of sickness. Expressing emotion also had a physical component, it was in part the expulsion of bad feeling, which ensured that destructive feelings did not get bottled up in the body. So tears assuaged grief and simultaneously indicated that the body was expelling harmful feelings that might otherwise cause illness. New medical techniques that stressed action rather than inertia sat easily with Caroline's belief in the value of emotion; getting out passion and getting out poison could go hand in hand.

During the month of January 1747, Ste got better, although his shuddering and twitching did not stop. Caroline filled her letters with his naughtiness and misdeeds and pronounced herself a satisfied mother. 'I feel great comfort and satisfaction in sitting in the room next to dear Ste,' she wrote to Henry one evening a few days before they left Bath. 'Indeed the greatest pleasure I shall have in life next to being with you is to take care of Ste and whatever other children I may have. For people of my stupid disposition who don't love the great world have nothing better to do than take care of their children.' While Caroline was convalescing, Henry had been busy politicking in London. Since their marriage he had risen fast. He was watched from a discreet distance with mingled dismay and amazement by his father-in-law who, through the medium of his friend the Duke of Newcastle, was well apprised of Henry's manoeuvring.

Once he had become a friend of Lord Hervey's and a Whig, Fox came under the aegis and tutelage of Hervey's political boss Sir Robert Walpole. By 1735, Walpole, as First Lord of the Treasury and effective leader of the House of Commons, had been in power for nearly fifteen years. He controlled the House with a masterful and heady blend of bribery, preferment and personal charm. With the King in one pocket and the Commons in the other, Walpole was virtually unassailable when no more was demanded of his pragmatic policies than they could supply. He realised that, by not moving into the House of Lords, as the man who became First Lord of the Treasury customarily had, he could hang on to the Commons and the Cabinet at the same time and, if the King's support was added to that, he could combine in himself all the most important bases of power.

Walpole had no party in the House of Commons, only a crowd of supporters who voted with the government, some from principle, others for profit, others, like the young Henry Fox, for political advancement. On the floor of the House and in the labyrinth of the Palace of Westminster, Walpole's most trustworthy and sturdy lieutenant in the Commons was Henry Pelham, younger brother to the Duke of Newcastle, and it was to Pelham that Fox attached himself. He had chosen the right man. In 1742, three years into a trade war with Spain that had escalated into a full-scale European conflict known as the War of Austrian Succession, Walpole was toppled. After a year of instability, Henry Pelham became First Lord of the Treasury and it was then that Fox got his Treasury post.

Pelham's authority was much less secure than that of his mentor. Unlike Walpole he did not have the complete confidence of the monarch. After Walpole's demise, George II relied on John, Lord Carteret, to conduct foreign policy, instead of Pelham's brother, the Duke of Newcastle, who was nominally in charge as the Secretary of State. Newcastle and Pelham begrudged the huge sums of money needed to wage a Continental war. But Carteret, a polymathic diplomat and famous drinker, endorsed the Hanoverian aim of a peaceful Germany at all costs. George was desperate to secure the peace and autonomy of Hanover from the territorial ambitions of other states, and he gratefully employed Carteret in the byzantine negotiations between crowned heads that went on behind the movements of money and troops.

For four years, between 1742 and 1746, the political turmoil at home matched the turbulence of the European war. George II fought and beat the French at the Battle of Dettingen in 1743, but the general drift of the war was in favour of the French and their allies, the Prussians and the Spanish. In 1745, Bonnie Prince Charlie, the Young Pretender ('our cousin' as the Lennox girls called him), took advantage of the confused and undefended state of the kingdom to land in Scotland. His advance south was ultimately destroyed not so much by the efficiency of the Duke of Cumberland as by apathy towards the Stuart cause. Gentlemen who for years had openly been toasting the King 'over the water' and marking the anniversary of the death of Charles I with theatrical mourning and demonstrations of grief, now feared for their property and their lives. Hasty conversions to the Hanoverian crown were seen all over the kingdom and the Young Pretender was forced to flee back into the land of sentiment and the imagination where he was immortalised as a romantic and unhappy splash of tartan in a Hanoverian grey reality. The King continued to rely on Carteret's advice and in 1744 Pelham and his brother threatened to resign in protest. Carteret was eventually dismissed, but with the war going badly and with the 1745 rebellion threatening national self-confidence if not the Hanoverian settlement itself, the King continued to consult him behind the scenes. Patience with the monarch finally wore out, and in February 1746 virtually the whole administration, including Henry Fox and the Duke of Richmond, whose Mastership of the Horse brought an honorary Cabinet post, resigned. George II was unable to form a government with the shreds of Carteret's support and he was forced, after a few weeks, to ask Newcastle and Pelham back on their own terms. Carteret was thrown into oblivion as a condition of their return. For the next eight years Pelham and his brother presided over a relatively stable administration.

At the beginning of the new government there was a period of shuffles and reshuffles of the Cabinet. It was in one of them that Fox got his chance. He became Secretary at War. The job brought a Cabinet post and a good deal of trouble. Europe was still in turmoil and no peace was in sight. Fox had wanted the post of Paymaster General of the Forces, a lesser though more lucrative and easier job, reckoning that it offered a step up the political ladder without the political risks involved in taking the War Office. But that had gone to Fox's rival Pitt, and ambition, of which Fox had a great deal, demanded that he accept the secretaryship. Refusal would signify faint-heartedness and signal the premature end of his political career. But faint-hearted was exactly what Fox was, as he freely confessed to his brother, 'I fear I must take it, to quarrel with the army and . . . to do business from morning to night.'

Before Fox was offered the post, Newcastle had thought it prudent to reassure the Duke of Richmond that he would not have to do any business with his hated son-in-law. A deputy could stand in for Richmond when he needed to work with the War Office. Richmond tried to stop the appointment but

Fox was by this time indispensable to the government and any duty of friendship that Newcastle owed to Richmond was rapidly cast aside by political expediency. Fox had become a more important political figure than his father-in-law and Richmond was made to realise it in no uncertain terms.

Having got the job, Henry and Caroline began looking around for a house to go with it. As a protégé of Walpole, Fox knew that splendid surroundings elevated a host and humbled his guests. Walpole had built Houghton, his country mansion, as a temple to power, a palace overflowing with the rewards of offices. Visitors there were stupefied by acres of plush damask and taffeta, sunk in the curves of French upholstery and overcome by the weight of gilded ceilings and golden picture-frames. Fox was looking out for a house on a smaller scale in which he could entertain and impress. What he and Caroline found, in the summer of 1746, was a house quite unlike the modern palaces successful politicians put up to demonstrate their exalted positions. It was a huge, decaying, unfashionable Jacobean mansion called Holland House, just on the western edge of London. Holland House came cheap, especially when its size was taken into account. It cost £102 16s. 9d. a year, not much more than the Foxes' house in Conduit Street, but the price reflected its dilapidation and unfashionableness. Henry and Caroline took Holland House on an extendable lease for ninety-nine years.

London was already marching relentlessly westwards when the Foxes leased Holland House. But the mansion still stood, a decaying anachronism, in a large park of sixty-four acres. When Henry and Caroline arrived, the park was unenclosed, bounded to the south and east by the gardens of Kensington Palace and its satellite cottages, to the north by the Acton road and to the west by open country dotted with artisans' dwellings and small vegetable gardens, gravel pits and farms.

Holland House appealed to Caroline because she had a passion for antiquities and although it was only a century and a half old the style of the house had been relegated to the scrap heap by most aristocrats and merchants who were building on any scale. It also reminded her of her father's house at Goodwood, from which she was now banished, which had survived only because he had spent a huge amount of money on Richmond House in London and plans to rebuild in Sussex had so far come to naught. Because Caroline's taste was for the old-fashioned and she was scornful of warmer, more modern, house plans, the Foxes renovated rather than rebuilt. When they first took it, Holland House was empty. Half a century earlier it had been split into apartments and rented out, but even these had proved unfashionable and the house had slipped into disrepair. It was built, like Goodwood, albeit on a much larger scale, in the H-plan common to many Jacobean mansions. The centre block rose, in gables and turrets, to four storeys; the two wings, running north to south, rose two imposing storeys high. A grand portico ran all the way around the inner walls of the house on the ground floor of the main, south-facing front, from which steps fell to an old-fashioned formal garden.

Holland House was so big that relatives and favoured friends could have their own apartments. Stephen Fox habitually stayed there on the increasingly rare occasions when he came up to London for parliamentary sessions. Charles Hanbury Williams, already renting his house in Conduit Street to the Foxes, was also given a room and took the precaution, made necessary by the tomb-like cold of the house, to pay for his own furnishings. Hanbury Williams had refused an embassy posting to northern Europe on the grounds that the weather there was too frigid and he was determined that Holland House would not prove a similarly inhospitable outpost. 'I have ordered my upholsterer to get my room in order at Holland House, where I am sure of being pleased and happy,' he wrote to Henry in 1746. His hosts, however, were notoriously careless of the cold, often leaving the doors open in the dead of winter. Less close friends were often scared into staying in town by tales of room temperatures that no hospitality, however warm, could mitigate. 'I can't venture to go to stay at Holland House yet awhile,' wrote Caroline's sister Emily one autumn day in 1761 while she was recovering from childbirth. 'I should be killed there, I know, for I could not (even for my first visit, which I thought a little unkind) get them to keep the doors and windows shut. I really found it very cold, but I saw it was thought affectation and fancy.'

Luckily, Holland House was near enough to Westminster to allow dinner guests to travel home at night, and big enough to accommodate both hardy souls and those too incapacitated to take to the road. Domestic and political life could thus go hand in hand. Fox could entertain in a manner normally only possible in the country and attend to government business the next day. Caroline could be with Ste and with Henry at the same time; in her own apartments she could read, write letters, entertain callers and play with her son. In the garden she could saunter about, supervise planting and muse amongst the flowers. Caroline frequently complained that their closeness to town brought all Fox's political associates to their door: 'Indeed when he is in business this place is quite like a coffee house.' Jealously, she felt that Holland House was too well placed for Fox's casual social life. 'Holland House is so convenient for his intimate friends to be constantly with him, that they take up all the time I could see him alone, and plague me ten times more than people who have real business with him.' But Caroline could and did retire from late-night carousing, and she realised that because Holland House allowed them to combine the spaciousness of the country with the business of the town she enjoyed a good deal more of Henry's company than politics might otherwise have allowed her. Fox became such a famous family man partly because his cronies and political associates saw him amongst his children at Holland House. For his children, equally, politics and nursery life were mixed together and the child and adult worlds fused hard and fast.

PART THREE
'The Lord Kildare is not the
most clever man in the world'.
Caroline to Henry, 15 January 1747.

It was soon after signing the lease of Holland House in 1746 that Caroline went to Bath, and it was from Bath that she sent Henry the news that her fourteen-year-old sister Emily was going to be married. For Caroline that meant a reunion, since Emily would now be free to see her as she pleased. But their intimacy would be short lived and henceforth at least partly epistolary, because Emily was marrying an Irishman who, unlike many Irish aristocrats, was determined to live in Ireland. His name was James Fitzgerald, Earl of Kildare. Once again, the Duke and Duchess were opposed to the match; this time on the grounds of nationality rather than social standing or political antecedents. Still bitter about her own treatment, Caroline reported to Henry, 'I think mother can't prevent the match, but I think she will delay it for a month or two if she can. I don't think she was ever so thoroughly mortified before as she is at this match for she must seem pleased with it in the eyes of the world at the time she would give her ears to break it.' As for the Earl himself, Caroline went on, he 'is not the most clever man in the world (and consequently not company for such a great man as you). Don't decline being intimate with him because I shall like seeing my sister a good deal and that pleasure will be much greater if I can be with you both at a time.'

Emily was the sibling Caroline knew best and in whom she had confided during the later stages of her courtship with Fox. Emily was also her parents' favourite. When she was a baby some of her bones were misaligned and she was laced in a 'swing' to let them fall free. This frailty increased her parents' adoration. She was a precocious child. 'Em is admirable but horribly naughty,' the Duchess of Richmond wrote with doting indulgence when Emily was a few years old. 'I saw her go to bed last night and asked her if the bed was a good one. She told me "c'est ce qu'on apelle en Englois comfortable" [*sic*] I dote on her as much as you do.' Elsewhere Emily's status as favourite was confirmed. 'Pray get the better of Emily if you can,' the Duchess wrote. 'I believe its very necessary she should be here for me to punish her, for you spoil her.'

In the autumn of 1746 Emily was approaching her fifteenth birthday. Fairer than Caroline, she had thick, curling brown hair, light-blue eyes (although they were sometimes wrongly painted grey by lazy portraitists) and her sister's small mouth that turned provocatively up at the ends. She was tall and well proportioned and, if the Earl of Kildare's partiality is to be believed, had beautiful legs. Her beauty, though, owed as much to manner as to features. Joshua Reynolds said she had 'a sweetness of expression' that was difficult for a painter to capture. To this charm were added a mental liveliness and a physical langour which called simultaneously for attention and pampering. Emily secured the indulgence of her friends and admirers by flirtatious demands, extravagant gestures and judicious apology if she overstepped the mark.

Emily was born in 1731 and was eight years younger than Caroline. When she was four, Charles, Earl of March, was born, and two years later the thankful Duchess produced another boy, Lord George Lennox. The family name and line was thereby secured and the second Duke and his wife were able to relax and enjoy their family. The atmosphere of sickness, death and anxiety that Caroline knew so well was dissipated as Emily grew up and she was entirely free from the sense of guilt and foreboding which haunted her sister. Her beauty and the obvious ease with which she manipulated her father and her two younger brothers endowed her with a lifelong sense of entitlement. Emily was complacent about others' feelings for her when she was young. 'I love to be doted upon vastly,' she wrote in her twenties and accepted devotion and adoration as her due. Yet while she never doubted her own powers of attraction, Emily was well aware of others' needs and dispositions. Caroline, she knew, was slightly censorious about vanity, regretting that she had 'more than a common share of that foible'. So Emily made her happy with loving flattery, writing on Caroline's thirtieth birthday, 'I think you are grown handsomer, younger and cheerfuller within these two years than ever I remember you, so pray don't be affected and say you are old.' Emily teased Henry Fox and was excited by his enjoyment of her company. 'I love his villainous countenance,' she wrote to her sister. To Fox himself she wrote high-spiritedly in 1756, 'I am glad your brother is made an Earl. He is a sweet man, worth a thousand of you; much better humoured, ten thousand times better bred, much livelier, and I believe full as clever, only that you have a cunning, black, devilish countenance and he has a cheerful, pleasant one; you are an ambitious vain toad and he likes to live quietly in the country.'

Sexy abuse of this sort was only suited to a man like Fox who was confident of his charm and did not stand on his dignity. Towards her husband Emily had necessarily to behave very differently but she used the same manipulative skills and displayed a similar confidence about her relationships. When she was young Emily exuded a delight in herself that rubbed off on other people. She surrounded herself with people, Caroline noticed, and amongst them she always had a few especially favoured female friends. With one she wrote poetry, as she had done with Caroline at Goodwood; with another she read and sewed and chatted. A dead horse gave Emily and Lady Drogheda, an intimate friend in the years after her marriage, a whole day of fun. She reported their enjoyment to Caroline with teenage exuberance: 'her verses are quite in our way and she and I writ poetry to one another all day long when she was here. Lord Kildare, who was in great grief (about the dead horse) begged they might be very serious and melancholy and suitable to such a subject, which accordingly they were, and I send them to Mr. Fox to show him I excel equally in the sublime as in the comical style. But my poetical genius can attain any height, nothing is either too high or too low for it.'

Emily liked women friends for company and service, admitting, 'as I . . . am lazy it is useful to have somebody to do a thousand little matters for me and give the many little assistances such as calling, fetching, ringing. All this you will say is very selfish and I allow it.' Of a friend who nearly died Emily wrote in the same vein to the Earl of Kildare: 'What should I have done without her? . . . that loves one as she does, that enters with such warmth into everything that interests one, all one's little views of pleasure, profit or ambition, in short one that has such a heart?' In her old age she looked severely upon her own self indulgence, writing, 'every young person should be brought up to be helpful; I never was,' but her youthful habits lasted her a lifetime.

Emily did not stand on ceremony. She was less worried than Caroline about behaviour and etiquette, happy to receive friends in informal clothes or undress. 'Colonel Sandford came here yesterday morning,' she wrote to her husband while she was confined after childbirth, 'I was in bed, but did not scruple seeing him.' Nor did she worry too much about social convention, within the limits peculiar to Protestant life in Ireland. From the countryside outside Dublin she wrote to her husband, 'Think how pleasantly Mrs. Crofton and Mrs. Crosbie surprised me Sunday night at nine o'clock. They were to go out and take the air after dinner together. One proposed coming here, the other assented and away they drove. They supped here, lay here and went away after breakfast again.' Caroline said, 'I should be miserable at the thoughts of a great many people in the house with me,' but admitted, 'I'm more personne d'habitude than you are.'

Caroline was also more thoughtful. Emily, at the time of her marriage, was still an 'engaging girl' as Caroline called her, only just out of the schoolroom. She filled her time with reading rather than dreary thoughts. 'I love to see everything new that comes out, either pretty or foolish,' she wrote, and had a standing order with the London bookseller Mrs Dunoyer for 'all the new books'. Like Caroline, she used books as an outlet for sentiment; she 'perfectly sobbed' at reading Murphy's play *The Orphan of China* when it came out, and declared that she would be 'killed' if she saw it acted on the stage. At some point she started reading political pamphlets as well as the novels, poetry and plays that were her staple fare. Emily also demanded novelty of other kinds, developing an expensive taste in furnishings, clothes of all sorts, buckles and jewels set in the latest styles, new games of cards.

As Caroline realised, Emily was still a child when she married, still searching for a comfortable personality to inhabit. She changed the way she signed her letters, she gave herself nicknames – her favourite being Patsy – and experimented with different sorts of handwriting. Her husband, in contrast, was already feeling all of his twenty-five years. His life was burdened with the heavy weight of an ancient dynasty and he took his familial duties tremendously seriously.

By the eighteenth century the Fitzgeralds, or Geraldines as they were popularly known, had an identity that was both august and schizophrenic. They were, as Kildare said, the oldest surviving and thus the 'first' peers of Ireland. By virtue of their long residence there and the marriage alliances they had contracted amongst the pre-Norman inhabitants, the Fitzgeralds regarded themselves as Irish. But by the mid-eighteenth century they were sufficiently powerful amongst the Protestants – particularly those in and around Dublin, whose families may have been there for two hundred years – to have become figureheads for Irish Protestant nationalism which was fundamentally at odds with the interests and rights of the Gaelic and Catholic Irish. Protestants, many of them in commerce and the professions, tended to advance their claims to the exclusion of all other groups. They were hostile to any whiff of emancipation for Catholics and Dissenters and were suspicious of any dealings by the Westminster government that might lessen their autonomy or control over national finances.

Kildare was very rich, with an estate that in 1820 was counted as 67,000 acres valued at £46,000. Low-lying fertile land spreading westwards from Dublin into the green heart of the country formed most of his estate. Fields of rippling wheat, scythed by cheap Irish labour for export to the lucrative English market, herds of milk cows and steers and rows of root vegetables represented high yields for tenant farmers and high rents for landowners. While England's hungry population was soaring, Ireland had yet to see the explosion that would make for so much misery in the future; Ireland was, in mid-century, in the full flush of a temporary prosperity that reached its zenith in the Napoleonic wars and crashed spectacularly thereafter. When he proposed to Emily, Kildare had a rent-roll of getting on for £15,000 a year and virtually unlimited credit with Dublin's bankers.

Kildare was an important figure in Irish political life because he controlled a large block of MPs in the Irish House of Commons. He was determined to use this influence, writing bluntly to Fox that he wanted, 'to be, if I can, of the first consequence here'. But his dynastic prominence carried him further in Irish politics than his own political talents. Confined to a totemic role as a figurehead of Protestant nationalism he might have been successful. But he lacked the acumen and flexibility that might have allowed him to make something of the active political role that he sought. Believing that the man of honour enumerated his grievances plainly and that plain justice would mitigate them, he appeared stubborn and unsubtle in the political arena. If officials side-stepped his demands, Kildare responded by asserting rank and taking the matter up with a higher authority, travelling, if necessary, as far as the King himself, and making enemies all the way up. He failed to understand that for men like Fox politics was a profession more than a dynastic responsibility and it was a profession which had increasingly complicated, subtle and devious rules of its own.

In and around Dublin, Kildare could set the social pace. In 1745 he chose a suburban site south of the Liffey for a grand new town house. It was not an area favoured by the nobility or by Dublin's rich merchants, but Kildare declared that 'they will follow me wherever I go'. Speculators, professionals and newly rich gentlemen poured across the river after him, sanctioned by nobility and credit to found a new fashionable centre for the city which gradually eclipsed the north side. In London Kildare was a much more uncertain figure. He had no lands in England and no English title that would give him social standing and a seat in the Lords. His wealth was to a large degree offset by his Irishness, because Ireland was already a focus for English anxieties about change and difference and colonialism. The Duke of Richmond for one made no distinctions among the heterogeneous population of Ireland, even though he himself had had Irish lands, preferring, in the interests of satirical prejudice, to lump them all together. The Duke declared, after Emily had a son, that his dark-headed hunter had more sense than any 'white Irish heads' and was slow to congratulate his daughter, prompting Caroline to write tartly (though without disagreeing), 'surely reflections on the Irish stupidity is not so civil in his Grace?' Prejudice of the same sort also dominated the Duchess's response to Kildare's proposal for Emily, the more so since she worked hard at forgetting the fact that she herself was of Irish extraction.

For both the Duke and Duchess of Richmond, Ireland was a country far more remote from their actual and imagined experience than continental Europe. Into this imaginary void they now tried to place their daughter; all they could conjure up were bogs, stupidity and the theatricality for which Irish actors, impresarios and playwrights were already famous in London. When Kildare first proposed in the summer of 1745 they baulked at the proposal on the grounds that Emily was still too young to know what she wanted or what marriage meant. Stubborn persistence kept Kildare determined and waiting. When the Duke could no longer put Kildare off, and unable to pass on a definite refusal from Emily herself, he drove a hard bargain. Emily came only with the promise of £10,000 when her parents died and the Duke demanded a handsome annuity or jointure for her in the event of Kildare's death. Richmond knew that Kildare was after the political rather than the financial advantage that went along with the bride and that his own part of the bargain would be to honour the political obligations that marital alliance brought with it. Especially galling was the knowledge that Fox, rising fast up the political ladder in the chaos after Walpole's fall, was equally the target of Kildare's overtures.

Knowing that politics played such a large part in Kildare's proposal contributed to the Duke's coolness. He also wanted Emily close by. Having lost one daughter to Fox, the Duke was reluctant to lose another to Ireland. But the Duchess was the real stumbling block, as Caroline had realised when she wrote to Henry from Bath. The Duchess was embarrassed about her Irish blood and the last thing she wanted was a connection which would perpetually remind her of it. Emily realised that her mother was hostile to Kildare, although at the age of fourteen she was uneducated in the anxieties of colonial identity. Ten years later she saw a parallel to her own case in another romance. 'Sir James Lowther has desired Mr Fox to propose him for Lady Betty Spencer. He is violently in love, poor man, and they don't behave quite well to him and are for putting it off two years . . . It is a vast match for her, but the Duchess is odd about it, the Duke would be reasonable enough if it was not for her, and, in short, the whole thing is just a second part of the affair between you and I, which makes me interest myself prodigiously about it.'

Despite her mother's objections, Emily was quite happy with Kildare's proposal and, with her consent, it was hard to find any grounds for objection to the marriage. Kildare, a model of persistent propriety, had waited eighteen months

for her by December 1746 and was no longer to be put off on
the grounds that she was too young. For the Duke to cite Kildare's Irishness would probably have resulted in a duel. It
lingered, an unmentionable miasma, in the background of
their negotiations, throwing a cloud of suspicion, prejudice
and mistrust over everything. Family honour was at stake on
both sides and there was no doubt that, strictly speaking, Kildare's was the more august and ancient family. Irishness
aside, nothing could be held against him. He was rich, young,
well educated and obviously in love. The only way that Richmond could make his prejudice about nationality obvious was
to drive a harder bargain than he would have done if Kildare's
land had been in Hampshire or Sussex, and Kildare tacitly
accepted that his Irishness had to be paid for with a penniless
bride.

Kildare was prepared to pay the price. He offered very
generous settlements, and wrote to the Duke, 'I have flattered
myself they are such as prove my value and esteem for Lady
Emily ... I hope and persuade myself that your Grace and
my Lady Duchess have by this time considered and seen them
in the same light too, and from reflection will be convinced
that I desire with ardour and sincerity to make Lady Emily
happy.' In arranged marriages, paying money to the bride in
the form of pin money and promises for a secure old age came
perilously close to paying money for her. For Kildare, at any
rate, money and desire were bedfellows. Emily and expenditure were always coupled together. Emily herself understood
this straight away. When she needed money she played on
Kildare's lust, and potential criticism of her extravagance she
diverted skilfully into desire.

Just negotiating about money made Kildare want Emily the
more, and some kind of sexual encounter took place between
them on Christmas Day 1746, in the Duke's empty summer
house on the Goodwood estate, Carné's Seat. Emily remembered it fondly when they were parted sixteen years later. 'If
you are at Goodwood, and the sun shines as bright as it does

here, I hope you will take a walk up to Carné Seat, sit down in the little room and think of that you took with Lady Emily Lennox, just returned from Bognor Church, sixteen years ago, and believe that I love you sixteen times better now than I did then.' This partially complete love making made Kildare, at any rate, long for the wedding which, the complex negotiations wrapped up to the satisfaction of both sides, took place at Richmond House on 7 February 1747. Gossips reported the ceremony as very magnificent, but Kildare later only remembered what followed. He reached a pinnacle of happiness that night and Richmond House was always associated in his mind with the first time he made love to Emily. 'I don't believe, if I was to lie at Whitehall, I could ever sleep, for thinking that in that house it was that I first took possession of that which for about fifteen years I have enjoyed.' Dynastic and national considerations fled; Kildare adored his wife and was an ardent lover. His love making was given confidence by the belief that sex was, as he put it, 'necessary to a woman's health and happiness'. (Caroline disagreed; when Emily relayed what Kildare had said, she retorted, 'its abominably indelicate and I don't believe a word of it. I'm sure one sees many an old virgin mighty well and comfortable.')

It was left to Horace Walpole to hint at the wedding's political dimensions. 'Lord Kildare is married to charming Lady Emily Lennox, who went the very next day to see her sister, Lady Caroline Fox, to the great mortification of the haughty Duchess mother. They have not given her a shilling, but the King endows her by making Lord Kildare a Viscount Sterling; and they talk of giving him a pinchbeck Dukedom too, to keep him always first peer of Ireland.'

Kildare had no objection to Caroline and Emily being reunited. On the contrary, their intimacy would pave the way to his political alliance with Fox. This alliance was by now worth risking the Duke's displeasure for: once again Richmond was made to realise that the political as well as the emotional initiative had passed to his son-in-law. None the less Kildare did not leave Caroline and Emily long to catch up on the missed years and interrupted confidences. By June, Emily was in Ireland.

In the minds of English visitors and observers, Ireland was a chimerical land, an island floating mistily in the sea of the imagination. Irish peasants and Catholic landlords alike seemed as unstable and deceptive as the foggy bogland itself. The Irish themselves clouded this picture by creating personae that exploited their capacities for theatrical, overblown and ironic narrative. Visitors confronted with the fantastic cloak of words within which the Irish hid themselves retreated, baffled, to their own prejudices and preconceptions. On the London stage overt Irish theatricality and the covert English sense of life as drama came together and an international reconciliation, smoothed by pleasure and profit, took place. Irish playwrights like Richard Brinsley Sheridan went so far, later in the century, as to pander to English prejudice with ironic creations of caricature Irishmen like Sir Lucius O'Trigger, and got hard cash and social cachet into the bargain. But in Ireland itself, particularly in the countryside, English rural fantasies replete with cosy cottages and happy swain could not be squared with the cottagers' way of life and domestic architecture. Turning their eyes away from the pockets of sophisticated agriculture and industry, observers fastened a horrified gaze on rural poverty, with its huts of wattle and thatch and scantily clad Gaelic-speaking families that subsisted on a diet of vegetables, milk and potatoes. Measured against an imaginary English rural idyll, this unregulated, uncertain and incomprehensible way of life seemed horrifying. After ten years in Ireland, Emily still measured the countryside against some notional English landscape of the south coast. Staying at Brockley Park, a small country house outside Dublin, she felt temporarily transported to that imaginary English land and wrote delightedly to Lord Kildare: 'You can't imagine anything more like the country of England than it is all round here; shady lanes with oak trees in the hedges, a river just under the windows, fields and meadows with paths through them, no stone walls, no miserable cabins near it – in short, just this spot is vastly pretty.' Like many English commentators, Emily looked at the countryside and saw it without any people. It was years before she noticed the poor around her, and when she did it was to register their change from the 'mob' (as Caroline always called it) to the 'people' as radicals described them.

Emily found the Irish nobility as unappealing as their countryside. She derided the interiors of their houses, her own included, as less well appointed than their English counterparts. To her mind no amount of well-fed, bibulous Irish hospitality compensated for run-down, badly furnished rooms. 'I wish to have our house look *sprucish*,' she wrote to Kildare from London in 1757, 'Every mortal's house here is so pretty and smart, and well furnished, that I do long to have ours too a little . . . How do people here, who can't afford it half so well as us, contrive to have things so pretty in their houses? I do believe the case is as Lady C[aroline] Duncannon said t'other day with a good deal of truth: "that everybody in Ireland spend all they have in eating and drinking and have no notion of any other sorts of comfort in life; they don't care whether their houses or anything in them is fit to receive company. Provided they can stuff them, that's enough." After all, my Dear Lord K., there is a good deal of reason in what she says. I own, it struck me – it's so generally the case amongst us.' The Irish nobility were, by the time Emily wrote this, working hard to rectify any lingering traces of seventeenth-century austerity from their domestic surroundings. Kildare had already started the massive landscaping and decorating project at Carton, his country estate outside Dublin, and other noble houses would rival anything in England for magnificence within the next thirty years. New building in Dublin was providing wealthy Irishmen with sumptuous modern town houses.

By the mid-eighteenth century, Dublin was settling into a

monumental grandeur. Town houses of the nobility – Leinster House, Tyrone House, the towering front of Powerscourt House, Charlemont House on the north side of the Liffey – dominated wide, boulevard-like streets lined with the regular red-brick façades of four-storeyed terraces. Some streets, like Fitzwilliam Street, led like avenues up to public buildings. Others ended in open spaces like Merrion Square and St Stephen's Green. Occasionally, on fine days, the purple Wicklow Mountains offered a spectacular natural back-cloth to man-made modernity. Dublin's public buildings were as splendid as its private houses. The Parliament House, begun in 1729, cost £95,000 to build and had a grandeur and completeness utterly lacking in its shambling Westminster counterpart. Trinity College, the focal point of Irish Protestant nationalism, was enlarged and rebuilt into granite impressiveness in the 1750s.

The exteriors of Dublin's terraced houses were as severe as anything going up on the Bedford and Grosvenor estates in London at the same time. But curvaceous fanlights hung with leaden swags and ribbons hinted at gorgeousness within. Wide halls led to generously turning staircases, top lit by fanlights, with smooth shiny mahogany rails and ornate banisters. In the grand public rooms upstairs, plaster work, white or particoloured, plump upholstery and rich carpets rioted in baroque splendour. In the grandest houses there was a hectic amalgam of pinks, purples and green, reflected and doubled in candelabra and chandeliers.

Such overblown raciness behind a dour façade was a feature of Protestant life in Dublin in the second half of the eighteenth century. Order and elegance might be one side of Ascendancy society, but outsiders were quick to see that they were matched by a taste for party-giving and going, bouts of heavy drinking, gambling and theatricals. Quarrels were often settled with blows or, at the opposite extreme, lawsuits of labyrinthine complexity. Outward restraint vied with an excess whose vulgarity was its own ironic comment on the uneasy social status of many newly wealthy Protestants. Social relations in Dublin society were equally confusing and contradictory. On the one hand the Ascendancy was enclosed within the wagon-circle of the Pale, impenetrable to those who were not Protestant. On the other hand, within the Protestant world a casualness about social class and distinction prevailed and humble origins were quickly obscured under rich French silks and layers of gilding and ormolu.

Emily settled down easily into the freewheeling raciness of Dublin society after her arrival in the summer of 1747. Dublin suited her theatrical and extravagant personality far better than it did Kildare's solemnity. Dubliners were happy to fall in with the combination of lazy domesticity and hectic party-going that characterised Emily's early married life. At Carton, Kildare's huge, unfinished Palladian mansion a few miles west of Dublin, Emily surrounded herself with friends and companions. She read, sewed and took a gossipy interest in country customs and scandals. 'We are mighty quiet and comfortable, live all day long in one room, muddle and dress in the morning for all day – in short,' she wrote to her absent husband, it was 'just the kind of life which you know once I get into I love mightily, and it is much better for you than if I was losing my money at loo in town.' But Carton was only a couple of hours drive from Dublin, and Emily readily dropped domesticity for an invitation to cards, a party or the play. In Dublin she stayed at Kildare House, monumental, charmless and also unfinished. From there she reported her gambling losses to her husband without a hint of contrition: 'Plagued by the servants, worried by the children, my dearest Lord Kildare, I have not been able to sit down and write to you till this minute. I did not stay to sup at Mrs. Hussey's, but played till twelve and lost £20, which is a great deal at plain crown loo.' As the losses and debts mounted, Emily took temporary refuge in gamblers' dreams. 'If I could have one good night ... it would retrieve my broken fortune.'

Good nights never did come and Emily went on losing with scarcely a qualm, writing complacently to her husband, 'amusement you know I cannot do without'.

In Dublin Emily played the *grande dame* to the hilt, matching her behaviour to the hectic conduct of the Protestant élite. She and Kildare were objects of fascination in Protestant Dublin. Bursts of rhetorical satire sometimes greeted their extravagance. But satirical acerbity was mixed with admiration: the Kildares' behaviour was too close to Dublin's mood to elicit anything akin to Swiftian savagery. Ten years after her arrival, Emily cheerfully sent such a satire to Henry Fox, knowing that like its author, he was still intoxicated by her gaiety. 'I send you a song that abuses us all and will divert you,' she wrote delightedly, and copied out the stanzas for him:

> The Tenth of November the Governor's ball
> My Lord Kildare of Carton,
> And there you shall see the Devil and all
> With Lord Kildare of Carton.
> For Bessborough's peer is not to be here
> With Lord Kildare of Carton.
>
> There close by his side see her Ladyship sit
> My Lady Kildare of Carton;
> For the mimic of majesty none so fit
> As Lady Kildare of Carton.
> The beaux they all bow when her Ladyship nods
> My Lady Kildare of Carton,
> Who thinks herself raised to the state of the gods
> By Lord Kildare of Carton.

Emily's queenly behaviour was not, however, derived from her social standing so much as her sexual confidence. 'If I was not your sister you would be in love with me,' she wrote invitingly to Fox. Emily brazenly used her sexual charms as barter for affection and indulgence and with no one did she barter more than her husband. This manipulation had a multiple purpose. Kildare stayed devoted, Emily remained adored and she was able to spend all the money she wanted. The more money she asked for and disposed of, the more excited Kildare became. Everyone, bankers included, were satisfied by the arrangement. Huge debts and a very large family were the inevitable result. By 1773, Emily and Kildare had debts of £148,000 and nineteen children.

Inevitably, when Emily and her husband were parted, money talk filled their correspondence and lust breathed hotly through it. Sometimes writing was troublesome for Emily because she had weak eyes; others were often inveigled into wielding the pen. But money was secret. In 1757 she wrote from Holland House to her husband, 'I employ a secretary out of prudence, my right eye being a little weak.' But after a paragraph about her debts and her need for a 'birthday gown and perhaps one sack, or two at most, for the winter', she forgot her blindness and seized the pen. 'I cannot, my sweet Jemmy, end this by my secretary; for I cannot let anybody but myself tell you what I always feel in regard to money; indeed it is what I should not attempt to express. Your goodness, your kindness to me always affect me so strongly when I talk or think on that subject, that I am too much moved to let any other person be witness to it.' Kildare was gratified by these tones of sexual conspiracy, and Emily got her debts paid. Sometimes Kildare was alarmed by the quantities of silk dresses, jewels, rolls of taffeta, yards of hand-painted wallpaper, bundles of books and expanses of carpet that Emily ordered. 'My love, my love, it is very great pleasure to write for things to be sent to one; but the paying is not so when it is inconvenient,' he wrote in 1759. But a few days later he was reporting, 'I have performed all the commissions that belong to you. As to pictures, tables, brooches, they have not been enquired after yet, and I am afraid to look for them. They will cost so much and this year I fear will be

my ruin. Carton will cost so much and no money coming in.'
Pleading poverty gave Kildare no defence against Emily's
charms. If he said he could not afford something, she had
only to hint that she might go elsewhere to procure it, and he
capitulated. Once she set her heart on having some diamonds
reset in the latest fashion and went slyly about getting her
way. 'You know, my dear Lord Kildare,' she began, softening
him up, 'you did once consent to my altering my buckle.
Now I wish it more than ever . . . such contrivances they have
now got to pick one's pocket, and you know your poor
Emily cannot resist temptation. So, my dear, my sweet Lord
Kildare, don't be angry.' Then she approached the problem
indirectly, mingling flattery and teasing, raising the sexual
temperature, 'it was very polite and right in you to invite
those ladies to Carton. I assure [you] I am not at all jealous of
any of them, unless it is Mrs. Clements; who is so pretty, so
young, so gentle and so unaffected that I think there is some
danger of your falling in love with her. If you do, Mr. Clements shall be my lover and then I may afford to new-set my
diamonds as often as I please.' Expensively reset, the
diamonds duly arrived. Emily declared them 'charming', and
wrote to Kildare, 'how good you are about the buckle'.

Sporadic attempts at economy punctuated this litany to the
heady new world of consumption. Emily did little to curb her
own habits, but every now and then she cast a weary eye over
household expenditure and made minute and totally ineffec-
tual adjustments. 'Yesterday . . . I looked over the house
accounts. It's well I did for you would have been ruined in
fruit cakes and tarts if I had not made a little regulation about
it.' 'I must tell you that I have made myself quite mistress of
the dairy knowledge . . . and have also got some hints about
soap etc that will be very useful to me; for since my dear Lord
K. leaves me so much at liberty to please myself about my
house I am determined to show him I can save his money as
well as spend it.' But Emily could not save and she felt much
more at home justifying extravagance than attempting econo-
mies. The passages at Carton dripped with water – in the

winter, she wrote, 'which shows, my love, the necessity of having very often fires almost all over the house. We must never be sparing in the article of coals.' So the debts mounted. Like many creditworthy aristocrats Emily schemed to juggle deficits so that they seemed to match incomes. During a ruinous visit to London in 1757 she wrote to Kildare: 'my scheme is to pay my old bills only, and any of the trifling new ones; but it would be too much to pay all indeed. Besides the people here never worry one for money you know.'

Kildare might grumble about paying for his wife's enslavement to novelty, but he pandered to it by making explicit the connection he made between sex and money, writing after the coronation of George III, which Emily had attended, loaded with finery, 'I gave . . . five guineas for Mrs. Ciber, for dressing you for the coronation, and would give more than I could name to have the pleasure of undressing you myself.' Indeed Kildare did not really want the spending spree to stop and he often contributed to the mounting debts himself with presents for his wife. Stockings were his particular favourite. They reminded him of the beautiful flesh they would so enticingly cover. Kildare knew that Emily was fond of stockings that had been 'clocked' or elaborately embroidered with silk. She bought them in London and from there her husband wrote excitedly in 1762: 'I find I exceed your commission in regard to your stockings with coloured clocks. I bespoke two pairs with bright blue, two pairs with green and two pairs with pink clocks . . . I am sure when you have them on, your dear legs will set them off. I will bespoke you six more pairs with white clocks; you mean to have them embroidered I suppose, therefore [I] shall make you a present of the dozen. The writing about your stockings and dear, pretty legs makes me feel what is not to be expressed.' When the stockings came back from the seamstress, Kildare was excited anew. 'I think they are very pretty and when upon your dear pretty legs will look much better – Oh! What would I give to see them. I must stop here, for if I was to let myself go on to express what

I feel by being absent, I should put my eyes out.' But he did go on, adding in his next letter, I 'long very much for the acknowledgment [your] dear, dear legs are to make for the trouble I have had upon their account, and make no doubt but that I shall be amply rewarded for the care I have had about them.' After the stockings had finally arrived at Carton, Emily wrote coyly, 'Henry [one of the little boys] admires clocked stockings as much as you do; he is forever peeping under my petticoats – what nonsense I do fill my letters with.' But she never made any declarations of passion to her husband, contenting herself with mildly titillating, fond and flirtatious replies to his declarations of need. Kildare once remarked with sober sadness, 'you have never mentioned or hinted at feeling the effect of my happiest moments.'

Emily's first child George, whose courtesy title was Lord Ophaly, was born in January 1748, less than a year after her marriage. Emily was sixteen years old. George was followed by a tribe of siblings so large that occasionally Emily and Kildare failed to recognise their children when they came back from sojourns in London or Dublin. Arriving home from a trip to London in 1762, Emily 'was sitting down by myself very quietly to write to my dear Jemmy,' when 'a dear little child run in to me and puts its arms round my neck; who should it be but sweet Henry! I did not know him the least in the world . . . Three months makes a surprising change at his age, but yet I wonder I did not know him.'

William followed George in 1749 and after him came Caroline in 1750, Emily in 1752 and Henrietta in 1753. Little Caroline died in 1754 and when Emily's next child was born, right on cue in 1755, she too was named Caroline, only to follow her namesake into a very early grave. A third son, Charles, was born in 1756. So the family grew. Now and then Emily and Kildare complained about the size of their family. They worried about how their younger children would survive when they grew up, particularly the girls who could not, given their parents' profligacy, count on much money. But they were proud parents all the same. Emily's mother-in-law noticed that they were very particular about their children's upbringing. Old Lady Kildare was exasperated with them, Emily reported to her husband and said, 'you and I were both so exact and had so much fiddle faddle about our children! You indeed were worse again than me, she would not be your servant nor your child for the world, you was so tiresome.'

Emily found the ever-repeating cycle of pregnancy, childbirth and confinement tedious. But she never regretted her large family and she was fond of each of her children. In 1762, three months after the birth of Sophia, she began to suspect – rightly as it turned out – that she was already pregnant again. She soon got the better of her annoyance and wrote to Kildare, 'I have resolved not to grumble! After all, are not my pretty babes a blessing? When I look round at them all, does not my heart rejoice at the sight, and overflow with tenderness? Why then repine? They are good, they are healthy, they are pretty; God Almighty bless them; if they gave me pain, they now make up for it by giving me pleasure.'

Emily loved the routine of the country and the nursery. She plunged herself into domestic life and extracted great pleasure from events that bored her husband. 'Henry naked is the dearest little being on earth,' she would exclaim and demanded regular bulletins from the nursery if she was away. 'Pray tell me something of dear little Charles – if he begins to walk, and how he likes his shoes and stockings.' 'My love to the dear girls. Kiss my Charles, my dear, dear pretty little Charles, and tell me something about him when you write.' 'Dear little Charles is lame; he has a sore leg. I have quite a hospital here. He is mighty comical about it and calls it the gout.' If Kildare was away, Emily regaled him with chatty details; she told him the story of her days for her own enjoyment rather than his. 'I am sure you will be glad to hear I have a fine bed of double jonquils in bloom, which delights me. You know I have a passion for them. You can't expect any news from hence I am sure; a chatty letter you don't love, but I can't help making mine a little so; 'tis quite natural to me, so pray excuse it.'

Writing was a great pleasure to Emily and she never went anywhere without her writing case. She once wrote to Fox, 'I believe I explain myself sadly but I have scribbled this in a minute while in the coach waiting for Lord K. . . . I had no intention of writing to you but having nothing else to do took up my pen and you know how I go on once I begin.' Exuberant letters of two or three sheets of paper regularly arrived for Kildare when he was away. Emily grumbled about servants, reported on progress from the nursery, flattered, cajoled and begged for money. She wrote out the story of her life with the panache of a born story-teller and sprinkled her letters liberally with terms of endearment. 'Believe me ever your tender, affectionate and dutiful wife,' she wrote, 'yours sick or well' or 'God bless you, my sweetest, dear Jemmy.' Kildare replied in kind. 'I am, my dear Emily, yours most tenderly,' or 'Adieu, my dearest Emily, till we meet. Yours ever, K.' Once he went so far as to write her a poem:

> Careless am I let who will reign
> O'er Britain's Isle.
> Nothing on earth shall give me pain
> So Emily smile.

It was not a success but Kildare was not interested in poetry or literature and never indulged in the versifying that went on at Holland House. He sat through a play willingly enough but he disliked reading. Political pamphlets, even when they concerned himself, he turned over to Emily. Reading was her province and, when she had her portrait painted by Reynolds in 1753, she chose to be seen with a book. At the centre of the picture lies a book. Emily marks her place in it with her index finger. She leans on her right hand and gazes out of the picture, lost in dreams. The viewer is shut out from her world and thoughts. Kildare, in the companion painting, looks straight at the viewer and, with a gesture of his right hand, invites him into the picture and to a tour of the Carton estate that nestles in the background. Kildare posed himself for Reynolds as a man of action, outdoors and in his military uniform, his hair brushed back and curled in a matter-of-fact manner. Where Emily is secluded and indoors he is engaged with the outside world, brisk, direct and beady eyed.

Conventional as these poses were, they showed the differences in temperament and occupation between Kildare and his wife. Politics and the care of his estates did indeed fill Kildare's days. He was proud of what he called his 'busy temper', and bustled about his estates, concerned for his reputation, rent-roll and, perhaps to a lesser extent, his tenants' welfare. None the less he relied heavily on Emily to guide him through the storms of political life. Under the guise of offering casual opinions, Emily often steered Kildare towards decisions or actions which he then adopted as his own. She was very careful, none the less, to disavow any influence in Kildare's politics, even to Fox. In 1757 she wrote to Fox, 'Lord K. is not governed by anybody in politics I assure you. In everything else he is as all good husbands ought [to be] by me.' To Kildare she was less behind-hand. 'I am glad to hear you say our affairs look well,' she wrote in 1757, casually assuming that politics was shared business. 'I hope you mean by that that the heads of our party are likely to be reasonable, which is all you can judge of as yet, and what I own I had my doubts about. Don't let them work upon you to expect too many concessions from these people. Nobody could be more inclined to peaceable measures than you are, and I hope you will continue so.' Then, moving swiftly to accommodate the well aired view that women had no part to play in public affairs, Emily concluded disingenuously, 'my dear Jemmy has always used me to talk to him upon this subject and tell my mind freely so I hope he don't think I have said too much.'

Emily liked the drama and the cut-and-thrust of political life. 'I long for a good fight,' she once wrote to Fox during an acrimonious phase in Kildare's political career. Political news and enquiries filled her letters. 'So much for linen. Now as to politics,' she began, or 'I long to hear some account of this day's transactions in the House of Commons'; 'Pray write me all the politics you can'.

At first Emily was interested in politics as a drama played out by relatives and acquaintances. But as the century wore on she started to read about political issues, perhaps prompted by Kildare's opposition to Westminster, perhaps by the pervading difference and strangeness of Ireland, perhaps simply from curiosity and conviction. She began to think about the constitution, about the rights and wrongs of the relationship between King, Parliament and people – what rights and what duties were involved in the compact into which they had engaged, and did Parliament exist for King or people? What happened if a government became despotic or unjust? Neither Fox nor Caroline were radicals; they accepted the status quo and concerned themselves with the business rather than the theory of government. Kildare was a reformer only in so far as he demanded more autonomy for the Irish House of Commons; government by Protestant oligarchy seemed right and proper to him. When John Wilkes attacked parliamentary prerogatives in the name of the people in the late 1760s, Caroline and Fox were vehemently opposed to him. But at some point Emily became a radical, not only idealistically interested in liberty but also prepared to countenance civil rights – access to offices, courts, information and religious emancipation – for a far wider section of the people than enjoyed them at the time (although in common with all her sisters, she never gave any indication that these liberties might belong to women as well as men). It may have been a gradual process, beginning in the late 1760s, gathering steam in the late 1770s when the foundation of the American republic offered a model of government that was an alternative to monarchical rule, and crystallising in the late 1780s with the French Revolution. Whenever and however the transformation took place, Emily was careful to keep it well hidden, revealing her preferences in omissions rather than declarations. In all her long correspondence she never praised the English monarchy. She never expressed regret (as almost every one of her contemporaries did) about the execution of the French royal family. Her beliefs and feelings revealed themselves in her children's views and the kinds of marriages she wished her daughters to make.

Kildare did not always follow his wife's hints about his political conduct. Obsessed with duty and probity, he was fatally hostile to expediency. Often he was so busy detecting a wrong that he neglected his own career. Friends noted that he would go out of his way to detect a politically insignificant subordinate in a lie and Caroline, with a touch of impatience, commented to Emily on Kildare's 'great veracity'.

Kildare was in London on political business several times in the years after he and Emily were married. Politics brought Kildare and Fox together and Emily and Caroline got to know one another again after a separation of four years. Caroline hoped that Emily would smooth the way towards a reconciliation with her parents, but Emily was soundly rebuffed. The winter of 1747 was a difficult one for Caroline. Rejected again by her parents, she began also to suspect that Fox was unfaithful. In the aristocratic circles in which Foxes and Richmonds moved, young unmarried men often had quite settled relationships with lower-class women, especially servant girls, women of the town and actresses. Fox was no exception; he now had two children by his mistress Ally, a barely literate woman whom he had installed in the west country with a small pension. After marriage, affairs were openly tolerated, although liaisons with childless wives, who might thus produce heirs of doubtful patrimony, were frowned upon.

This was changing; notions of domestic felicity and a greater marital fidelity were beginning to make inroads into Caroline's circle amongst both men and women. They were creating a schizophrenic outlook towards men's behaviour.

Caroline approved of 'gallantry' for her brothers, and she was to encourage her sons' affairs, saying that being 'in love' was very good for boys. But from her own husband she wanted a commitment that any affairs he might have would be confined to the level of sex with servant girls. She was not prepared to tolerate a mistress, certainly not a mistress from her own circle. Mistresses were fine, she suggested, but not in her household or life.

In the winter of 1747 she suspected that Fox was straying. That year her annual trip to Bath made her feel lonely and depressed. She disliked herself for her peevishness but for several weeks she was unwilling to confront Fox with her anxieties, and she turned her anger on herself, writing only, 'if you was ill natured I should be better to you'. The preparation of bark and bitters that her doctor prescribed suited her mood but did nothing to cure her suspicions. Finally, on 20 February 1748, three weeks after her arrival, she told Henry what was on her mind. She dated her letter 'Ste's birthday' and noted by the date, 'this time three years [ago] you began not to love me so much'. The accusation poured out, jumbled and confused by misery. 'I was never so much convinced of your being tired of me as I have been for a month before I left London and ever since I came here. Nothing but your coming to see me can convince me you wish to be with me. I'm vexed to the greatest degree in the world and don't care whether I ever get well or no.' Caroline was certain that Henry had 'particular reasons' for wanting her out of London. She wrote on, underlining her words with angry certainty, 'give me your word and honour not to vex me (you know what I mean).'

Caroline's accusation of infidelity arose as much from her need to create a scenario that would put her in the wrong as from any evidence of Fox's waning affection. The plan succeeded to perfection. Fox sent off a furious letter of denial and, hard on its heels, an assurance of his love for her. It was one long, ungainly sentence, as bulky and inelegant as its writer. During a meeting of the Privy Council Fox scribbled to his wife, 'wherever I am, whatever doing, you are always in my thoughts, deservedly their object and the object of the fondest and, except about dear Ste, the only fond ones my mind admits of.' Caroline was crushed. 'In the first place my dear, dear life, I beg you a thousand pardons for my two simple foolish letters. Do forgive me and tell me so and never reproach me again and I'll endeavour to mend.'

Caroline was right that she had been neglected for the past couple of years. But Fox's attentions were paid not to another woman but to the duties of office. Conflict in Europe still raged and as Secretary at War, Fox was in the thick of it. Logistical and financial arrangements took up most of his time. If troops moved or went abroad the War Office staff took them from place to place on paper. Horses, carts, matériel, food, clothing and medicines travelled with them. Camps, billets, stabling, fuel and food were prepared at their destinations. Troop ships, slapping emptily at naval docksides, had to be waiting for regiments travelling to Europe or to far-flung and dangerous imperial outposts: Bermuda, the Bahamas, Antigua, Jamaica, Nova Scotia, New York. The War Office drew up army budgets, the Treasury issued money and the Pay Office spent it. Although the War Office came with perks like lodgings and patronage, large sums of money did not pass through the Secretary's hands. Fox did not grow rich there. In a will made round about 1748, he left the relatively modest sum of £8,000 and a pension for Caroline of £1,100 a year. He disliked the job, moreover, on grounds of morality as well as expediency, understanding that distilled into the ledgers in his office were the disease, death and frustration of armies on the move and at war. He quoted Voltaire on war's human cost. 'Amongst all the variety of wishes for peace or war, the lives of mankind have never once been mentioned' and, without being prepared to lose his job for it, believed in peace. Caroline was much more forthright in her denunciation of war, declaring that war was 'a disgrace to human nature'. She called the military profession 'the murdering trade' and said, 'it would grieve me beyond measure to have any of my sons take to it.' But the War Office was a good position from which to launch a bid for the highest political office. Because all military appointments went through the Crown, Fox saw a good deal of the King. He was active in the House of Commons and close to officials in the Treasury. So he determined to make the most of it and work out a *modus vivendi* with the Commander-in-Chief of the army, George II's unpopular brother, the Duke of Cumberland. Gradually Fox came to like Cumberland who was, like himself, a corpulent and clever man, and they struck up a political alliance that lasted the length of Fox's tenure.

During the War of Austrian Succession, Cumberland, or the Captain-General, as he was called, was in charge of a British army that was busy but not notably successful. By 1747, seven years after the outbreak of war, there was a military stalemate and Henry Pelham was determined to end the war. In 1747 he decided to call a general election before making any pacific overtures to the French. Capitalising on the anti-Jacobite mood after the defeat of Bonnie Prince Charlie, he campaigned on an anti-Tory rather than an anti-war ticket, and was returned with an increased majority. Secret negotiations had in fact been under way for over a year and in 1748 they were successfully wound up in the Treaty of Aix-la-Chapelle.

After Aix-la-Chapelle, Pelham and his ministers quickly cut the size of the army. Fox was busy moving troops back to Britain and disbanding regiments. When the first flurry of decommissioning subsided, dust began to settle again on the ledgers at the War Office and Fox had time for Holland House and family life.

The Duke of Richmond had been keeping a shrewd eye on the career of the Secretary at War. As Fox rose in prominence he also rose in his father-in-law's estimation. By the early spring of 1748, Richmond was prodding his friend Newcastle to move Fox up from the War Office. 'I have but one word to trouble you with,' he wrote during a Cabinet reshuffle in February 1748, 'which is to tell you that if Harry Fox should be Secretary of State, the Duchess and I should be vastly happy, though we still wish him the Paymaster's place, as it is less precarious and a better thing for his family's sake.' Fox had been changing in the Duke's mind. 'Mr. Fox' now sometimes gave way to 'Fox' and even to 'Harry Fox'. Fox was successful, popular and no longer a man to scorn. The Duke acknowledged as much, writing, early in 1748, to an ex-mistress from whom he had been separated for many years. 'My family is numerous; four girls and two boys. The eldest girl, Caroline, married against our wishes a man infinitely beneath her, so we do not see her; but I must tell you this man by his merits and talents is bound to make a name for himself in this country.' Now that he was a grandparent, Richmond felt that second-hand news about the family in Holland House, passed on by Emily, was no longer enough. He wanted to see Ste and to chat with Fox. So the Duke and Duchess admitted defeat, swallowed their pride and allowed Henry Fox into their family. The preceding four years had turned the tables of affection and need. The Duke's long letter to Caroline, sent via Fox on 26 March 1748, was ostensibly a gracious offer of reconciliation. But although Caroline and Fox were careful to send grateful replies that fell in with this fiction, both the Foxes and the Richmonds knew that the contest between Henry and the Duke had finally been settled in Fox's favour.

Because his letter to Caroline was in effect a declaration of love and a document of surrender, Richmond was as careful to lay out the ways in which Caroline had delayed the reconciliation as he was to emphasise that he was prepared to forget the past. The Duke began his letter with a résumé of Caroline's faults, a face-saving device that did little to make her feel loved. His long letter opened: 'My dear Caroline, Although the same reason for my displeasure with you exists now, as much as it did the day you offended me, and that the forgiving you is a bad example to my other children, yet they are so young, that was I to stay until they were settled, the consequence might in all likelihood be that we should never see you as long as we lived, which thoughts our hearts could not bear. So the conflict between reason and nature is over, and the tenderness of parents has gotten the better, and your dear mother and I have determined to see and forgive both you and Mr. Fox.'

Richmond went on to criticise Caroline's attempts at reconciliation through the intercession of her grandmother Lady Cadogan and then of Emily and Kildare. He warned her not to corrupt the morals of his remaining children and then finished his letter with hopes of seeing little Ste and holding his daughter in his arms once more. 'One thing more of greatest importance to the future happiness of your family I must mention and recommend to you, which is that I trust to Mr. Fox's honour, probity and good sense, as well as to yours, that your conversation ever hereafter with any of my children, especially my dear March, may be such as not to lead them to think children independent of their parents. We long to see your dear innocent child, and that has not a little contributed to our present tenderness to you . . . When we meet, let our affection be mutual and you may be sure that seeing you is proof of the sincerity of ours. So, my dear child, you and Mr. Fox may come here . . . and both be received in the arms of an affectionate father and mother.'

Caroline and Henry duly displayed the contrition and gratitude that satisfied the demands of family etiquette. Although Caroline never lost a trace of bitterness towards her parents and although the Duchess never fully forgave Fox, the benefits of reconciliation outweighed their nagging grievances. Caroline was reunited with her siblings and saw Sarah, who was born in 1745, a year after Caroline's elopement, for the first time. The Duke and Duchess happily assumed the role of grandparents. Caroline and her mother were mothers together. The Duchess gave her daughter advice about Ste, who was only five days older than Sarah, and consoled her during the new pregnancy she soon announced.

Within a few months Richmond was a regular guest at Holland House. Fox once again played a masterly hand. In the hour of victory he adopted a flattering attitude of deference and gratitude towards his father-in-law. 'I beg your Grace the moment you arrive to let me have your orders touching this turtle, which is now alive in salt water in Long Acre, and pray tell me what cook I must have.' He sent the Duchess an expensive present, a snuff-box – both she and Caroline were fond of snuff – ordered from the Meissen factory by the devoted Hanbury Williams whom Fox seemed determined to include in both the beginning and the end of his rejection by the Richmond family. The little box, roughly two by two-and-a-half inches, had a gently domed lid. Its porcelain panels, set in Dresden gold, were painted with bouquets of flowers and the box was sealed with a shell-shaped clasp. But Fox's present had a secret. Inside the lid was a portrait of Caroline herself, copied in the Meissen factory from a miniature Fox sent Hanbury Williams. But it was only Caroline's image Fox gave back to her mother. Its original, he hinted, he kept for himself.

The Duchess accepted Fox's present, but was never at ease with her son-in-law. Richmond and Fox, in contrast, were soon on excellent terms. They already knew one another well and their political interests were broadly similar. Notionally separated by a generation, there were in fact only four years between them and both were devoted fathers of young children. Richmond, fonder of his girls than his boys, liked to boast of his toddlers' precociousness. Of Sarah he wrote delightedly to Fox at the end of 1749, when he was forty-eight and she four, 'There is a cursed hard frost which is very hard upon fox hunters and planters. You are one of those I know that don't comprehend anybody's loving hunting, so I must entertain you with a question. Sha Sha ask'd her Mama, upon my being gone out in a bad rainy day, "Esceque Papa est obligé d'aller à la chasse ou escequ'il en a envie?" [*sic*].' Henry was for the moment unable to compete with this infant bilingualism. But he had happily reported, at the beginning of that year, the birth of another son born on 24 January 1749. The baby was christened Charles James in honour both of his Stuart ancestry and his grandfather, and his name was a public declaration of the reconciliation between the Fox and Richmond families.

Peace was officially declared in February 1749 and celebrated in late April with the first performance of Handel's 'Fireworks Music' and fireworks in Green Park. The display was a failure. Huge Catherine wheels, nailed to posts near a specially constructed pavilion, obstinately refused to turn. Part of the building, replete with colonnades, statues of Greek gods and a bas-relief of the King, caught fire and burned to the ground. The Duke of Richmond, in an uncharacteristically economical gesture, bought up all the unused and unsuccessful fireworks and used them for a gigantic entertainment of his own. Richmond's fireworks were a codicil to the peace and a declaration of his new happiness. Caroline and Fox, Emily and Kildare, and Richmond's own younger children were all together for the first time. Emily had just presented her father with another grandson, born at the beginning of March, bringing his total to four. Fashionable London, invited to Richmond House, celebrated peace, fecundity and family unity.

Charles Frederick, Controller of His Majesty's Fireworks, organised the show. In the middle of the garden stood a triumphal arch with lamps burning on its roof. It was a symbol of unity and of military might. At the four corners of the garden conical pyramids, like miniature helter-skelters lit up with spiralling lights, each supported an illuminated crown in honour of the Duke's royal guests. Between them, ranged along the terrace, were huge Catherine wheels. Wooden rings, anchored to the river bottom, bobbed on the water. Further out into the river lay a barge laden with sky rockets, and from there Mr Frederick orchestrated the fiery performance: '200 water mines, 20 air balloons, 200 fire trees, 5000 water rockets, 5000 sky rockets, 100 fire showers, 20 suns and a hundred stars' lent lustre to the occasion.

The show started on the river. Rockets shot dizzyingly into the black night sky. The hot jets sped upwards until their tops exploded into golden palm trees, whose leaves fell towards the water. At the surface they crashed into their reflections, hissed and expired. Their ghosts, wraiths of steam, drifted like white muslin handkerchiefs over the upturned faces of the crowd. In an interval the plop-plop of the roman candles, burning on the wooden rings beneath the railings, accentuated the calm. Then explosions from a battery of mortars reeled against the side of Richmond House, rebounded and collided with oncoming waves of sound. Noise sprays rose in the air and then followed the tracks of their fiery brethren towards the burning water. Next the Catherine wheels were lit on the terrace. As they turned faster and faster they whistled and creaked. Their whirling petals gave off showers of incandescent pollen that fell to the ground in shimmering arcs. Faces glowed and then faded away. Finally the triumphal arch was illuminated and, as the noise died down, light spread across the crowd packed into the garden and lit up the royal barge on the river. Music and dancing began. At two in the morning the Duke leant against the railings on the terrace and sang patriotic songs for his guests and family.

8 August 1750
With alternate thrills of hot and cold the Duke lay shivering in a fever at Godalming. Sedgwick, his secretary, sat anxiously by him. Wormwood, *Artemisia absinthium*, dark, bitter and oily, was prescribed to bring down the Duke's temperature. The Duke drank it, hardly aware of his surroundings. He lay between damp sheets, confused by fever and weakened by dehydration. Days and nights passed blurrily in the darkened room. Gradually the house filled up. From London, Truesdale and Middleton, the family doctors, came with medicines and assistants. The Duke's landau brought the Duchess and her servants from Goodwood. Relatives and friends came in and went quietly out. In the midst of

this muffled commotion the Duke travelled alone into the dark extinction of death. Slowly but surely fever pulled him into the void from life, light and happiness. On the tenth day the Duke died.

A few hours later Middleton took off his frock-coat and rolled up his fine white cotton sleeves. He picked up his knife, pressed it against the dead Duke's soft, resisting stomach and then pressed harder until the skin broke and parted. Middleton cut a deep, straight line down the Duke's navel. He sliced through the pinky-grey skin, the gelatinous yellow layer of fat and the thick red muscle wall. From the thin skin of the peritoneum Middleton's warm, gloveless hands pulled out the cold intestines and burrowed down into the pelvic cavity to reach the bladder. Picking up a small steel scalpel he slit the bladder open. The bladder was irritated and inflamed like a small balloon but there was no trace of any stones.

Left alone in the room to refine and practise his diagnostic skills, Middleton rummaged about amongst the dead Duke's cold and solidifying organs. He split open a section of intestines and examined the stomach. After some time he carefully put the pieces back again, pressing down the grey, sausage-like intestines, and threaded a length of cat gut through the eye of a large needle. He tied a knot in the end of the thread and, pulling the severed skin together, sewed the body up with a line of stitches that ran in parallel down the abdomen. Then he washed his hands in a basin standing on the floor. The Duke's body, cleaned and dressed, was prepared to make its final journey to a dark vault in Chichester Cathedral.

A year later the Duchess, too, was dead. Two sons and three daughters passed into her eldest children's care. Caroline and Emily were no longer daughters in the world's eyes. They were mothers, wives, sisters. At first grief drowned out their parents' voices and to bystanders the Duke and Duchess became paintings on the wall and remembered voices that faded to the written word as the years went by. But as their grief died down, Emily and Caroline, still daughters in their minds, began to hear their parents speak. So began a colloquy that would go on until they in their turn left the world to their grieving children. Caroline and Emily joined in the huge mute conversation humanity carries on with the dead that stretches back through the ages as, with silent self-justifications and voiceless wrangles, children whisper to parents and they, children in their turn, lisp confidences to lost mothers and fathers. On the walls of Holland House and Goodwood, the Duke and Duchess were immobile and mute. In their children's minds they flitted in and out, watchful, loving, censorious, always listening, and still alive.

LEFT: The Lennox girls' father, Charles, second Duke of Richmond, painted by Charles Philips in the late 1740s as a courtier and collector.

ABOVE: Louise de Kéroualle, Charles IIs 'young wanton' and subsequently Lennox family matriarch.

LEFT: The second Duke of Richmond with Sarah his wife by Godfrey Kneller, early 1720s. The Duchess wrote to her husband, 'I love you exceedingly' and he called her 'the person in the whole world I love the best'.

ABOVE: The Privy Garden in 1741, much as it would have looked to Caroline as she ran away from home in 1744. Richmond House is to the right of the trees in the middle distance.

BELOW: The Thames from Richmond House Terrace by Canaletto, 1747.

ABOVE: Looking the other way from Richmond House,
Canaletto's view of the Privy Garden, with a servant bowing
to the Duke of Richmond by the gate of the stable yard.

BELOW: The shell house at Goodwood, designed by
the Duchess and her daughters in the 1740s.

LEFT: Caroline, voluptuous in Turkish masquerade costume shortly before her elopement. 'Her eyebrows and forehead are charming,' Emily wrote.

BELOW: The north front of Holland House, sketched in 1898, but much as it was when Caroline and Henry lived there.

RIGHT: Henry Fox as a self-promoting gigolo, painted in Rome by Antonio David in 1732, when he was on tour with his mistress, Mrs Strangways-Horner.

BELOW: The south front of Holland House showing the portico outside Caroline's dressing room where she had a greenhouse and an aviary.

LEFT: Emily in masquerade costume before her marriage; the undisputed beauty of the family.

BELOW: Grandeur without style: Carton House, County Kildare. Now the back, this was the front when Emily lived there.

RIGHT: James Fitzgerald, Earl of Kildare and then Duke of Leinster, painted by Ramsay in 1762. Kildare liked Ramsay because he 'had not a picture of anyone I ever saw, but I knew'.

BELOW: Leinster House, Dublin. Another gloomy mansion, it was built between 1745 and 1747 and originally known as Kildare House. Emily's children were mostly born here.

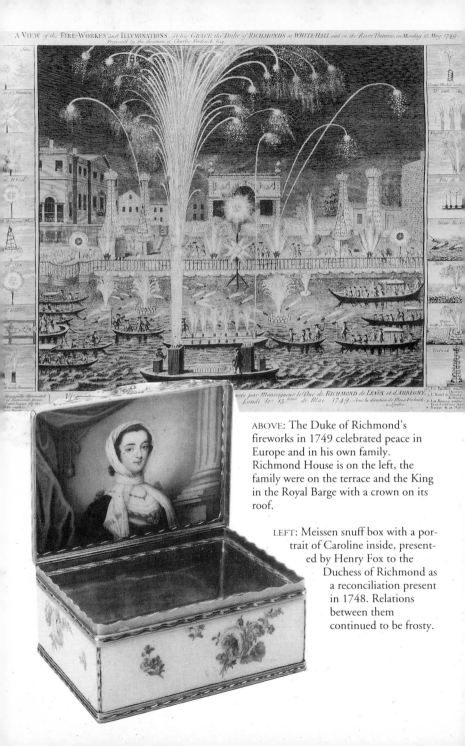

A VIEW of the FIRE-WORKES and ILLUMINATIONS, at his GRACE the Duke of RICHMONDS at WHITE-HALL and on the River Thames, on Monday 15 May 1749. Performed by the direction of Charles Frederick Esq.

ABOVE: The Duke of Richmond's fireworks in 1749 celebrated peace in Europe and in his own family. Richmond House is on the left, the family were on the terrace and the King in the Royal Barge with a crown on its roof.

LEFT: Meissen snuff box with a portrait of Caroline inside, presented by Henry Fox to the Duchess of Richmond as a reconciliation present in 1748. Relations between them continued to be frosty.

CHAPTER
TWO

LOUISA
AND SARAH

PART ONE
'You have been very good indeed
to the family on this occasion'.
3rd Duke of Richmond to Henry Fox,
30 November 1750.

'Poor dear Lady Kildare is in the utmost affliction, for she loved her father extremely, and is very unhappy about the poor Duchess of Richmond, whom I pity very much. I am doing all I can to keep her from sinking under her grief, as she can't cry enough to ease herself. I have had her out in the one horse chaise alone three hours this morning, which I think she is the better for. I don't leave her for a minute.' The Earl of Kildare thus reported Emily's misery to Fox after the Duke's death in 1750.

Kildare deferred to Fox because Fox was now *de facto* head of the family. With the Duchess's death in 1751, all family relations changed again. In his will, the Duke, who had forgiven but not forgotten Caroline's elopement, passed over his eldest daughter in assigning homes and mentors for his younger children and entrusted the three little girls to Emily's care if the Duchess died. So now Louisa, aged eight, Sarah six and

Cecilia little more than a year old, were sent to Ireland. Carton House became their home and Emily became a second mother to them. The two boys, Charles, now third Duke of Richmond, and Lord George Lennox, continued their education in England and abroad. Richmond was an amorous and pedantic schoolboy of fifteen when his father died and he looked to Fox for guidance, calling him his 'best friend' and his 'second father'.

Despite his youth, the third Duke had gradually to assume his father's mantle. As he grew up his brother and sisters endowed him with the age-old rights accompanied by the duties and responsibilities that rested with heads of families. He would help search for suitable husbands for the younger children and reserved the right of veto over any they chose for themselves. Marriage settlements, annuities and wills were his to discuss and settle. In quarrels he acted as arbiter and at times of crisis he provided safe haven and money. Exasperated though they might be by his preachy stubbornness, his siblings deferred to their brother and depended on him to defend the family's interests. Caroline was now a Fox and Emily a Kildare, but neither in their own minds ceased being a part of the Lennox family. So the Duke's influence was considerable.

The third Duke went on the Grand Tour when his father died, and he stayed abroad until January 1756. Fox, sometime renegade and outcast, now protected the interests of an extended family created by two generations of Richmond marriages. For the moment the family was united. Kildare and the third Duke of Richmond joined Fox's political circle as did Kildare's brother-in-law the Earl of Hillsborough, an Irish peer who lived largely in England and spent a good deal of time at Holland House, to Caroline's occasional chagrin. At the periphery of political although not always of family affairs were Henry's brother Stephen Fox and, from the other side, Lord Albemarle, a career soldier and diplomat who had married the second Duke of Richmond's sister. Albemarle and Stephen Fox spent little time in London, but they lent weight to the Fox and Richmond interests in the west country. Other relations, Cadogans, Digbys and Brudenells, also stood within the pale. Beyond them the family branched into a plethora of 'cousins', as more remote relations were indiscriminately dubbed. Such relationships grew fainter with distance, spreading out like ripples in a pond, but the blood tie remained; Caroline and Emily even acknowledged the Old and Young Pretenders, descendants of their great-grandfather's brother, as cousins.

Members of this extended family might vote with the Pelham ministry if they had parliamentary seats and might support one another's extra-parliamentary ventures if they did not. They met socially and, as time went on, they intermarried. In return for votes and support those, like Henry Fox, who had powerful offices, expected and were expected to look after the family interests with places and emoluments. When the second Duke died, Fox, as Secretary at War, prepared the Duke's younger son, Lord George Lennox, a schoolboy of thirteen, for a military career by buying him a commission and getting him sinecures to supplement his modest army pay. Similar distributions of pensions and offices amongst the family, and amongst those to whom the family felt beholden, went on throughout the century.

Complicating this picture of state-funded largesse were serious and lasting political quarrels which affected the women of the family just as acutely as its active politicians. There were also occasional disputes between women that spilled over into politics. By the end of the century family alliances were intact in some places and irrevocably fractured in others: the extended family was by no means synonymous with the happy family or with the political coterie.

The year 1751 saw the family grieving but united. The third Duke was surveying battlefields, studying botanical, geological and biological specimens in Europe's newest museums, and seducing women in its most illustrious drawing-rooms, pleasure gardens and brothels. He was accompanied by Abraham Trembley, a biologist and educationalist who had made a name for himself in one of the most contentious debates that convulsed scientific circles in the eighteenth century. Biologists and botanists, seized with taxonomic fever, were trying to establish the differences between plants and animals, carving up the natural world into mineral, vegetable and animal fiefdoms with the same enthusiasm that European nations were dividing each new-found uncolonised land. Trembley's proof that the marine polyps that drifted on the Solent tides were not plants but animals made him famous, and his renown opened museums and cabinets, gardens and menageries to the young Duke in his charge. Of Richmond himself Trembley wrote, with some restraint, 'he loves dogs prodigiously; he loves also the human race and the feminine race.'

While his older brother was learning military and amatory strategy, Lord George Lennox continued his own education at Westminster School. In London, Henry Fox's job was made easy by peace. When Parliament reassembled after the summer recess in November 1751, Fox wrote happily to Hanbury Williams, 'There never was such a session as this is likely to be. The halcyon days the poets wrote of cannot exceed its calmness. A bird might build her nest in the speaker's chair, or in his peruke. There won't be a debate that can disturb her.'

As the duties of the Secretary at War declined, Fox's interest in his two children, and particularly in his younger son, grew. Charles had inherited his father's hairiness, as Fox reported the day after he was born. 'He is weakly, but likely to live. His skin hangs all shrivelled about him, his eyes stare, he has a black head of hair, and 'tis incredible how like a monkey he looked before he was dressed.' From this inauspicious beginning, Charles grew into a handsome child. Abandoning any claims to disinterestedness, Fox wrote to Hanbury Williams when the boy was a year old, 'Charles is playing by me and surprises me with the éclat of his beauty every time he looks me in the face.' Two years later Hoare painted him, resplendent in bandana and silks, plump and swarthy like his father.

When politicians came to Holland House they saw and reported on Fox the father as well as Fox the Secretary at War. MPs who knew Fox as a brilliant administrator and a ruthless manager of men were astonished at his fatherly sentimentality and concern. In the 1750s, England was at the beginning of a love affair with children and with domesticity that was swelled by and in turn fuelled an outpouring of sentimental novels, paintings of sweet infants and happy family groups and books of advice about raising and educating children. Visitors to great houses noticed children everywhere; they were spoiled, deferred to and adored. Astonished callers at Holland House were among the first to see affairs of state supplanted by childhood illness and parental pride and care. Richard Rigby, a protégé of the Duke of Bedford and soon of Fox himself, came to Holland House one afternoon in the 1750s to talk politics. But he stayed to administer alcoholic relief to an unhappy father. 'I dined at Holland House, where, though I drank claret with the master of it till two o'clock in the morning, I could not wash away the sorrow he is in at the shocking condition his eldest son is in, a distemper they call Sanvitoss dance (I believe I spell it damnably), but it is a convulsion I think must kill him.'

Ste's illness produced a more than usual leniency in his parents. Caroline gave and forgave him anything, longing only for him to get well. At the age of six Ste was a regular visitor to the Haymarket and Drury Lane. 'I did give Ste a general leave to go to the play whenever he chose it,' she wrote to Henry in 1751. Charles soon joined his brother in the box. By the time Charles was five he was reading every play he could find. At six he had graduated to novels and poetry and Caroline began to teach him Roman history. Stories about the Foxes' indulgence were legion. Charles declared his intention of taking apart a fob watch. His father stood by murmuring, 'well, if you must, you must'. Once a grand dinner was held at Holland House for some visiting foreign dignitaries. The Fox children were brought in for dessert. Charles, still a toddler in petticoats, said he wanted to bathe in a huge bowl of cream that stood on the table. Despite Caroline's remonstrances, Fox ordered the dish to be put down on the floor and there, in full view of some of Europe's most powerful politicians, the little boy slopped and slid to his heart's content in the cool, thick liquid. Another time Fox lifted Charles up on the table and put him on top of a prize joint of roast beef so that the child could sit astride the symbol of England itself, a living image of Fox's hopes for his sons. This indulgence scandalised more disciplinarian parents, but Fox insisted that it had a rationale, saying of Charles, 'Let nothing be done to break his spirit. The world will do that business fast enough.' Caroline wrote to Emily with a mixture of pride and apology, 'you know this is reckoned such a house of liberty for children.'

In the Spring of 1753, politics swept Fox away from the jollity at Holland House. For the first and perhaps the last time in his life, Fox took a principled rather than a pragmatic stand on a political issue. He lost his temper and his case, and he came to feel that the episode marked a turning point in his career. The proposal that caused such anguish did not seem to many to be worth the time and passion that Fox lavished upon it; it was a Bill to regulate and tighten the marriage laws, introduced and sponsored by the Chancellor, Lord Hardwicke.

Hardwicke's initiative was purely administrative, designed to stop the abuses which widespread clandestine marriages caused. But Fox took it personally as an attack on his elopement with Caroline and on the honour of his family. He was a committed libertarian in social matters (more so, indeed, than Caroline), believing that people should suit themselves and the state should not meddle in affairs of the heart. He fought vehemently against the Bill in Parliament. He shouted and gesticulated towards the House of Lords, where Hardwicke sat, and astonished fellow MPs (who thought of him as a consummately pragmatic politician) by his anger and imprudence.

The vote, when it came, was resoundingly in favour of the Bill. When he had calmed down, Fox was horrified to realise that he had made an implacable enemy of the Lord Chancellor. 'I despise the invective and I despise the recantation; I despise the scurrility (for scurrility I must call it) and I reject the adulation,' Hardwicke declared, adding that Fox was 'a dark, gloomy and insidious genius who was an engine of personality and faction.'

This disastrous foray into the politics of belief left Fox shaken. Abstract notions like liberty and conscience, which he had used in the debate, had not been conspicuous elements in his political creed. Stepping off the safe ground of pragmatism Fox had cast himself onto a sea of self-doubt. While he continued to assert his veracity his confidence in his own political style was damaged, as if, having once lost control of himself, he might do it again and again. Rather than let that happen Fox imperceptibly but inexorably began to reduce his ambitions. During the next crisis of his political career in 1755, he appeared to outsiders to be artificially constrained from fulfilling his ambition and talent. His family were in no doubt that the affair of the Marriage Bill had weakened his confidence. Emily wrote to Kildare on that occasion, 'he seems in vast doubts how to act and always says he has committed one fault never to be retrieved; and that I believe is what prevents his acting with as much spirit as he would have done once. I know this is my sister's opinion.' Fox had risked and perhaps lost his political career for his beliefs. Henceforth he stayed within the compass of the familiar: quid pro quos, payoffs and pragmatic dealings.

Superficially Fox's ambitions were not blunted by the events of 1753. He seemed as bullish and as eager for the highest political office as he had been a year earlier when he confided in Lord Hillsborough that 'he resolved to push for his turn: not by opposition, for he said he had a family and could not afford to part with his emoluments, but if accident should happen he pretended to succeed: that, indeed, Mr. Pelham's life was as good as his, and he could not oppose him; but that he should endeavour to look upon himself as next.' Fox's chance came in 1754 when Pelham suddenly died of a seizure, and peace, both at home and abroad, died with him. Two candidates vied to fill Pelham's positions of head of the Commons and First Lord of the Treasury: Fox himself and his rival William Pitt. Fox was Secretary at War, Pitt was Paymaster of the Forces. Between them and high office stood the Duke of Newcastle, whose determination to bring neither into prominence was stiffened by the Chancellor Lord Hardwicke. Hardwicke naturally opposed any move to bring Fox into the upper echelons of the government. The King disliked Pitt. So Newcastle took the Treasuryship for himself. His own position of Secretary of State for the Northern Department (the equivalent of the American Secretary of State or British Foreign Secretary) he ceded to the diplomat Sir Thomas Robinson, who thus became the government's chief spokesman in the Commons. The combined force of Fox and Pitt acting together in the House was too much for Robinson; Newcastle decided that he must break up the strange alliance they had struck up. A Cabinet position and other sweeteners were offered to the one who would stop tormenting the government. It was Fox who accepted Newcastle's offer. Unable to wait until the Treasuryship fell into his lap, convinced that Hardwicke would block him at every turn and afraid of Pitt's steely, prim reserve, Fox decided to leapfrog over Pitt and try to approach the Treasury by degrees. In December 1754, Fox became a member of the Cabinet and one of the Regency Council appointed to govern when the monarch was in Hanover.

At first things went Fox's way, helped it seemed by the disintegration of peace in Europe and the North Atlantic.

Disputes between France and Britain about the way to carve up the North American continent broke out into naval skirmishes and land confrontations in May 1755. The House of Commons, still without any official leader, was in equal disarray. Once again either Fox or Pitt would have to be appeased if Newcastle was to hold his fragile administration together and once again it was, in the end, Fox who rose to the bait. Despite Hardwicke's opposition Fox was elevated to the office of Secretary of State and Leader of the House of Commons. Pitt was dismissed in November 1755 for his opposition to government policy and returned to the sidelines to await his turn.

On the Continent the merry-go-round of alliances was whirling faster and faster. The European powers were once more making fervid preparations for war. By March 1756 the French had assembled expeditionary forces to strike both at the English mainland and at Minorca, Britain's chief Mediterranean base. The British sent reinforcements too late. Minorca fell and the reverberations threatened Newcastle's government. 'The rage of the people increases daily,' Fox wrote, certain that as Secretary of State and Leader of the House he would be blamed. Fox was anxious and dithering; Caroline reported that he was in very low spirits. He was beginning to lose stomach for the fight. Facts and figures not international affairs were Fox's strong points, and taking on the burden of government foreign affairs with only lukewarm support from the King and the Duke of Newcastle was a catastrophic error from which he could find no way out. Fox knew that his career was drawing to a crisis and that the prize of the Treasury had slipped from his grasp. Rather than carry the can for the government in the Minorca affair, he resigned. Newcastle and Hardwicke were unable to find anyone to replace him in the Commons and, with war going badly and Pitt menacing them in the House, they both handed in their resignations as well. Only the King now stood between Pitt and power. In desperation George turned back to Fox and asked him to form a ministry. Fox tried, but not very hard, because he knew that Pitt would refuse to join. 'I can't much blame him,' Fox wrote. He abandoned the attempt. On 4 December 1756, Pitt, with the Duke of Devonshire as Treasury minister, took over the government. Fox's political career was all but over: the next year he took the politically worthless job of Paymaster of the Forces.

Thwarted in his political ambition, Fox was determined to become rich. The war that had broken out on the lands and seas of Europe and America was to be the most expensive ever fought. At any time the Paymastership was one of the most lucrative of government offices, as Fox's father knew well. In wartime, and particularly in this war, the key to the Pay Office unlocked enormous riches. Because the price for his wealth was to be political oblivion, Fox was determined to milk the Pay Office for everything it could provide. In the next seven years he garnered a fortune rumoured to be £400,000. Despite public hostility and detailed enquiries, nobody then or since has been able to prove that it came from anything other than the accepted practice of lending out and reinvesting the vast sums of government money that went through the Paymaster's hands in wartime. In this way, dripping with money and loaded with opprobrium, Fox ended his political career. The 'boisterous and impetuous torrent' as Pitt called Fox, was diverted into the political backwaters. In 1757 he set his course towards an ocean of money upon which he intended to float his sons towards the power he had lost. Henceforth his hopes rested with his family.

In 1755 Caroline had had another son, named Henry after both his father and the Foxes' second son who had died as an infant in 1746. Henry, or Harry as his parents always called him, could not displace Charles in his father's heart. None the less, Fox could never resist a baby. He wrote to Caroline in 1756, 'Charles is very well and very pert and very argumentative. I rode to Holland House this morning and found Harry ... in the park, looking cold but very well. I called him Squeaker and he looked at me and laughed, but upon the whole seemed to like my horse better than me.'

Caroline reported similarly trivial but treasured incidents to Emily in Ireland. By the early 1750s they were writing every week or fortnight, usually on folio or half-folio sheets of paper, but sometimes on several smaller sheets. Before dispatch, letters were folded and sealed with wax into a compact parcel about the size of a pocket diary. The recipient's address was written on the smooth side of the packet. 'Ly Car. Fox. Pay Office,' Emily wrote, while Caroline addressed letters to 'Countess of Kildare, Carton. Co. Kildare'. In cities, letters were collected and delivered, usually by the same person, at given times during the day, centrally sorted and dispatched by coach to their destinations. Caroline and Emily could confidently assume that London news would reach Ireland in five or six days and that letters would rarely go astray. Letters posted outside London – from Bath to Dublin, for instance – went by the 'cross post', a sorting and dispatching system that bypassed London.

Post to and from the Continent was equally simple, although it was sometimes disrupted by war, weather or quarrels between post masters and heads of state. Letters from Europe came addressed in the language of their country of origin. 'A Miladi Car. Fox, A Londres,' they announced, or 'A la Comtesse de Kildare, A Dublin.' In wartime letters from Europe were often entrusted to friends or naval officers, but in peacetime the ordinary post was fast and efficient enough to guarantee a regular correspondence.

Emily and Caroline saw themselves as self-conscious letter writers with 'formed' styles. Like polite conversation, letter writing was an accomplishment with its own complex rules, as Caroline revealed when she told Emily how ashamed she was that Ste Fox still wrote like a child at the age of seventeen. 'His letters are quite a schoolboy's. He is well, hopes we are, and compliments to everybody. Adieu. Yours Most Sincerely.' Emily's daughter, in contrast, received Caroline's praise for epistolary skill. 'I wrote to your daughter Emily . . . She is a delightful correspondent, her style quite formed. I have given her some account of Voltaire.'

The Lennox sisters believed that epistolary style should conform to an aesthetic and that letters were to some extent performances whose success could be measured against a set of rules. They were public displays in other ways too. Letters were for family consumption, to be read aloud. Thoughts that were exclusive to writer and reader would often be included on a separate sheet of paper that could be removed before the rest did its round of the drawing-room. In 1756 Emily wrote a flirtatious note to Henry Fox teasing him for flouting this convention. 'What a creature you are! I receive your letter before a thousand people. "A letter from Mr. Fox, oh we shall have some news." Everybody waits with impatience till I have read it. I open it with an important face and then behold it's full of nonsense and indeed such stuff as is not decent to shew to any creature.'

What were the elements of epistolary style, the 'forms' that the Lennox sisters set so much store by? Commentators described letter writing as an art that at once informed, entertained and revealed the self. The most perfect style was both artless and arch, intimate and allusive, with frequent gestures towards a rarefied culture of print. Male writers backed up their revelations and observations with Latin maxims and verses. Women like Caroline and Emily, lacking a classical education, used contemporary French and English writers for the same purpose. Emily liked jokey allusions to French comic novels and English plays and poetry. Caroline inclined towards aphorism. She often quoted from the *Spectator*, which she said she 'knew by heart' and also favoured La Rochefoucault, La Bruyère, Rousseau and, inevitably, Voltaire. 'Voltaire says somewhere, la dévotion est la ressource ordinaire des âmes sensibles. Perhaps there are people good to do their duty without it. I know I am not.' 'I like Martin's answer to Candide's asking, pourquoi ce monde a-t-il été fait? Pour nous faire enrager replies Martin; which thought comes naturally into one's head on several occasions, tho' its a false maxim.' Pride of place as both moral authority and stylistic model went to Madame de Sévigné, whose letters were required reading for self-conscious English letter writers in the eighteenth century.

Madame – La Marquise – de Sévigné was born in 1626. Her letters were published posthumously in 1725 and then more fully in several new additions over the next three decades. 'I have got a new volume of that divine woman's letters,' Horace Walpole wrote when another volume appeared in 1773. Over a thousand of Madame de Sévigné's letters survived, mostly written to her daughter, Madame de Grignan. While many commentators praised her descriptions of Parisian life, it was her love for her daughter and her opinions about everyday life that captivated Caroline and Emily. Madame de Sévigné was, for them, the quintessential rational woman of feeling.

Madame de Sévigné wrote about books and people. She commented on the act and art of letter writing and she indulged in moral reflections about time and death. But it was maternal love that she described and celebrated most of all. Her style, with its asides, snatches of dialogue and exclamations was praised by self-conscious letter writers as both natural and perfected, its art consisting precisely in its artlessness. Like Caroline and Emily, Madame de Sévigné moved deliberately from the ponderous to the domestic and, in so doing, heightened the emotions she wished to convey. 'What are you reading, my dear?' she asked her daughter in April 1672. 'I am reading the discovery of the Indies by Christopher Columbus, which I am finding extremely entertaining. But your daughter appeals to me still more. I love her and don't really see how I can help it. She makes a fuss of your portrait and pats it in such a funny way that you have to rush and kiss her.'

Caroline and Emily aspired to this sort of style. Madame de Sévigné became their authority and, because they knew no Latin, their alternative to the Catullus or Ovid that male writers used to give their letters a canonical grounding. 'Dear

Madame de Sévigné,' Emily called her. 'I love you for calling her "dear Madame de Sévigné". I'm quite glad to think I shall have forgot her letters enough to read them over again,' Caroline replied. Caroline was fond of quoting Madame de Sévigné on the nature of life: 'as Madame de Sévigné observes, le temps s'en va et nous emporte avec lui si terriblement vite.' She sent friends in France on a pilgrimage to find her heroine's descendants, and she envied Horace Walpole, who in 1766 had 'a pretty snuff box sent him with a miniature portrait of Madame de Sévigné on the top, and her cipher at the bottom set in . . . stones.'

Like Madame de Sévigné, the Lennox sisters often described their letters as conversational and sprawling, even while they aspired to a 'formed' style; so their writing was characterised by a deliberate sloppiness. 'Since you are so kind as to complain,' Sarah wrote to Emily in the mid-1770s, 'I am encouraged to begin one of my monthly magazines; for I think my letters very like them, a compound of unconnected stuff and a little sense par-ci, par-là.'

First and foremost, they believed, letters were conversations between writer and recipient in which both could construct and (paradoxically) display a private self. In letters they shared thoughts, troubles, jokes and gossip. Finishing off a long letter written to cheer Emily up during a troublesome pregnancy, Caroline wrote, 'Adieu, I'm tired of writing. I hate to be so much in arrears, a constant regular correspondence is so much more comfortable. I don't expect you tho' to write much now, poor soul. Let me know just how you do and I'll write constantly to you, for believe me, conversing, sweet siss, with you is one of my greatest pleasures.' Emily agreed. 'When one receives a letter,' she wrote, 'sitting down immediately to answer it is like carrying on a conversation.' Once they started writing, Caroline and Emily were prolix. Often they felt they could not stop: Caroline wrote in 1759, 'Since you love a folio sheet of paper, dear siss, you shall have one. I'm sure I shall fill it, for when once I get into a talking or writing way there is no end of me.' Caroline called Emily 'the only person in the world I can freely open my mind to on all subjects, except Mr. Fox.' All her life Caroline got up early in the morning, and before breakfast she would sit down in her dressing-room and write letters. Towards the end of the 1750s she started wearing spectacles for reading, writing and sewing. Peering through them at the thick creamy paper, she scribbled the story of her life, troubles and all in what her husband and sons described as atrocious handwriting. 'I must wear you to death, sweet siss, with my complaints, but it is so comfortable to unburden one's mind.' 'Adieu, my dearest siss, I must always unburden my mind to you which is the only purport of this letter.' In happier times than these, Caroline and Emily swapped declarations of love. In 1762, Caroline wrote, 'believe me, except Mr. Fox and my children, there is nothing I love in this world in the least to compare to you; nobody but Ste is so often in my thoughts; your happiness and peace of mind is one of the things I have most at heart.'

Confessions of misery and expressions of love occupied the beginnings and ends of letters. Between them was stuffed a ragbag of news and anecdotes. In the 1750s, talk of children – their illnesses, intelligence and education – covered many pages. Emily's children had coughs, colds, fevers and occasionally more serious complaints. Ste Fox's shaking and trembling agitated Caroline's heart and pen. But in spite of regular purges, diets and treatments with mercury and tin, he survived. In 1756 Ste was sent to Eton College, his father's old school, and was soon 'very jolly' there. At about the same time Charles, discovering that Caroline had made an error in Roman history, decided to go to school as well. Fox and Caroline gave him free rein in his choice of school. After a week's deliberation the seven-year-old child plumped for Mr Pampellone's Academy at Wandsworth. The same year Emily sent her two sons, George, now eight and William, now seven, to England. George joined Ste at Eton and William went to

Wandsworth with Charles. Caroline took charge of them in the holidays and the sisters commiserated over their loss. 'I pity you, dear siss, from my heart, being obliged to part with them, but I do think Wandsworth School is the best nursery for delicate children in the world. I pity you, for I can hardly accustom myself to the absence of my two boys (Ste indeed I live in continual fears about), but sweet Charles I miss vastly.'

Other family news was dispersed amongst accounts of children's health and schooling. The third Duke of Richmond married in 1757. His bride was Lady Mary Bruce, only daughter of the late Earl of Ailesbury. Relations between the new Duchess and her sisters-in-law were to be extremely volatile. In 1758, one of the sisters' second cousins, Caroline Brudenell, married 'an immense rich citizen' Sir Samuel Fludyer. Their first cousin, Lady Caroline Keppel, Lady Albemarle's daughter, ran away with the celebrated surgeon, Robert Adair in the same year. 'I pity the poor girl very much,' wrote Caroline, remembering her own elopement. These and innumerable other tidbits of London and Dublin gossip passed to and fro. Sometimes such domestic news was more emotionally charged. In 1759 Caroline hinted obliquely to Emily that Fox and she were quarrelling, but she didn't give any details, thus admitting that she could not tell everything in her letters. In her next letter she decided to come clean: the trouble was about one of Fox's illegitimate children, Lizzie, now a pretty teenager. It was difficult for Caroline to write about Lizzie but she needed to share her feelings. 'I don't know why I scrupled naming Lizzie in my letter as the person I was so silly as to be uneasy about.' Caroline struggled with her feelings of guilt and jealousy. Although she acknowledged Lizzie's charm and her claims on Fox, Caroline insisted on being first in her husband's heart. She refused to allow Lizzie to live in Holland House. Many aristocratic women tolerated illegitimate children in their houses, sometimes on the same footing emotionally – though not legally – as their own offspring. Such tolerance, celebrated

by the novelist Samuel Richardson in *Pamela*, was impossible
for Caroline. She wanted Lizzie out of sight. 'I can't bear her
being here as one of the family. Mr. Fox would dote on her if
she was and I am unreasonable enough to be unhappy about
it. He don't want her here on the footing of a fine lady, but to
dine with us when alone, be sent for to play at cards with the
boys, and to be with us in that sort of way. She loves and
courts Mr. Fox very much, which is mighty natural, and I
own to you my feeling in my own mind how hard it is in me
to want to deprive her of that pleasure makes me imagine
myself wicked sometimes, and the dread I am in of not behaving quite well to her is one of my greatest reasons for keeping
her away as much as possible.'

Caroline's jealousy got the better of her guilt and Lizzie did
not come to live at Holland House. Lizzie's claims on her
father had no chance when they were pitted against Caroline's
need to be the centre of Fox's world. Materially Lizzie did as
well as any illegitimate child of an aristocrat could hope. She
married a cleric, Edward Young, who was tutor to the Fox
children. In 1761 Young was appointed to an Irish living by
the Lord Lieutenant Lord Halifax, probably at Fox's prompting. He and Lizzie, safely out of Caroline's way, prospered
and had a daughter. But Lizzie died in 1765. Caroline, now
able to show compassion, wrote of Young to Emily a year or
so later, 'poor man, he felt the loss of his pretty wife severely'.

To Emily such matters were more simple. By the end of the
1750s she had six children of her own, besides her sisters
Louisa, Sarah and Cecilia in the household. A few more did
not matter very much. In her husband's affections Emily was
supreme. Casual affairs and their tiny human consequences
simply made up the sexual imbalance in their relationship.
Writing to Caroline in 1751, Emily made it clear that Kildare
was sleeping with a woman in their household who was now
pregnant. But she treated the affair more as a joke than a
threat. 'I must tell you by way of n.b. that things can breed in
this house as well as her Lady K. You will hear more soon –

and 'tis to be hoped that my turn for getting a lover will come in good time; but you know hope deferred maketh the heart sick and that is my case; but adieu, I won't tire you any longer.' Emily's hope was eventually to be realised. When it was, far from being a joke, it had a profound effect on the whole family.

Letters were not just channels for gossip and confessions. They also gave writers opportunities to make statements about the world around them: comments on books, on the nature of humanity, on society. Caroline in particular was given to a running commentary on life. Once Emily declared that human happiness consisted in taking pleasure from 'trifling amusements'. Caroline commented in reply that she was 'philosopher enough' to think Emily wise, 'for after all, how trifling are most of the serious amusements and concerns of human life'.

Despite comments of this sort, Caroline and Emily did not consistently present themselves as 'philosophers' or 'bel-esprits' as they called salon thinkers. Unlike Lady Mary Wortley Montagu or their friends Mrs Greville and Mrs Vesey, Caroline and Emily did not think of themselves as 'blue stocking' women, part of whose self-definition (and reputation) was as women dedicated to demonstrating that their sex was capable of intellectual endeavour. Caroline and Emily described themselves as 'women of fashion', thus emphasising social position rather than any set of beliefs. They could not be described as 'feminists', but they participated actively in debates about the role of women.

Caroline was frequently scornful of men, her own husband excepted, and in 1766 wrote acerbically to Emily, 'some pursuit is necessary to man, particularly to an Englishman; 'tis an animal quite incapable of leading a rational life (that is what we should call so) and quite insufficient to itself. It must always be running after a fox, a hare, a blue ribbon, a place or some such thing, or given up to play. I do think nature has given us women the best lot in this queer jumble of life.' What women's lot was, Caroline made a little clearer in her comment on her friends who disliked Rousseau's *Émile*: 'Mrs. Greville and several others don't like what he says about women, nor his notions about them, so unwilling are our sex to give up being bel esprits, politicieux, gamesters and fine ladies, and to allow that a woman shines most in her own sphere.' Adding up the two statements, Caroline suggests that women were more rational than men (or Englishmen, whom she looked upon as inferior to the French). She admitted that women were taking part in the sort of gambling, political intrigue and social climbing she derided in men, but insisted that their talents should be used where they shone brightest, their 'own sphere'.

In theory this seemed to reserve the 'public' world for men and confine women to the 'private' or non-public. But exactly what Caroline meant was vague; her domestic space was both familial home and political base; she read without qualm or comment the works of hundreds of women who earned their living in the 'public' world of print; she patronised female business women so frequently that it was probably by preference, buying her books and prints as well as her watches, toys and clothes from women; and she went constantly to watch actresses on the stage. Her working definition of a 'woman's own sphere' was fluid, changing its boundaries to suit the shape of her own life. Both Emily and Caroline read novels and advice literature which demanded a circumscription of women's roles, but they were under no social pressure to comply with this growing body of thought. Their response was gestural rather than significant, a matter of taking what they wanted and discarding the rest.

Beyond saying that women had a better life than men (something she only half believed) Caroline made no general statements about women's roles or aspirations. Emily was too wrapped up in the drama of her own life to do so, although when the time came to seize the initiative and act out newly fashionable ideas about the virtues of domesticity, marriage for love and marital fidelity, she did not hesitate. All the Lennox sisters were open to new ideas, and their wealth and education gave them instant access to the newest books, most fashionable thinkers and latest ideas about women. But this openness was not specifically 'feminist'. It was a reflection of the Whigs' political philosophy; a way of life (refined and articulated as the century wore on) in which a belief in amelioration (or 'progress') was central. The Lennox sisters believed in improvement and, for the most part, responded to change positively, as an indication of it. Religious toleration; expansion and new methods in trade, commerce, agriculture, medicine and the arts; a greater role for Parliament in government: all these were welcome novelties and changing ideas about women were just part of the package, one set of new ideas among many. This was a modish and mannered culture in which ideas were talked as well as lived and the relationship between talk and life was complex and personal.

Sometimes the flow of news and ideas faltered. Twice in the 1750s Emily and Caroline disagreed and their letters became more formal and less frequent. The first coolness, in 1754, was about politics. During the 1740s, the Irish exchequer had accumulated a large surplus which the Westminster government demanded. The Patriot Party, to which Kildare belonged, claimed the surplus and treated it as a symbol of Ireland's right to greater local autonomy. To get redress, Kildare decided to bypass 'the Castle', as the Westminster government in Dublin was called, and take the matter directly to the King.

In the spring of 1754, Kildare arrived in London with a long petition addressed to the monarch which justified both himself and his party and laid out their joint grievances. Kildare's presence was an embarrassment to Fox, who had already written angrily to his brother: 'Lord Kildare has deceived himself or been deceived most egregiously, and must be much mortified.' The duties of Fox's office bound him to rebuff his brother-in-law, while the duties of family bound him to support him.

Fox was unwilling to lose even the smallest political [...] on behalf of his brother-in-law. So he tied Kildare up [...] bureaucratic knots, sending him to fruitless appointments with ministers, but persuading him not to push his luck as far as the King himself. The long petition languished unread in Kildare's trunk. But Kildare's mission was not wasted, because the memorial raised his reputation among Dublin's Protestants. Scorned in Westminster, Kildare became something of a figurehead in Dublin. A medal was struck, showing him like a dragon, guarding Ireland's money from the English predator. Bonfires were lit in Dublin that gave off golden sparks of Irish defiance. Yet this local triumph had a familial cost. From the 1750s onwards Irish politics were to be a difficult matter for the whole family.

The second dispute, in 1758, was conducted more in innuendoes than open accusations; but feelings ran high on both sides. Ostensibly about the futures of Louisa and Sarah, now almost fifteen and thirteen, its real subjects were Emily's comfort and Caroline's self-esteem. Caroline had always assumed that Louisa and Sarah would be sent to London to be floated on the English marriage market. In the autumn of 1758 she began to make arrangements for Louisa's arrival, hoping to reclaim her father's posthumous good opinion by finding her sister an eligible husband.

Emily had few intentions of letting Louisa go. To Louisa and Sarah, Emily, at twenty-six, was at once mother and sister. They looked up to her as a figure of authority and confided in her as an equal; Sarah called her both 'dearest siss' and 'Queen of Ireland'. Emily was determined not to lose the pleasure of this enviable position. So she and Kildare began looking round for a suitable Irish husband for Louisa. Caroline was hurt and the dispute was referred to their brother. Trying to keep the peace, the third Duke declared that Emily and Caroline would be equally good guardians. Emily, used to being flattered, was offended; Caroline was hurt at Emily's offence which she construed as a slight to her: 'the thing I

our seeming to think my brother's having
ion of me as you was an offence to you. I
hat in any other light.' The hurt rankled.
ered that her elopement was held against her
sister and she wanted Louisa with her pre-
e could wipe away what she saw as the stain of
her ii.....ll.

Emily declared they might disagree even more if they lived
closer together. But Caroline swept away this attempt to
smooth over their differences. 'I believe the contrary, at least I
know myself I'm much oftener disposed to be angry at people
when they are absent; its easier to explain things when together.' But Emily disregarded Caroline's claims and pressed
on in the search for a husband for Louisa. Her first choice
Louisa rejected out of hand. The second, twenty-year-old
Thomas Conolly, Louisa accepted. From the Kildares' point
of view, Conolly was the perfect match. He was the richest
man in Ireland and, although he was without political experience himself, his family had been connected with
nationalist politics for half a century and so he could be
counted on to support Kildare and the Patriot Party. Out-
weighing all this, for Emily, was the fact that Conolly's park
was next to her own and Castletown, his mansion, was the
nearest big house to Carton. Married to Conolly, Louisa
would scarcely even be leaving home, and Emily could look
forward to a lifetime of comfortable chats and sisterly service.

PART TWO
'I can never deserve all he does for me'.
Louisa to Emily, 10 April 1759.

Thomas Conolly had an education appropriate to a young
man of vast fortune. Painted by Mengs in Rome, Conolly
dressed for the occasion in an elaborate brocaded coat. He

gestured towards a line of marble muses whose attire, in-
struments and place under a huge marble column vaguely
suggested a knowledge of classical learning and antiquities.
Beyond such a gesture, Conolly had little interest in the
ancient world. Rome and the rest of the Grand Tour made
little impression on him. When he returned to Ireland he took
up the life of a country gentleman with unaffected pleasure.
He cut his hair short and curling round the ears and swapped
his grand clothes for a simple cravat and riding-coat. In Conolly's portrait by Reynolds, painted in about 1760 for the
Holland House gallery, the classical props are abandoned.
Conolly wears an olive-green overcoat and a white shirt. In
the background a rapidly brushed swirl of clouds, good practice for a studio assistant, suggests only the out of doors. No
books or speeches show that Conolly aspires to be a dilettante
or politician. Reynolds painted Conolly open faced and
slightly open mouthed, an honest man in a country setting.
Eight years later, firmly established in his identity of 'Squire
Conolly', he was painted again, by the Irish artist Healy. This
time one of Conolly's race horses, huge and gaunt, fills the
centre of the painting, while Conolly, modestly taking a subsidiary role, is almost edged off the side.

By 1768, when this last picture was made, Conolly was
thirty. He was a formidably strong man, liable to fits of hypochondria if deprived of hunting, racing and 'rough riding'
over his estate. As this painting showed, horses were Conolly's greatest pleasure; he was quite content to share any
canvas with his charger, his trainer and a groom. His house he
shared with sporting companions from many walks of life.
Happy days in his calendar were those marked by equestrian
achievement in the field or on the track.

Conolly scrawled enough figures in his account books to
show that racing, hunting and gambling on horses cost him a
great deal. In 1776 he lost a small fortune at Almack's Club in
London. As Louisa put it, 'the dear soul was so often called
there by bets upon his horses that it drew him into a little

gambling. The money he lost (happily) won't really hurt him ... It was reported he had ruined himself, but I am sure his losses altogether were under £10,000.' Such a reverse would have ruined many prosperous country gentlemen, but Louisa could afford her insouciance; by the 1770s Conolly's rent round was bringing in around £25,000 a year.

This wealth was new, made by Thomas Conolly's great uncle, William 'Speaker' Conolly in the years after the Battle of the Boyne in 1690. Land sequestered from defeated Jacobites was bought up by William III's supporters; fortunes were made and the Protestant Ascendancy secured. In the turbulence humble men, William Conolly among them, pushed their way to prominence. The son of Protestant innkeepers from Donegal, Conolly trained as a lawyer, but soon moved from settling land deals to making them. At the same time he acted as Collector and Receiver of revenue for the government, thus ensuring a steady supply of cash to finance his purchases. After his election as MP for Donegal, he quickly built up a political machine that rivalled his landholdings in size, and ended his career as Speaker of the Irish House of Commons, spokesman for Irish Protestant nationalism and the richest man in Ireland. He had extensive lands in the north and west of the island, a large Dublin house and Castletown, a magnificent 'pile of building', twelve miles to the west of the capital. In 1729 Conolly died and his property and fortune passed to his brother Patrick and thence to Louisa's Thomas Conolly, who inherited in 1754.

Despite the fact that Thomas Conolly's mother was an English aristocrat, from the Wentworth family, he was seen as irremediably Irish and had to pay a high premium for a well connected English bride. The settlement for Louisa, made before their marriage, was his exchange for entering ducal and courtly circles. Lands with an annual rent-roll of £6,178 were settled on Louisa to provide a widow's pension and fortunes for younger children. For the time being these rents supplied the £3,000 a year Conolly paid his mother. On top of this money, Louisa had several hundred pounds a year of 'pin money' to do what she liked with. On the Lennox side, the Duke of Richmond handed over to Conolly Louisa's £10,000, owed her from her father's will. For Conolly the marriage meant an alliance with the Kildares, Richmonds and Foxes. For Louisa it meant wealth and proximity to her sister. The young couple were married on 30 December 1758. Louisa was fifteen, her husband twenty. Still smarting from her defeat in their recent quarrel, Caroline wrote tersely to Emily with her 'sincere congratulations to you on this happy occasion,' adding, 'I will not interrupt your present joy by entering into any more of the particulars now subsisting between us.'

When Louisa married Conolly she also married his house. In the years to come she bestowed immense devotion on the fabric of each. In 1758 Castletown was, like its proprietor, a sturdy but undecorated structure, outwardly complete but unfinished inside. It had no hothouses, nurseries or landscaping.

Castletown has an exterior as severe as those of many Dublin town houses. It stands on flat ground by the banks of the Liffey, which meanders sluggishly through the park. The south-facing front is a flat rectangle of shining, dense, cream-coloured limestone, four storeys high, thirteen windows and 140 feet wide. A simple columned porch outlines the entrance, from which two shallow flights of steps flow to the driveway in wide undulations. The same stark regularity is repeated round the sides of the house and along its north front. From the upstairs windows the blue humps of the Wicklow Mountains dominate the southern skyline.

Castletown house, as originally planned in the 1720s by its Italian architect, Alessandro Galilei, was a Palladian box on such a huge scale that its geometry was transformed into monumentality. It did not stay so simple long. Very soon an element of the rococo crept into the design; a hint of the sumptuousness that was played off against plainness in

Ascendancy life. Edward Lovett Pearce, an Irish architect, added two curving colonnades that, with a suggestion of caprice and two necklace-like rows of sculpted urns, link the main house to its satellite offices and kitchens. To the right and east of the main block sit the stables and kennels, to the left are the kitchens and household offices. Castletown's unfinished interior offered Louisa endless scope for what she and her sisters called 'business'. Decoration, landscaping and building occupied Louisa for 25 years.

But it was in England, not Ireland, that Tom and Louisa spent the first couple of years of their married life. Early in 1759 they left Dublin for Park Gate in Cheshire, arriving there on 13 March after what Louisa called 'a charming passage of thirteen hours in the night air'. Park Gate was a small port with a large custom house and a harbour deep enough to take the ships that churned back and forth across the Irish Sea. Now it lies mired and silted up in the muddy chocolate skirts of the Dee estuary. But two hundred years ago it was the favourite landing place for passengers from Dublin. The alternative was Holyhead in Wales, which was closer to Dublin but further from London. Park Gate made sense for Tom and Louisa because their first destination was Stretton Hall in Staffordshire, the Conolly family seat in England. At Stretton Louisa looked around her with the eagle eye of prospective ownership and pronounced the house 'a sweet, dear, lovely, pretty place'. Her new Conolly relatives, delighted with the marriage, used much the same adjectives about her. But Louisa was also lost without her sisters and she clung to Conolly for comfort, writing to Emily, 'I hate to have Mr Conolly leave me at all . . . for then I feel quite forlorn, as if I wanted somebody. You have no notion, my dearest sister, how happy I am to have so sweet a picture of you as I have to wear constantly; its the greatest pleasure almost I have, to look at it so constantly as I do.' Louisa's initiation at Stretton over, she and Conolly proceeded nervously to London, to be presented at Court and at Holland House.

Henry Fox, quick to serve the family interest, had written to Conolly at Park Gate, offering him the vacant parliamentary seat of Malmesbury, which was up for sale to a suitable candidate at four or five hundred pounds. But although Malmesbury was the primary subject of his letter, Fox was also writing to make sure that Louisa and Conolly would not upset Caroline by appearing visibly taken aback when they saw Ste's twitching and trembling. Ste was still very ill. 'As yet there is no amendment in my dearest child,' Caroline told Emily. 'He will be better for some hours, almost a whole day sometimes, then be as bad as ever again. Wilmot, Duncan, Truesdale, Ranby and a Doctor Reeves out of the city attend him; he is now taking tin. As yet nothing seems to have any effect.' Fox's caution was in vain; Louisa was horrified by Ste and Caroline noticed it. But Caroline, in her turn, was shocked by Conolly. On 3 April, a week after Louisa's arrival, Caroline wrote carefully to Emily, 'Mr Conolly seems vastly good natured'. But by 17 April she had thrown this caution to the winds: 'You must indeed be partial to Conolly not to think him immensely silly, dear siss; sure, he is a tiresome boy, and one feels sorry he is so, he seems so exceedingly good natured. I can but think how miserable I should have been at Louisa's age to have had such a husband. I hope and believe she won't find it out ever, but I should have thought it dreadful.' Caroline's criticism offended Emily, who replied that Conolly did not 'want sense', although to Kildare she wrote, 'I should never think of comparing you to poor Conolly in anything'. Memories of the recent quarrel still lingered and Caroline hurried to make up for her blunder. Conolly, she agreed, was not stupid, but 'in company he is dreadful sometimes'. By the middle of June Caroline had decided that Conolly was bumptiously childish rather than simply empty headed. 'To be sure he is reckoned a mighty silly boy, but ... I feel to love him, he is so good natured, neither is it a kind of silly way I dislike so much as others. I look upon him as a boy of ten or eleven years old, and treat him as such. I only dread her feeling ashamed of him sometimes.'

Louisa was not ashamed of Conolly. She had already decided how to treat him. He was her 'flea', her 'tormenting flea' and also her 'dear flea': a constant irritant of which she was nevertheless fond. He hopped about, guileless and full of muscle. As time went on Louisa adapted herself to 'flea'. She came to depend on his presence and to dread his trips away from home when, let loose from her restraint, he might gamble, drink and make foolish political decisions. At home she watched over him, nursing his ailments and entertaining his sporting guests. Sarah once wrote to Emily about the way in which Louisa came to implicate herself in Conolly's hypochondria: 'if Louisa has written at all, I am sure she has given you an idea of his being very ill, which you must not say I deny, for it is really so odd a fancy of his, and so rooted, so much adopted by her, that I'm convinced both of them would think me very unfeeling if they hear how lightly it is treated by every soul . . . His weakness admits of three hours ride and two of walking every morning, and the spitting increased by what he terms want of appetite; -viz: two plates of soup, three pork steaks, half a chicken and tart. Dearest Louisa is deaf; but why she should be blind I cannot guess.'

Simultaneously artless and inscrutable, Louisa baffled her family. Caroline, Emily and Sarah reached for superlatives to describe her, as if exact language was inadequate to her merits. Writing to a friend in the mid-1750s, Emily said, 'As for Louisa, I really think that in my life I never knew or heard of anything equal to the sweetness and gentleness of her disposition. She is indeed as yet quite an angel. She is mildness itself. It is not in nature to ruffle the sweetness of her temper one single instant.' Emily continued, indulging in her fondness for 'storybook' analogies, 'one may say of her as Lord Hastings says in the play of Jane Shore,

> Without one jarring atom was she formed
> and gentleness and joy made up her being

which I think the prettiest character that can be given any woman.'

Caroline and Sarah agreed with Emily that something otherworldly surrounded their sister. 'That angel Louisa', 'that sweet angel', Caroline called her, and Sarah said she was 'a dear angel' whom people 'worshipped'. Louisa's place in the Lennox family was that of a lodestone of virtue, a standard of goodness against which her brothers and sisters measured their waywardness and depravity. Sarah, in particular, used her older sister for self-chastisement and encouragement. 'She is an angel and I'm a weak, unsteady, thoughtless, vain creature.' 'My angelic sister's character ... raises me above my own weak nature sometimes.'

Quietness was one of Louisa's greatest strengths, the more so because her siblings believed in expressing their emotions forcefully. Sandwiched between Emily's queenly claims to emotional dominance and Sarah's volubility, Louisa became at an early age mistress of the judicious silence. Sarah would have liked her sister to join in gossipy dissections of people and events, partly because Louisa's reserve made Sarah feel tarnished and guilty. But Louisa never did, and Sarah wrote with a touch of exasperation, 'dearest Louisa! How does she contrive to keep out of all scrapes? Why, by holding her tongue, to be sure. She is closeness itself, for the deuce a word will she utter that can be turned into any form but that she gave it.'

Louisa believed in battening down strong feelings. Towards the end of her life she wrote to her brother, 'nobody is more likely than me to be drawn out of the right path where their passions are engaged. I am sensible of possessing very strong ones by nature, in so much, that I have made it a constant duty with myself to regulate them, and trust that upon the whole I have been able to subdue them very much. But on some occasions throughout life I confess they have been stronger than my good resolutions.'

Louisa managed her silent gestures and eloquent reserve with great skill. They were her ways of securing attention and love. Early on in her life Louisa had forged a connection between doing good and being loved. Unlike Emily, who demanded love as a right, Louisa came to believe that love had to be earned, something not inevitable but hard won and reciprocal. Louisa had far lower expectations of her desserts than Emily or even Caroline, uncertain though the latter might be in some respects. Almost all her life her ambition was to please first Emily, then Conolly, Sarah and her other brothers and sisters. Yet the rewards, she felt, were great and lasting because she did not, like Caroline, feel happiness must inevitably be snatched away. 'Thinking good of one's fellow creatures is the most heartfelt satisfaction,' she said, and described herself as 'one of the happiest and luckiest of women'. By making herself useful, Louisa made herself important and beloved in the family. In return her family doted on her. When pressed to name a favourite sibling, all her brothers and sisters named her. Louisa was, as Sarah said, their 'sheet anchor in all things'.

As a young woman Louisa wanted nothing more than to please Emily and be loved by her. She was a very willing subject in Emily's empire of charm. When they parted in 1759, Louisa sent her sister declarations of love that were supplications before the altar of a deity. 'No one can love another better than I do you, my dear sweet sister. I beseech you believe this from your ever loving and most affectionate L. A. Conolly.' 'I don't know how to express my obligations to you for such kind advice as you gave me in the beginning of your letter. Indeed, I take it so kindly, and feel so happy with it, that I read over your letter with the greatest pleasure imaginable to find you still continue the same goodness to me you always had and which I shall never be so ungrateful as to forget. You know, my sweet sister, how sincere I always am in my professions of love or gratitude towards you.'

Louisa made her mark by absenting herself emotionally in the midst of her more volatile and expressive siblings. Sarah noticed that Louisa did not like to make 'a fuss' and that she enjoyed 'doing good to all around her'. Louisa claimed she disliked 'affectation' by which people drew attention to themselves; so much so indeed that if she was upset she would take extra pains not to show it. 'When my mind is occupied with vexation,' she wrote to Emily in 1776, when she was thirty-two, 'I do not love to speak of it to anybody . . . and think my safest way upon most occasions is to hold my tongue.'

This silence, a dam that restrained high feeling and bad temper, created its own emotional drama. Louisa used her stillness to have others scurrying around her, wondering what they should do for her, wondering what her opinions and needs were. During one family crisis she wrote to Emily, 'remember, my dearest sister, I will not be considered,' thus deftly adopting a stance which put Emily in the wrong whatever she did. Sarah watched the same diminutive play of emotion unfold when Louisa paid her a visit in 1776. Louisa, Sarah wrote to Emily, was 'very naughty, I assure you, about her health . . . I wish you would give her a serious lecture about it. Do you know that if I had not had a fire made in her room here she would have come to this damp . . . house from town with the colic and never ordered one, because it did not signify, she said.' Once or twice Louisa's reserve drove Sarah beyond guilt and into exasperation. 'Louisa carries her delicacy too far,' Sarah burst out to Emily in 1776. 'She ought to express the whole of her feelings and let us judge ourselves at what rate we value them.' Most of the time, however, Sarah felt simply guilty.

When the fifteen-year-old Louisa arrived in London in the spring of 1759, Caroline was impressed. 'I can't say enough of sweet Louisa. Indeed, my dear siss, she does you honour. There never was anything so natural, so easy and pretty as her behaviour is, she dances charmingly.' Two weeks later she added: 'Louisa is vastly liked, not thought near as handsome as you, but she is so well behaved, gentle, modest and civil, and seems to have so much sense and propriety about her its impossible but that she should please. I shall think her handsomer than Sal because she has so very pretty a figure.'

Louisa described herself as tall and well built. Others thought her handsome but not pretty, the distinction lying in her having a good figure rather than a beautiful face. Caroline praised her sister's 'presence', a bosom whose size and amplitude conformed to the taste of the times. While she was in London Louisa went to Allan Ramsay's studio and posed for her portrait. The picture was paid for by Caroline and destined for the gallery at Holland House. Caroline may have insisted on Louisa standing to show off her figure, even though a full-length portrait, especially if both hands were showing, was extremely expensive. Ramsay made a quick sketch of Louisa, taking note of her dark hair drawn tightly on top of her head, her plump hands and forearms, and the tipped-up nose, small mouth and soft chin she shared with her sisters. In the finished portrait, Louisa looks a good deal older than her fifteen years. She holds a bunch of grapes which hint at the wine and youthful merriment she was enjoying during the London season, and is wearing a salmonpink court dress with three deep ruffles on the sleeves, two ruched frills round the skirt and seven rows of gathered ribbon across the stomacher.

Ramsay's studio was only one site that had to be visited in the busy weeks of the London season. Louisa and Conolly plunged into a round of assemblies, balls, trips, plays and operas. Many of these had some sort of political intention or overtone since politics and pleasure were indivisible; the Conollys were being presented at Court and initiated into the world of the Whig aristocracy at the same time. On 23 March, the third Duke of Richmond gave a ball for his sister, and by 10 April Louisa and Tom Conolly had kissed the King's hand, attended three operas, two plays, numerous assemblies and one *ridotto*. The latter, a mixed entertainment of music and dancing that combined an informal concert with cheerful dances, the shy Louisa declared she liked 'of all things'.

Despite this social whirl, Louisa was miserable. She was lonely for Carton, for Sarah and, above all, for Emily. When Emily hinted that she might accompany Kildare to London when he came on business in the summer of 1759, Louisa replied, garbling her words with delight, 'be so good as to excuse this scribbling, but I really am so excessively overjoyed to think I so soon shall be so happy as to see you that I really don't know what I am doing or what I'm about. This is so charming a surprise. I really want words to express my joy.' Emily did not come and Caroline reported that 'poor dear Louisa cried sadly the whole afternoon about it'.

Louisa did not forget the anxiety and loneliness of her London sojourn. Years later when she was decorating the long gallery at Castletown she selected an engraving called 'La Nouvelle Épouse' and had it copied in oils and placed on the wall above her husband's portrait. The engraving came from a seven-volume illustrated encyclopedia of the ancient world, Bernard de Montfaucon's *L'Antiquité expliquée et representée en figures* (1719–24). The book's plates were accompanied by an explanatory text; in this one, Montfaucon wrote, the bride was weeping because she was leaving home for the first time. In the Castletown panel, she sits on a tomb-like wall, covering her eyes with a cloak, while a cupid stands awkward and unemployed near a servant who is trying to wash away the bride's unhappiness.

As the spring of 1759 matured into summer, it was Emily's turn to feel anxious. She suspected that Conolly was planning to live in England for good, and she wanted Louisa back. At the end of May Emily wrote impatiently to Kildare, who had arrived without her in London, 'I am sure you might easily dissuade her from buying a house in London. And you might at the same time commend your own wife to her for readily agreeing from prudent motives to give up that you had in London, tho' she was fond of it and had still more reason to love England than Louisa can, having been bred up there.'

But not for nothing had Emily kept Louisa and Sarah so close to her. By the time she left Ireland for London, Louisa had grown into the uneasy mentality of the colonist. She loved Ireland but was ashamed of it in the face of English snobbery and distanced from it by virtue of her English birth. Yet she was unhappy anywhere else. Louisa lived in a colonial limbo mistrusted by both the English she lived amongst and the Irish she had left. She tried to overcome her dislike of England, writing to her sister in 1759, 'now though one may be partial to Ireland, as I am, yet one need not find fault with this place . . . Are you not of my opinion, my dear sister, that one should try not to make oneself disagreeable to any nation?' But England was not her home and she came to think of herself as Irish, a definition that was to bring her great anguish in the years to come.

Louisa was home by the autumn. But for the next few years she and Conolly went backwards and forwards between England and Ireland, spending the sporting seasons at Castletown and going to London for parliamentary sessions. In 1761 Conolly was elected to the Irish Parliament as MP for Londonderry, and after that unless Irish affairs were on the Westminster agenda, he seldom attended the English House of Commons. Castletown became the focus of the Conollys' lives. They became more and more reluctant to leave it, even for social occasions, preferring to hold open house rather than accept invitations. As time went on Louisa and Tom fused with their house in the minds of their friends and Castletown became one of those almost-living symbols of Ascendancy life so lauded by apologists and decried by opponents.

Life at Castletown changed with the weather and the seasons, closer at all times to the demands and offerings of the land than the hectic amalgam of town and country life at Holland House. Louisa gave her guests hospitality rather then wit. After a day's riding friends looked forward to immense dinners followed by a gentle hand of cards. They did not expect Charles Fox's prodigious brilliance, Henry's wit or Caroline's serious conversation.

In summer, when Dublin was empty, Castletown life re-
volved around racing and, after 12 August, shooting, both
predominantly but not exclusively pleasures for men. Early
rising was called for on days of organised sport which would
take them a considerable distance from the house. On other
days, guests and their hosts got up about eight o'clock, several
hours after their servants, and they came together for breakfast at nine-thirty or ten. Before breakfast Louisa often wrote
letters or went over her accounts. After breakfast the party
would divide. Some went out to ride, pay calls or walk
through the grounds, Louisa's favoured outdoor occupation.
'This is a most lovely day,' she wrote in February 1768, 'a
white frost with fine sunshine. I am going out with all the
dogs to take a long *trudge* all over the place, which is a pleasant thing to do.' Women and old people settled down to
several hours of work accompanied by readings, mostly from
novels, poetry, histories, sermons and books of travels. Sewing of all sorts was the main occupation for women, but it was
varied by drawing, which Louisa enjoyed, copying and
colouring prints or making plans for houses, offices and
rooms. Women embroidered bed hangings, chair seats, fire
screens, waistcoats and gowns. They worked lace into ruffles
and wove silk into ribbons. When they got bored they passed
their work on to servants to be finished. 'I have begun my
gown, its vastly pretty, the stripes go on like lightening, but
the flowers are a little tedious,' wrote Sarah on a country
sojourn in 1760, holding out little hope that the finished garment would be all her own work. In another letter she added,
'I am grown a great workwoman lately.'

At three o'clock everyone dined. In the long summer evenings after dinner the party walked into the gardens, taking tea
there if it was warm, watching the Liffey ooze its way to
Dublin. Sometimes they drove out into the green countryside. Card tables were put up for their return, and as night fell
people broke up into small groups. Some played cards, others
chatted, worked, looked at prints, planned sporting and political strategy or played chess. Supper was served at ten

o'clock and by midnight everybody except hardened drinkers and busy gamblers had gone to bed.

This summer timetable carried on through long visits by family members and constant exchange between Castletown and Carton. Two or three times in spring and summer Castletown was decked out for what Sarah described as 'fêtes', outdoor parties for servants, locals and workpeople, and grander affairs to benefit charitable institutions. Through all this activity, week in week out, Louisa kept up the running of the house. She made up accounts in a small, meticulous hand with scrupulous care. Growing, buying, provisioning, cleaning, cooking were not her responsibility, but she had to keep track of what was being done and how much was being spent. Whenever there was an empty house, decorators moved in to make an alternative bustle and Louisa kept watch over them too.

Winter routines were different because Dublin was full of parliamentarians and government officials and the season was in full swing. Louisa rarely stayed at the Conollys' Dublin house, preferring to issue invitations to Castletown instead. Guests drove out from Dublin for dinner. As usual the list was long and mixed. Relatives, huntsmen, clerics and sometimes a carefully vetted actress or two sat out the long winter evenings. In December, Louisa held what Sarah called 'a month's round of different parties', and discharged the social obligations she had incurred by refusing invitations. If Parliament was sitting, Conolly might stay in their town house. If not he was usually chasing foxes across his acres. Louisa went into town to the theatre and to charity concerts (although she admitted preferring cheerful ensemble singing to any instrumental playing), and occasionally visited friends there.

But it was at Castletown that Louisa was most happy and content. On a quiet winter's day eighteen years after her marriage she sat down and wrote to Emily, 'I always was very fond of this place, but living so much at it as I have done of late has made my partiality increase for it, and 'tis amazing

what constant amusement and employment I find for myself.
We have been a great deal alone, which has made it still more
delightful for me, as I find that is what Mr. Conolly likes
best.'

PART THREE
'He is in love with her'.
Henry Fox, Memoir, April–May 1761.

Sarah made her London début at the age of fourteen in circumstances totally different from those that had smoothed
Louisa's path. Louisa had much to give her confidence
besides her own pretty figure. Her marriage had made her
rich and secure. She had nothing to ask of her brothers or
Caroline and she was ready, despite her shyness, to take her
place alongside them as a hostess and a companion. London
was a glorious playground and money no object. Sarah, in
contrast, came unmarried to London with £10,000 and a good
name. Everyone understood that she was there to find a suitable husband and that the pleasures of the capital must be
inseparable from that arduous search.

Sarah's greatest asset was her sexual allure; her greatest
handicap was that she was unaware of the effect she had upon
others. Like her sisters, Sarah construed life as a drama or a
tale. For Caroline, life cast itself as a fable or a morality tale in
which she and her family were the principal sufferers. Emily
saw life as a full-blown Rousseauian melodrama of which she
was heroine and subject. Louisa, in contrast, used the life of
Christ as her narrative model. To Sarah life was a comedy of
manners that existed to reveal her follies. She was the shrewd-
est and coolest observer of human folly in the family, but life
did not become real for her until she had told it to others. She
was in consequence a compulsive gossip and story-teller.
Gossip and intrigue, solidified into stories, were also ways of
temporarily arresting the flux of sensation and event through

which she felt herself drifting. But when she retold her own story, Sarah made herself into a figure of fun, a character for ironic and comic treatment who acted, or fumbled, her way through life more according to social and familial dictate than her own desires.

From her earliest childhood Sarah had been a pawn in the scandal-ridden mix of politics and personalities that constituted the Court of George II. The second Duke of Richmond had been proud of Sarah's prettiness, her way with words and her 'rough and showy' Lennox complexion. One day in the late 1740s, as a band of courtiers accompanied the King and Queen through the Broad Walk in Kensington Gardens, Sarah broke away from her governess, toddled up to the King and burst out in her prettiest French, 'Comment vous portez vous, Monsieur le Roi? Vous avez une grande et belle maison ici, n'est-ce pas?' Then, in imitation of an elaborate and much practised court ritual, she dropped a low curtsey in front of the monarch and made a temporary conquest of his heart.

As a result of this infant indiscretion, Sarah became a royal plaything. She was often summoned to Kensington Palace to amuse the old King. Once, George II picked her up, put her in a tall Chinese jar and closed the lid. Sarah came through this trial of spirit splendidly, discerning like a seasoned diva the inmost wishes of her audience. She sat down in the bottom of the jar and launched into a song that was bound to warm a Hanoverian heart, 'Marlbrough s'en va-t-en guerre'.

While it was unusual for a child and a monarch to play together in such a way, kings were anything but magical beings to court families. For salaried officials like Lord Hervey and the second Duke of Richmond the sight of the monarch was often accompanied by the descent of overwhelming boredom. Despite the fact that King and courtiers alike knew that they were participating in the rituals by which majesty transmuted itself from the ordinary to the magical, and that knowledge lent gravity to court occasions, life at Court was dull precisely because its purpose was to divest the King of the quotidian.

As Caroline Fox observed, the King had to 'play the King', and in the act the pettiness and idiosyncrasies that form the compelling interest of human lives had to be shorn away. Courtiers, bound up in this alchemy of ritual, soon stopped associating the monarchy with glamour or mystique.

Sometimes the stultifying sameness of courtly life was shattered. New reigns and royal marriages brought an invigorating sense of excitement to courts, as credulous appointees and inexperienced monarchs fumbled with the machinery of kingship. But when the engine of ceremony began to run smoothly once again, befuddlement and stagnation would settle over the royal palaces.

Sarah remembered and retold the stories of her youthful encounters with George II not because they were remarkable but because they served to confirm her place in the world. She was a royal plaything, a drifting flibbertigibbet who caught the scenarios others threw her and acted them superbly well. Not until she was middle-aged was Sarah able to choose and set a course through life to which she held in the face of family disapproval and that she arrived at from some degree of self-knowledge and self-interest.

Everyone agreed that Sarah was a pretty girl. But to her sisters she was very little more. Emily declared, 'to my taste Sarah is merely a pretty, lively looking girl and that is all. She has not one good feature . . . Her face is so little and squeezed, which never turns out pretty.' Caroline noticed that Sarah's attractions did not lie simply in her face. 'Her manner is vastly engaging and she is immensely pretty,' she wrote soon after Sarah arrived in London in the autumn of 1759. 'Sarah seems to have more observation and cleverness about her than Louisa,' she added. But she was very critical of Sarah's way of coming into a room: Sarah held herself awkwardly, she said, stooping her shoulders and dropping her head forward. She also danced badly and had a scrofulous scalp. 'I'm seriously hurt tho' with her disguising that sweet little figure of hers by holding herself as she does . . . She has not the least air; its a thousand pities.' Sarah was equally disparaging when she talked about herself. She had, she said, small eyes and a long and turned-up nose that managed both to grow longer and to turn up more as the years went by. Her legs were bad and she was in constant danger of passing over the fateful border between plumpness and fat.

Despite all this, Sarah bore comparison with her sisters well. 'In England and in Ireland you will find ten to one people who will give it to her before any of the others,' Emily wrote in surprise. It was left to men, to whom the codes of gallantry gave narrative licence, to explain that Sarah's manner made an ordinary face and figure into an overwhelmingly attractive one. Henry Fox, after ticking off her good points, added in exasperation, 'but this is not describing her'. She was, he concluded, 'different from and prettyer than any other girl I ever saw.' Horace Walpole, eager as ever to breathe scandal into innocence, saw, farsightedly as it turned out, the potential for social disaster in Sarah's resplendent sexuality. 'No Magdalen by Correggio was half so lovely and expressive,' he said.

Sarah arrived at Holland House in November 1759. Charles Fox was away at Eton, Harry was at Wandsworth and Ste, much recovered from his last bout of illness, was preparing to travel abroad. Caroline and Henry had provided a companion for Sarah none the less, Lady Susan Fox-Strangways, daughter of Henry's brother Stephen. 'She is not pretty. She is very fat, has a good complexion, large heavy eyes, a wide mouth and very fine light hair. I don't know her yet,' Sarah reported to Emily. Susan was decisive and confident and quickly swept Sarah away on a tide of schemes and imaginings. Sarah's need for a confidante quickly got the better of her first impressions and she began to think of Susan as her bosom companion, her 'true, sincere and amiable friend'. Very soon she agreed to allow Susan to vet and veto any suitors she might have, thus sharing control over the overriding priority of her London début, the search for a husband.

Other surprises were in store for Sarah when she came to Holland House from Carton. She was amazed to find Fox and Caroline so engaged in one another's lives, reading and gossiping together, disagreeing and arguing in public. Used as she was to Emily's effortless superiority, Sarah was horrified to see Caroline working to make Fox laugh, and disgusted that they made jokes together at Emily's expense. Fox teased her about Emily's financial profligacy, knowing that the joke would be passed on, which it duly was: 'All this he sat telling me last night, grunting and groaning every minute, and saying, "Lord have mercy upon me. What an extravagant jade she is! How she does love buying! Lord help her!" And so he goes on for an hour like an old man in a play.' Sarah was even more indiscreet about Ste. 'Ste Fox is going to Geneva in three weeks. He is a very disagreeable boy and frightfully ugly.' Caroline, enchanted with Sarah like everyone else, was simultaneously writing to Emily, 'I hope Sal loves me. I do her, vastly.'

At the end of November Sarah was presented at Court, wearing blue and black feathers in her powdered hair, a black silk gown, cream lace ruffles ('that Louisa gave me') and white shoes. While she was renewing her acquaintance with the old King, the Prince of Wales, hovering behind his grandfather, caught her blushes and stammered replies to the King's questions and fell head over heels in love with her.

When Sarah and the Prince of Wales first met, she was a seasoned campaigner in the social mêlée of Ascendancy Dublin, despite being only fourteen years old. The Prince, at twenty-one, was far less experienced in the ways of the world. Yet in a sense they were made for one another: neither was in control of their destiny. George's father, Prince Frederick, died in 1751, leaving the young Prince caught between the demands of his mother, a series of tutors and the needs of the nation. He was slow and withdrawn. Casting round for a father figure, he fastened on Lord Bute, an impecunious Scot whose friendship with his mother was attributed to a 'good

person, fine legs' and 'theatrical air of the greatest importance'. Bute quickly became everything to the lonely Prince of
Wales: tutor, adviser, friend. He treated George with a mixture of deference and ferocity that played on the dual senses
of majesty and worthlessness that were at the core of the
future monarch's character.

In June 1759, the Prince of Wales celebrated his twenty-
first birthday. He was still a virgin and still ill at ease; less unhappy than he had been before his attachment to Bute, but
none the less a pitiful figure, solemn, tortured and priggish.
When Sarah was presented at Court a few months later he
said very little to her. But what little he did say was more
than enough for Sarah, who was hoping for a quick escape
after the ordeal of talking to the King. 'But what was worse
than anything was that the Prince of Wales came when the
King went,' she wrote to Emily. The Prince was, however,
too dazzled by Sarah to speak to her for long. Instead he
walked over to where Caroline stood. After some time,
George began to talk about Sarah. He was not used to paying
compliments to women and his gaucherie was complicated by
his sense of betrayal: he associated expressions of emotion
and vulnerability with his feelings towards Lord Bute. Sarah,
he told Caroline with awkward directness, was very tall and
very pretty. When she was older and fatter she would be very
handsome. He liked Louisa 'very well', but he liked Sarah
better. She had lively eyes and 'when she laughed they were
little and pretty'.

Sarah was 'very proud' but nonplussed by such undressed
expressions of admiration. She was more at ease flirting with
wits and responding coquettishly to carefully turned phrases.
Horace Walpole she pronounced 'charming': 'One thing is
that he commends me prodigiously, I mean flatters me.' She
also revelled in the company of a poet, 'who I disliked till I
heard he said I was like a rose and now I like him.' Such men
paid Sarah exaggerated compliments whose over-ripeness fitted perfectly with her ironic presentation of herself. 'Lady

Rochford and he [Horace Walpole] have found out the last beauty in me that anybody else would think of finding, which is that my hoggy paws are pretty.' The difficulty with the Prince of Wales was that he was sincere. As Caroline put it, 'he coloured as he spoke to me of her.'

Sarah continued to appear at drawing-rooms throughout December 1759 and the Prince of Wales grew increasingly excited and miserable. He became 'grave and thoughtful' and put his change of mood down to a 'daily increasing admiration of the fair sex'. But this admiration was anything but pleasant. George described it as a 'combat in my breast' and a 'struggle' between 'the boiling youth of twenty one years and prudence'. He was overwhelmed with guilt and fantasies of marriage at the same time. Lonely as he had been for so long, George was unable to conceive of love as expandable and inclusive. Side by side with his infatuation ran an inner dialogue of conflict and betrayal in which, as he put it, 'I must either lose my friend or my love'.

By the end of 1759 Bute was becoming suspicious about the Prince's feelings and intentions. He pressed George for a confession. But although he sent Bute two letters of anguished contrition, George kept his secret and went on seeing Sarah. They had a long conversation at the Twelfth Night Ball on 6 January 1760, an elaborate function which rounded off two weeks of Christmas entertainments at Court. To keep Sarah talking, and to build up a favourable picture of her that he could present to Bute, George asked her about her sisters. Did Louisa govern Conolly or the other way round? What was life like in Dublin? At Carton? What did Sarah do when there was no company at Carton? Sarah replied to the last question that either she or Louisa had been used to read to Emily because of her eyes. George construed the conversation thus: 'her voice is sweet, she seems sensible, has a thorough sense of her obligations to Lady Kildare,' and concluded miserably, 'in short she is everything I can form to myself lovely.'

By this time, the Prince's attentions to Sarah had caught Henry Fox's eye. They gave him perfect material for his teasing and 'worrying'. 'Mr. Fox says he is in love with me and diverts himself prodigiously,' Sarah reported to Emily. Nobody, except for Bute, realised that the Prince was serious, although Sarah uncharacteristically hid details of the Twelfth Night conversation from Caroline and her husband. 'I would not tell it [to] Mr. Fox and my sister for fear of Mr. Fox's worrying me about it.'

In early January 1760, Sarah need not have been too concerned. Caroline, in particular, was too busy sifting through the social, political and material prospects of London's eligible bachelors to think much about the Prince of Wales. By the end of January she had fixed upon George Spencer, the young and immensely wealthy Duke of Marlborough. Her researches had shown that there were some drawbacks to the match, she told Emily, but 'his fortune, title, figure are just what one would wish'. Caroline had gone to a ball at which the nineteen-year-old Duke 'seemed charmed with Sal'. Before long Caroline's hope had been transformed into a rumour which reached the Prince of Wales. 'The other day I heard it suggested as if the Duke of Marlborough made up to her. I shift'd my grief till retired to my chamber where I remained for several hours in the depth of despair.'

The addition of jealousy to the explosive mixture of passion and guilt in George's heart finally drove him to confess his feelings to Bute. One night during the spring of 1760, the Prince sat down and trustingly confided his troubles to his friend, 'feeling culpable in having kept you so long in the dark'. George's story made sad telling. He was, he wrote, 'struck' with Sarah's first appearance at St James's and since then he said, 'my passion has been increased every time I have since beheld her.' But despite having 'flattered himself' that Bute would permit him to marry Sarah, the Prince protested 'before God that I have never had any improper thought with regard to her.'

The Prince added to his confession an abject appeal. 'If you can devise any method for my keeping my love without forfeiting your friendship, I shall be more bound to you than ever.' Then, in a suicidal gesture, he resigned everything, casting himself into Bute's hands in a gesture of pathetic self-abasement. 'On the whole let me preserve your friendship, and tho' my heart should break, I shall have the happy reflection in dying that I have not been altogether unworthy of the best of friends, tho' unfortunate in other things.' Bute was not moved by this desperate call for help and replied with brutal insincerity, 'God knows, my dear Sir, I with the utmost grief tell it to you, the case admits not of the smallest doubt.' The Prince of Wales wrote back humbly, 'my Dearest Friend has thoroughly convinced me of the impropriety of marrying a countrywoman.'

Lord Bute had good reasons for expunging the Prince's hopes. Marriage between George and Sarah Lennox would raise the Foxes and Richmonds to even greater political eminence, and Fox's triumph would be Bute's annihilation. Bute recognised that his best hope for continued domination and thus for political office was to urge upon the Prince a loveless marriage with a German princess, and as soon as George had written to renounce Sarah he began to hint that the Prince should look abroad for a suitable wife. George agreed to a search but refused an immediate marriage; and although he had abandoned hope of Sarah, he continued to indulge his love for her even while his courtiers ransacked the Almanach de Gotha for a German bride.

Now that he had confessed and renounced his infatuation, the Prince's guilt lifted and his attentions to Sarah became more marked. They continued to meet throughout the spring of 1760 until the end of the season in May. The season over, and husband hunting temporarily suspended, Sarah and Caroline left London for a prolonged country perambulation. They spent some time at Goodwood, where Sarah was 'exceedingly pleased and happy' and Caroline kept a wary and disapproving eye on her sisters-in-law. In September they went to Woburn, the country seat of the Duke and Duchess of Bedford. By the beginning of October they were back at Holland House, Sarah to plan and perform private theatricals with Susan Fox-Strangways, Charles and Ste Fox and Emily's oldest sons George and William Fitzgerald, and Caroline to supervise repairs on the house. In the years since Henry Fox became Paymaster improvements to Holland House had proceeded apace. Caroline had put a greenhouse and an aviary on the flat roof of the portico outside her dressing-room window so that she could wander out and look at birds and plants while she was reading and writing in the mornings. She was fitting up the chapel and starting a picture gallery, commissioning portraits of the family as they passed through London. 'We are so busy here, you can't imagine, spending an immense deal of money,' she told Emily in the autumn of 1760.

This cheerful activity was interrupted on 25 October by the old King's death. George II had got up early, had breakfast and retired as usual to the lavatory. While he was sitting there he had a massive heart attack and died *in situ*. The manner of the King's demise hastened his descent from the heights of majesty to the level of the ordinary man. A few weeks after his death the *Gentleman's Magazine* printed a large and detailed engraving of his ruptured heart.

The King's eventual death had been much debated, not least by his heir and Lord Bute, but the suddenness with which the Prince of Wales was translated into George III surprised everybody. 'A young King opens a new scene here, which excites one's curiosity and causes great speculation,' wrote Caroline to Emily, as if she had never known the awkward, shy Prince who lurked behind his grandfather's shoulder at drawing-rooms and birthdays. Sarah and Susan were delighted by the new reign too. They looked forward to a young and lively Court, to the coronation and even to the burial of the old King. Intoxicated by the prospect of balls and parties Sarah declared with self-conscious exaggeration that she was 'absolutely in love with the King'.

The King was certainly still in love with Sarah. Now that he had confessed to Bute his love seemed legal, and he was determined to savour the sensations of romance even while he was throwing it away. George began practising the language of love – which he mixed with the peremptory speech of those used to being obeyed – on Susan Fox-Strangways. At a drawing-room in March 1761, he told Susan that he would like an English queen and then added, 'what do you think of your friend? You know who I mean, don't you think her the fittest?' Emboldened by this start, the King progressed to Sarah herself. At a drawing-room a week later he asked Sarah if she had seen Susan and if she had, had Susan told her about their conversation. 'Yes,' replied Sarah, and then fell silent.

Much to Henry Fox's chagrin, Sarah did not play her part well on this occasion, and she was unable to make good her failure because, on a visit to Somerset in March 1761, she fell off a horse and broke her leg. The injury kept her in the country for several weeks so Fox, despite his vestigial scepticism, went to Court in her stead and engaged the King in conversation. After some small-talk, Fox skilfully brought the conversation round to Sarah, noting in a memo he jotted down the next day, 'Now I have you'. The King's face twisted in sympathy as Fox described Sarah's fall and pain. Fox pressed his advantage home, playing the King like an instrument and harping on the theme of Sarah's injury. 'Then came the same countenance and expressions of uneasiness, which I rather increased by talking again of the pain the motion of the coach gave; and then relieved by assuring that she had nothing hard to bear now but the confinement.'

Fox had been the first to laugh at George's marked attention to Sarah and to treat it as a pretext to tease her. But after this conversation he was certain that the King was deeply infatuated. Fox decided that if Sarah played her cards right she could be a queen and that he himself would, at the very least, secure an earldom. By 1761 Fox had few ambitions left. He was immensely wealthy and he had abandoned his hectic pursuit of the highest political office. But he desperately wanted to seal his career with a title, for himself and for his family, and Sarah's elevation would make an earldom easy fruit.

Once Fox decided to enter the fray, he went about it with the skill and attention to detail that was the hallmark of his political success. He sent strict instructions about how Sarah was to behave on her return to London. As she convalesced, Sarah learned her lines, repeating them for Susan with an irony that bordered on self-hatred. 'I am allowed to mutter a little, provided the words astonished, surprised, understand and meaning are heard.' 'What a task it is! God send that I may be able to go through with it'. 'I am working myself up to consider what depends on it ... The very thought of it makes me sick in my stomach already.'

On 22 May 1761 Sarah returned to London, her leg mended and her speeches prepared. 'Well today is come to nothing,' she wrote to Susan after her first appearance at Court. The next meeting seemed more propitious. She went, chaperoned by Fox, to the play and the King appeared in the box next to theirs, showing 'great pleasure on seeing her'. Two days before she came back he had finally picked a bride, Princess Charlotte of Mecklenburg-Strelitz, a plain, unremarkable girl of seventeen. So when Sarah reappeared George felt, if not lighthearted, at least free to immerse himself in the tide of love that swept over him. At a birthday ball on 1 June, he 'had no eyes but for her and hardly talked to anybody else.' Henry Fox was jubilant. 'He is in love with her,' he wrote triumphantly in his running notes. Sarah, eager to please and by now fully in Fox's confidence, reported faithfully everything the King said to her.

Fox's manoeuvring and the King's dog-like devotion did not go unnoticed. When Fox left London for the country in the second week of June, it was rumoured that he had deliberately left Sarah alone and unchaperoned in Holland House.

Horace Walpole reported that while Fox was absent, Sarah had orders to dress up every morning in simple country dress, go out into the grounds of Holland House by a road along which the King drove every day, and rake hay becomingly *déshabillée*.

This Marie Antoinettish story was fabricated or exaggerated, although Sarah did ride out in the Holland House grounds each day, perhaps in hopes of intercepting the King on his way to Court. Walpole's report may have originated in a print that was doing the rounds of the Court which showed a courting couple in the grounds of Holland House. The engraving was cheekily entitled 'Palemon and Lavinia': Palemon was one of the noble lovers in Chaucer's 'Knight's Tale', while Lavinia was a legendary princess given in marriage to seal a political alliance. In the 'Knight's Tale', Palemon only triumphed because his rival fell from his horse, so his name on the print added a sly reference to Sarah's recent accident. The engraving shows Palemon clasping Lavinia's hand to his bosom in a stagy gesture of ardour while she, casting her eyes demurely towards the ground, avoids his passionate gaze. Lavinia wears a straw bonnet and a simple country dress without hoops or lace. In the background, Holland House, half concealed behind a magisterial royal oak, identifies the lovers as George III and Sarah Lennox.

In fact when the Foxes went to the country, Sarah was anything but alone. The whole family had assembled in London in anticipation of the coronation, and now they watched the final act of the drama. In the absence of Caroline it was Emily (heavily pregnant as usual) who took Sarah to Court on 18 June and Emily who wrote to Fox that the King had said to Sarah plainly and fervently, 'for God's sake remember what I hinted to Lady Susan Strangways before you went to the country'. Emily and Fox believed that this speech must be followed by a declaration. They did not realise that the King was saying goodbye. It was the last time he would talk to Sarah intimately and, like a child denied a wish, he raised his voice and then repeated his statement: 'For God's sake remember what I said to Lady Susan before you went to the country, and believe I have the strongest attachment.'

For the next three weeks, while the formal proposals for Princess Charlotte's hand were being made in Germany, Sarah went regularly to Court. But although the King 'spoke and looked with great fondness', Emily reported to Fox that he said 'nothing in particular'. On 1 July a Privy Council meeting was called for the 8th, and on the 4th Fox was told that its purpose was to announce the King's marriage.

Sarah was mortified by Fox's news, not because she was fond of the King but because she had been deceived. 'Luckily for me,' she wrote to Susan, 'I did not love him, and only liked him. Nor did the title weigh anything with me . . . The thing I am most angry at is looking so like a fool.' The trial was over, Sarah had played her part as best she could, and now she wanted, she said, to enjoy the marriage and coronation festivities like any other woman of fashion. 'I wonder if they will name me train bearer,' she wrote to Susan on 16 July. 'I wish they would, tho' they abuse me and call me names, for its the best way of seeing the Coronation.'

But try as she might, Sarah could not forget the affair. She felt and continued to feel tainted, as if the King's duplicity had been her own. Her failure confirmed her self-hatred and her role as the plaything of others. In the weeks leading up to the wedding Sarah diverted herself by looking after a sick squirrel, translating the damage done to herself on to the care of another frail creature. But in a bathetic comment on her loss of dignity the squirrel died. Sarah hurriedly found a hedgehog, an animal whose prickly self-defence she could have used with gratitude. The hedgehog came down to breakfast with her and she kissed it constantly. Fox noticed the hedgehog's analgesic role with a mixture of irony and concern and Sarah herself remembered it tenderly thirty-five years later.

As time went on Sarah's memory erased some parts of the humiliation and distorted others to fit the King's later history.

In Henry Fox's account, written as the drama unfolded, Sarah's conversation with the King in March 1761 was extremely brief. In reply to his enquiries about the exchange with Susan Fox-Strangways, Sarah had simply answered 'nothing'. But Sarah, retelling the story much later embellished it, weaving her knowledge of the King's madness through the eighteenth-century cult of Shakespeare and playing Cordelia to his deranged despotic Lear. Sarah described the King taking her into a large window recess and saying, '"has your friend told you my conversation with her?" "Yes, Sir." "And what do you think of it? Tell me for my happiness depends upon it!" "Nothing Sir." . . . upon which he left her abruptly, exclaiming pettishly, "Nothing comes of nothing".'

It was half a century before Sarah overcame her sense of humiliation. In 1805 she wrote to a friend, 'Why do you ask me if ever the King had much sense? Read his reign, good madam, and judge for yourself.' Sarah did eventually move with the times, sharing in a general softening of attitudes towards the Crown in the aftermath of the French Revolution, and after the end of the Napoleonic wars she surprised friends by the warmth of her monarchism. But she always insisted, 'I still rejoice that I was never Queen, and so I shall to my life's end.'

George III did not forget Sarah, although he did not talk about her for many years. But when he fell ill with porphyria in 1788 his raving mind travelled back to his youth and disinterred the love which had been safely buried for thirty years. The salient feature of George III's illness was what Robert Fulke Greville, one of his equerries, called his 'talking very fast on [a] variety of subjects, incoherently and imprudently'. The King was not so incoherent, however, that his doctors and minders could not discern that this imprudence consisted of an avalanche of sex talk: random sexual fantasy, disgust at the Queen, spicy allusions to Lady Pembroke, a woman he had greatly admired in the early 1760s, and now and then sly asides in which he seemed to shake off his raving and reach a hidden truth that served his amorous ramblings. On 16 January 1789, for instance, the King asked Greville 'to go and look for Paley's Philosophy, in which he told me that I should find that tho' the law said that Man might have but only one wife, yet that Nature allowed more.'

In this mix of sense and nonsense Sarah was not forgotten. On 22 February, the King told the Lord Chancellor that 'he had had an attachment thirty years ago' and earlier he declared that he had renounced the woman he loved and married another chosen from the Almanach de Gotha. In 1805, many years after his recovery, the King put that memory to the service of patronage. After a solicitation which Sarah described as 'a letter full of details of my situation with some remarks on the sympathetic feelings of one blind person to another', he awarded her a pension of £800 a year.

Thus in her old age, Sarah was prepared to turn her place in the King's heart to her advantage. In the months immediately succeeding the announcement of the King's marriage, however, it seemed to brand her as an outcast and a failure. Caroline made matters worse by saying that it would be wrong for Sarah to attend the royal wedding especially because, as the eldest unmarried Duke's daughter, she would be premier bridesmaid and well within sight of the King throughout the proceedings. Henry Fox approved of Sarah's being there for exactly the same reason. Forcing the King to compare Sarah with Charlotte of Mecklenburg was Fox's only available revenge. 'Well Sal,' he said to Sarah, 'you are the first *vargin* in England and you shall take your place in spite of them all as chief bridesmaid, and the King shall behold your pretty face and repent.'

The royal ceremonial over, Caroline and Emily, with their attendant husbands, turned back to the serious business of the next few months, finding Sarah a husband. In Caroline's scheming to catch the Duke of Marlborough she had paraded Sarah at Ranelagh. But although the Duke came he 'walked all night' with Lady Caroline Russell, whom he eventually married. 'Is this not quite mortifying?' Emily asked Kildare in September 1761, adding, 'this is an unlucky year for our poor little Sal.' Caroline came up with a substitute, Lord Errol, a Scottish peer of vast stature, moderate income and small attraction for Sarah, who dubbed him 'Ajax' and refused him. Caroline smarted from her failure and wrote waspishly to Emily in mid-December, 'that's over so we will say no more about it. I hope she will be happy when she marries, and that she may get married before her pretty face gets too common.' A few weeks later she added, 'here are all the good matches going by her . . . some girls have all the luck.' Although Sarah was still only sixteen, her spinsterhood was becoming a liability for everyone.

Caroline's self-esteem was bound up in finding a good match for her younger sister, especially since Emily had succeeded so spectacularly with Louisa and Thomas Conolly. But as one bachelor after another passed Sarah by, Caroline retreated from the fray, saying self-righteously that she was not fit to pronounce on suitable candidates because her own marriage was so extraordinary as to make her forget the common lot. 'One so likely to make a woman happy as Lord Errol she will probably not meet with, as I believe they are very scarce. But my ideas of happiness in marriage are I find so different from most women's that I can't judge for anybody else, but feel more thankful every day of my life for my own happy lot.'

Nobody came out well from this scramble for marital security; not Caroline who first took up and repudiated the challenge; not Fox, who initially pushed Sarah towards the King and then declared that marrying for love was devoutly to be wished; not Emily and Kildare, who nurtured her in Ireland and then abandoned her to her fate in London; and not Sarah herself, who against her better judgement allowed others to take control of her life.

Even before the end of the débâcle with the King, Sarah

was feeling tainted and unloved. She said that the only reason she was not married was 'that I am not liked'. Although still only fifteen, she felt that time was running out although, she confided to Emily, 'I don't quite despair as seventeen is generally the age people are married in England; for they look upon 15 as quite a child. I don't quite approve of that custom. But after 17 I intend to go to Ireland, and take Massie Hall, by Carton, and so settle myself for life.'

By the late autumn of 1761, the marital pool was drained. Sarah was anxious enough to note down carefully some advice from Ste Fox, who with the sagacity of sixteen told her: 'Don't refuse a good match when you can get it, and don't go to plays and operas too often.' In December a new suitor, Thomas Charles Bunbury, had emerged out of the crowd of Whigs and gossips who came to talk politics with Henry Fox at Holland House. Bunbury was MP for the county of Suffolk. He was, at twenty-two, noted as a dilettante and wit but regarded as a politician of such ineptitude that he once divided the House of Commons and found himself in a minority of one. Sarah described him as like 'a Marquis in a French story book', smooth, handsome, foppish and lugubrious. When Bunbury began to pay her attention, Sarah hurried to tell Susan about it, 'to lay the case before you and ask for your advice'. But this time she added with the defensive caution born out of repeated failure, 'we don't always agree about these sort of things you know'.

Bunbury came constantly to Holland House in December 1761 and he followed Sarah on the round of Court and social events as well. Caroline took heart from this langorous shadowing and began to enquire about his background, employing her aunt Lady Albemarle as sleuth. Lady Albemarle reported that Bunbury's parents, Sir William and Lady Bunbury, had an estate of five thousand a year and two good houses at Barton and Mildenhall in Suffolk. They were 'very retired people, very fond of their children, and very good kind of people.' Sir William was prepared to give Charles, as his heir, £2,000 a year and 'a house in town and country'. The Foxes, Kildares and, later, the Duke of Richmond, all regarded such financial provision as nugatory, especially for young people of fashion who lived in London and went to Court. 'Both so young as they are, and in high life, they will not have the prudence to live within their income,' Caroline wrote to Emily when Lady Albemarle's report reached her.

None the less the affair progressed. At the end of January Caroline noted on the bottom of a letter to Emily, 'today a long copy of verses (he is a poet), full of sighs, miseries, pains etc etc etc.' Initially Caroline was ambivalent about the courtship. Bunbury was without Fox's driving ambition, Kildare's name or Conolly's fortune. On the other hand, 'it is a thing one can't advise her against,' she said, because there were no more eligible bachelors queuing for his place.

As the marriage began to look more certain, Caroline warmed to it, pleased that her duties as matchmaker would soon be over. 'I have quite made up my mind to like it. He seems a grave young man of elegant, ingenious turn; now he is in love, mighty delicate and sentimental. He is a scholar and a poet.' Sarah too warmed to her task, flirting outrageously. 'I do suspect, now she sees she is sure of him and of our consent, no difficulties in the case, that she has a mind to coquette a little and tease him,' Caroline wrote disapprovingly.

By the middle of February 1762 the formal proposals had been made and a marriage settlement drawn up between Henry Fox, the Duke of Richmond and Sir William Bunbury. As the details of the Baronet's financial affairs emerged a new consensus formed amongst Sarah's relations: the marriage could only be described as a 'love match' because the couple were bound to be very poor. Caroline said that 'nothing but liking him immensely can make the match tolerable. They will never have more than £2,500 [a year] in hard money.' Henry Fox also conceded that Bunbury was 'not rich enough', but sanguinely said, 'tis a match of her own making and happiness don't depend on money.' In reply to Fox's details of Sir William Bunbury's fortune, the Duke of Rich-mond, with his characteristic blend of pedantry and concern, sounded a prophetic note of caution. 'I can only observe how very bad a match this is. And 'tis the greater pity as I think one may say from past observation that Sarah's temper is not so unalterable but that she might have done without him . . . How difficult it is to persuade one's friends to do what is for their own happiness.'

In the midst of this barrage of commentary the principals in the affair made their way slowly towards the altar, revealing nothing to their families of their feelings. Their silence was drowned by the mounting chorus of criticism from Sarah's siblings. As Bunbury's financial prospects were gradually re-vealed to be less than glowing, so observers discovered that the lovers themselves seemed cool and distant. Lord Kildare arrived in London on business at the end of April 1762 and found Bunbury less a 'beauty' than he had been told and less ardent than he expected. 'Lady Sarah is just the same as she was; but neither she nor Mr. Bunbury seem to be much in love according to my notion of being in love.' Caroline, Fox and the Fox children all agreed: 'the young pair, as our boys observe, are the coolest of lovers.' By the middle of May Caroline began to see defects in Mr Bunbury's character, although for her own sake as much as for Sarah's she still gave him the benefit of the doubt. 'I believe he is one of those kind of people one can't find any fault with, and yet that don't grow more pleasing upon acquaintance . . . With regard to her happiness one very great fault he has which I must mention, he despises story books.'

At the beginning of April 1762, the wedding had been set for the middle of May, but neither the bride nor the groom seemed impatient for the ceremony. On 15 May Henry Fox wrote to Dr Francis, the minister who was to officiate at the wedding admitting that 'it is impossible to say with exactness when the wedding will be'. The tentative date of 25 May came and then Bunbury put off the wedding for a week, prompting

Caroline to write angrily to Emily, 'I feel most exceedingly peevish with him, am convinced myself 'tis that he don't chose to miss the B[ute] House ball ... happily for her she is not the least in love with him.' But, inexorably, the reluctant couple approached the altar.

2 June 1762

A small party, richly dressed in silk and velvet, walked out of the damask-lined drawing-room of Holland House, into the entrance hall and through the iron gates of the chapel. The chapel was two storeys high, with round arched windows down the east side and an Inigo Jones ceiling. It had new pews and fresh paint and gilding, white like a bride, twinkling in the evening light.

The Duke and Duchess of Richmond, Susan Fox-Strangways and a crowd of Holland House servants took their seats. Dr Francis walked to the altar and turned round, waiting for Sarah and Bunbury to come and stand in front of him. They came up hesitantly, Sarah stooping, Bunbury carrying himself with self-conscious dignity.

'Dearly beloved,' Dr Francis began, shifting his gaze from Sarah and Bunbury to the guests, 'we are gathered here together in the sight of God.' Everyone relaxed, soothed by the familiar incantation. Nobody listened closely to the words of the marriage service. Dr Francis read through the reasons for matrimony. 'First it was ordained for the procreation of children,' he chanted. 'Secondly it was ordained for a remedy against sin, and to avoid fornication. Thirdly it was ordained for the mutual society, help and comfort that the one ought to have for the other.' Children, constancy, companionship: they were solemn undertakings and ones which Sarah and Bunbury had hardly considered.

Dr Francis turned to Bunbury and asked the famous questions: 'Wilt thou have this woman as thy wedded wife, to live together after God's ordinance, in the holy estate of matrimony? Wilt thou love her, comfort her, honour and keep her in sickness and in health and forsaking all other keep thee only unto her as long as ye both shall live?' 'I will,' Bunbury replied; and 'I will,' said Sarah too.

The service continued – the ring, the blessing, a prayer and holy communion. Bunbury slipped the ring on to Sarah's finger and she became a wife. As the married couple turned away and walked down the aisle, a tear, reflecting the panes of the chapel windows, rolled slowly down Dr Francis's plump cheek.

CHAPTER
THREE
HOMES,
EDUCATION
AND ADULTERY

PART ONE
'Our gallery advances so much, 'twill
soon be ready for all the pictures'.
Caroline to Emily, 8 August 1762.

The day after the wedding Sarah wrote to Emily, signing
herself 'Sarah Bunbury' for the first time. It was a short
letter merely announcing her marriage and Bunbury's intention to leave London immediately for his country house in
Suffolk. Unlike Louisa, Sarah was settling where she had no
friends and no family. She was a hesitant traveller. 'I go to
Barton tomorrow or the next day to stay the rest of the summer. I don't quite like going to a strange place for so long, but
Mr. Bunbury has set his heart upon being there this summer.'
A cryptic postscript read: 'I was not as frightened as Louisa
was yesterday, but I make good what Lady B[arrymore] used
to say, that we lively people were much more afraid than
grave sober folks, for I am ten thousand times more terrified
now than she was the second day. Hers was shyness at first,
which one always gets the better of; but real dislike I am sure
is not so easy to get over.'

Sarah's fear had grown up swiftly after the ceremony. The
wedding night, the slippery loss of virginity in the flickering

candle-light, had terrified her. Between the removal of the gown that Caroline had given her and the squawking of the peacocks and pheasants on the Holland House terrace, Sarah was transformed. Innocence gave way to experience, the maiden to the wife and the bibulous optimism of the wedding breakfast to the settled despair of 'real dislike'. As soon as they became man and wife the couple dropped their courting characters. Bunbury's flood of letters and verses abruptly dried up and Sarah's lively flirtations were overcome by a melancholy restlessness.

To everyone's surprise, Sarah took to following Bunbury about like a dog. Through the long summer recess she stayed at his side as he went about his daily life as county MP and country squire. 'I am in a constant fear of making him angry,' Sarah confessed to Emily in September, 'for though he loves me, yet not one in ten like to have their wives tagging after them constantly; and that is what I cannot help doing, for, whenever he is absent an hour even, I am watching for his return and follow him to the stables etc, and, in short, am vastly troublesome . . . I can see he don't like it and I will get the better of it.' Sarah eyed her husband incessantly, scrutinising him for signs of tenderness, appalled at his distant beauty. She attributed her vigilance to jealousy and interpreted her jealousy as a sign of love. 'Pray do not tell anybody of my jealousy, for if it came to Mr. Fox's ears – Lord have mercy upon me!' she begged Emily, adding, 'I don't know if, in the main, it is not better for me, as it will keep up my love for him.'

Already Sarah was edging towards unpleasant conclusions. If her jealousy was a sign of love, what did Bunbury's complete lack of jealousy mean, and what could be the reason for her own sudden disinclination to flirt? For Sarah's hound-like shadowing owed less to jealousy than to a need for signs of love; even a hint of tenderness on Bunbury's part would do. As the summer of 1762 wore on, Sarah stopped writing and she stopped flirting. Her need to act flamboyant parts and to tell stories was squashed under a larger fear that Bunbury might treat coquettish behaviour with a benign indifference. That might confirm what Sarah already suspected – that her husband neither loved nor desired her.

At first her sisters were sanguine about Bunbury's equanimity, hopefully attributing it to the new fashion for homeliness. Caroline told Emily that 'Mr. Bunbury is sobriety itself, and very domestic, and don't appear to have any little teasing ways with him, so that she may be just as happy with him as if he was more lively.' Louisa reported back to Sarah herself that Bunbury 'has, by all accounts, one of the most amiable dispositions that ever was; is very sensible and good natured.' But to the third Duke of Richmond, she passed on a very different report. 'Don't say I said so, but I hear terrible accounts of his coldness and reservedness.' None the less, she qualified her anxiety by asserting, 'he is vastly fond of her though and I know she dotes upon him.'

Thus it was that Sarah's marriage rapidly became an experience of collective self-deception by her siblings. Everyone maintained that Sarah's marriage had been a love match forged in freedom, but they all knew that Sarah had been forced into a quick choice by familial as well as social pressures. So all the sisters dulled their foreboding with recitations of Bunbury's good nature and Sarah's happiness. But everyone – Caroline, Emily, Fox, Kildare and Louisa – had created Sarah's marriage, commending Bunbury and urging her on; and everyone would bear responsibility if the fragile ship of her felicity was swept towards the rocks.

No one connived more eagerly in this act of collective delusion than Sarah herself. Like her sisters, Sarah was determined not to delve behind the façade of her cheerfulness and jealousy. She began to live a life of the surface, busy at Barton and in Bury St Edmunds. She entertained friends and neighbours and set about planning flower gardens, walks and shrubberies. 'I must be in pursuit of something,' she said. But she was running rather than chasing, fleeing from the spectre of a lonely life and trying frantically to escape from herself. She lacked money, which in big enough doses could keep aristocratic marriages alive, so her distractions had to be modest. First she asked Emily to send her an Irish wolf-hound. Then she found a loquacious parrot. She abandoned reading alone and, in the summer evenings, worked feverishly on handkerchiefs and a gown while Mr Bunbury's sister read volumes of French memoirs. She tried to make Barton feel like home, tending her garden as a way of rooting herself in her new environment. 'I have set my heart upon being *settled*,' she said. To Susan Fox-Strangways she wrote, with her accustomed note of supplication, 'I have planted all the trees you bid me and others that I have thought of. I have fished out two cedars as high as a chair and flourishing charmingly; is not that a treasure?'

When horticulture paled, Sarah turned to the opiate of country society. Bury was a thriving market town. Two small streams, the Lark and the Linnet, rippled past the ruins of an abbey sacked in the fourteenth century by a citizenry who had since settled into model constituents. Around the flinty remains were the town houses of local landowners, the assembly rooms and a theatre. Behind and above these grand buildings was a grid-based town with houses of brick and stucco; white, cream and yellowy pink, all wreathed in the heady smell of malt and hops drifting out from the town brewery. Just above the abbey stood the imposing Angel Hotel where successful local candidates, Charles Bunbury amongst them, distributed dark local ale to their cheering supporters. In October, Bury fair brought a noisy mixture of animals, performers and mountebanks to the town centre; for two weeks a closed and secretive rural society opened itself up to the latest scientific curiosities, the newest travelling quacks and a caravan of horse dealers, prize fighters, print sellers and trinket merchants. Away from the packed squares and streets the local gentry ate and drank in town houses and inns. 'Sally in her letters seems quite worn out with visiting. She was engaged in no less than eight different turtle feasts in the town of

Bury last time I heard from her,' Caroline reported to Emily in October 1762.

Despite the turtles and the visits, life in Suffolk lacked the excitement and cosmopolitan diversity of both Carton and Holland House. Sarah fought isolation and self-knowledge with a string of visitors. Caroline and Fox came first, in the middle of July, barely six weeks after Sarah's wedding. Although Sarah was 'as pert or more so than ever', delighted with Fox's familiar and reassuring bawdy talk, Caroline was quickly bored with country life. 'The people there pass their whole life in dining and visiting about,' she complained. In August Bunbury went to a house party, leaving Sarah and his sister alone at Barton. Soon after his departure, thirteen-year-old Charles Fox came for ten days. Then Susan Fox-Strangways arrived and stayed until mid-October, when races at Newmarket and the Bury fair filled the house with gamblers and horse-fanciers. Gossiping and versifying with Susan and jaunting from track to town with Bunbury's friends kept Sarah from watching her husband too closely. A little while after Susan left, Sarah felt courageous enough to put self-deception to paper. 'You have made a mighty pretty discovery, Miss, truly! "I can think there is happiness in the country with a person one loves." Pray now who the devil would not be happy with a pretty place, a good house, good horses, greyhounds etc for hunting, so near Newmarket & £2,000 a year to spend? Add to this that I have a settled comfortable feel that I am doing so right, that all my friends love me and are with me as much as possible; in short that I have not one single thing on earth to be troubled about.'

Missing from this catalogue of bliss was Bunbury himself. At the heart of Sarah's life was a blank space where her love for her husband and his for her might have been; a no-go area of anxiety and unhappiness carefully cordoned off from mention or examination. The nearest Sarah came to admitting the existence of this emotional black hole which, in spite of her best efforts kept pulling everything towards it, was to complain of boredom or 'wretched spirits' that could be attributed to temporary domestic disappointment. 'You need not have envied me,' she wrote to Susan in October, 'for my devil of a horse is as lame as a dog and Mr. B. has been coursing, hunting and doing every pleasant thing on earth and poor me sat fretting and fuming at home.' She longed to see Emily's children and dreamed of Carton and home. 'Believe me, dear sister, when I think of you it is not to be conceived how I long to go to you and see my dear little girls, and in short twenty people and things . . . I sit here and fancy myself there and think of what I shall do and where I shall go.'

At first Sarah hoped that Fox and Kildare might be able to fix Bunbury's appointment as Secretary to the next Lord Lieutenant of Ireland, but his chances were destroyed by a change of administration. A later scheme that he should accompany the British Ambassador, Lord Hertford, to Paris also fell through. The historian David Hume took the job and also took Paris by storm, surprising and enraging his upstaged employer. Sarah and her husband stayed in England, she to dream of Ireland, he of training a Newmarket winner. Gradually she came to realise that her husband's first love was for horses; the more indifferent he became to Sarah's body the more absorbed he was by horseflesh.

Unable to go back to Emily, Carton and her childhood life, Sarah did the next best thing. As soon as she decently could, she left for Holland House. 'Sal and Mr. Bunbury are here,' Caroline reported to Emily on 7 December 1762. 'She is just as she was, pretty and good humoured as an angel.' The House was sitting; Conolly had come over (although he spent most of the time out with the Charlton hunt at Goodwood); Kildare was expected. Emily's heir George, her second son, the slow and amiable William and Charles Fox were all about to come back from Eton. Susan Fox-Strangways was on her way up from the west country. Holland House was alive with political gossip and plans for the coming season. While Bunbury went to the House of Commons, Sarah plunged gratefully back into her former life.

The third Duke of Richmond, already a lover of dogs and women
on the grand tour in Rome, painted by Batoni.

LEFT: Thomas Conolly, painted by Reynolds in 1759, when he was 21. 'Sure he is a tiresome boy,' Caroline exclaimed.

BELOW: Tom Conolly in his natural habitat, painted by Robert Healy in 1768, leanly muscular in racing gear and jockey's cap.

ABOVE: Castletown House, loved and decorated by Louisa for 60 years, at the turn of the century.

RIGHT: Louisa Conolly in magnificent court dress, painted by Ramsay in 1759: Caroline praised her height, bearing and 'pretty' figure.

Four faces of Louisa:

LEFT: 23, sweet and plump, painted by Reynolds in 1764.

BELOW: Practically dressed and on a 'trudge' through the Castletown grounds with a gamekeeper in 1768.

Sarah in her teens, dressed as 'the mourning bride' for a session of amateur dramatics. Although Emily said she was 'merely a pretty, lively looking girl and that is all', Henry Fox thought she was 'different from and prettier than any other girl I ever saw'.

Ramsay's official portrait of George III in Coronation robes of 1762:
a far cry from the 'boiling youth' who had fallen in love with Sarah a year before.

ABOVE: *Palemon and Lavinia:* a print that did the rounds of court, purportedly showing the King wooing an uncharacteristically demure Sarah in the grounds of Holland House.

LEFT: Sir Charles Bunbury, painted by Reynolds for the Holland House gallery shortly after his marriage to Sarah in 1762. When his nephew was offered this picture, he refused it, saying that he did not want to be reminded of his uncle.

Although Holland House still belonged to the Mr Edwardes from whom it had been leased, the Foxes continued to make interior alterations, to buy up parcels of land around it and to plant the grounds in expectation of the estate eventually becoming their own. With the help of the naturalist Peter Collinson they moved walls and paths, laid down a bowling green and planted trees and shrubs throughout the sixty-four acres of the park. Caroline decorated the lawns with pheasants, peacocks and pedigree cows, whose white bulks moved slowly against the green of grass and trees, manuring as they went. Gardening, with its biblical overtones of Edenic tranquillity and its English associations with virtue and peacefulness, hardly needed literary justification. But Caroline quoted *Candide* all the same. Writing to Emily in the autumn of 1764 she said, 'My chief work is now clearing and cutting down trees to let in peeps here and there, and also to prevent the trees killing and over-running one another as they did at Goodwood . . . nothing truer than *il faut cultiver son jardin* to relieve the many cares of human nature.'

No such philosophy dignified the accumulation of interior furnishings. Gratification, display and (in cases like Caroline's) francophilia were the deities who presided over the decoration of great houses. But Caroline did not alter the interior of Holland House. She took an unfashionable delight in its heavily coffered plaster ceilings, dark oak panelling and mullioned windows. Emily privately disliked Holland House, decried Caroline's taste and avoided commissioning her to buy furniture, wallpapers or chintz for Carton. Caroline resolutely went her own way. She was well aware that she was regarded as eccentric in her love not simply of the quaint (which might have been praised as newly fashionable Gothicism) but the outmoded. 'I love these old-fashioned comfortable houses,' she said.

Concessions to modernity were made in furniture and painting. Caroline chose fashionable Parisian furniture and accumulated, by commission and purchase, a large and up-to-date picture collection. Like many of her aristocratic con-temporaries, Caroline favoured upholstered French furniture decorated with gilt or ormolu; pieces that were light but loaded with gold. In 1764 she told Emily that she was 'all for the magnificent style – velvet, damask etc. I have three im-mense looking glasses to put in my drawing room, and propose hanging it with a damask or brocatelle of two or three colours.' In niches and cupboards, on mantelpieces and bureaux stood curvaceous Sèvres nicknacks. 'I hope Lord Kil-dare has made a good report of my blue gallery and my dressing room fitted up with a great deal of pea-green china and painted pea-green. I have been extravagant enough to buy a good deal of china lately, but I am in tolerable circum-stances,' she reported to Emily in 1759, adding a few years later, 'My dressing room in London is thought pretty; with Horner's paper and the carving, of which there is a good deal, painted two greens and varnished.' As Fox's fortune accum-ulated so did Caroline's china. By the mid-1760s her dressing-room was chock-a-block and the mantelpiece was 'covered with small pictures, china [and] Wedgwood's imit-ations of antiques'. There were three large 'mazarine china bottles', two blue and one pea-green, their handles hung with chains and stoppers in their mouths. There were five 'fish shaped' Sèvres vases, painted in the bluer, less harsh 'sea-green', ornamented with ormolu and intricately painted. Their sharp bottoms rested on gold circular mounts. Four gold-spangled cups festooned with golden flowers completed Caroline's collection of display pieces. But she also had a Sèvres tea and coffee service painted in blue wreaths of flowers from which to take breakfast and serve visitors. The whole collection was rounded off with a complete blue dinner service.

Caroline took a sometimes guilty delight in the accumula-tion and display of furniture and ornaments that were redolent of wealth. But she did not invest much of herself in them. They were not heirlooms, which came replete with ghosts and responsibilities. Neither were they gifts reminiscent of friendship. Some reminded her of jaunts to Paris in the mid-1760s, others reassured her of her own wealth and taste. But for that one object could serve as well as another.

The picture gallery at Holland House was quite another matter. It was designed to show to the world the image of a happy and successful marriage, family and career. Caroline invested time, money and herself in it. It constituted a kind of self-portrait. Displayed on the gallery walls were those people, those lives, that made up her own life and personality. Everyone who really mattered to her was there.

Round the gallery hung the extended Richmond-Fox family, augmented by friends and mentors and presided over by ancestors. Charles II and Louise de Kéroualle looked down from the walls. So did Sir Stephen and Lady Fox, carefully painted by Kneller. Caroline's parents, her brothers Lord George Lennox and the third Duke of Richmond, the latter painted by Batoni on his grand tour were also there. Fox's brother, the Earl of Ilchester, his wife Elizabeth and their daughter Susan Fox-Strangways hung close by. Hoare had painted Ste as a little boy and Reynolds painted him as an adult. Caroline and Henry themselves, Charles and Harry Fox, Louisa, Conolly, Emily, and Kildare, Sarah and Bunbury: all those whom Sarah called 'one of us' eventually crowded on to the walls.

In a world where dynastic considerations counted for so much, reverently arranged family portraits were everywhere from the grandest nobleman's house to the parlours of modest merchants and shopkeepers. But Caroline's gallery was not simply a tribute to the Fox and Richmond families. It stressed particularly her beloved children and her sisters. Louisa's full-length portrait by Ramsay hung over one fireplace. Over the other went Reynolds's triple portrait of Sarah, Susan Fox-Strangways and Charles James Fox. This huge canvas celebrated the young Etonian's poetic precociousness. Round the walls of the gallery connecting the two central portraits like beads on a necklace were all the other paintings, links in Caroline's familial chain of alliance, love and friendship.

Of course paintings and sculpture were scattered throughout Holland House. Caroline had a portrait of her mentor Madame de Sévigné in her private rooms and Fox had a bust of his, Voltaire. There were paintings by Steen, Van Loo, Murillo, Salvator Rosa and Hogarth, as well as a very large collection of English, Flemish, French, Dutch and Italian prints that the children used to dip into. But the gallery housed the family, the portraits of her relatives that Caroline thought 'most like' their originals and those that reminded her of past happiness. When she started the gallery in 1761 there was already a fine family gathering to be moved in. Caroline had been painted by Reynolds in 1758, Fox by Reynolds and by Hogarth. Louisa was there (in Ramsay's sumptuous portrait of 1759), so were the third Duke of Richmond, Charles, Ste and all the august ancestors. But Caroline was choosy. She wanted only the best and she did not want pictures that no longer met the criterion of likeness to their originals. Her own portrait by Reynolds was a case in point. Reynolds had painted Caroline as a woman of fashion. She wears a ribbed and ruched bodice and sleeves with extravagantly deep ruffles. Around her neck is a tippet of shining blue ribbon which tucks into her bodice behind a nosegay of two fresh old-English roses, pink with yellow stamens and centres. Nestling between Caroline's bodice and petticoat was the little water bottle in which the roses sat. With nervous determination Caroline stares out at the viewer as if she has looked up for a moment from the work on her lap: her right hand holds a needle which she is pulling through her embroidery.

Since the completion of Reynolds's portrait in 1758, Caroline had decided she was getting old. Already in 1759, when she was thirty-five, she had written to Emily, 'I never liked a racketing life, but now I grow old and I think when one is nearer forty than thirty, which is now my case, one has an excuse to indulge oneself in the way of life one chooses. That among many other reasons I think makes the middle age the happiest time of one's life. I'm sure mine is; and middle age everyone must allow thirty-five to be, though many women choose to put themselves on the footing of being young at that time.' By 1763, when she was forty, Caroline had settled into the persona of a woman of ripe years, looking forward to a 'long and comfortable old age' and declaring that she no longer need 'drag *un visage de quarante ans*' into the ball-room. Caroline asked Ramsay to paint her for the gallery in a manner that fitted this new image of herself. Ramsay obliged; Caroline sits in a gilded and upholstered French chair, turning her face and half turning her body towards us from her work-table. The intense gaze that Reynolds gave her has softened. Now she appears further away, deeper into the picture's space and her own world, dignified and a little aloof. Her sewing – something Reynolds favoured for its sumptuousness, but Caroline rarely took up – has been discarded in favour of a letter. Reynolds painted Caroline as she thought she ought to be, a woman of fashion. Ramsay painted Caroline as a digni-fied grey-haired woman, a letter writer and reader, dressed in warming furs and distanced from us by her social position and experience of life. Both paintings contained elements of fantasy. Caroline was more bookish than Reynolds showed but far less comfortable and serene than Ramsay suggested. But this was Caroline as she liked to think of herself, and it was the portrait destined for the Holland House gallery.

It was rare for women to ask painters to make them look older than they were. Usually, as Caroline herself pointed out, painters erred on the side of youth and towards the standards of beauty agreed by the age. When Emily declined to sit for her gallery portrait in 1762 on the grounds that at thirty she looked too old and tired, Caroline replied, 'as for its being not so young and blooming as it once would have been, that makes very little difference in a picture, except quite old people and children. Painters make their other portraits, I think, look much the same age. You'll be handsome enough these twenty years to make the best picture in our room if the painter does you justice.' Emily prevaricated. She was almost continuously pregnant in the 1760s, producing Louisa in 1760, Henry in 1761, Sophia in 1762, Edward in 1763, Robert in 1765, Gerald in 1766 and Augustus in 1767, and could justifiably claim exhaustion and incapacity. Eventually Caroline settled for a copy of Ramsay's 1765 portrait of Emily which tucked her pregnant form under a table and a large, folio volume. 'Your sweet face is come home and put up in my gallery,' Caroline wrote in June 1766. Once the picture was hung, Caroline became more hopeful about the painter's capacity to produce a good likeness (or perhaps the image came to stand for its original and Caroline began to think that Emily was like her picture rather than the other way round). 'Opinions about pictures are so various I never mind any but my own with regard to portraits. I like it of all things and think it very like.'

Sarah did not have her own portrait in the gallery and Reynolds's triple portrait was still unfinished when she came back to Holland House in the winter of 1762, although she had had nine appointments. It was proving very expensive. Painters charged according to the proportion of the sitter they showed, bust, half, three-quarter or full length. The triple portrait had Sarah in half length and Charles and Susan in three-quarter. When the painting was eventually delivered in 1764, Henry Fox received a bill for £120. But the same year this figure was put in the shade by an even more spectacular portrait bought from Reynolds by Charles Bunbury. As the first president of the Royal Academy on its foundation in 1768, Reynolds championed history painting as the highest form to which painters could aspire. History paintings displayed – usually with classical plots and props – heroes who sacrificed themselves for their countries, men and women who gave their children to save friends or cities from destruction and many other personifications of the virtues conventionally believed to be necessary to a good citizen. Critics and painters alike spilled much ink on the value of history painting, but few buyers wanted pictures of minor deities or classical heroes throwing themselves about stony ruins, and painting was dominated by economic rather than moral forces. What patrons like Fox (who bought eight paintings from Reynolds, at least four from Ramsay and three from Hogarth) wanted were portraits of friends they loved and icons of political mentors and heroes.

With his patrons' connivance Reynolds gradually merged the subject matter of history painting with the figures of his portraits, coming up with a hybrid known as 'sublime portraiture'. In sublime portraits modern subjects posed as classical figures in appropriate costume. Sublime portraiture became a way of marrying nudity, theatricality and the unimpeachable virtues of the history painting. 'Lady Sarah Bunbury Sacrificing to the Graces' was one of Reynolds's first and most flamboyant examples.

Reynolds painted Sarah throwing a libation into a smoking serpent-ringed urn. Statues of the three graces stand on a carved pillar just beyond her; behind her a handmaiden pours the next offering into a shallow dish. Sarah is wearing a pink gown lined with blue, tied under her bosom with a blue-fringed sash, a garment Reynolds designed especially for the painting. Like the costumes worn at some Holland House theatricals (and this painting is nothing if not theatrical) the gown displays as much as it conceals. The invitation the painting offers to admire Sarah's body is only partly retracted by the prominently displayed wedding ring on her left hand. Whatever the painting's ostensible theme – a tribute to friendship, a sacrifice to love, an elaborate compliment to her beauty – its effect is more fleshy than ethereal, redolent of boudoir rather than temple. For this magnificent concoction Bunbury paid £250, an eighth of his annual income and a sum that would have bought a small Salvator Rosa, a clutch of Old Master drawings or a passable Rembrandt. Sarah's portrait was admired by men and women alike. Louisa wrote to her, 'my sister Kildare has set me quite distracted about a picture of you that she says is quite delightful, done by Reynolds . . . and when I see it, if it answers my expectation, I will go to gaol rather than not have it, but I'll persuade Mr. Conolly to buy it for his gallery – I mean a copy, for I hear Mr. Bunbury intends to have this. In short I am wild about pictures of you and my sister Kildare, I don't think I shall ever be satisfied without dozens of them.'

At Reynolds's large studio on the west side of Leicester Square, he and his sitters were the still centre of an ever-moving crowd of onlookers. The artist frequently held open house. Visitors chatted and milled about, moving between his painting room and his gallery where his latest portraits and collection of paintings were put up on the walls and furniture was scattered about to give the air of a gentleman's residence rather than a place of business. In tiny back rooms along corridors a small army of assistants worked on backgrounds and drapery, disgruntled and out of sight. In Reynolds's workroom servants handed books of engravings to prospective customers. Politicians leafed through these volumes searching for poses and props that would lend them an air of statesmanship. Women also looked for the symbolic detritus so necessary to society portraits: books to show that they were critical or absorbed readers, sewing, embroidery, lace, flowers and, increasingly, children. Reynolds's engraving books offered patrons a chance to create an image of themselves to show the world. Orchestrating this show, chalk in hand, was Reynolds himself, equal parts artist, gentleman and host. Despite Reynolds's air of worldly propriety, his studio was a place where everyday social conventions were flouted or ignored. Because entry was without invitation to Reynolds's clients, carefully planned meetings could take place there and be passed off as chance. Women who had lost their reputations might meet estranged friends for hurried conversations. Lovers bumped into one another, assuming stagy poses of indifference and surprise that concealed churning stomachs and beating hearts. Actors, actresses and courtesans came face to face with their audience, each side agog with curiosity.

Reynolds had to be careful. Notorious courtesans like Kitty Fisher came to sit at an hour early enough to avoid the crowds. But even if she didn't mingle with more respectable clients her portrait was evidence enough that she had been and its engraving was all over the town. Kitty Fisher was a star and young women like Susan Fox-Strangways, who were fascinated with the theatre and the personal power that actresses and courtesans like Kitty Fisher occasionally attained, copied her eagerly. They aped her extravagant dress and manner – what Caroline disapprovingly called 'the Kitty Fisher style' – and, with her portrait as a guide, they could model their own pose on hers when they came to sit themselves. When Susan sat to Ramsay for the Holland House gallery in 1764 she declared her interest in the theatre and its murky underworld by copying the pose in Reynolds's picture of Kitty completed three years before. Both women sit with their heads turned slightly away from their viewers. Their hands lie loosely across their forearms, allowing their triple lace ruffles to billow across the lower half of the canvas. Ramsay's addition of a shadowy classical pillar behind Susan does little to dispel the similarities between the two paintings. Such iconography ratified and intensified the kind of social mixing the visits to the painter's studio allowed. If Susan could copy the dress and pose of a notorious courtesan, who knew what other aspects of low life she might next decide to emulate.

The public acceptability of courtesans stopped at their images. Actors, who shared the courtesans' milieu, had already by the 1760s breached the walls of the aristocratic home. Young men from Drury Lane and Covent Garden helped out at private theatricals, while their elders, led by Garrick, entertained adoring fans at assemblies and dinners. Inside their own houses aristocrats may have felt safe from the sort of social dilution they noticed at the painter's studio.

But amateur theatricals and the studio made one another acceptable because they had a good deal in common. Young men and women like Sarah, Susan and the Fox brothers stood or sat in rich and often revealing costume watched by friends and servants alike. Moreover, seeing Sarah 'en déshabillé' acting Jane Shore, as she did at Holland House in 1761 was not so different from going to see Reynolds paint her sacrificing to the Graces three years later. Horace Walpole hit not only on the connection but also the moral. Sarah's acting called to mind a painting, but it also hinted at the kind of social impropriety that could hover about the painter's studio. 'When Lady Sarah was in white with her hair about her ears and on the ground, no Magdalen by Correggio was half so lovely and expressive,' Walpole wrote in January 1761. His choice of image was prophetic: Sarah looked not only like a cinquecento masterpiece but also like a fallen woman.

When Sarah came back to Holland House in December 1762, Fox had a sadder description for her. She was the 'widow', left in London while her husband went to a house party at Woburn. But she was far from bereft, slipping happily back into Holland House life, its games of cards and political chat, Fox's bawdy teasing and Caroline's anxious intensity. In the mornings the sisters read by their own firesides. Books were companions and friends. 'I think it a very happy thing to have reading,' Caroline wrote. In the long winter evenings after dinner everyone gossiped over cards. On 4 January 1763 Sarah wrote to Susan Fox-Strangways: 'Dear Ly Sue – sitting by the quadrille table, where Mrs. Greville, Charles, Mr. Fox and my sister are playing, you must expect to hear about their games.'

Besides making up the numbers at cards, visitors to Holland House expected conversation on both the political and cultural news of the day. Caroline had strong views about social gatherings; as a hostess she attempted to achieve, as she did in her letters, a careful informality. The atmosphere was studiedly casual, a mixture of the modish and the bawdy;

serious talk, dominated by politics, literature and the latest philosophical ideas, mixed together with flattery and scurrility. Many of the Foxes' friends put themselves forward, in their own social circle and sometimes on a more public stage, as wits and writers. Over the card table Caroline and Mrs Greville might argue about Rousseau's attitude towards women. Fox praised Sterne's *Tristram Shandy* while Caroline admitted that she 'could make neither head nor tail of it, tho' I tried because that same thing of the clock caught my fancy at the beginning.' Fox and his friends traded copies of their occasional verses.

Of the Foxes' most intimate companions, Sir Charles Hanbury Williams, Molly Hervey, George Selwyn and Lady Townshend were originally Henry's friends. Horace Walpole, Lady Diana Bolingbroke and Mrs Vesey were held in common, while Frances Greville had originally been a friend of Caroline's mother and aunt. Other Holland House *habitués* like Lady Albemarle and the Hillsboroughs were part of the extended Richmond family; the Countess of Hillsborough was Emily's sister-in-law, Lady Albemarle was Caroline's aunt. Sarah was often at Holland House after her marriage, choosing to go to spend time there rather than wait for visitors to her own house in Spring Gardens. In the 1760s, Charles Fox brought a stream of young Etonians to his parents' table. From amongst them, Richard Fitzpatrick and Lord Carlisle quickly became absorbed into the Holland House milieu.

Henry Fox's friends had several features in common. They were writers, wits, agnostics and sexual adventurers of various hues. Hanbury Williams, described by Dr Johnson as 'our lively and elegant though too licentious lyric bard', was the companion of Fox's youth and bachelordom: it was in his house that Caroline and Fox were married in 1744. Although nominally a west-country MP, his real interests were women, poetry and drinking. From 1766 onwards, Hanbury Williams was often abroad on diplomatic missions.

After an unsuccessful posting to St Petersburg in 1757 he broke down completely and in 1759 he killed himself. Once Hanbury Williams had gone, his cousin George Selwyn took his place as the favoured oddity among the Foxes' friends. Selwyn began his career of infamy getting himself thrown out of Oxford for blasphemy. He went on to develop more epicene tastes: a sexual obsession with corpses and executions (to which, it was rumoured, he sometimes went dressed as a woman) and an equally strong interest in young men, among them the Earl of March and Charles Fox's friend the Earl of Carlisle. Rumours abounded that he was a hermaphrodite, born without genitals. Selwyn carried with him a love of life as well as a whiff of the grave. Fox, who enjoyed flirting with his male friends – from Hervey to Selwyn and Walpole – teased him in his letters with sexual innuendo. Caroline and Sarah wrote to Selwyn as an avuncular friend.

Horace Walpole was often at Holland House, sometimes in Selwyn's company, always hoovering up political chat and matrimonial gossip, an onlooker rather than a participant, continually reworking the raw material of his leisured life into letters, commentaries and political treatises. Caroline shared his cult of Madame de Sévigné and his Francophilia, but she expressed more respect than fondness for him. Fox, always less discriminating, called him his beloved 'Hory'.

Besides these three, a host of other men moved in and out of the family circle at Holland House. Lord Shelburne's lawyerly mind briefly captivated both Caroline and Fox at the beginning of the 1760s. Richard Rigby, the Duke of Bedford's secretary was, until 1763, one of Fox's favourite drinking companions. Clotworthy Upton, a gentle and cosmopolitan friend of Louisa's from the north of Ireland, became intimate with Caroline in the 1760s. Topham Beauclerk, wit, rake and dope-fiend, was a frequent visitor at the end of the decade after his marriage to Lady Diana Bolingbroke. Charles Fox's friends Richard Fitzpatrick and the Earl of Carlisle had settled in a few years earlier.

Fox favoured women who were witty or beautiful. To those, like Lady Townshend or Lady Hervey, who were (or had been) both he offered lubricious flirtations and scatological verses. Caroline had few very close women companions outside her own family, but she liked women who were socially skilful, 'amiable' and clever. In her letters to Emily she singled out Lady Diana Bolingbroke, Lady Bateman and Mrs Greville (although, in deference to the epistolary art, she would rarely mention friends that Emily did not know). Lady Bolingbroke was clever, long suffering and a gifted painter, at least two of whose works hung in Holland House. After her marriage to Beauclerk in 1769, she tolerated his constant infidelity and nursed him to his drug-induced death in 1780 with saintly devotion. The Batemans, mother and son, were two intimate friends whom Caroline praised for their good humour and affection rather than their wit or cleverness.

Mrs Greville was one of the four daughters of the Irish Earl Macartney. After her marriage to Fulke Greville in 1748 she and her husband – gambler and wit enough to satisfy Fox, author enough to interest Caroline – were often at Holland House. Mrs Greville wrote verses which Caroline sometimes tucked into her letters to Emily. 'Prayer for Indifference', which Mrs Greville wrote about 1756 was the most celebrated poem written by a woman in the eighteenth century, frequently printed in miscellanies and anthologies. The 'Prayer' was an attack on the newly fashionable notion of sensibility, but an attack which, by virtue of its length and intensity, tended to emphasise the emotion it claimed to reject. 'Take then this treacherous sense of mine/ Which dooms me still to smart;/ Which pleasure can to pain refine/ To pain new pangs impart.' Mrs Greville was one of a generation of men and women, Caroline and Emily amongst them, for whom sensibility, with its attendant notions of romantic love and eventually propriety and domesticity, was a newly defined emotion. Her poem was constantly read because it recognised both that sensibility was here to stay and that it was bringing about a sea change in the notions women (and to a lesser extent, men) held about themselves.

For all her uneasy acceptance of sensibility, Mrs Greville was far from conventionally feminine. She had matured in the 1740s, a time when, in certain aristocratic households, women traded witticisms and critical opinions with friends of both sexes. Fanny Burney, product of a more careful class and age, was shocked at Mrs Greville's assertiveness and noticed her habit in company of 'lounging completely at her ease', lying on a chaise-longue, 'with her head alone upright'. Caroline loved her, but when Mrs Greville's forthright presence clashed with her own anxious oppressed spirits, found her difficult. 'Mrs. Greville was here a few days with her pretty daughter,' she wrote at a low point in January 1763. 'I love Mrs. Greville, but I don't enjoy her company as I formerly did.' Their friendship recovered with Caroline's equanimity. Mrs Greville's nephew, George Macartney, accompanied Ste Fox to Geneva in 1763 and Caroline briefly harboured hopes that Ste might marry her daughter, the 'pretty' Miss Greville. Nothing came of that plan, but the friendship prospered. By 1766 Mrs Greville, along with Sarah and Clotworthy Upton, had her own bedroom at Holland House, 'to come and go as they like it'. Despite Sarah's marriage, private theatricals, either at Holland House or in the country, continued. Charles Fox and his friends could be relied on for male parts; Susan Fox-Strangways was often there; Miss Greville and Sarah's brother-in-law, the caricaturist Henry Bunbury, sometimes lent a hand. By the middle of the decade they had added Dryden's *All For Love* (in which Sarah played the doomed Cleopatra) and Fletcher's marriage comedy *Rule a Wife and Have a Wife* to their repertoire.

At the end of 1764 Caroline sent Emily an account of Holland House life. 'Mr. Bateman, besides being more entertaining than most people in my opinion, is really the most valuable friendly man I know. Little Lady Bateman and him I do love exceedingly and the more I see them the more I value them; without anything brilliant she has understanding enough to make her conversation agreeable and has a better heart and more good humour than almost anybody I know, free from caprice or touchiness. The Hillsboros in their queer way are in good humour with us, and agreeable enough. I have seen Mr. Walpole pretty often and Tatty Upton. We breakfast at nine, dine as soon after three when people dine here, as they will come, and so to bed about eleven. So you see we keep time with you; and you have now a full account of our life and conversation.'

Despite the crowds of friends and relations – Albemarles, Hillsboroughs, Ilchesters, Cadogans, Brudenells – who filled the Pay Office and Holland House, Caroline's sympathies and anxieties were largely reserved for her husband, sons and sisters. In the early 1760s she felt easy about all her children. Harry was at Mr Pampellone's Academy at Wandsworth. Ste was travelling on the Continent, picking up polish, women and the first of many gambling debts. Charles was finishing at Eton; he was already the creature of paradox who was later to puzzle his admirers: shy and worldly, extravagant and painstaking, dissipated and studious.

With her sons occupied, Caroline's anxieties were concentrated on her husband, particularly when, in 1762, he suddenly re-entered the political arena. Lord Bute and the King asked him to help bring about an end to the expensive and long-running war with France. Fox agreed to come out of his semi-retirement at the Pay Office and force what he knew would be an unpopular peace through the House of Commons. The King and Bute needed Fox as the only man with the ruthlessness and authority to bring the House of Commons round. Fox agreed to do their bidding. Temperamentally he had always been a servant rather than an opponent of the Crown. Besides, he disliked war and wanted to secure the earldom he felt his services merited.

In the autumn of 1762, while Bute's ministers negotiated

with the French, Fox set out to gain the necessary votes for peace in the House, helped by a deep pocket of government money. He bought peace in the time-honoured way, with promises of offices and sinecures, with flattery and with bribes. He was rapid and efficient: the Peace of Paris was ratified in the Commons in February 1763. Taking the opportunity offered by victory, Fox also advised the King 'to make his reign easy' by stripping his opponents of offices and emoluments. He was prepared to mastermind such a purge and accept the inevitable enmity of those involved in return for public recognition by the Crown. Shelburne, however, realising that Fox's 'massacre' had left him relatively friendless in the House of Commons, determined that he should bear public responsibility for an unpopular peace. Fox's earldom was withheld and, to emphasise his tactical victory, Shelburne demanded that Fox give up the Pay Office.

In the end Fox had to settle for a barony, hanging on to the Pay Office for a couple of years but forced to retreat to the House of Lords to lick his wounds. He gained the title Lord Holland, Baron of Foxley, Wiltshire, but lost all political credibility. Realising his error, Fox broke with Shelburne, and when Rigby and Calcraft, his two closest friends in the Commons, sided with Shelburne, he quarrelled with them too. Baffled and mortified, Fox sought refuge in verse, and Caroline as usual in a letter to Emily: 'You have no conception,' she wrote, 'of the court Lord Shelburne has paid us all last year, trying every means to get into our utmost confidence and into Mr. Fox's favour by Charles, Sal and me; it appears now so plain I'm surprised I was the dupe of it ... 'Twas a most unlucky thing for Mr. Fox he came in last year, and I should for ever lament the share I had in it (prevailed on and persuaded by Mr. Calcraft and Lord Shelburne) did I not think without his coming in Peace would not have been made; indeed it seemed right at the time.' She was horrified by Fox's fall from grace partly because it exposed her emotional investment in his success. 'I can't help feeling mortified at his ceasing to be of consequence, though I would neither have him in power nor in opposition. Such is the frailty of the human mind; but my vanity is hurt.'

Fox tried to hide his bitterness, writing to Caroline in April 1763, 'I have done right and am got to that ease I always wished for; not with the grace I had a right to expect, but I am got there.' But ease was not to be his lot. Exposed and out-manoeuvred by Bute and Shelburne, he was left to soak up public wrath over the Peace of Paris. It did not escape the notice of the press that Fox had made a huge fortune from the war. Pushing through a treaty which many felt gave too much territory to the French was, so the satires ran, adding insult to the injury done to the country by his ambition and greed.

With the end of every war in the eighteenth century came a period of political turmoil that was accompanied by calls to reform the processes of government. For several years after 1763, Fox was pilloried as the 'public defaulter of unac-counted millions'; a man who epitomised not only the corruption of those in high places but also the baseness of politicians who reaped rewards and then sold the impover-ished nation short. So Fox's dreams of peaceful retirement were misplaced. Wherever he was, in Belgium or Paris, Naples or Florence, newspapers and pamphlets brimming with vitriolic attack reached him. Satirical poets had a field day; Charles Churchill attacked him in his 'Epistle to William Hogarth', Thomas Gray lampooned him in 'On Lord Hol-land's Seat near Margate'. Fox said that hostile verses were 'unanswerable and must be endured'. But after he retired from active politics in 1763, and particularly after he gave up the Pay Office in 1765, he seemed listless and diminished. Politics had been his bedrock and stimulant for thirty years, fuelling his self-esteem, good humour and domestic happi-ness. Without it he gradually lost the will to live.

Fox's troubles brought back Caroline's stomach complaint and low spirits. After the final humiliation she decided they should go abroad. They would see Ste, take the waters at the

Belgian resort of Spa and spend several months in Paris. The peace of 1763 opened up the Continent to aristocrats and those Caroline called 'rich citizens' whose zeal for travel had gone unassuaged for seven years. The British came as swaggering victors, representatives of Europe's new dominant political and economic power. For twenty years after the Peace of Paris English aristocrats wandered Europe buying up pictures, furniture, clothes, statues and ideas with an economic bravado that only just concealed their cultural humility. Even Caroline, part French and almost bilingual, wrote to Emily before she set off, 'we shall return all fine and foreign'. Francophiles like Fox looked towards French philosophers – Voltaire in particular – for ways of thinking about the world. Many spoke and read French fluently and could compete creditably in the contests of wit and gallantry that dominated Paris drawing-rooms. None the less they came as humble supplicants to the temples of the arts. In the salons they gulped in the latest theories and literary controversies that divided the 'philosophes'. In Italy, connoisseurs with golden pockets prostrated themselves before the compositions of Italian baroque painting or the delicacies of 'Etruscan' vases. In Switzerland devout Voltaireans made their way to Ferney outside Geneva to attend the master's own amateur theatricals or catch a gem-like phrase as it fell from his lips. Some came away with a curt greeting from the decrepit sage; others were treated to an orotund aphorism. Second-generation adherents like Ste Fox were warmly greeted as the sons of Voltairean fathers. Almost everybody left with their faith restored, adoring the old cynic whose creed counselled against faith and adoration.

The English travelled in style, with clothes, medicines, horses and servants. Caroline took two maids to France, along with a personal hairdresser. Fox took his own valet, as did Charles and Harry, plucked out of school for the trip. During the 'tedious voyage of fifteen hours' between the North Foreland and Calais, Caroline sat in her post-chaise on the deck of the cross-Channel packet. The carriage was strapped firmly to the deck and Caroline's stomach rolled with the boat as it ploughed its way from Kent to France. Once travellers had landed on the Continent, they made rapid and calculable progress if they stuck to the post-routes; they simply planned and checked their journeys by the printed timetables for the post-coaches. After they landed the Foxes gaped not only at the battlefields of Ramillies and Malplaquet, as if to certify their national identity before a long season amongst the French, but also at the lace shops of Brussels. A week after landing the Foxes were comfortably installed in the Hôtel Treville, the first of their three Parisian addresses.

Before long the whole family had moved to the Hôtel de Montagu. 'I was much determined against liking Paris,' Caroline wrote to Emily, 'but I find I do; 'tis a pretty place indeed, so full of fine hotels and large shady gardens to them, the streets so well paved and no black smoke in the town . . . I'm sure you would all . . . be diverted to see me go by in my berlin all over glass and gilding, with my hoop and my millions of curls and my rouge and my lace liveries.' As they began to pay calls – on the liberal and Anglophile Duc d'Orléans, on the Prince de Conti and, for form's sake on the English Ambassador – Caroline realised that Parisian life was just as she had hoped: replete with gossip and intrigue, but less riven by political faction than life in London. In the shady gardens of the 'grands hôtels', with their formal walks and crunchy gravel, and in the airy drawing-rooms where curtains billowed from long, open windows, the talk was anything but political, prompting Caroline to the conclusion that France was a 'pretty quiet country . . . where people so sensibly trifle away life with ease and good humour, the same people contented keeping company with one another for sixty years, no parties or interest to divide them.' Fontainebleau, where the monarch held court, was the centre of such party intrigue as the nation's political and social systems allowed. Paris had its own life and rules. Caroline entered eagerly into the niceties of salon life, able to admit now that she was not on home ground, that those people she was most curious about were the philosophers and writers whose work she had read. She soon became an *habituée* of Madame Geoffrin's famous Wednesday salon in the rue Saint-Honoré, where Diderot, Marmontel, d'Alembert, Grimm and other literary lions went through their paces for the benefit of admirers. 'Madame Geoffrin n'est pas noble, but very fond of the English, is constantly at home of an evening, and sees all sorts of company, dévots, savants, beaux-esprits, petits-maîtres robins, etc, etc,' Caroline wrote, explaining to Emily that 'these are what make a dévote, elle ne porte point de rouge, elle fréquente les églises, elle ne joue point, elle ne soupe point, elle ne va point aux spectacles'.

Caroline relished the ostentatious austerity of the dévots, she was curious about the savants and she was happy to forgo the habit of a lifetime and eschew political talk. Her great-grandmother's legend, her father's memory and the good offices of Horace Walpole and Lady Hervey furnished them with many contacts and, as one of the architects of the Peace of Paris, Fox was cordially treated in the French capital. Two or three times a day they paid visits or received guests. Mornings were often turned over to shopping for china, clothing and furniture. Caroline had a good many commissions from Emily, and Henry Fox, back in England briefly in the autumn of 1764, sent her a long shopping list. 'Send me at least two vases like the Duchess of Hamilton's and, if you wish, two more that you may like, for ourselves. Send me the large clock at Poirier's which I thought too big for Sir Jacob Downing with a long genteel figure in bronze reclined ... You'll say I'm extravagant. But why should not I treat myself as well as other people? Send a spring gown, a negligee for Lady Suke too.' Besides these commissions Caroline bought a large quantity of furniture for Holland House and clothes for Sarah and herself. Her sisters, nieces and nephews in Ireland were not forgotten; assorted presents for Emily and her children went in the diplomatic bag. 'By the French

Ambassador's things I have sent you two biscuit china figures which I admire vastly, but you'll not get them this great while. I hope dear little Charles will by this time have got his knife, which I sent him. There are also three geneva stone necklaces for the girls, and a new-fashioned pincushion and scissors, one for Emily t'other for Harriet.' 'Let me know if you are fond of china set in ormolu. I admire it vastly and, if you do, will send you some, but would know your taste first as 'tis very dear.' 'I send you two story books.' 'Indeed you shall have the green vases, set your heart at rest.'

In between bouts of hectic spending, the whole family went to Spa in Belgium, where crowds of English, gouty, bilious or just worn out by the exertions of travel, went to drink the waters and lounge about. 'The account of our life there I can give you in a few lines,' Caroline wrote to Emily. 'Ste made distant and humble love to Lady Spencer, rode out with Lord Spencer; Lord Holland s'ennuyait beaucoup, but could talk a lot of nonsense to Lady Bateman about drinking the waters in order to breed. Charles attached himself to every French coxcomb that came ... As for me, I gambled with the gentlemen.'

After Spa the family went back to Paris, settling down for the winter at the Hôtel Rouac in the rue de Grenelle. Now that she had her husband away from politics and her beloved eldest son by her side, Caroline was temporarily content, weaving for herself a vision of Paris that chimed with her tranquillity. Her Paris was an easy city, where good conversation took precedence over the political intrigues she spurned with exaggerated dislike. 'I'm not French like Lady Hervey,' she wrote, 'but I do think they are the only people who know how to put society on an agreeable foot; they don't like us run after diversions, nor think themselves ennuyé unless something clever is going on; they are trifling, chatty and easy ... Upon the whole I think every woman past thirty that really lives a Paris life among the French, and understands the language, and who likes conversation better than cards, will prefer Paris to London.' In her temporary calm, Caroline was able to forget the bitterness that she had felt towards her parents and to look back to her childhood, one of the very few times she ever did so in twenty years of correspondence with Emily. 'I can easily account for my partiality to the French,' she wrote, 'it was early taken. You know my father had it strongly. We went when I was quite a child to Holland and France; the servants (and children of consequence) hated Holland and the Dutch and were violently fond of the Duchess of Portsmouth. It seems foolish but these early impressions remain with one.'

After their extended Parisian sojourn of 1763–64, Caroline and Lord Holland (as she reluctantly began to call Mr Fox) acquired a taste for continental travel. Caroline came back to Paris in 1765; the whole family travelled through France to Naples in 1766, and they were back again in France in both 1767 and 1769. Winters were spent at Holland House or in Piccadilly, summers at Kingsgate, Henry's newly acquired estate on the windswept coast of Kent. Holland House still provided a London base for the whole family, although each of the sisters had their own London town house: the Kildares' in Arlington Street, near Grosvenor Square, the Conollys' in Whitehall and the Bunburys' in Spring Gardens on the north-western side of the Privy Garden.

It was important for all the members of the family to come to London from time to time. Bunbury, Kildare and Conolly came to deal with business affairs and to attend Parliament. Emily and Louisa returned to reassure themselves about their family identity and their fast-fading sense of Englishness, although Emily's growing band of children meant she came less and less often. Everybody came for the pleasure gardens, the gambling, the print sellers, the theatre, the shopping and the social life.

The idea of London produced self-fulfilling edicts about the pace of metropolitan life that gave visitors a sense of self-importance and were especially attractive to those like Sarah who had much to forget. Sarah plunged herself into the social whirl as soon as she arrived at Holland House or in Spring Gardens, declaring loudly that London was responsible for her full calendar. 'My Dear Netty,' she wrote to Susan in the spring of 1766, 'I have been in town about a month and am not settled yet, for I have not a moment's time to myself. The hurry of this town is inconceivable, for I declare I have been only once to the Play, Opera and Oratorio, to very few assemblies, and yet I cannot find a moment's time to myself.'

London was the Western world's first great metropolis. By the 1760s it lay sprawled over many square miles, reaching out of the old centres of Westminster and the City along riverbanks and coach routes like an octopus uncoiling its tentacles. On its outskirts half-joined villages were interspersed with a pea-green and chocolate-brown patchwork of vegetable gardens. Closer in were scrubby patches of ground spattered with red, magenta and ultramarine from dyers' vats, and tenter grounds where taut ropes swayed in the sooty air like giant hairy worms. From these outlying settlements through the half-urban spaces of manufactories, vegetable gardens and stable yards the poor trudged miles to work in the city. In summer they walked in clouds of dust. Sand from London's unmade roads, stirred up by feet and carriage wheels, turned and twisted in the half light. Everybody choked and complained. In winter they walked in the dark, on roads whose pot holes and ridges froze into slippery moraines.

The poor came in early. Fruit sellers made their way to Covent Garden to buy fruit to sell on the streets of the City and the West End. Labourers arrived to look for work on building sites in Piccadilly or around Oxford Street where the city was growing rapidly up its shallow northern rim towards the villages of Hampstead and Islington. Going in they passed night-soil men carrying their fertilising loads away from the city to the nursery gardens and farms around.

As they arrived commercial London was coming to life, prostitutes and their clients were at last going home to sleep. The smell of meat and manure rose with the sun over Smithfield market in the east, joined above the old Fleet ditch by the marine odour from Billingsgate fish market. In Covent Garden fruiterers laid out their stalls as the last of the night's revellers stumbled drunkenly by.

Haloed by dust in summer and soot in winter, the sun rose. The light filtered into the attics of Spitalfields falling on to Huguenot weavers as they bent their backs at the loom. On the floor below them prosperous merchants said prayers with their families. At street level the Spitalfields bird sellers opened up their shops. As covers came off rows of wicker cages, goldfinches and greenfinches, linnets and woodlarks drew their beaks from the warm haven of their wings and began another day in captivity. Soon afterwards in the narrow houses of St Paul's churchyard, along Fleet Street and out into the Strand master printers and their compositors set to work. Pressmen put on their stiff ink-blackened overalls. From scores of open boxes the compositors plucked metal letters and punctuation marks, rapidly assembling them into words, paragraphs, pamphlets. Proof-readers checked finished copy. In another room, surrounded by stacks of paper from Holland and France, the pressmen inked the type with viscous leather lollipops. As they worked they read, commented and criticised, members of an unenfranchised but politically active group.

Round about ten o'clock government clerks sat down at their desks. Some were careful men who lived a life of orderly service. In sheet after sheet of paper they laid down the foundations of a bureaucracy, identifying themselves more with the nebulous processes of government than with the Crown whose nominal servants they were. With ink, words and figures they created a shadowy world; its civil lists, budget estimates and revenue figures were silently assuming a central place in national life. As these government offices opened, so did the shops that served the wealthy. Apprentices in Ludgate Hill removed the wooden shutters from wallpaper emporia and mercers' shops. In the Strand and St James's booksellers unwrapped bulky parcels from continental publishers and checked their shelves for sufficient stocks of the latest novels and histories. From New Bond Street smells of lavender water, pomanders and expensive fragrances wafted from the doors of perfumeries over the open drains that transported soapy liquids slowly down to the Thames. In the streets post-chaises rumbled over the paving stones, rolling backwards and forwards on thick leather braces. Heavy delivery carts lurched behind. Phaetons and cabriolets bounced along towards Hyde Park. Chair-men lifting the closed leather boxes of sedan chairs twisted in and out. Above the clatter of wheels and the smack of hooves street sellers shouted and sang. All the time beggars and children huddled immobile in doorways and church porches and stared out at the cacophonous mass moving past them.

It was about this time of day that merchants' wives, gentlemen and ladies of fashion set out for the shops. They were carried towards the city to buy wall coverings or cloth, to the jewellers of New Bond Street and Hatton Garden, the drapers and lacemen near Covent Garden and the book and print sellers of the Strand, St James's and Ludgate Hill. Caroline and her sisters invariably went shopping in mid-morning, after reading, letter writing and (for some) accounting. 'Let me have any order you may have,' Caroline wrote to Emily in October 1764, 'as I don't at all dislike jaunting to town in a morning from Holland House at this season of the year, tho' I detest it in spring or summer; but in winter 'tis an exercise that agrees with me.' Caroline believed that commerce brought improvement; shopping, apart from being a pleasant pastime, was a rational exercise, a commitment to the civilising powers of trade.

Inevitably Emily sent large numbers of commissions. In 1759 Caroline sent to Ireland one set of chairs with damask with which to upholster them, a 'short dressed cloak', an ermine gown, a taffeta gown, some china and a pair of silver buckles from Mrs Chenevix, a fashionable jeweller and 'toy woman' in Suffolk Street. She also sent a pair of pearl earrings as a present for Sarah. From Mrs Harriet Dunoyer, a bookseller in the Haymarket with whom Emily had an account, Caroline ordered several books that Dublin could not immediately supply, among them Voltaire's *Candide* and *Orphan of China*, Clarendon's *Memoirs* and the latest political pamphlets.

Caroline was far from the only person who executed commissions in London for Emily. When Kildare and the newly married Conollys came over in the same year, they too had long wish-lists from Carton. Almost as soon as she arrived in London, Louisa obediently set out on what was to prove a long and expensive search for a hundred and fifty yards of painted taffeta with which Emily planned to cover beds, windows and chairs in her principal bedrooms. 'I have seen a vast number of taffetas which Louisa is looking out for you,' Caroline wrote in May 1759. Kildare, watching the samples pile up, began to show alarm at the cost. 'I am sorry to put my dear Emily in mind of anything which she don't like to hear of. The great expense that all your commissions (which are very numerous) will come to is the occasion . . . The hundred and fifty yards of taffeta is a commission that people are surprised at and say they believe you don't know what an expensive thing it is, and there is hardly any such thing to be got as even a hundred yards of the same pattern.' But a week later he wrote in his customary blend of financial and sexual language, 'the taffeta is bought by my desire'. Louisa added more prosaically, 'Lord Kildare goes on Monday . . . He carries your painted taffeta in his own trunk and has paid sixty-five guineas for it.' Emily had got what she wanted. 'Since 'tis bought I must tell you I am out of my wits at the thoughts of being in possession of what I think the loveliest, sweetest thing in the world. You have no idea how delighted I am at the kind manner in which you tell me it is bought. And now, my Jemmy, what do you think is the difference between this and the frightful Nassau damask they sell in Dublin? You wou'd not have thought that a very unreasonable demand; well, nine shillings a yard is what they ask here for that. Comes' *Commerce*, which I just now consulted to be certain of what I am going to say, tells me that 150 yards of that comes to £67:10s, and the sweet India taffeta stands us in £70:00; what a vast difference in beauty! And how little in the price! . . . In short it is as cheap *silk* furniture as one can have. I know you will smile at this, but 'tis really true.'

Occasionally desire ran faster than memory. Kildare wrote with some astonishment from London to Carton in 1766: 'I was this day looking for glass cream pots and in Swallow Street I saw some that were bespoke by a lady about two years ago, and the man had them as the lady was gone to Ireland. Upon asking what lady it was he said Lady Kildare, so I supposed they were what you liked, desired he would pack up a dozen and send them to me.'

Once Emily's gargantuan appetite for commodities had been temporarily satisfied, purchases had to be paid for. Kildare banked with La Touche in Dublin. Neither he nor Emily had a London banker so they had no ready source of cash in London. Commissions were often paid for in kind; some of Emily's debt to Caroline in 1759 was repaid with a white lutestring gown, a length of green ribbon and buckles for Ste. Caroline also favoured soft Irish leather gloves which she ordered several dozen pairs at a time. None the less the balance was invariably in Caroline's favour and since both were haphazard mathematicians, tended to remain so for months at a time. Only Louisa was a careful accountant, jotting down debts and credits in her household accounts and carefully settling bills with her sisters. In 1763, after a summer in London, she wrote to Sarah, 'By the account I send you, you are indebted to me £0:3s:0d, but I rather fancy I owe you £0:10s:0d. For one article that I have put down £13:0s:0d, I am not sure whether it ought not to be £13:13s:od. In that case I shall owe you ten shillings. If its the other, the three shillings you know will be no matter.'

Although Emily or Louisa often asked Caroline or Sarah to find something in London which they themselves were unable to get in Dublin, shopping and spending were not entirely the province of women, as some contemporary commentators asserted. The world of goods was very roughly divided into two hemispheres of consumption. Women bought clothes for themselves and their children, and they were responsible for housekeeping and interior decoration. Men took care of goods that were used outside the house. They bought horses and tackle and in London it was they who went to Long Acre and ordered carts and carriages. Caroline waited for Kildare to come over to London before she ordered a carriage, evidently believing that he was a specialist in their design and purchase: 'I have a pretty pair of spotted horses, and must have a pretty light chariot, which I hope Lord Kildare will give himself the trouble to bespeak for me when he comes,' she wrote to Emily in 1760. Men and women alike bought furniture and books and both sexes bought presents of all sorts.

This rough-and-ready sexual division of purchasing varied from couple to couple. While Emily often commissioned quite expensive items from friends and relatives, Louisa habitually waited for Conolly's approval. So, when Sarah planned a trip to Italy in 1766 (a trip she never actually made) Louisa sent a commission from Emily but delayed including her own until Conolly could be persuaded to part with the money. Emily 'begged' that Sarah would 'lay out twenty guineas in any pretty little marble thing that strikes your fancy ... For my part I will try to coax Mr. Conolly to let you lay out a certain sum in pretty things. This week is Curragh meeting, so I must wait till that is over, and if he wins, I will ask him to let me commission you.'

Even fashion, which fuelled a constant demand for luxury

goods, was not exclusively the interest of women, although women's fashions changed more quickly than did men's. But men were less likely than women to record their sartorial longings; loving descriptions of clothes were largely absent from their letters. For women who habitually wrote letters, clothing the body in language as well as dress was an essential ingredient of a chatty page. The very last act of dressing was describing the dress. Sarah excelled at this *coup de grâce*. In a long letter to Susan in the winter of 1765–66, she described the prevailing fashion: 'To be perfectly genteel you must be dressed thus ... The roots of the hair must be drawn up straight and not fruzzed at all for half an inch above the root; you must wear no cap and only *little, little* flowers dab'd in on the left side; the only feather permitted is a black or white sultane perched up on the left side and your diamond feather against it. A broad puffed ribbon collier with a tippet ruff or only a little black handkerchief very narrow over the shoulders; your stays very high and pretty tight at the bottom; your gown trimmed; ... the sleeves long and loose, the waist very long, the flounces and ruffles of a decent length, not too long, nor so hideously short as they now wear them. No trimming on the sleeve, but a ribbon knot tied to hang on the ruffles. The men's dress is exactly what they used to wear latterly.'

When Sarah or Caroline were looking for expensive items such as Sarah described to Susan, they would sally forth to finger and price material themselves. If they needed household goods other than silver or the finest china, they would send a servant on a preliminary sortie. Trusted servants like Caroline's housekeeper Mrs Fannen took charge of all household goods, and Emily wrote directly to her when she needed crockery and china from London. Much shopping was also done from home. Dressmakers, tailors, booksellers and jewellers all took their wares to aristocratic houses, presenting themselves with samples and order books. 'I diverted myself very much with making the shop keepers bring me all sorts of pretty things to look at,' Sarah wrote about a London visit in the mid-1770s. Tradesmen gave especially deferential service to aristocratic customers. As a quid pro quo for home visits and extended credit they used their elevated customers to advertise their wares and services. Such visits also provided convenient opportunities to bring bills which might have been unpaid for months at a time.

Most tradesmen and tradeswomen came in the morning, late enough to ensure that their customers were up, but not so late that they had left the house to dine out or were preparing to receive visitors themselves. Round about one or two o'clock people of fashion came home to dress for dinner. Business in the shops and workrooms of the city slowed down. Shops emptied gradually, pens and presses moved more slowly. Sometime after two o'clock, tradesmen and government officials left their cramped offices and followed their noses through meaty vapours to the chop houses and taverns. In workshops all around the town, masters and apprentices downed tools, clustered round tables and dined in their shops. Beer was delivered daily by brewers' draymen, who decanted the frothing liquid from barrels into jugs; their food was produced by the household cook or brought in. Clerks and labourers, unable to afford a seat in a coffee house or tavern, dined upright on the streets, buying beer and pies from street sellers or shops that opened on to the pavement.

After the dinner hour the city slowed. Gentlemen made for their gardens and firesides, gathering themselves up for the climax of the day. Merchants, clerks and artisans marked time too. They knew they had several hours at desk or press before the evening was theirs. The rumble of traffic dimmed and the city waited for the streetwalkers and pimps whose appearance signalled the start of the evening and the beginning of the night's entertainment.

London at night offered little to the exhausted labourers who turned their backs on the darkening city and made for home. As they walked, some dreamed of their children heaped up on truckle beds fast asleep; some conjured up steaming cauldrons of soup with bread and ale; others hoped for better times. In Spitalfields the weavers straightened their backs, sat up stiffly and then went downstairs. Fluffing up their feathers the birds on the ground floor settled down for the night. Doors closed; link boys stretched up to light flaring street lamps; children mumbled, cried and fell asleep.

A little while later other doors began to open. From the basements of houses in the City, Whitehall and St James's, apprentices and servants emerged, running eagerly up the steps to the lighted streets and an evening out. With their gowns and coats trimmed to the latest fashion, servants could pass for their social betters, which astonished foreign visitors and made employers regret the custom of paying part of their wages in cast-off clothing.

Other servants stayed indoors. They arranged chairs and card tables, straightened carpets, lit fragrant bees-wax candles in sconces and chandeliers. Ladies' maids tucked imitation flowers into their mistresses curled hair and discreetly dabbed rouge on to cheeks made sallow and hollow by years of sedentary gourmandising. Far below the liveried butler announced the assembly's first arrivals.

The streets filled and revellers made choices. Some headed for taverns to drink the hours away; some walked the length of Oxford Street watching the urban parade. Others milled outside the theatres in Covent Garden and Drury Lane or strolled to the river where, at Westminster and Whitehall Stairs, barges and rowing boats waited on summer evenings to take customers across to Vauxhall Gardens. On a warm night as many as fifteen thousand people paid their shilling entrance fee to the pleasure gardens on the south bank of the river opposite Westminster. Peers rubbed shoulders with stable hands, well dressed courtesans might be mistaken in the gloom for women of fashion. Ladies' maids met their lovers in the lamp-lit walks and leaving the gardens' crowded centre drifted amorously to the periphery where mock rockeries and clumps of shrubs covered their flirtations. Music from the orchestra floated over them as they kissed and loosened fastenings.

The middle of Vauxhall was an elongated quadrangle formed by four covered colonnades. It was sprinkled with trees pollarded in the French manner to make them elegantly tall and thin, and optimistically called the grove. Festoons of lamps undulating along the colonnades lit up the grove and its jostling crowd. At nine o'clock visitors hurried to the north side of the garden to see the cascade, where a curtain was drawn aside to show a sculptured rustic landscape illuminated with concealed lights. In the foreground were a miller's house and waterfall. As the crowds clustered round, the 'exact appearance' of water seemed to flow down the slope, turn the mill wheel, rise up in foaming billows at the bottom of the race and glide away.

For the next couple of hours visitors strolled about and stared at one another. In the boxes along the colonnades friends met up and chatted, keeping one eye on the crowd, hoping to spot a famous beauty, a minor political figure or a fashionable courtesan. Soon afterwards tables were set in the alcoves of the colonnades and diners sat down to supper. It was part of the evening's entertainment to complain about the food: the old joke went round that you could read the newspaper through a slice of Vauxhall beef or ham. Poorer visitors bunched round the booths of wealthy diners, commenting on their manners and dress. In the early hours of the morning, boatmen ferried the weary back to the northern side of the river. In the gardens servants extinguished the lights and the illusion they created. Soon only the marble statues of Milton and Handel were left to survey the scene.

In 1742 a more respectable pleasure garden opened on the north side of the Thames at Ranelagh, by the Chelsea Hospital. The high entry price to Ranelagh of 2s. 6d. allowed its proprietors to claim that the garden was genteel and socially exclusive. In the summer there were regular concerts, fireworks and promenades; but it was the constant display of

London's social élite that really drew the crowds. At the centre of Ranelagh an enormous rotunda was built, a round Romanesque structure ringed inside with two tiers of forty-eight wood-panelled boxes. At one side of this huge space stood a canopied orchestra box from which players serenaded the couples and groups who walked solemnly round the floor. Brass chandeliers with candles enclosed in glass spheres hung from the distant ceiling; sound disappeared into the dome and the building was sometimes eerily quiet. Walkers' conversation sounded like the murmuring of lost spirits and women's dresses swished along the marble floor. To diners in the upper boxes it seemed as if the promenaders were purgatorial wanderers, condemned to walk for ever round in circles.

Dawn broke over the city. Ladies and gentlemen back from balls and masquerades flopped into bed. But in some houses the candles still burned, fading to blue flames as the white morning light filled the rooms. The clubs of St James's were still crowded. Young men sat at baize-topped tables, piles of guineas to one side of them, glasses of wine and brandy to the other. In front of them and in their hands were cards. By the morning hours only these inveterate gamblers were left at the tables, men who lost (and occasionally won) hundreds or thousands of pounds a night. Stories circulated of their depravity; to a nation which became ever more addicted to risk as it became more commercialised, they epitomised both the lure and the shame of playing life itself for high stakes. These pallid young men, emotionally exhausted and financially ruined by night-long bouts of gaming, were only the visible representatives of a country in the grip of gambling fever.

Almost everybody who had any spare cash, and many who did not, gambled. Servants and labourers put away part of their meagre wages to buy shares in lottery tickets, hoping against hope that chance would free them from a life of unremitting servitude. Farmers gambled at rural race meetings.

Apprentices, merchants and their clerks held bets on political events, on which merchantman would arrive first at the Port of London, even on which woman would first turn the corner at the end of the street. Dowagers and gentlemen sat over games of faro or whist through long winter evenings, regularly losing twenty pounds a night to their hosts who took the bank. Virginal, unmarried women were not supposed to play – one loss, it was thought, might lead to another – but they did, out of the public gaze. 'Sarah is fond of loo,' Caroline wrote before Sarah's marriage, 'but I have desired her, except in private parties with the Duchess of R[ichmond] not to play.' After her marriage Sarah came of age as a gambler. Caroline noticed with alarm that when Bunbury was not in London she played with the Duke and Duchess of Richmond and other young men at Richmond House. Emily regularly lost moderate amounts without a qualm. Caroline, drawn towards something she thought of as dangerous and wrong, was both attracted and worried by the idea of playing for considerable sums. In 1760 she wrote, 'I can't help when I play deep having an unpleasant feel about it, as if I did something wrong; perhaps a little vanity at not acting consistent with the rest of one's character. In short, I don't quite know, but 'tho I love it I don't feel pleasant at it, and fear encouraging myself in it.'

But it was those who played for very high stakes who held the nation transfixed. Everyone agreed that in moderation gambling was an innocuous pastime but that too much gaming was a vice. Parents and commentators alike puzzled over the cause of this excess, the more so because the line between enjoyment and ruin seemed so permeable. At the beginning of the century, writers regarded games of chance as a kind of pleasure. They trusted to reason and conscience to exercise moderation, and they saw excess as a failure of will, especially since in games like faro the players took turns at being the banker and thus at recouping their losses. Later on, the focus shifted from individuals to the larger world. The habits of gilded youth seemed to offer up a mirror to society; gambling became a symbol of national corruption and imperial decline. As troubles with the American colonists brewed, Horace Walpole wrote, 'the gaming is worthy the decline of our Empire. The young men lose five, ten, fifteen thousand pounds in an evening. Lord Stavordale, not one-and-twenty, lost eleven thousand last Tuesday, but recovered it by one great hand. He swore a great oath – "Now if I had been playing deep, I might have won millions."'

Gambling on this scale was confined to a few dozen young men, *habitués* of Newmarket, denizens of Almack's and White's. They gambled to display their wealth, to identify themselves as part of a group and, increasingly, to indicate a way of life that had political as well as social parameters. Caroline's sons were at the heart of this cadre. To her horror, Ste and Charles Fox, trading on the expectation of very large fortunes, were ostentatious in their huge gambling losses and others in their circle followed their lead. Lord Stavordale was their cousin. Lord Carlisle and Richard Fitzpatrick, Lord March and George Selwyn were the Fox brothers' companions at the gaming table. These men, with their associates of club and turf, developed a culture of gambling. Winning was exhilarating but losing, and losing well, was equally important; a member of Brooks's who left the club with winnings of £12,000 (probably gained as the banker) was vilified by those who remained. By his name in the club books they wrote, 'that he may never return is the ardent wish of the members'.

As Charles Fox made his way in Parliament in the 1770s, gambling became part of his political personality. Fox's admirers lovingly repeated what Horace Walpole wrote about a great extempore performance in the House after a gaming bout. 'Fox was dissipated, dissolute, idle beyond measure. He was that very morning returned from Newmarket, where he had lost some thousand pounds the preceding day, . . . had sat up drinking all night . . . had been running about the House talking to different persons,' and yet spoke with 'amazing spirit and memory.' Where his rival Pitt was cautious and costive, Fox and his supporters were excessive and carelessly brilliant. By the time Fox took on the mantle of 'Champion of the People' in the 1780s, his gambling had been transformed by legend into an aspect of his populism, a form of generosity and symptom of political openness, English liberties and, eventually, for his supporters, of Liberty itself.

Caroline, who was to see nothing of Charles's deification, continued to think of her sons' gambling as a corruption of reason. While Charles and Ste made huge inroads into their father's fortune, and broke every resolution of better conduct, and while onlookers blamed their vice on a lack of childhood discipline, Caroline still trusted to reason and 'confidence' to get the better of their unbridled passion for cards. 'Oh Ste,' she burst out in 1773, 'you have neither of you the excuse of having harsh or hard parents. Too indulgent ones is no excuse for bad conduct, as our indulgence never tended to, nor our example to encourage, sin; but we hoped to reclaim folly by gaining confidence.'

When fortunes were lost and credit ran short, other amusements had to be found. A shilling a night took anyone to the theatre. There audiences asked over and over again the same questions that dominated the gambling dens: 'What will happen next?' and 'how will it all end?' Suspense and resolution were the stuff of the playhouse; in a melodrama everything might depend if not on the fall of the dice, then on an act of the gods or the flick of a tyrant's wrist. Emily had a box in the Dublin theatre, Caroline one at both Drury Lane and Covent Garden. When she came to London in 1760, Sarah went to the play several times a week, often in the company of Charles and Ste Fox, who had been regular visitors since they were five or six years old. At home plays were read silently in the morning, out loud in the evenings and acted by the younger members of both the Fox and Fitzgerald families. Everybody joined in the cult of Garrick. Caroline invited him to assemblies, Louisa had him to dinner when she came to London and Sarah and Susan followed his career with minute attention until the day he died in 1779.

Time spent at the playhouse and reading plays testified to the allure of the theatre not only as an oratorical training ground for budding politicians but also as a metaphor for life itself. It was, of course, an old metaphor, stretching back through Shakespeare to classical writers. But in the eighteenth century it was given new impetus. Actors and theatres were growing in popularity and commentators began to hint at the double role that everyone played in the world, at once actor and audience, all watching the unfolding drama. As early as 1719, Addison's *Spectator*, weighing up the merits of the metaphors of life as a journey and life as a stage, plumped for the latter on the grounds that it was more suited to the bustling and crowded condition of modern life. For the younger generation of Foxes and Fitzgeralds, though, the theatre was more than metaphoric. They worshipped actors and actresses as minor deities, confused actors with their roles and cast themselves as heroes and heroines. In the spring of 1764 the social and metaphorical distance between the aristocratic and the theatrical house broke down altogether. Susan Fox-Strangways eloped with William O'Brien who compounded the error of being an actor by his Irish, Catholic descent.

From the time she appeared in London society Susan had been regarded by her family as unpredictable, headstrong and 'cunning'. 'I fear Lady Suke,' Caroline had written during the negotiations with the Bunburys over Sarah's marriage settlement, afraid that Susan might induce Sarah to call off the wedding and damage her reputation. 'She has too much of the reverse of humility in her composition,' Louisa added. Susan said, 'I thought myself fitter to advise and govern than to soothe and cultivate', and when George III fell in love with Sarah, Susan had hopes of unprecedented influence in national affairs. 'I almost thought *myself Prime Minister*.' She was baulked in this ambition and unable as she said later 'to talk, to confide' in her family. She summed up her childhood thus: 'my father in one room reading – my mother in another playing cards – the ennui I felt – then very little communicating of sentiments or opinions'. Susan turned her attentions to the theatre. There communication between actors and audience created a magic web of confidence and there, too, powerful women like Kitty Fisher stalked the aisles. Home was all reserve, the theatre all engagement.

For a determined girl like Susan it was an obvious step to move from aping Kitty Fisher's clothes and worshipping actors from the distance of her box to falling in love. O'Brien epitomised the glamour of the stage: he trod the boards in major roles and lived on friendly terms with Garrick and Foote. Each night he pandered to the romantic dreams and sexual longings of a thousand adoring fans. Susan wanted his stage declarations of love to become real and she wanted him for herself. Wrapped in the lascivious gaze of the Covent Garden crowd, O'Brien seemed to her more desirable and a greater prize than all the dukes of St James's.

William O'Brien was a rising star, a protégé of Garrick who had come from Dublin in the late 1750s taking leading roles in Farquhar's *The Recruiting Officer* and one of the century's smash hits, Townley's *High Life Below Stairs*. *High Life Below Stairs* was, like Gay's *Beggar's Opera* and Foote's *Mayor of Garrett*, a comedy which used low life to criticise high society. O'Brien played Lovel, a rich young colonial, who disguised himself as a servant and took employment under his own butler. Thus O'Brien, who was an actor pure and simple, took the part of a West India merchant who played the role of a servant. For Susan, who had already toyed with reversing the roles traditionally played by men and women, this confusion was at the heart of his attraction.

O'Brien could impersonate a gentleman just as well off the stage as on it. As a result of his success he quickly found his way into his audience's houses. By the early 1760s he was at Holland House helping out with private theatricals, and he and Susan came face to face. Susan was already in love with

O'Brien's stage persona. Now that he was at Holland House the socially disruptive nature of his presence in her world, a mocking commentary on the supposedly separate milieux of drawing-room and stage, made him irresistible. On a visit to Barton in the summer of 1762, Susan seized the initiative. With Sarah's connivance she wrote O'Brien a note which invited him to contrast the reserve of her world with the enchanting expressiveness of his. It ran:

> In my silence see the lover,
> True love is by silence known
> In my eyes you'll best discover
> All the power of your own.

O'Brien responded to this verse with a torrent of language which exactly suited Susan's desire. 'There never was a more eloquent, unaffected mark of love than your last letter – the tender simplicity of it enchants me – I have done nothing but write and tear answers to it continually – I can't find language strong enough to express the feeling of my heart. What return can I ever make you for your economy . . . Can my whole life spent in attention to you be any kind of equivalent – take it – do what you will: I shall resign my whole soul to your keeping. I will hear, see, and believe nothing but what you would have me. You was determined to fix me yours to the last period of my days, and you have.'

O'Brien recognised immediately that Susan wanted to overturn the notional sexual order. She would 'govern', he would 'cultivate' and sign over his will to hers. Everything about the affair overturned accepted principles of courtship and social order. Instead of a gentleman picking up an actress, as was the accepted custom in the theatres, a woman of fashion was seducing an actor. Through the winter season of 1763–64, Susan and O'Brien met often. O'Brien would check each night in the theatre appointments book to see whether the Foxes' box was filled by the family or whether they had sold on their seats to somebody else. Trusted theatre employees smuggled Susan notes in the box as she sat apparently attentive to the show before her. O'Brien also often appeared at Miss Read's studio, where Susan was sitting for her portrait clad in a fur-trimmed gown and a wide-brimmed hat.

In the spring of 1764, Susan's parents discovered the affair. O'Brien's reaction was suitably histrionic, and his subsequent letter to Susan was a skilful blend of sexual directness and the sorts of gestures expected of a tragic hero. 'I am distracted – I don't know what I do or say. I sit down ten times in a day [and] write a sheet of paper full of incoherencies and almost madness which when I read over I throw into the fire – start up and walk ten miles in the hour in my room, backwards and forwards with you in my heart, in my hand, in my mouth . . . Do forget me, give me up at once – don't let me dishonour the happiness and elevated joys that you were born to – let me despair and die – it's no matter. I was born to be unfortunate – to know you, to love you, to lose you – to – and to lose you? No, I must not, cannot, will not give you up . . . Can't I supply the place of father, mother? You would be that and more to me, and what is all the world if the mind's unhappy, if we must sigh for *something unpossessed*?'

At this point, Susan had either to finish the affair or push it quickly to its logical conclusion, a dénouement in which O'Brien would become by proxy the sort of gentleman he had so often played on the stage, and Susan, sinking down to Kitty Fisher level, would be debarred from London drawing-rooms as a ruined woman. Once they had taken the decision, O'Brien provided the stage directions, complete with mysterious stranger. 'Your coming away I have planned in this manner; for you to be at Miss Read's at ten o'clock and send away your servants and bid your man go home and bring you a cap or something which may make him think you are sitting for your picture and will take him one way while you go the other. Then walk to the china shop at the corner of

St. James St., where you will find a friend of mine who will put you into a chair, or if you think it better I'll be there myself in a Hackney coach and bring you away to the church ... my friend, if you think it the best way, will be dressed up in a plain green suit of clothes, by which you will be able to know him.'

Susan and O'Brien were married on 6 April 1764, in St George's Covent Garden leaving hastily as soon as the ceremony was over for the safety of O'Brien's villa at Dunstable in Bedfordshire. There they stayed for a few days not knowing what to do: no script had been written for this sort of affair. Five years before, the Lennoxes' cousin, Lady Caroline Keppel, had eloped with her doctor, Robert Adair. That had been smoothed over eventually. Adair was, after all, a popular and successful surgeon. But an actor provoked desperation in Susan's relatives. Lord and Lady Ilchester immediately denounced their daughter. Sarah thought it prudent to deny her own part in the affair, telling Susan, 'I hope you will own I try'd to prevent what I hope in God will turn out better than is likely (in all human probability) this unfortunate step will.' Louisa with no guilt to bear was more charitable. As she told Sarah, 'I cannot think her wrong; you know my opinion of them kind of things is not a usual one, and I know it is an opinion that does not agree with the common ways of doing well in the world; but I do think that marrying the person you like is so much the first thing to be considered that everything else ought to give way to that.' Henry and Caroline Fox, remembering their own elopement, said the same. Everyone else demanded that, as a first step, O'Brien leave the stage. Even when he had done so, however, nobody could countenance the newly wed couple in the family circle.

The O'Briens considered moving to Ireland, but Kildare and Conolly refused to receive them. Next a scheme was canvassed to find O'Brien a job in the East India Company and then pack them off to Madras. Susan angrily rejected this suggestion and scandalised everyone not only by failing to show remorse for her actions but also by demanding support and money. Her parents refused both. After several tense weeks, Fox came up with a compromise that would placate his angry brother and satisfy the errant couple: he would give them a yearly annuity of £400 and buy them some land in New York if they would go to live in America and O'Brien left the theatre to set up as gentleman farmer. Outcast and penniless, Susan had little choice but to agree, but she made up for her capitulation by displaying the minimum of gratitude. The O'Briens landed in New York in September 1764 and for the next few years Sarah regularly received letters denouncing the philistine barbarity of the colonists, the lack of opportunity for newcomers, the harshness of the climate and their own extreme poverty. The O'Briens gradually came to share the colonists' political views, but they disliked New York and failed to prosper. Most of their energy was dissipated looking eastwards, plotting their return.

Crises like that of Susan's elopement with O'Brien produced a flurry of letters. Letters went between Holland House and Carton, Carton and Goodwood, Goodwood and Castletown, Castletown and Barton; each day the post brought fresh out-pourings of sympathy and anxiety. While the sisters did not express any kind of joint opinion, they wrote round to report the news and to reassure one another of their constancy, shocked into a renewed appreciation of their loving relation-ships and family solidity. Support was especially important in this case for Sarah, because she had been implicated in Susan's affair. In the face of London gossip about her complicity, and in full knowledge of her guilt, Sarah needed her sisters to demonstrate their love for her. So she wrote to Louisa, ex-pressing her distress at the reports that were circulating about her, trusting her sister to bolster her self-esteem. Louisa re-plied on cue: 'if people's cursed tongues go on talking, make yourself easy, for as 'tis impossible for anything to behave better than you did, you may be sure 'tis only spite and envy of your dear, sweet face; it can be nothing else when they find fault with the best heart, the most heavenly good mind and the strongest attachment to their husband and the best disposed creature in the world, all which I most sincerely think you are my dear sweet Sally.' Ominously, only two years after Sarah's marriage, Louisa felt it necessary to lay particular stress not only on Sarah's innocence but also on her good wifely behaviour.

Bolstering Sarah's flagging sense of her own worth in this way was one of Louisa's roles within the family. Whenever there was a period of difficulty Louisa had always offered unconditional love. But such expressions of affection were integral to the Lennox sisters' idea of themselves; very few of their letters were without them. In spite of their marriages and children, Caroline and Emily, Louisa and Sarah continued to think of themselves as sisters, whose lives were complementary and entwined. 'It is such a pleasure to have a dear sister one's friend,' Emily wrote once to Caroline. Sarah cherished the idea of her sisters being her friends in old age, saying 'nothing but a mother or a sister can inspire that sort of friendship that occupies the mind so much late in life.' Sisterhood and the love it brought was always there. They thought of one another in good and bad times alike; in disaster they wanted to be close together.

Louisa's position amongst her siblings was the most serene. In her long life she never had any lasting quarrel with any of them. None the less, Emily held the emotional high ground. Caroline loved Emily with great intensity; she was her confidante and childhood companion. Caroline, unlike Emily, had known very little of Louisa and Sarah as they grew up at Carton, and she tended to see Emily and herself as a pair to which the younger sisters were subsidiary. There were twenty years between Caroline and Louisa and, for Caroline, they made a distance which could be greatly lessened by familiarity but never erased. Emily was the bridge between Caroline and the younger members of the family. Caroline was her special friend, and yet she also commanded the affections of her younger sisters as second mother and sister. Louisa was eight when she came to Carton, Sarah six and little Cecilia scarcely a year old. Emily became the linchpin of their lives, mother and sister combined. Louisa, writing to her brother the third Duke of Richmond in 1768, when she was twenty-four, he thirty-three and Emily thirty-seven, explained their feelings. 'It is one of my sister's pleasures, the being with her, but if it was not my inclination, I should think it my duty to contribute as much as possible to make her comfortable, for added to the love I have for her as a sister, I owe her that due to a mother and do feel it for her. I must say that I do find her everyday more deserving and more comfortable and more pleasant than anybody.' Sarah felt the same. Cecilia, born in 1750, had no memory of her English life, and simply called Emily 'Mama'.

When it came to sharing secrets, Caroline confided in Emily. Everyone else confessed to Louisa when the burden of their own lives became too heavy. But sisterhood was not simply a matter of sharing troubles; sometimes it was found not in confidences but in lies. Nobody, for instance, told Louisa what they thought of Conolly. When she first arrived in London with her husband in 1759, Louisa wrote to Emily: 'Pray, my dear sister, let me know honestly what my sister Caroline, and Mr. Fox say and think of Mr. Conolly ... Though I have watched them I have not cleverness enough to know how it is with them.' In her heart Louisa knew the answer. She called her husband 'poor dear Tom Conolly' as well as 'my angel' and 'my dear Thomas'. But she would never hear these epithets offered by one of her sisters. Thus a fiction of regard was created, a fiction that maintained Louisa's self-respect and cordial sisterly relations and, in the course of time, allowed fondness to supersede initial disdain. This fictitious web bound the sisters together; by 1768 Caroline could say of Conolly, 'he seems to have the best heart in the world.' So love grew on a carefully nurtured bed of concealment. Hoping for a similar transformation, Louisa constantly expressed a fondness for Sir Charles Bunbury which she did not feel, saying, 'my love to Mr Bunbury', 'I beg you will give my love to him.'

Despite several serious rifts the Lennox children never surrendered their closeness. It was tested and strengthened by their parents' early death and it survived the sisters' absorption into other families. Even Lord George Lennox, often abroad with the army, was welcomed by his siblings whenever he returned to the family fold, although few of his sisters spent much time with him and Sarah said he had 'a remarkable, obstinate, vain and ponderous mind'. During serious illness or moments of danger like childbirth, the siblings called on one another for comfort and distraction. In crises the family closed ranks and did its best to stay together. Even comparative strangers noticed and commented upon what Louisa called 'the Lennox affection for one another'.

Yet the family operated within a distinct and carefully observed hierarchy, with the Duke of Richmond at the top and Sarah and Cecilia at the bottom. Sarah criticised her brother's 'high flown ideas of right, which are apt to soar above nature and of course never come to anything.' None the less she and the rest of her siblings approached him with the deference owing to the head of the family. None of the Duke's siblings ever referred to him, in letters at least, by his Christian name. They called him, 'my brother Richmond', 'brother Richmond' or sometimes 'my dearest brother'. Lord George Lennox, on the other hand, was described as 'Lord George', 'my brother George' or simply 'George'. Between themselves as well, the sisters also observed a hierarchy of deference that found expression in their forms of address. As the eldest, Caroline could refer to all her sisters by their Christian names. But they usually called their elders by their married names or titles. So Caroline called Emily 'dearest Patsy', 'my dearest sister' and 'dear siss', while her younger sisters were 'Louisa', 'Sal' and 'Cecilia'. But Louisa usually called Emily and Caroline 'my sister Kildare' and 'my sister

Holland', only occasionally using the more familiar 'my sister Caroline'. Only with one another did Louisa and Sarah consistently use their Christian names.

This hierarchy was based first on sex and then on age and thus position in the family. But it was potentially susceptible to shifts brought about by changing circumstances. If, for instance, Tom Conolly had acquired a title and some political stature, Emily and Caroline might have referred to Louisa less familiarly. But it so happened that outward events did not disturb the family's own ordering. Even when, in 1766, the King fulfilled the long-standing promise to Kildare and made him a duke, Emily's new title of Duchess of Leinster only confirmed her pre-eminent status amongst her sisters.

Certain rights and duties attached to the family's hierarchy. The Duke of Richmond was both allowed and bound to comment on his siblings' behaviour. His opinion was sought as much because he was head of the family as for any perspicacity of his own. It was his duty to present his feelings on family matters to the world and to unite the family, if possible, in the face of public disapproval of any member's conduct. Along with the Duke, older sisters had the right to comment freely on their juniors' conduct. 'So, dear sweet Louisa grows a little vulgar with her Irish companions,' Caroline wrote to Emily in 1764. Louisa was temperamentally more circumspect than Caroline, but it was duty as well as character that lent caution to her pen. She felt she had no right to criticise Emily; when she did, in a letter to her brother of 1769, she immediately qualified her judgement away. 'She is a valuable dear soul! I wish you were more with her. She would do you good, her humility about trifling faults (for indeed hers amounted to no more) is beyond what one can conceive.' But she hastily added, 'I feel myself quite culpable for saying such a thing as that my sister L[einster] had trifling faults.'

The conventional family hierarchies of sex and age were broadly accepted and honoured by the Lennox children. But they could also be nullified and set aside – by great changes of fortune, for instance, and by love. Love shifted its focus and altered its forms. But as a trust given and returned it levelled family distinctions. Criticise as she might, Caroline called Sarah 'a sweet companion' and Louisa 'one of the most rational, amiable and discreet women in the world'.

In 1765 family duties and loyalties were put to the test by the unexpected illness and death of George, Lord Ophaly, Emily's eldest son and heir to the new Leinster dukedom. Ophaly was seventeen, a year younger than Charles Fox, and had just left Eton. He was, by his parents' own admission, the only one of their ever-growing brood, apart from 'little Eddy', who showed much intellectual acumen, and he was destined for the army. In the summer of 1765 he was lounging lazily in London waiting for a commission. He was past the age when children died suddenly; besides, disaster was far from everyone's minds. Louisa and Sarah went on a six-week jaunt to Paris in the early summer, accompanied by Caroline and Charles Fox. What was uppermost in Emily's mind then was not her son but the emporia of the French capital. 'I have not yet heard from the Paris ladies,' she wrote to Henry Fox in May, 'and nothing could comfort me for not being of the party but thinking of all the fine china you intend they should buy there and make me a present of.'

When Sarah and Louisa returned they found Ophaly practising being a juvenile rake in London clubs and drawing-rooms. But by the beginning of September he was 'very ill', confined to Richmond House with a consumptive fever. They stayed with him until he died on 26 September, and all through his illness they sent letters to Carton in which hope and caution were carefully mixed. In this way they led Emily to expect Ophaly's death without presenting it as a certainty. Cecilia reported to them that Emily was 'quite resigned', but Emily only half understood what was going to happen.

It fell to the Duke of Richmond, as head of the family, to

write to Ireland with the terrible news. Ophaly's death was the first family crisis he had had to deal with; despite their political differences, notably over Wilkes's attack on general warrants, Richmond wrote to his old mentor Fox, anxiously seeking to share his worry and responsibility. 'Which ever way she hears it I dread the consequences. You know how much she had placed her affections on him in particular . . . I have been obliged to determine what was to be done about his burial. I told his servant it should be in a decent private way and in St. Martin's church where my grandfather was buried. I hope I did right.' Richmond also wrote to Kildare. 'I tortured my brain to find out some soft and easy way of telling it simply, but at last resolved on the plainest way.' Kildare got the Duke's letter just as he was going to bed on the night of 13 October. He kept the news from Emily until the morning, 'by which she slept well and was better able to bear what she was to go through.'

Richmond and Kildare tried to protect Emily from the news of Ophaly's death. But for her it was the fact and not the announcement that mattered, the creeping understanding that she would never again feel her child's warm body against her own, that his voice, his smile and her hopes were gone. Years before, when George was a toddler and Emily a doting mother of nineteen, she had written to Caroline: 'I just ask'd George if he had anything to say to you, and he says, no nothing to aunt Caroline but my compliments to Master Ste, 'cause 'e did send compliments to me, and me can say all my letters, and can master Ste say all his letters?' Now the lisping student of two and the cheerful Etonian of fifteen were gone, rotting in St Martin-in-the-Fields hundreds of miles and an ocean away.

PART TWO
'This house stinks enough to poison one of paint'.
Emily to Kildare, 15 May 1759.

When Ophaly was buried, part of Emily went with him. She
felt miserable and exposed, safe only at Carton in the company of those she trusted. Louisa and Sarah, who had been at
her son's bedside, hurried over to Ireland, arriving in mid-
October. Emily was pleased to have Sarah at Carton (and
Sarah was delighted to be back in her childhood home), but
grief and the early months of a new pregnancy made her listless and torpid. She had no enthusiasm for life and at times,
she told Louisa, 'she wished her existence in this world at an
end'. She had to go to Dublin, as she always did, for her
lying-in, and the town plunged her into even lower spirits.
Not until May, eight months after Ophaly's death, was Emily
able to tackle everyday life. Louisa told Sarah, 'my opinion is,
that she will [never] recover her spirits so as to enjoy a town
life or what is called gaiety, but I think that, at Carton, where
she is quiet, she will grow to have a contented calm feel and be
very much amused with the improvements and works going
on.'

Louisa was mistaken. Emily did recover her 'gaiety' and
her high-spirited sense of occasion. What she lost was her
equilibrium. After Ophaly's death, Emily was more anxious
and less satisfied with life. Pray as she did, irritation, anger
and a sense of incompleteness kept forcing themselves upon
her. She worried about her children and became a victim of
what she called '*sinkings* and horrors' that seemed 'at times to
deprive one of every power but that of feeling wretched'.

Emily came back to Carton with her new baby son in the
summer of 1766. Gradually her grief receded and she began to
take an interest in the alterations being carried out in Carton
Park. An artificial lake had been constructed with an island
and fashionable landscaping of hillocks and informal clumps
of trees. Workmen had built a gently hump-backed bridge

across one end of the newly dug lake. Raw piles of reddish earth from the lake bottom were covered in saplings, and a labourer's house where Emily often dined with her children was being transformed into a shell cottage. Waterstone, as the shell cottage was named, was planned as a joyful re-creation of the shell grotto at Goodwood, a celebration of family continuum. But because of Ophaly's death, it became the site and expression of Emily's grief for her son.

In the spring of 1766, Carton builders took the roof off the single-storey cottage and built a dome with a skylight that allowed light to filter into the single room below. The cottage was almost square, with a mullioned window looking out at the lake. Work on the interior began at the far wall opposite the window bay around the panel between two deeply embrasured gothic windows. Emily, with Louisa's help, designed and oversaw the construction of the shell ornamentations. In the first section to be completed, sections of bamboo, stained and arranged in a geometric pattern, were surrounded by shining mussel and oyster shells gathered into flower heads.

Although it had none of the rococo prettiness of the shell grotto at Goodwood, the back wall at Waterstone was ordered and regular, with its rows of concave oysters and fluted scallops angled up into petals. But as the workmen moved to fill in the segments of the dome, this regularity began to break down. Huge conches from tropical seas, corals with a myriad of tentative fingers, ceramic apples whose tips blushed red, twinkling crystalline specimens hewn roughly from their parent rocks, lumps of fool's gold, smashed chunks of green-glazed pottery and fronds of seaweed like matted hanks of hair: all these were stuck into the walls, first in loose lines and rectangles, but then higgledy-piggledy. They were jammed together, smothering the walls in a thick array of nature's offerings, as if an enraged collector had tipped out his cabinet of curiosities and pressed them feverishly into the waiting cement.

Looking upwards into the dome visitors saw bulging cowries and conches like giant wrapped-up ears sticking out of the sides. Ceramic fruits, lumps of crystal as big as a child's head and pieces of white coral, frozen stiff after their languid seabed life, hung from the dome's rim, suspended loweringly, as if they might pull the whole edifice down.

In the embrasure of the mullioned window, all attempt at panelling and floral patterning was abandoned. Shells and stones were crushed together. They overlapped and stuck on top of one another. One or two sponges were set in the walls, filamented, pursed, anus-like. Around them were slabs of crystal, like purple heaps of snow, lumps of ore, calcified worm cases, scallops shaped like ladies' fans and, in the crevices, humble winkles from Dublin Bay. From out of the embrasure wall came four shell-encrusted candelabra, each sinisterly twisted like arthritic bony hands. In one rock-covered corner were three miniature ceramic Chinese villages, with tiny painted figures, pagodas and a wooden bridge. They sat in a grotto of their own, balanced precariously on sea-weed-covered boulders, chiming with the broken porcelain stuck on the walls, but seeming otherwise remote and out of place.

Emily worked on Waterstone with maniacal haste. As the walls were covered something brooding and irrational took over from the delicate floral surfaces of the original design. Rococo prettiness became a solidified chaos whose patterns and broken surfaces were inscriptions of anger and grief, repeated over and over again, threatening to draw the visitor into the death-encrusted mouth of the tomb. Yet amongst this riot of morbidity were everyday objects: a seventeenth-century fireplace with blue-and-white tiles and barley-sugar columns supporting the mantelpiece; tables and chairs, a carpet, a dinner service and a spinning wheel belonging to Cecilia Lennox.

Waterstone struck visitors as charming and commodious rather than intense or oppressive. They dined in the small room and out of the window watched the lake sparkle through the trees. On fine days they sat by the lawn outside.

Louisa, for one, did not feel that Emily had lined the walls of the cottage with her anger and her grief. Writing to Sarah in September 1766, six months after the decorating had started, she said that Emily 'has amused herself very much with Waterstone, which is just finished and a dear thing it is, as you never saw. I am sure you would dote upon it. Its the most comfortable looking place that can be.'

Waterstone was Emily's own project. She conceived and designed it. Louisa, Cecilia and the elder Fitzgerald children helped in arranging groups of shells and rocks. Workmen from the Carton estate carried and lifted and stuck the specimens in place. But all the time they were also busy elsewhere: Waterstone was only one of many alterations carried out at Carton in the mid-1760s. Emily had to the full what Sarah called 'the Lennox passion for improvements' and the Duke of Leinster, in keeping with new, technocratic (and often seen as 'Whig') attitudes towards landscape was eager to try his hand at creating the sort of informal park that Capability Brown had made fashionable. At the beginning of the decade the Duke (then Earl of Kildare) had the park surveyed and set about redesigning it himself. Emily and he seemed to have divided up the task of alteration in the conventional manner. She, as the mistress of the house, had charge of the inside, the layout, decorative schemes and choice of furniture. He, as man of the wider world, took the park, the offices and the gardens as his domain. But this division was honoured more in the breach than the observance. While the Duke was the original designer of the park, its final shape owed a good deal to Emily's whims and her famous lack of patience. Moreover, when in 1755 Arthur Devis painted the couple seated outdoors surveying their domain, it was Emily and not her husband who was holding the plan of the grounds.

Before they began on outdoor work, Emily and Kildare decided to alter Carton House itself. Carton had disappointed Emily when she first arrived in Ireland as a young bride. Despite its interior magnificence it lacked grandeur on the

Holland House scale. On the ground floor was a suite of state rooms and a series of smaller rooms facing the garden in which the family lived during the day; Emily's parlour and a bedroom she sometimes used were there. The house had no basement, so the kitchens and offices were housed in two wings. The first floor was entirely taken up with family bedrooms while the attic storey housed the servants. At first Emily and Kildare considered massive alterations, including the creation of a 'great room'. But large amounts of money had already been spent. The ceiling in the salon, where plaster putti stuck their icing-sugar legs over the cornices and wrapped their fat arms round gilded swagging, had been installed in 1739. The grand staircase, hallway and interior panelling were all complete. So they decided to redecorate, supposedly a cheap alternative to redesigning, and to concentrate their resources on bringing the park up to date.

'I really think Carton House when 'tis spruced up will be vastly pretty and full as fine as I wou'd ever wish a country house to be,' twenty-seven-year-old Emily wrote as the decorating got under way in the spring of 1759. She was full of enthusiasm for her schemes, dreaming about the magnificence of newly painted rooms hung with Chinese prints or bedrooms hung in blue paper and upholstered in silk. But she did not enjoy the process of transformation, quickly losing patience with the army of carpenters, plasterers, paper hangers and painters who swarmed about the house. 'Here are my painters all going away and leaving the work half done, half undone. I am plagued to death with them and poisoned into the bargain. My paper man, too, has used me very ill . . . I am quite sick of them all,' she complained in May 1759. Refurbishment demanded patience and persistence, neither of which were Emily's virtues. Not only did she demand the instant realisation of her plans but she also got carried away by whims which diverted her from the management of the whole task. While the painters and stone masons were hard at work, Emily's energies were dissipated by the search for 150 yards of taffeta and the Chinese wallpaper and prints she called 'India paper' and 'Indian pictures'. 'My dear Lord Kildare,' she wrote, 'don't let Louisa forget the India paper, and if you see any you like buy it at once, for that I have will never hold out for more than three rooms, and you know we have four to do; for I have set my heart upon that which opens into the garden being done, for 'tis certainly now our best and only good living room.' The India paper arrived, although it wasn't enough. Emily spread it thinly, cutting out the prints and sticking them directly on to the painted walls.

Outside, under Kildare's punctilious direction, things progressed more smoothly. By the summer of 1761, the stream that ran between the house and the Dublin road had been dammed, dug and widened into a kidney-shaped artificial lake, with sloping banks and an island in the middle. Emily called the lake Kildare's 'piece of water' and was full of praise for her husband's ingenuity, claiming that he was the equal of the most celebrated landscape gardeners. 'The new river is beautiful; one turn of it is a masterpiece in the art of laying out, and I defy Kent or Brown or Mr. Hamilton to excel it. This without flattery; and now that you may not feel too vain, the shape of the island in its present state is not pretty. It wants that grace and easy pretty turn that you really have without compliment given to all the rest, and in one part especially. The end is extremely well hid at present, and when the banks are dressed and green it will be altogether a most lovely thing. I had great pleasure in seeing ten men thickening up that part of the plantation between the Dublin and Nine Mile Stone Gate with good, tall showy trees – elm and ash; but there are still quantities of holes not filled, and I suspect that to satisfy our impatience last autumn Jacob Smith dug more than he will get trees to fit this winter.' The holes were rapidly filled. Indeed too many trees were planted throughout the estate. By 1766, Kildare had pruned, clipped and trimmed to let light in to the plantations. Then Emily complained. The trees in the walks to the flower garden were now too sparse, she said. Kildare replied wearily, 'As for the walks to the flower garden, I cannot but say they were my doing, and am concerned that my Emily dislikes them. Since she does, I can say no more, but that she may alter them if she pleases, for pleasing her is what I [would] wish to do: what I am going to say is not in the least to prevent your altering of the walks as you have my consent. But trees in a year or so would cover the walks to the flower garden in such a manner as would prevent the cold winds from blowing as you say they do, and look thick again. But then, patience is required for that.'

Patience, in short supply at Carton, was found in abundance at Castletown. Louisa never committed any of Tom Conolly's money to a scheme until she was absolutely sure she wanted it. Then she went about building and decorating in a steady and concentrated way, enjoying the process because she was utterly certain of its purpose.

At the beginning there had been talk of demolition. Castletown, with its wainscoting and long gallery, its formal garden and flat park, was old fashioned. But once Louisa had put in the new staircase in 1760 she saw that the house could be at once publicly imposing and privately informal. So the original structure was reprieved and a process of decoration begun that was to last for more than twenty years. 'I am glad you like what has been done at Castletown,' the Duke of Leinster wrote to Emily in June 1766. 'I told Lady Louisa that when she came to live here after the alterations were made, that she would be obliged to me for finding out that the alterations could be made without pulling down the house.'

Castletown's alterations were Louisa's labour of love. As the years passed and she and Tom remained childless, Castletown absorbed some of Louisa's spare familial feeling. She fussed and worried over it and loved it like a member of the family. It was her creature and her creation. Away from the house she felt bereft and incomplete.

The hall at Castletown was paved like a huge chess board in

shining marble slabs of black and white. Once the staircase was in, Louisa finished off the entrance with walls of white plaster bas-relief. The Lafranchini brothers, who were responsible for a number of loaded Dublin interiors and the sugary excrescences of the Carton salon, were called in to do the plaster work. But Louisa used their modelling skills with a characteristic restraint. They created scores of shells, cornucopias, dragons and swaggings on the Castletown staircase wall, but she drew the line at fat putti with dimpled knees and acres of gold leaf. Characteristic too was Louisa's choice of subject matter, hunting for Tom and the family for herself. Emily and her husband, suspended in profile in winged roundels, face each other on the staircase wall. Between them is a hunting scene of stupendous carnage, a metonym for Tom Conolly himself. The effect is monumental rather than magnificent because the great expanse of the walls is white and the strongest pattern comes from the chequered simplicity of the hall floor below. The only gold in the entrance was reflected from the regiment of brass stair-rails, which march from ground to first floor in upright regularity.

Louisa kept the existing rooms on the ground floor: a dining-room to the left of the entrance hall that was connected by a curving passage to the warm and muggy kitchens in the west wing and, running along the back of the house, a series of state rooms that looked over the gardens to the distant vista of the Conolly Folly, an immense brick structure on the northern horizon. These rooms were furnished in conventional grandeur, although Louisa put up relatively unadorned white plastered ceilings. The only room downstairs on which she lavished care was the antechamber to the state bedroom where 'Speaker' Conolly held morning levees in royal fashion. This Louisa made into her print-room.

The print-room was assembled by pasting prints on to cream-painted wallpaper, surrounding them with elaborate frames with bows and swags cut from printed sheets and then hanging whole sections on to the walls. The work suited

Louisa's careful temperament and her interest in drawing and copying. Like most aristocratic girls Louisa was given drawing lessons, but unlike most she continued them long after they had done their work in the marriage market. Caroline pronounced Louisa an 'ingenious' girl and praised her copies from old master drawings. Louisa took lessons from Mr Warren, a Dublin drawing master who taught the Carton girls the delicate art of copying and the Carton boys the kind of geometrical drawing that would help them if they took up a military career or wanted to survey and alter their parklands. Louisa sent her sisters some of her copies, with instructions to hang them high so that the mistakes would not show. She also tried her hand at oil painting, painting directly on to distempered walls and handiwork of all sorts. From Paris she brought a number of wood blocks for printing on cloth. 'I am so busy painting some flowers with the French stamps upon white satin to hang a little closet with, that I should scarcely find time to write to you if I did not begin of a Sunday,' she told Sarah in 1768, adding, 'its the quickest work that I ever saw, quite a work suited to your genius, and, when done, altogether it looks very pretty, tho' coarse when you examine it.'

From the early 1760s onwards, Louisa was also patiently assembling prints of suitable subjects and sizes to create a print-room. Prints were sold either individually or in packets of four, six, ten or more. In 1766 she wrote to Sarah: 'any time that you chance to go into a print shop, I should be obliged to you if you would buy me five or six large prints. There are some of Teniers, engraved by Le Bas, which, I am told are larger than the common size. If you meet with any, pray send a few.' Word went out amongst the family that Louisa was building a collection. On his grand tour, William, Emily's second son who became the Duke of Leinster's heir after the death of Ophaly, was a dutiful searcher. He sent a large batch of prints from Rome in 1767 with carte blanche for Louisa to take her pick. Louisa's own account books show that she went on buying prints, in twos and threes, throughout the next decade. 'Paid Mr. Bushell for prints, £1:2:2½' appeared in 1766, as did 'paid for Lady Sarah Bunbury's print £1:1:0', '£1.2.9 for a subscription for prints' in 1771, '3 prints at 15s' in 1773, and so on.

Louisa was not alone in making such a place. Print-rooms were sufficiently numerous for printers to produce pattern sheets from which borders were cut out and assembled. Gentlemen coming into their property often had a closet with engravings picked up on the Grand Tour: a reminder of their youthful adventures and an advertisement of their completed education and supposed learning. Women had print-rooms too, often more intimate affairs, with genre scenes to supplement classical landscapes, and engravings of friends and relations. From the grandest houses to the humblest hovels prints were stuck on the walls; storybook illustrations, vignettes from Bible stories, moral tales and cartoons that savaged the governments of the day. Emily had some sort of print-room at Carton, made while Sarah was still there in the 1750s. Lady Clanbrassil, an active mutual friend of Emily's and Louisa's who lived at Templeogue on the outskirts of Dublin, had prints of her friends stuck up in her private closet. Amongst them was the engraving of Reynolds's portrait of Sarah sacrificing to the Graces. From Templeogue Louisa wrote to Sarah in the summer of 1766: 'I am with Lady Clanbrassil, who desires a thousand loves to you. She has employed me in cutting out a border to go round your print which she has put up in her closet. It was pleasant work for me as I looked at your dear Fiz. all the time.'

Louisa's print-room satisfied her immoderate desire for swagging (she also had swagging on her mantelpieces and purple ribbons round her bed) and her pleasure in planning, ordering and balancing. Each of the four walls was arranged around a central image. On the north wall was a Van Dyck of the children of Charles I in which the Lennox sisters' great-grandfather stood between his two sisters. Opposite them was Sarah, sacrificing to the Graces. On the east and west walls were two prints of Garrick. The first showed him between tragedy and comedy, after Reynolds, the second with Mrs Cibber, after Zoffany. Other prints were set in symmetry round these images. Some were included because they fitted a space (a portrait of Pitt the Younger, for instance); others because they were part of a set. But many carried a moral or showed an activity that played a part in Louisa's life. Like the gallery at Holland House then, the print-room had an autobiographical element; it was in part a self-portrait as well as a disparate collection of images. There were vignettes that showed maternal and filial responsibility, images of hunting and card playing and many genre scenes that carried moral messages and hints of mortality.

On the north wall, for instance, around the Van Dyck print there were five occasional pieces, six genre scenes and two overtly moral pieces, 'The Death of Seneca', extolling stoicism, and 'Le Bon Exemple', which offered an example of industriousness. The occasional scenes included a mother and child, a courting couple, Vermeer's 'Lady Writing a Letter', a print after Rembrandt called 'The Philosopher in Meditation' and a French print, 'Mlle. sa Soeur'. Genre and rural scenes, people drinking in taverns, family groups or hunting parties, almost always contained visual messages which undercut any jollity they might display. Fallen trees, peeled fruit, spilt milk, broken egg-shells, snuffed candles – all these delivered reminders of death and sermons against vanity and folly. 'The Pretty Kitchen Maid' (after Boucher) on the north wall, for instance, spiced a seduction scene with hints of deflowering (the prominent key hanging below the maid's waist, the lacy cabbage laid out on the table) and reminders of death and decay (the empty pan and glass, the guttering candles and the broken sticks in the foreground). Louisa's print-room was full of images like this. It was at once an entertainment and an encyclopedia of examples and warnings.

The print-room was only one of several improvements to

Castletown that were being made simultaneously through the 1760s and 1770s. As the Castletown account books show, plastering, gilding, glazing, tiling, carpentry and painting in various parts of the house continued unabated for decades. Conolly's incomplete and haphazard accounts record a steady stream of large disbursements: in 1766, £150 for 'carpenter's bill for work at Castletown', in 1767 'plastering £14', 'slating £42.14.4', 'Bowers paid in full on account of carpentry work £175.8.1', 'paid Tilbury the bill for glazing this house £67.3.3', 'paid Tilbury his bill in full for glazing hot houses, melon beds etc', 'paid Mr. Carnoss his bill of painters' work done on the whole house £251.0.2½', 'paid Cavinagh his bill of iron work £101.1.1'; in 1768, 'paid Bowers on account of hot houses, espaliers etc £150.0', 'paid Mr. Cranfield for carving and gilding drawing rooms, dining room etc, £223.1.5'. Year after year the payments went on, until by the turn of the century, Conolly had spent £25,000. It was a huge sum but, for him, little more than a year's income. Besides, Castletown, as he made clear in a letter of 1773, took the place of children. 'I had no occasion to save money, having no children, and I flatter myself that the money I spent annually was rationally employed by living, not extravagantly, but like a gentleman.'

In the 1770s, Louisa's major decorative project was the Castletown long gallery. The long gallery ran the length of the house at the back. Its eight windows looked north across formal gardens and parkland to the huge brick folly known as the Obelisk that looked like nothing more than a giant factory chimney. Louisa turned the gallery into an informal living-room that made the state rooms almost obsolete except for the grandest of occasions. The original gallery, bare and cheerless, was transformed into a painted room which, by virtue of its length and two fireplaces, could be used for several occupations simultaneously. By the end of 1774 the gallery was complete except for the painted decorations. The coved ceiling was heavily gilded but otherwise left blank. From each of its three compartments hung a big two-tiered Venetian chandelier, swagging solidified into glass, in pink, blue and clear crystal. The ends of the room were dominated by fireplaces, over which hung portraits of Tom and Louisa, his by Mengs, hers by Reynolds. On the walls were French mirrors, several bookcases and plinths with classical busts. The spaces in between were to be filled in with paintings by an English decorative artist, Mr Reily. Louisa had seen Reily working at Goodwood and engaged him to come to Castletown as soon as his job for the Duke of Richmond was completed. Reily arrived, somewhat reluctantly, in Ireland in the summer of 1775. Unlike most painters he worked not at piece rates but by the month. At less than £100 a year he was reckoned a bargain. As Sarah put it, 'his taste, his execution, his diligence and his price are really a treasure, and will not be met with again. For Mr. Conolly and Louisa [cannot in conscience] to give him so little as a £100 a year and [they] mean to add a little more to it.'

Sarah and Louisa chose the subjects for the long gallery decorations together. Their sources were the books of engravings from the antique and from Renaissance painters which were staple fare of gentlemen's libraries, frequently brought back from the Grand Tour. *L'Antiquité expliquée*, the books of engravings by the French engraver Montfaucon, provided Louisa and Sarah with many of their originals. They knew it well; Reynolds had used the volumes to provide him with patterns for the jug and serpent-ringed urn in his portrait of Sarah sacrificing to the Graces.

Sarah and Louisa picked out four engravings from Montfaucon and Reily turned them into oil panels: a marriage ceremony taken from a Roman marble frieze, which showed the bride and groom being prepared for their wedding; the young bride weeping as she leaves her home for the first time; the wife and her first child; and a group of women spinning and preparing cloth. The two remaining panels, derived from engravings of Sir William Hamilton's collections of Greek

vases, showed the daughters of Atlas, captured and taken
from their homes by pirates in the service of the King of
Egypt because of their beauty and wisdom.

Together these panels, framed in gold and grouped across
the south wall and around the portraits of Tom and Louisa at
each end of the room, offered a melancholy commentary
upon marriage from the woman's vantage point. Beautiful
and intelligent women captured by barbarians, a daughter
mourning her childhood home, a bride nervously awaiting
the ceremony and, finally, wives carrying out their marital
duties of child-rearing and domestic husbandry – none of
these offered a positive gloss on an institution that was central
to women's lives. There are no pictures of courtship, no snug-
gling couples or classical lovers and no happy family groups.
Together they seem to provide an alternative narrative to the
publicly joyful union between Tom and Louisa, suggesting at
the very least that married life is built on a sacrifice of childhood happiness. Sarah's bleak vision of her own marriage
may, especially by 1775, have contributed to the pessimism of
the images; even so, Louisa made no attempt to stop this
negative picture taking shape on her walls. On the contrary,
she was delighted with the scheme, and even took the lion's
share of the credit for its selection, writing to Emily in June
1777, 'Mr. Reily is now painting our gallery in a most beautiful way. Sarah's taste is putting the ornaments together and
mine in picking them out so that we flatter ourselves that it
must be charming as Mr. Reily executes them so well.' Discreet as ever, Louisa, even if she was aware of the sad portrait
of marriage she was putting up, remained silent about it and
never offered a hint about her own interpretation of the
pictures.

As if to take the sting out of the message of the panels,
Louisa and Sarah planned a plethora of more lighthearted
decorations in the gallery, vignettes, roundels and statues
which gestured towards happier aspects of married life at
Castletown. Tom Conolly's passion for sport and its attendant revelries was given ample due. In a niche between the

two doors on the south wall stands a busty statue of Diana, goddess of the hunt. Dotted round the room are panels showing bacchanalian rites, medallions with Cupid and Bacchus, small paintings of a lion adorned with grape and vine leaves, a lady with silver dishes, a peasant pouring wine from a sack and dancing women.

Sarah arranged Louisa's selections in groups, Reily copied them and another decorative artist (perhaps Thomas Ryder) filled in the blanks with leaves, flowers, swags and scrolls. Complementing the allusions to Tom Conolly's convivial sporting life were indications of Louisa's more contemplative aspirations: busts of Homer, Venus, Hesiod, Plato, Cicero, Niobe, Sappho and Julius Caesar. Supporting this gallery of distinguished ancients were Pindar, Hesiod (again), Philemon, Gracchus, Cato, Hypocrates, Zeno and Socrates, whose painted eyes gazed out over their heads from medallions on the wall. Opposite them, on the north wall, Apollo and the nine Muses, each surrounded by their props and symbols, stared back. Joining all the figures were layer upon layer of temples, masks, cornucopias, eagles, griffons, leaves, cupids and bows. When Louisa, Sarah and their decorators had finished not a square foot of wall was left uncovered. The paintings surged round niches, over bookcases and up mirrors. They were stopped only by the wainscoting and cornices. The effect was idiosyncratic and amateurish, but it gave the room exactly the informality that Louisa wanted. When it was finally finished at the end of 1775 she wrote delightedly to Emily: "tis the most comfortable room you ever saw, and quite warm; supper at one end and the company at the other and I am writing in one of the piers at a distance from them all,' adding it 'really is a charming room for there are such a variety of occupations in it that people cannot be formal.'

The same desire for informality governed Louisa's schemes to transform the forbidding flatness of Castletown's park. Just as she broke up the length of the gallery into several spaces, so she began to fragment the surface outside, putting a shrubbery here, a lake there, creating vistas, walks and flower gardens. In the early 1760s she built herself a 'cottage' by the river, a garden house which served some of the same purposes as Waterstone at Carton. The cottage – really a well appointed little house that theatrically declared its modesty – was a place where Louisa went without her servants. Multi-coloured pheasants strutted stiffly about; the Liffey wandered sinuously by.

Observers came gradually to notice a contrast between this sort of cottage and those beyond the Castletown gates. But Louisa, when it was first built at any rate, saw her cottage as a symbol for a rural idyll whose contrast was with the city and the Court rather than a mean subsistence life. Sitting in her cottage one warm June morning in 1764, when she was twenty years old, she wrote to Sarah (who was still smarting from rumours of her complicity in Susan's elopement): 'You say in your letter Do I think there are no liars but in London? I think that there are in every great town and I therefore detest a town and wish to live as little as possible in them. I must only describe to you my delightful pleasant situation. I am sitting in an alcove in my cottage with a park before it, in the wood three quarters of a mile from the house, a lovely fine day, the grass looking very green, honeysuckles and roses in abundance, mignonette coming up, seringa all out, the birds singing, the fresh air all about ... my work and my book by me, inkstand as you may perceive and a little comfortable table and chairs, two stands with china bowls, filled with immense nosegays.' The only thing lacking from this bucolic picture was a rippling stream. The sluggish Liffey had to do the duty of a babbling brook and Louisa soon became impatient with its dilatoriness, calling it 'my troublesome tho' beautiful Liffey', and tried to make the river foam by piling up rocks on its bed. The river continued unperturbed, held up very little by her efforts.

Castletown and Carton, with their cottages, lakes and

Emily and her 'dear Jemmy', painted by Arthur Devis
in 1755 with an imaginary Carton behind them.

Emily, aged 22 by Joshua Reynolds, 1753.

The Most Noble
Prince James
Duke of Leinster
Lord
Marquis of Kildare
&c &c &c

By Sir Joshua Reynolds

Kildare in the companion portrait of the same year.

ABOVE: Sarah, voluptuously painted by Francis Cotes when she came to London at the age of 15.

BELOW: The south front of Carton House.

Sublime and ridiculous: *Lady Sarah Bunbury Sacrificing to the Graces*, by Reynolds, 1764–5.

Louisa's print room at Castletown.

ABOVE: The Long Gallery at Castletown with Tom Conolly's portrait by Mengs over the fireplace.

BELOW: Castletown from the air, with the 'Conolly Folly' on the horizon.

ABOVE: Emily's 'India paper room' at Carton.

BELOW: The shell cottage at Carton: morbid excrescences a
world away from the curlicues of the Goodwood shell house.

Emily in ermine by Reynolds, early 1770s.

ABOVE: Louisa: ample in middle age.
BELOW: Sarah's house in Celbridge, now part
of a church school for the handicapped.

'Dear Edward': Emily's favourite son with
a democratic cravat and hairstyle in the
early 1790s, by Hugh Douglas Hamilton.

Emily at 77, by Sir Martin Archer Shee.
'The most beautiful woman your age in the kingdom',
her adoring husband declared.

shady walks, stood at the centres of complexes of buildings whose scale was industrial rather than domestic. Around the main houses were offices, wash-houses, kitchens, coal-houses, stores, hothouses, ice-houses, potting-sheds and stables. Beyond them stood bakehouses, breweries, the granary, the tannery, the kitchen gardens and, by 1766, at Castletown, 'very comfortable' 'octagon water closets'. In the park of each was a home farm which produced foodstuffs for consumption in the main house. Carton even had in the coach-house courtyard, a carriage wash. This lozenge-shaped arrangement of stone walls enabled the stable boys to reach up and polish the roofs of the Duke and Duchess's carriages. As they drew up to grand front doors, their hosts, standing on the steps above them, would see the Leinster carriage gleaming from top to bottom.

Keeping this immense, almost factory-like unit going was the responsibility of its master and mistress and the task of their senior servants, the steward and the housekeeper. Emily and Louisa approached and executed their managerial duties with very different expectations and abilities. Emily was absorbed by her children and bored by household management. Louisa, on the other hand, was a meticulous housekeeper. She prided herself on the efficiency and loyalty of her staff or 'family' as they were known. Rich though she was, she worked closely with her housekeeper, butler and steward to cut costs and keep the household running smoothly. Nothing came in or went out of the house without her acquiescence and she made up the household accounts herself.

Households like those at Carton and Castletown had a complex command structure. At its apex were the master and mistress themselves. Beneath them came the steward who was both the main household officer and the bridge between the household and the world outside. Under him worked the housekeeper, the butler and the clerk of the kitchen. At Leinster House in Dublin a 'maître d'hôtel' took the place of the steward.

Bere, the Carton steward, was a man of considerable power. He collected rents (often not all that the Duke was owed) and, from the sanctuary of his office on the ground floor of the house, he ran the estate and paid the servants. In his charge were not only his own personal servant but also the pantry boy, the gentleman of the horse and the small army of servants who worked outside: lodge keepers and labourers, the farrier, the miller, the chandler, the brewer, the carters, wheelwrights, smiths, grooms, stable hands and even the shepherd who gazed glassy-eyed over the sheep in the park. The mill, the granary, the brewery and the tannery were all his province. On baking days it was his job to open the mill, weigh the grain as it went in, weigh the flour as it came out and to check those amounts against the weight of the finished loaves, in order to ensure, as the Duke of Leinster himself put it, 'that nobody has stolen the flour'. In the same way Bere weighed the tallow and the candles into which it was made and he marked each cask of ale and small beer with levels and dates.

Bere had a heavy ring of keys that denoted other incarceratory duties. Keys to the gates of the park, keys to the mill, the granary, the brewhouse, the chandlery, the smithy, the carpenters' shop, the stables and the offices: all these had to be unlocked and relocked, their contents checked against pilfering and their floors cleaned and polished. If something broke down – a carriage, a kitchen range or a bell pull – it was Bere's responsibility to summon the wheelwrights, smiths or handymen and see that it was mended. Coaches and carriages – the heavy four-horse chaise for long journeys, the lighter, more compact landau for jaunts to Dublin and Emily's beloved one-horse chaise in which she was driven on fine evenings around the Carton grounds – needed constant maintenance; many journeys were interrupted by broken axles or shafts and the Duke was a demanding traveller.

Day after day, as the huge household worked, ate and played, Bere had to tabulate all that it consumed: numbers of candles used by stable hands, the quantities of loaves, the weight of butter, the barrels of beer and bags of apples. When supplies ran short it was his job to restock the pantry and the stores. Wherever possible supplies came from the Duke's own tenants who reared cattle and grew grain in the rich lands of county Kildare. Once a month Bere took his accounts to the Duke, who signed them promptly, only to complain later to his wife about the cost of his own extravagance. 'Bere has not brought near so much money from his circuit as he used to do,' he complained in 1759, as if this rather than his own expensive habits and schemes for improvement explained the parlous state of his finances.

In compensation for his arduous duties Bere had a substantial salary, his own servant and a parlour to himself. He lived on a friendly footing with the family and often dined with them. But the Duke took care that Bere remained a servant. He was forbidden to shoot or hunt, he was told 'not to encourage visitors' and his first duty was 'to live always in the country'.

The housekeeper, the butler and the clerk of the kitchen were collectively responsible for the day-to-day running of the house. The housekeeper took, or anticipated, commands from Emily herself. Her provinces were the laundry and the rooms in the main house. The housekeeper's maids, divided into upper-house maids and lower-house maids, washed and cleaned, laid fires and made beds. Immediately below the housekeeper in the female hierarchy were the wet nurse (one was more or less continuously resident at Carton in the 1760s), Emily's own maids and the nursery staff. Lastly, grouped among the lower servants – who were the cleaners and washers rather than the fetchers and carriers – was the plate maid. Her job was to wash the plate in bran and water, and then polish it to a sparkle with lamp spirits, whiten and alcohol. She worked for the butler but came under the housekeeper's protection.

The Carton housekeeper was paid £30 a year. She had a

maid of her own and, in deference to her gentility, she was in charge of the tea caddies and sugar loaves. After 1762, she also had a bell pull, a luxury which, Emily explained to her husband, had become a necessity because of the laziness of the maids. 'Mrs. Clarke grumbles sadly about the maids; they won't get up in a morning and she catches her death with cold going to call them. I have given her leave to have a bell, which she is mighty desirous of, tho' as I told her it will do no good, and that the only way to make them get up early was to make them go to bed early; that they won't do – why, because they have nothing to do, and so sit up gossiping and prating – give them work to do, make them mend and make the linen, you'll find they will be ready enough then to go to bed as early as you please.'

Working closely with the housekeeper was the butler Stoyte. Stoyte operated from his sanctuaries the pantry and the stillroom, where the plate, linen, tableware, bottles, candles, condiments and groceries in everyday use were stored. The pantry and the stillroom formed the command centre for provisioning the household. Under-servants brought candles there from the chandlery, bread from the bakery and butter from the home farm. Maids carried freshly washed and ironed damask tablecloths and napkins from the laundry. Pantry boys took empty wine bottles out, brought new ones in and replenished the ale casks. Footmen, to the fury of the Duke, hurriedly put on their uniforms there, as guests arrived and bells began to ring. The Duke, aware of the noise and merriment issuing from under the pantry door, once sent the butler a stiff reminder that 'he must not by any means admit the pantry to be a meeting or gossiping place for the under servants'.

Such laughter and intrigue were snatched and hurried, at least until the household was settling down for the night. Footmen and other liveried servants had to be in constant readiness to attend the family, as did the Duke's personal servants, his groom of the chambers and valet. They lurked in corridors and antechambers waiting for a bell or a sign: footmen in the public rooms, the valets de chambre in the family's bedchambers and dressing-rooms. Eight pounds a year, board and lodging and an allowance for their splendid uniform was their reward. Not surprisingly it was a job for young men; married men could not live in the house and, besides, one of the job's few compensations was the after-hours social life.

In the late 1760s Carton footmen wore black worsted shag breeches, tailored coats and fine felt hats with a silver chain loop, a button and a horse-hair cockade. Thus attired they waited on family and guests alike, expecting from the latter handsome tips for their assiduity. The abolition of tips, or vails, cost the Duke £4 a year for each footman by the 1770s, a sum they could add to their wages. Still, they left in numbers, tired of the drudgery, moving on to other houses perhaps or departing for matrimony and family life. In a desperate attempt to keep his servants with him the Duke introduced a bonus scheme in the 1760s, adding a year's wages to the pay packets of those who would stay with the household for five years.

If the pantry was one social centre for servants, the others were the kitchen and the servants' hall, run by the clerk of the kitchen, the cook, the confectioner (a specialist sweetmeat and pudding maker recruited in France) and their staff. It was the duty of the clerk of the kitchen to make sure that all the Carton servants, both indoor and outdoor who lived in the house, got fed. Married servants who took board wages to pay for their board and lodgings elsewhere – outside the gates in Maynooth, for the most part – were only fed on Sundays, 'to live in harmony' with the rest of their workmates.

Planning, ordering and co-ordinating meals was a complicated business. Like much of the work around the house, meals were timed by the ringing of bells and they were eaten in shifts and at different times according to circumstance and season. A simple rule of thumb prevailed: the lowlier the servants the earlier they ate because the earlier they began work.

For those at the bottom of the heap, the Carton labourers, the day began as soon as the sun crept up above the park gates. 'It is my orders,' the Duke wrote in 1765, 'that all the workmen and labourers do come to work as soon as day in the morning, at which time the bell is to ring as warning and a quarter of an hour after that time to go to work; the bell to ring at nine o'clock for them to go to breakfast; quarter past ditto to go to the place of work, and twenty minutes past ditto to go to work. The bell to ring at one o'clock for them to go to dinner, half an hour past ditto for them to go to their place of work and three quarters past ditto to go to work and to work as long as they can see till further orders from me . . . NB any workmen or labourers that don't conform to these orders let them be discharged.'

From daybreak to dusk with only an hour and five minutes rest was a punishing stint, even allowing for the Duke's anger being in proportion to his failure to enforce the rules. Other servants, particularly upper-servants in the public and family rooms of the house, had a better time. They too rose early, to set and light fires, and to clean rooms before their master and mistress got up for breakfast. But their duties were less exhausting than those of outside labourers or the staff in the kitchen and laundry. For maids and footmen there were times of quiet, after meals, or when the family went out, when they could loiter in anterooms, tell jokes and swap gossip and stories.

When meal-times came round servants made for different rooms according to their rank. At the 'second table' in the steward's parlour sat the higher servants and any guests they might have. The wet nurse and all the maids dined in the still-room, while the other servants headed for the servants' hall or the kitchen. Though meals were snatched, food was plentiful and loaded with good cuts of meat. The Duke was careful to prescribe a hearty diet for his workforce and eager to impress visiting stewards or factors with the quality of his servants' table. 'Particular care must be taken that all meat is well and cleanly dressed and good of the kind.' Servants dined at one o'clock if the family was in residence, at four if they were away. On Saturday, Monday, Tuesday and Wednesday they ate 'boiled beef, cabbage and roots'. On Thursday they were given 'boiled mutton with turnips etc, if convenient, or boiled pork, pease pudding and potatoes instead of mutton'. Friday was a fish day, in deference to the religion of the vast majority of Carton employees; usually it was salt fish with potatoes and cheese. On Sunday they enjoyed 'a piece of beef roasted and plumb pudding or any kind of pudding'.

Supper, served between nine and ten, was bread and cheese: a quarter of a pound of cheese for each servant, with a pat of butter for the men. While the servants waited for supper the butler or the clerk of the kitchen held a roll call, checking off the servants' names against a list. After supper the servants' hall was supposed to be locked, but secluded as they were in their own wing of the house, it was easy for servants to flout the Duke's orders. Sometimes there was gaiety, drinking and dancing. House parties in the main part of the house meant parties for servants too. Ladies' maids, valets de chambre and coachmen all came with their employers to house parties and they brought with them bustle and fun, new faces for intrigue and fresh material for gossip. In the turbulent summer of 1769, when every post and every visitor seemed to bring bad news, the servants' merriment was too much for the Duke, and he sent his steward a curt note. 'I will not for the future permit any dancing to be in any part of the house without my leave or the Duchess of Leinster's, which occasions neglect, idleness and drinking.'

Almost every year, to the delight of the staff left behind, the Duke and Duchess left Carton. If Emily was about to lie in she went to Leinster House in Dublin, where she remained for the birth of her child and her month-long confinement. Sometimes Parliament was sitting. Sometimes (though less and less) they went to England. With the state rooms closed and the family away, the housekeeper and her charges had little to do; they might mend and sew, she sometimes showed visitors around. But life slowed and they were able for a few weeks to ape their mistress's habits, getting up after sunrise and eating dinner in the afternoon.

When the family were away, Carton servants dined at four o'clock, even later than their employers. They ate the very best that the Carton kitchen gardens offered, feasting like merchants or squires on melons and peas and jugs of milk and cream. 'Dinner to be on the table at exactly four o'clock. To consist of one or two dishes such as roast or boiled [beef] with garden things, mutton and broth, mutton chops, harricot or hashed roast or boiled pork with pease pudding and garden things or steaks roast and boiled, veal with garden things when veal is killed at Carton. Once a week to have mutton or beef pie and on every Sunday roast beef and plumb pudding or any other kind of pudding. Supper and breakfast to be of such meat as is left at dinner, either cold hashed or broiled as they like adding some potatoes or any kind of garden stuff, cheese or eggs.'

While they ate, everybody drank. Ale, strong and dark, was served, a pint to each servant. Throughout the day, from the time the breakfast bell rang, servants could drink unlimited quantities of small beer, a very weak, pale beer brewed for refreshment rather than nourishment or intoxication. Those whose duties were hot or demanding were given extra rations. The cook had a quart of ale at eleven o'clock and at two o'clock, laundry maids had a quart twice a week and the wet nurse a pint at night.

The rules which the Duke laid down for the government of his household conjured up an imaginary scene of order, in which servants came and worked to the ringing of bells, goods were weighed, measured and written up and punctuality and good manners universally cultivated. But try as he might, the Duke could only create a dutiful household on paper. Whenever he lifted his eyes from his desk he saw pilfering, disloyalty and disobedience. Powerless and enraged he would hurry back to his desk and compose lectures to his staff on their professional conduct. 'The way to perform and get everything done is to be regular and not to do anything but that all the world may know it; for once that anything is done that Lord or Lady Kildare is not acquainted with, and should be displeased if known, he puts himself in the power of others and then all authority is over and not to be got again.'

For higher servants such disquisitions might have served some purpose. With lower servants it was useless, despite ringing calls to loyalty: they worked for the money, the food, the lodgings and the social life. The Duke disciplined them with threats of punishment and dismissal. 'Carton Dec. 23 1764. I desire that the shepherd be stopped sixpence for every sheep and lamb that is found in the plantations and that he goes round the fences everyday to see that they are not broke or damaged. If they are he is to put a hurdle or bushes in the place and give notice immediately to the office when they are broke or damaged, for no excuse will be allowed for the sheep getting in. Signed K.' 'Jan. 10 1767. I desire that after this day Mary Kelly (commonly called Cocker Kelly) be not admitted within my park gates without my order in writing . . . If I find she has been admitted I will stop half a crown from the Gate Keeper at whose gate she has got in and if I cannot find out, from each gate keeper half a crown.'

The disorder continued. Footmen, young and unmarried, were spotted loitering without leave in the countryside; other undesirable women, Anne Strong and Mary McDannatt, got into the park against orders. Labourers pretended to be sick or left without explanation. Carters, allowed five and a half hours for the journey between Carton and Leinster House in Dublin, unaccountably took longer, throwing the Duke into a rage and bringing down heavy fines on their heads. He suspected that they diverted their carts between leaving Dublin and arriving home. Despite the rules and regulations, the ringing of bells and the docking of pay, the Duke felt barely in command. Sometimes he lost control of himself, too, and his anxiety about the estate peeped wickedly out from behind his unbending, authoritarian prose. At the end of an angry letter to Mr Brown at the home farm he wrote: 'I expect these things all done and not altered or changed without my being first acquainted with it, as I shall lay all blame upon you and will take no excuse for neglect.'

Cumbersome, leaky and above all expensive, the household at Carton creaked through the years like an ageing man-of-war, industrial in its scale and cost, a centre of employment and production that had few parallels for size and scope. When major works were under way two or three hundred people might be employed there (although the permanent members of the household, employers and staff numbered about a hundred); even the largest linen manufactures in the country had not yet grown to that size. Only armies and fighting ships, with their crews of four hundred, were bigger.

When there was serious trouble at Carton among the servants, Emily sometimes came to their rescue. Interceding with her husband to save their jobs, she was like a monarch issuing a royal pardon, or at least a temporary stay of execution, to an unfortunate subject. Sometimes, too, she turned her extravagant attention to details of household management. These bouts of interest in domestic economy usually occurred when her husband was away and time lay a little heavy on her hands, as it did after the birth of her daughter Sophia late in 1762, when she spent £150 (about the annual salary of a middle-ranking government servant) on linen. 'You don't imagine, I hope, that I have been buying any fine suits of damask linen for the £150; none but useful and necessary things I assure you, such as coarse sheets of two sorts, children's sheets, a few fine ones for ourselves, coarse table linen for the steward's parlour, pantry linen, . . . beef cloths and mutton cloths which Stoyte said were wanting.' 'The table cloths are not bought yet, so I wish you wou'd bring over some of that pretty kind, of a proper size for a table for six, which is what we most want; two for a table of ten would not be amiss, and ten of the others . . . Napkins we also want, about eight dozen will do. We have not a napkin or a table cloth in the world that I have not examined, and I am a perfect mistress of the state of our linen at present.'

Such impulses towards household management usually ended up as yet another contribution to the Duke's mountain of debt. As Louisa put it to Emily after a spending spree, 'you was never *famed* for your economy.' Over at Castletown things were very different. Louisa not only played a considerable part in running her household but she also thought carefully about the relationship between servants and their employers.

Louisa regarded social differences, exemplified in the positions of mistress and servant, as part of the divine plan. Her strong faith in God's power was balanced by a belief that the universe was rationally ordered and thus that God's purpose fitted in with modern ways of thinking. God created high and lowly, she said, in order that the exalted, like herself, should display their benevolence and in order that all ranks of society could perform their reciprocal duties. Difference was created so that man could show himself good in accommodating it. 'The little circumstance you tell me about servants, I quite agree with you in,' she wrote to Sarah in 1772, 'for certainly the not letting a person feel *leur dépendance* may be done without taking them out of their station; for it depends on the delicacy of your manner more than in what you require them to do and surely 'tis due to them, . . . for what merit have we in being placed above them?' None, she went on, for 'my opinion has always been that the difference we see in the station of human creatures (certainly all made for the same purpose) was never intended for the indulgence of some and the dependence of others, but for the use of calling forth our good qualities and the exertion of our several duties . . . As to servants I think we treat them too much as if they were dependents, whereas I cannot think them so much so, for I am sure they give us a great deal more than we give them, and really, if we consider it, 'tis no more than a contract we make with them.'

As she often did in her letters, Louisa was thinking aloud. The notion that social class was ordained was conventional (and convenient) enough; the idea that servants, though humble, were not dependent, that indeed the dependence was the other way round, was much less commonplace. With it Louisa edged towards the opinion that servants were people who offered their services freely for a reward, not simply an anonymous class pre-ordained to live in servile dependence upon the rich.

This sort of reasoning could make employer–servant relationships personal as well as contractual. Unequal though the relationships between servants and their mistresses remained, they were also personal in Lennox households. Caroline's maid Milward lived with her, first at Goodwood and then at Holland House, all her life, and Caroline often wrote about her (sometimes in anger but always with engagement). Mr and Mrs Fannen, steward and housekeeper at Holland House, became personal friends, not accepted in the drawing-room but consulted, visited and above all needed. Equally, Emily's housekeeper in the 1770s and 1780s, Mrs Lynch, became as Emily put it, 'a second mother' to her children. As Louisa suggested, it was the mistresses rather than the servants whose dependence was greater. Mrs Lynch and the Fannens had contracts to provide services for money and with that their duties ended. Caroline and Emily had a duty to pay and to respect their servants, but they also built up an emotional dependence which did not end with their employees' contracts. When the Fannens retired after a lifetime of service in 1766, it was Caroline who felt the blow most severely. 'Mr. and Mrs. Fannen grew infirm and old; were, as 'tis very natural, desirous of a house; they have a small, neat house just this side of Kensington. He is still steward and manages all, and she is to the full as great a comfort to me as when she lived with me. Her health is good and she will, with the quiet life she now leads, I hope be a stout old woman, and last years. I frequently walk to see her; sometimes one of my sons and I dine with her [in her] snug. She always comes if I want her, which I do when I want to alter, change or settle anything in the house with regard to servants' furniture etc.'

Louisa never had this kind of intimacy with her house-keepers or maids. Instead, as Caroline disapprovingly noticed, she ran a household that was informal from top to bottom. Tom Conolly, mindful of the welfare of his precious hunters and racehorses, was on easy terms with his trainers and grooms. On feast days Louisa and Conolly shared their servants' merriment, dancing with them in the servants' hall. Outside Louisa was actively involved in the management of the home farm. While the harvest was gathered in the autumn of 1796, she wrote to Tom: 'we have finished that immense stack of oats . . . in the barnyard, and yet could not put up all the corn, so that another small stack (or rather cock) will be made today . . . and by two o'clock I hope every grain of corn will be at home.'

Louisa was the only one of the family interested in day-to-day domestic management. Watching the haystack rise or noting a fall in the price of tea were as much a part of her everyday life as reading or writing in the long gallery. As she strode about, dressed in her heavy-grey or brown-serge walking clothes, shadowed by her dog Hibou, she rubbed shoulders with her servants constantly. When some of them supported the Irish rebellion in 1798 she felt a sense of personal betrayal. She could not understand that betrayal was almost inevitable because they were servants and she the mistress, because they were poor and she was rich, because they were Irish and she was English, a Protestant and a colonist. In her response to betrayal, she unwittingly demonstrated the truth of her pronouncement of thirty years before, that she was more dependent upon her servants than they on her.

Louisa did everything she could to show herself a conscientious mistress of her household. Besides going out and about amongst her tenants and servants, she regularly stayed indoors checking and cross-checking the Castletown accounts. At Castletown there were accounts for everything: there were tradesmen's receipt books, servants' wages books, books that showed the costs of Conolly's hounds, dairy accounts, books showing taxes paid and due, monthly, quarterly and yearly account books which tabulated all the household disbursements and, finally, memoranda of quantities of food bought and consumed in selected years. Louisa went over them all.

Running Castletown, with its 46 servants, over 90 hearths, three four-wheeled carriages, running water and constant improvements, was a costly and time-consuming business. Louisa's steward discharged between two and fifteen bills every day. Outgoings accelerated towards the end of each month when accounts were made up. Monthly, quarterly and annual accounts tabulated expenditure into categories – foodstuffs, wages, apothecaries supplies, taxes, charitable donations and so on. Totals varied more according to extraordinary expenses and personal extravagance than to rises or falls in prices and consumption of ordinary goods although, towards the end of the century, a bout of inflation did mean higher prices. Aside from building expenses and Conolly's personal spending (mainly on horses and gambling) Castletown and a Dublin house cost between £2,500 and £3,000 a year to run. The accounts for the year 1787, typical in that Louisa rarely left Castletown except to go to Dublin in the spring and typical too in that building work was in full swing, show how the total was reached.

In 1787, £656 was spent on servants' wages, £254 on their clothes, £221 on 'Dublin bills' and £400 on charities. Louisa's personal expenditure came to £321, 'sundries', which were regular but uncategorisable expenses like polishing the Castletown banisters and cleaning the clocks, came to £107. Food and drink added considerably to the total. Marketing and groceries cost £210 and 'country bills' for flour, wheat, oatmeal, peas, butter, candles and letter carriage came to £354. Some £202 was spent on the barley, malt and hops used for brewing, £445 on wine and £598 on oxen, cows, sheep and hogs. The year's total, as Louisa calculated it, '£2956:11:7½', was made up with £77 on servants' travelling expenses, £42 on 'physicians and drugs' and £195 on 'extraordinaries'.

Into the category of 'extraordinaries' went part of whatever building and decorating was done at Castletown that year. Thomas Conolly often discharged a proportion of these costs and his payments were entered into his own, irregularly kept personal account books. In 1787, when Louisa was forty-four, several new buildings were put up at the home farm. Louisa described them in a letter to Emily who was in London. 'My dearest sister, it is really such an age since I wrote to you that I expect you to be angry, and yet I hope you won't ... I only comfort myself that your hurry in London had made it less perceivable; and that when you come to eat some of the excellent pork, bacon and ham that I hope our new piggery will afford, the good butter, cream and cheese that our new cow house (I hope) will produce, and the fine beef that our new bullock hovel will (I make no doubt) also furnish, I think you will pardon my neglect of writing, and that my time has been well bestowed. Joking apart, we have engaged in a great deal of building of that sort, which has required my constant attention, being the chief overseer and having, as you know, great amusement in it. I am very proud of having made fifty cheeses this summer, which next year will nearly keep the family in that article, and my dairy is grown quite an object with me.'

Notwithstanding Louisa's descriptions of the new buildings as 'hovels', they were spacious and expensive, as the 'extraordinaries' in the account books show: over 30 tons of slates and more than 30,000 bricks went into them, at costs of £62 0s. 8d. and £30 11s. 0d. respectively. Constructing the buildings cost £222 11s. 0d.

A lot of bacon, ham, beef, butter and cheese would have to

be produced to justify these costs. But the household at Castletown was indeed a voracious maw, consuming huge numbers of animals, dozens of consignments of groceries and hundreds of tons of fuel a year. From the dairy came 19 cwt of cheese, 7,934 gallons of milk (some of which went to feed calves), 1,496 gallons of cream and 1,454 lb of butter, which had to be supplemented by 1,951 lb from outside suppliers. The slaughterhouse and the butcher provided 524 lb of veal and sweetbreads, 160 sheep, 204 cwt of oxen, 94 geese, 112 turkeys and 1301 'fowls and chicken'. These and other chickens produced 10,460 eggs for consumption, but they were not enough: 6,206 more eggs had to be bought.

Home-produced food was never enough because enormous numbers of people were constantly dining at Castletown. Sarah explained that towards the end of the century as many as 82 were regularly fed there: '60 in the servants' hall, 12 in the steward's room and never less than 10 in the parlour or long gallery.' This figure was reached by adding on to the Conolly's own establishment labourers working in the park, tradesmen visiting the estate, guests of the family and the servants they brought with them.

Like Carton, Castletown had its own brewhouse where both ale and small beer were produced. In 1787, 182 hogsheads of small beer and 85 hogsheads of ale were brewed, although some small beer and 85 hogsheads of ale had gone sour and undrunk by the end of the year. Higher servants, guests and the Conollys themselves also drank imported English beer – porter and a special brew from Dorchester – and wine. The vinter's bill for 1787 was £445, a testimony to long evenings with convivial company, tall tales and steady drinking.

Keeping Castletown warm and light was another major undertaking. Fat stripped from sheep carcasses provided some of the tallow for the 2,127 lb of common candles used during the year. The rest came from the local butcher. About 250 lb of bees-wax candles were burned, mostly in the long gallery, the dining-room and parlour. The Merrion Street house, sitting empty for most of the year, used far fewer candles and by the 1780s it was equipped with oil lamps for the public rooms. Coal was used exclusively for heating. Local brown coal from Kilkenny was supplemented by Welsh coal sent from Swansea; both reached Castletown by way of the new canal that ran west out of Dublin along the edge of the Duke of Leinster's estate. Castletown's hearths, which included not only the fireplaces in the house but also those in the brewing house, the laundry and the hothouses, burned over 300 tons of coal a year, at a cost of £282.

A good deal of coal was consumed heating water for washing. Bed linen, cotton clothing and underwear were all regularly washed in hot water. Silk stockings and gowns were washed in cool or tepid water. In 1783, 78 lb of soap powder and stone blue were used in the Castletown laundries, along with over 75 lb of starch and whiting. Only the richest clothes were spared soaping and pounding: they were brushed and aired.

Foodstuffs that could not be produced at home or bought locally were supplied by the grocer. He delivered to Castletown a glorious multinational shopping basket of goods: sugar, tea, coffee, chocolate, cocoa, currants, raisins, almonds, sago, barley, rice, vermicelli, macaroni, anchovies, mustard, brawn, saltpetre (and salt), nutmeg, citron, cinnamon, caraway seeds, pepper, white ginger, ground ginger, cloves, allspice, mace, capers, brandy (13 gallons), oil, vinegar, alcohol, isinglass, hops, drops, oil for the blacksmith, stone blue, starch and powder blue (all for the laundry), prunes, biscuits, split peas, lentils and treacle. Chocolate consumption was small at 20 lb a year. But the 21 cwt 3 stone 22 lb and 4 oz of sugar the two households used added up to about 2,400 lb which came out at about 40 lb a year for each occupant of the house (although that total did include any sugar eaten by visitors and outside servants). Some of this sugar went into the preservation of local fruit but the rest, combined with eggs, butter and cream rounded off the splendid richness of the Conollys' diet with syllabubs, trifles, sorbets, fruit tarts and meringues. 'Being thin ... is not a natural state for any of our family to be in,' said Louisa, although even she expressed some annoyance one summer when she found that the winter's gourmandising had increased her weight by 9 lb. Sarah, the plumpest of them all, went on a diet in 1776, only to decide that it was bad for her: 'I took it into my head to be thin ... I heard by chance that Lady Ancram had succeeded in making herself thin, and yet not hurt her health, by eating everyday a little bread and butter half an hour before dinner to damp her stomach. I did the same and so effectually damped mine that in a fortnight's time I grew ill with not eating at dinner. So I left off this scheme.'

Castletown's servants were a small cost in proportion to the food and wine bills. In 1787 Louisa paid £80 19s. od. for 153 dishes of fresh seafood and £47 2s. 7d. for her cheese from the grocer. Eighty pounds bought her the annual services of 10 footmen or maids, while £47 was almost half the yearly cost of her steward. There were other costs incurred in the employment of servants. They were fed, warmed, clothed and housed and, as part of their wages, they received uniforms and, sometimes, cast-off clothing. They also got 2 lb of sugar a month each (but had to buy their own tea to go with it). None the less labour was cheap, so cheap that employing local people became a form of charity. At times of great economic hardship in Ireland, Louisa employed scores of local families on the Castletown estate, seeing the offer of employment not as a gain to herself (which it undoubtedly was) but as her contribution to the relief of suffering.

If one rhythm sounding through country houses was that of the bell and another that of the seasons, a third was that of life itself. It was in the country house that children were mostly conceived, educated and groomed for the world. There the pleasures and griefs of family life were played out. One measure of the quotidian was the account book with its record of constant small disbursements. Another was the letter book. Scarcely a post went by without a letter from Caroline to Emily, from Emily to her husband, from Louisa to Sarah, which did not record the most ordinary events – good nights, bad nights, bumps, scratches, rashes, headaches, flowers coming up and hay coming in. Day after day, week after week life accumulated in tiny, steady droplets, giving the sisters, as the years went by, a rich medley of commonplace events to remember and write about.

Carton ran to the body's time as, with annual or biennial regularity Emily gave birth, endured her monthly confinement (from which she was welcomed impatiently by her amorous husband), ovulated and became pregnant again. 'You will always be breeding; I wonder you are not ashamed of yourself,' Caroline wrote.

Whether she became pregnant or not, every woman was conscious of her body's clock, and charted her transition from childhood to womanhood by its monthly rhythm. Louisa began to menstruate at fourteen in the year before her wedding, thus becoming 'a woman', as Caroline put it, before she was married. A few years into her marriage she had a miscarriage and, although she occasionally took the waters in hopes of returning fertility, she never conceived again. By the end of the 1760s, when she was in her mid-twenties, she had almost given up hope of ever having a child.

Sarah also failed to produce a baby. As the 1760s wore on her sisters began to suspect that the reason lay in her marriage rather than her body. Whereas Louisa compensated for her childlessness by becoming an extra mother to the Carton brood, Sarah shunned young couples with children. Instead she sought the company of single men and childless couples like the Duke and Duchess of Richmond and continued, as much as possible, to lead a rakish, metropolitan life.

None the less, like her sisters, Sarah was attentive to her body's changes. For all of them, menstruation was associated with physical and mental distress. 'At *certain* times, my poor nerves are very bad, and it would be hard to say how they are affected. I am so full of *odd* whims, I will try the lime flower tea,' Louisa wrote. Periods were habitually referred to as the 'French lady's visit' and having one's period was 'being the French lady', being that is, in a familiar but different state. As Emily's daughter Charlotte wrote in 1779, 'I have within these few days been rather worse by being the French lady, at which time there is no telling how very ill I am.'

Periods were at best a slight discomfort, at worst a serious inconvenience. Menstrual rags made ordinary life difficult. Some women, like Charlotte Fitzgerald, took to their beds. Others, like Caroline, stayed at home and raged at their body's bad timing. In 1759, when Louisa was first in London after her wedding, Caroline wrote to Emily, 'I must tell you Louisa and Conolly come here Monday, stay till Saturday, then go to Goodwood, where they stay two days. I shall not be able to go with them, I much fear, which is a great disappointment to me. But 'twill be a time I can't. I shall be glad to be old, to be rid of *that* plague. Yours C. Fox.' By the late 1760s Caroline's discomfort increased and she began to think that the menopause was upon her. While old age might have seemed attractive a few years before, getting to it promised to be difficult, as she hinted in 1766. 'I seem to have been out of order a week, ten days and a fortnight's end, never get beyond three weeks scarcely. I own I dread disorders of that kind, particularly as I am now past forty-three, something of that kind may be beginning.'

Only Emily looked forward to her period. Any discomfort it brought was offset by the emphatic message that for the moment at least she was free from pregnancy. Despite her love for her children, Emily often longed for a respite from childbearing, so she was happy to be able to report to Kildare in 1762 (barely three months after the birth of her daughter Sophia) that her fears of pregnancy were unfounded. 'The complaint I mentioned in my last letter goes on very well and puts me quite out of all doubt, which is a vast comfort; but I

am exceeding low with it, more so than I ever was in my life.'
Others waited anxiously with Emily for her period to arrive.
'I shall be fidgety about you till I hear of the next French
lady's visit,' wrote Louisa in the 1770s.

All too often, though, Emily's predictions were right, and
she began another pregnancy. As time went on and her family
grew, she developed a thorough knowledge, fashionable and
practical, of the protocols and procedures of childbirth.
Rather than give way to worries about the dangers of childbirth she organised her pregnancies around a series of
practical rituals which allowed her to go her own queenly
way and to become the undisputed obstetric authority within
the extended family. Her plan for pregnancy and childbirth
was very simple and very effective; in all her labours she never
had a still birth and only lost one new-born baby, Caroline in
1755, who died after four weeks.

A successful pregnancy, Emily believed, was one which
was lived as usual. 'More people have hurt their health by fear
of miscarrying than by its happening,' she declared. She
advised good food and plenty of rest and exercise. If walking
was out of the question (as it certainly was for Emily with her
regal indolence and her muscles slackened by multiple pregnancies), a daily rattle in a bouncing carriage was a necessity.
Some '7 or 8 mile everyday' in a post-chaise 'along a jumbling
road . . . to jumble you' could, Emily asserted, make 'labour
so much easier.' She herself was often to be seen being driven
about the Carton desmesne by her hump-backed coachman in
her beloved pea-green one-horse chaise.

When she suspected that her lying-in was close (or, as
Louisa put it, she was 'about to pig'), Emily moved to Leinster House in Dublin to prepare for the birth. Following
contemporary aristocratic fashion Emily always had a man
she referred to as 'the doctor' in attendance at the birth. He
was a surgeon or an 'accoucheur', as especially trained male-
midwives called themselves. Hovering outside the door of the
birth chamber would be a nurse-keeper, whose job it was to

wash and clothe the child, and a wet nurse. Inside, apart from
the doctor and any other attending servants, would be Louisa,
Cecilia or Sarah. The Duke of Leinster never mentioned being
in the birth chamber, but if he was in the house at all, he was
probably near at hand: Henry Fox was close enough to Caroline when Charles Fox was born to be able to see his son
before he was dressed, which since it was mid-winter must
have been as soon as he was washed and dried. Emily's older
childen would be near by too, eating cake and drinking what
her son William described as 'this delicious caudle'. Caudle
was a rich spicy wine prepared especially for the attendants to
drink during and after childbirth.

As she became a connoisseur of childbirth Emily concentrated more and more on the circumstances rather than the
process of labour. She insisted that her room be light, with the
curtains drawn back if it was daytime, and plenty of candles if
it was night. This was contrary to the common practice of
darkening the birth chamber, as was her belief in open windows and fresh air. As her confidence grew she continued
daily life, and the story she wrote of it, right up until the onset
of labour. 'Only think how delightful it is, my dearest sister,
to have a letter of yours to answer, wrote on the day that you
were brought to bed,' Louisa wrote in 1770, when Emily was
thirty-nine, adding, "tis a sign of your having been so well.'
Once or twice Emily described her labours as 'tedious' but,
although she said her children had caused her pain, she never
referred to childbirth itself as a painful process, psycho-
logically or physically.

As soon as her children were born, Emily handed them
over to servants. Following the advice of John Locke in his
Thoughts on Education, she insisted that they should be
lightly clothed, without pins or swaddling. Although she was
a believer in breast-feeding, Emily did not breast feed any of
her own children. There was a popular belief that breast-
feeding could damage the eyes. Emily, who suffered all her
life from painful and debilitating eye inflammation (alleviated

by applying leeches), handed every one of her children over to a wet nurse on her doctor's orders. It was something she regretted all her life. 'Mama,' said her son George to her one morning in the late 1770s, '"don't the mothers of calves give them suck?" "Yes", says I. "And why then did you not give me suck for you are my mother like the cows are the mothers of the little calves." Was not this quite cutting? It went to my heart and I was ready to cry, but I told him that the naughty doctors and people would not let me and so I got Ryley to do it for me.'

Once her labour was over and the child dispatched to the nursery, Emily entered into her month-long confinement. Confinement was not only a time to rest, it was also a time to relish because all duties, both social and managerial, were suspended. Emily lay, sat and then lounged first in her bedchamber, then her dressing-room and finally her parlour. She was cosseted by her family and servants and visited by friends and relations. Because of the anxiety about her eyes, reading was proscribed for a week or two, so Emily chatted and played cards. On 10 August 1761, 11 days after having given birth to her fourth son, Henry, in London, Emily had got out of her bedchamber and into her dressing-room. She had just begun to write, and received a constant stream of visitors and relatives like her aunt Lady Albemarle. 'I write a little a day ... that I may not make my head giddy by too much at a time. Sarah's being with me is mighty comfortable. The boys sit with me the whole evening. Last night I had my two Viscounts. Lady Harrington and her daughters the night before, besides Lady Albemarle and hers; which, added to my sister [Caroline] who has been here every evening, has kept me in a continual hurry of company and tired me a little; but I make up for it ... by sleeping in a morning till twelve or one o'clock.' Three days later she had got into her 'outward room', hired a new housekeeper and was dining on pheasant.

Confinement held two other joys for Emily. In the first place it was characterised by a social informality and jollity and in the second it made her the cynosure of all eyes. Everybody came to her and their duty was to entertain their hostess rather than, as usually, the other way around. On 17 August Emily wrote again to her husband. 'I have never been alone, some one body or other continually dropping in; . . . I had a Dutch cousin Bylande to see me t'other day, who the last time he was here in England found me lying-in "apparemment la famille de Mi Ladi doit être assez nombreuse," says the man, which diverted Sarah and Lord Powerscourt prodigiously. They told him it was true for that I had done nothing but lie in ever since. Lord Powerscourt lounges away some part of every evening here. If he comes early we make him read *Tom Jones* to us, which diverts the boys.'

After her month's confinement Emily went through the ceremony of churching, when women were readmitted to the outside world after childbirth. 'For as much as it hath pleased Almighty God of his goodness to give you safe deliverance, and hath preserved you in the great dangers of childbirth: you shall therefore give hearty thanks unto God,' intoned the Maynooth minister or the Holland House chaplain at the beginning of the service. To which Emily was supposed to reply, 'I am well pleased that the Lord hath heard the voice of my prayer; the snares of death compassed me round: and the pains of hell got hold upon me.'

Churching brought women back into daily life. It signalled that the ritual of childbirth was successfully completed and, in Emily's case, that the cycle might begin again. After churching came sex. The Duke of Leinster had no hesitation in acting upon the service's injunction that 'children and the fruit of the womb are an heritage and gift that cometh of the Lord, . . . Happy is the man that hath his quiver full of them.' Most of his children were born between 11 and 15 months apart. In May 1766, two months after the birth of Lord Gerald Fitzgerald, the Duke wrote to Emily from London, 'I long, and yet fear to hear, if any consequences has happened from my being so happy with my Emily.' This time they were lucky: Emily had a year's respite between the birth of Gerald and the conception of Augustus.

Emily loved her huge family. She cherished each child (although George, and after his death Charles and 'Eddy' were her favourites) and mourned even those lost at a very early age. When tiny Caroline died at four weeks she told her husband that although she had recovered quickly from the shock, she had been very upset, which convinced her 'that there is a great deal more in what is called nature or instinct than I ever imagined before, for what else but such an impulse could make one feel so much for a poor little thing that does but just exist?' Parents, nurse-keepers, family doctors, maids, relatives and even siblings all kept an eye on young children, watching anxiously for fevers or wasting diseases. Even the most trivial of childhood complaints – sores in the mouth or boils on the skin – were cause for alarm, because any infection could spread throughout the body and there were constant fears that a minor problem could be the token of something much more serious.

Little children did die. Vulnerable at birth, they were in danger throughout the early years of their lives. Emily lost many children in their early years. Caroline, born in 1750 died in 1754; Henrietta, born in 1753 died at the age of ten; Augustus, born in 1767 died in 1771; Fanny, born in 1770 died five years later; Louisa, born in 1772 died about five years later; George, born in 1773 died in 1783. Only half her huge brood survived into adulthood.

Parents prepared themselves emotionally and mentally to expect the deaths of their toddlers. In 1749, when William was three months old, Emily then aged eighteen, wrote to her parents on the subject, which had been lingering on her mind since his birth. 'Since I know what it is like to be a mother I can feel it more strongly and surely nothing can be so dreadful ... when they do happen He that sends them will also send us strength to go through these trials. This is the only and greatest comfort on such an occasion, for if it was not for this thought, people that have tender hearts must lead a miserable life only from the apprehension of what might happen to those they love.'

Love and anxiety went hand in hand; mothers accepted that they came together. In Caroline's case the one fuelled the other. Ste, who was by her own admission her favourite child, was a constant source of worry to her; the older he got the dearer he became and, as his health continued to be precarious, with corpulence and deafness taking the place of his earlier twitching, the more she worried. 'One's children ought to turn out very well, to recompense one for all one suffers on their account,' she grumbled, adding, 'I have never been six months without some anxiety or other about Ste since his birth.' Harry Fox, in contrast, who had always enjoyed rude good health, got less than his fair share both of illness and of love. 'As for Harry,' Henry Fox wrote in the mid-1760s, 'he is the happiest of mortals,' and left it at that. The same equation between love and anxiety held in Ireland too. Charles Fitzgerald was seriously ill in 1764 and his condition bound Emily ever more closely to him. In 1764 Louisa wrote about Emily's daughter Louisa Bridget: 'I am sorry to think how much I love her, for a little child of that age must be liable to so many dangers.' Louisa had good cause for her anxiety: Louisa Fitzgerald died a year later at the age of four and a half.

Children did not always die. Charles Fitzgerald was taken to Malvern, a spa recommended for its air and its waters. Against all expectations he recovered, only to go down with smallpox when he got back to Ireland. Smallpox was a devastating and deadly disease. But it, too, was survivable. After initial anxiety about the strength of the virus, whether it was, as Louisa put it, the 'good' kind (where the spots remained few and far between) or the 'bad' kind (where the spots joined up, covered the body and moved to the lungs), eight-year-old Charles progressed well. Isolated in Dublin he told jokes and stories and made light of the soreness of his spots.

Congratulating Emily on Charles's recovery, Caroline took the opportunity to recommend inoculation for the rest of the Carton brood. Horace Walpole's friend Lady Mary Wortley Montagu had brought back the practice of inoculation (in which the patient was injected with a mild dose of the virus from a sufferer) from Turkey in the 1720s. Her example garnered the support not only of the Whig aristocracy and their doctors but also of another authority with equal influence in the Fox household, Voltaire, who had praised her in his *Lettres philosophiques* of 1733. Not surprisingly, Caroline was warmly in favour of the innovation and had her own children inoculated at early ages.

Inoculation was a tedious business, involving a month's preparation on a low diet to bring the child to a suitable physical state and an anxious period of waiting for the spots to appear after the injection. It was not without danger either. Children given a mild dose of the virus as protection against a full-blown attack did every now and then succumb and die. But quite apart from her fondness for advanced medical practice, Caroline regarded it as the lesser of two evils.

Emily was less enamoured of doctors than Caroline, preferring her own methods of caring for children to professional advice. She prescribed children a good diet, exercise (especially sea bathing at all times of the year) and plenty of physical affection. Hugs and kisses – what Louisa called 'delightful mumbling' – were never in short supply at Carton. Seeing Edward Fitzgerald act *Tom Thumb* one afternoon in 1771, Louisa wrote to Sarah: 'Eddy did *Tom Thumb*, and you can have no idea how pretty it was to see him. His figure, his voice, his action and grace, with a vast deal of spirit was really enchanting, one was ready to eat him up . . . I dined at Carton today and mumbled Lucy pretty well, she is just of the right age.'

When children did fall sick Emily was prepared to send for the doctor. But both she and Caroline fished in their store of folklore and consulted their own medical textbooks as well.

The Foxes' library at Holland House was well stocked with medical opinion. Besides two editions of Tissot's *Avis au Peuple sur la Santé*, a volume Sarah mentioned consulting at Carton, were Mead on poisons and the smallpox, Cheyne's *Essay on Regimen*, Manderville on diseases and Barry on digestions. There were five volumes of miscellaneous medical tracts, a book on sea-water bathing, Pringles' *Diseases of the Army* (bought not because of any interest in the army but because army doctors were renowned for their advanced medical techniques), Quincy's *Dispensary* and, for sick travellers, guides to continental spas. As the children grew up they could consult Venette's *Tableau de l'Amour conjugal*, a sex manual complete with advice, anatomies and amorous illustrations. After 1769, Buchan's *Domestic Medicine* nestled snugly on every shelf, joined in 1771 by Cadogan on gout. Sarah sent Buchan to Louisa who, along with thousands of other grateful readers, pronounced it 'very sensible'.

If children survived the worst that nature, the doctors and the apothecaries could throw at them, they had to be educated. Emily and Caroline were both interested in education and Caroline started out by educating her sons herself at home. Her children knew their letters by the age of two. By five they could read fluently, browsing not only in children's books but also in novels and plays which their parents were reading. Caroline did not just teach reading and writing. She used prints to train her children's understanding and maps to help them with geography. At the age of three Harry Fox was thumbing through Hogarth's works (of which the Holland House library boasted a complete set) and explaining the contents of engravings (even, his doting father said, their meaning) to his nurse. By 1762, when Harry was seven and Rousseau had made his mark at Holland House and Carton, Caroline had added exercise to his regimen and she taught him geography using jig-saw puzzles, recently invented for that purpose. She reported to Emily from Kingsgate in Kent:

'Dear little Harry is a pleasant child to have here; he really works very hard all day out of doors, which is very wholesome and quite according to Monsr. Rousseau's system. He eats quantities of fish and is so happy and pleased all day. At night we depart a little from Monsr. Rousseau's plan, for he reads fairy-tales and learns geography on the Beaumont wooden maps; he is vastly quick at learning that or anything else.'

In the winter months Harry was at school at Wandsworth. Caroline believed firmly that 'school is the best place for boys' and all her children progressed from Wandsworth to Eton. In 1764 Charles Fox, then fifteen, left Eton for Oxford. He had outgrown Eton but was too young to enter Parliament. Besides, Caroline was not in favour of his choosing a political career, hoping to steer him instead towards the law and see him Lord Chief Justice in due course. She was not really keen on Oxford either, but could not come up with an alternative educative scheme for her precocious boy. Somewhat to everyone's surprise, Charles loved Oxford. His passion for literature and his intermittent but fierce concentration on other subjects, particularly mathematics, astonished his fellow gentleman-commoners and his tutors. 'I really think,' he wrote, 'to a man who reads a great deal there cannot be a more agreeable place.'

By their own and their parents' admission, the Fitzgerald children had few of the intellectual interests of their Fox cousins. Emily could see little profit in pushing her boys fruitlessly towards scholarly pursuits, and she had a bevy of girls for whom a domestic education was the only one ever planned. Nobody expected that girls should have anything but a basic grounding in the classics and mathematics, and despite the acknowledged variety and excellence of her own education, Emily concentrated as much on their dancing, deportment, drawing and singing as on more scholarly pursuits. Her daughters grew up to be excellent French speakers and they had the usual drawing masters, singing and music teachers, and dancing masters. This standard education for girls of their station was supplemented by hours of varied reading in the Carton library.

Boys' education could not be so easily dealt with. After Ophaly's death and Charles Fitzgerald's illness, Emily turned against formal schooling because it meant English schooling and she no longer wanted her sons to leave Ireland. So she began to search for alternatives to Wandsworth and Eton. She had already read Rousseau on education and now she turned to him as an authority to endorse her own decision to educate her sons outside school. Rousseau wrote two works about education: *Émile*, published in 1762 and *La Nouvelle Héloïse* of 1761. *La Nouvelle Héloïse*, one of the most sensational and popular novels of the century, was about the relationship between a tutor, Saint Preux, and his pupil Julie. It was, as well as a work about moral and sentimental education, a steamy love story. Julie and Saint Preux fall passionately in love. Forbidden to marry by the unwritten laws of society, they part, he to wander the world in despair, she to accept the hand of a suitor found and sanctioned by her father. This arranged marriage brings Julie tranquillity and the happiness of motherhood, and it is an education in sociability and responsibility. But when Saint Preux reappears, Julie dies tragically, knowing that their forbidden passion is unextinguished and burning bright.

Like its prototype *Clarissa*, which dwelt with sadistic enjoyment upon the violent sexual conquest of a young woman, *La Nouvelle Héloïse* condoned what it appeared to condemn. The illicit love between tutor and student, rejected as not only unworkable but also a threat to class and property, was yet the only relationship in the book that seemed attractive. Rousseau implicated his readers in the forbidden, exciting them and involving them in the couple's love by describing, with hyperbolic realism, their beating hearts and stolen kisses. 'I felt,' wrote Saint Preux, in a passage calculated to cause havoc in parlours and drawing-rooms, 'My hands shook – a gentle tremor – thy balmy lips – My Eloisa's lips – touch, pressed to mine, and myself within her arms? Quicker than lightning a sudden fire darted through my soul.' *La Nouvelle Héloïse* was a brilliant book, written with fast-moving, rhetorical flourish, and it took Europe by storm, scandalising and seducing as it went.

As seasoned readers of sensational fiction, Caroline and Emily were sure targets for some of the novel's more melodramatic flourishes. But its endorsement of social propriety and its apparent condemnation of illicit romance were less likely to have struck a chord. Caroline complained in 1764 that Rousseau and Richardson, with their long-drawn-out love affairs, millions of words and high-flown sentiments, had destroyed the earlier vogue for melodramas like Prévost's *Le Doyen de Killerine* which she and Emily had read so avidly as children. 'The Marquis de Roselle, a new stupid story book, shall be sent to you with your other books ... It's *rempli de beaux sentiments*, the style of novel I hate, unless its very excellent of its kind, and I think Rousseau, Richardson and Crébillon have quite ruined the good old-fashioned story books like Doyen de Killerine and Mlle. de Salens etc etc; now they all pretend to wit or sentiment.' Emily passed a judgement on Richardson that was succinct and severe. When *Clarissa* was finally published in its entirety in 1749 she dubbed it simply, 'that stupid book'.

This short verdict on a long work was not simply aesthetic. It was also rooted in Emily's experience. Clarissa's tragedy turns on her refusal of an arranged marriage, the kind of union that Emily herself had happily accepted two years earlier. Clarissa's insistence that marriage should be founded on romantic love as well as respect, and must rest on fidelity, seemed pig headed to a woman who was well aware of her husband's philandering and cheerfully wrote in 1751: 'my turn for getting a lover will come in good time.'

In the early 1750s, taken up as she was with her growing brood of children, the improvements at Carton and her husband's political career, Emily could easily reject the claims of sensibility that Richardson advanced. Besides, her marriage was happy and admirably successful within its own lights. But by the 1760s the cult of sensibility had reached even aristocratic circles; it swept all before it and brought romantic love, female modesty and marital propriety in its train. The cultural and emotional climate was changing and changing Richardson's way. Life and literature were beginning to march hand in hand to Richardson's tune, and Rousseau added fuel to the fires of romantic love. Hundreds of second-rank novelists, lacking Rousseau's subversive instincts and Richardson's sadistic streak, baldly promoted female virtue and modesty and plot lines were resolved either in tragedy or in marital fidelity based on romantic love. If in the upper echelons of literary endeavour Fielding's vision of literature and life as a tragi-comedy of manners won out over Richardson's sense of life as spiritual melodrama, in the realms of the storybook, the shilling magazine and the mental lives of readers Richardson was the winner. Women who rode to hounds, told dirty jokes, flirted, argued vigorously in drawing-rooms and carried on open affairs became anachronistic curiosities. The new plot lines through which many aristocratic women dreamed their lives were those of the novel of sensibility.

Caroline, whose romantic life had been decisive and subversive, was relatively immune to the siren call of sensibility. Emily was not. When, in the midst of misery and grief after Ophaly's death in 1765 she became dissatisfied with her life, she turned not to the storybooks and conventions of her youth, which might have prompted a low-key affair with an Irish peer, but to newer works which advocated romantic love and total, absorbing passion. *Clarissa*, in which the passion between Lovelace and the heroine oozes unexpressed beneath the surface, remained a novel that no self-loving woman would want to translate into her own life. But *La Nouvelle Héloïse*, which contained passages of genuine sexual abandon, was more capable of emulation. On Emily, for one, the story of the love between Julie and the tutor made a great impression.

After *La Nouvelle Héloïse*, Rousseau turned his attention to the education of young children and produced *Émile*, a semi-novelised manual of moral and practical education, subtitled prosaically *de l'Éducation*. *Émile* sets forth the way to bring a boy from babyhood to married life, with digressions upon the nature of humanity, society and religion. In some respects, Rousseau wrote in unbridled form what John Locke had advocated in his *Thoughts Concerning Education* of 1683; that, for the most part, people 'are what they are, good or evil, useful or not, by their education'. As Rousseau put it, 'we are born totally unprovided, we need aid; we are born stupid, we need judgement; Everything we do not have at our birth and which we need when we are grown is given us by education.' Education for Rousseau began at birth with the mother's milk. Rousseau insisted that a mother's place was by her children's side and argued that women should forsake the drawing-room and the wider world for the nursery and the country, offering their children the love and support upon which family and thus national morality depended.

But there the mother's role ended. Characteristically flinging out a premise which flatly contradicted his emphasis on nurture, Rousseau said that because women were shallow creatures governed by their passions, children should be handed over to tutors for education. Once isolated from the family the little boy will be taught reason, not by insistence and punishment but by example and experience. At the heart of Rousseau's system was the axiom that children should 'learn nothing from books that experience can teach them'. Complicated games were devised to teach boys mathematical, physical and moral truths. Rote-learning was forbidden. Books of all sorts, including the prayer book, were discouraged until nature's lessons had been thoroughly learned.

In Rousseau's time-consuming and intensive educational plan there was much that Caroline and Emily could endorse.

But there was much also that they disregarded. Rousseau's hatred of the theatre where, he said, actors exhibited themselves for money and women for sex and money, fell on deaf ears. His diatribes against courts, assemblies, doctors and 'learned and brilliant' women, they managed (though not without some difficulty on Caroline's part) to disregard. 'I have just finished Rousseau's Sur L'Éducation,' Caroline wrote in August 1762, 'there are more paradoxes, more absurdities and more striking pretty thoughts in it than in any book I ever read that he did not write.' But she baulked at Rousseau's denigration of book learning, and thought his scheme of practical education wildly impractical, concluding in her tartest manner, 'there is certainly a small objection to putting his scheme of education in practice, viz. that its impossible – there are a number of contradictions in his book but its immensely pretty.'

Emily thought so too. She took what she wanted from *Émile* and abandoned the rest. The elevation of the countryside, of games, exercise and loose clothing for toddlers fitted in both with her own practice and her wish to keep her children close at hand. Rousseau's hatred of academies endorsed her decision not to send any more of her children away to school. Offering *Émile* as her model and justification, Emily decided to set up a school for her children at Black Rock on the coast south of Dublin. In 1766 the Duke of Leinster bought a bathing lodge close to the sea with several fields for hay making and gardening. Eventually some of the rocks by the water's edge were blasted away to make a bathing pool and an alley was built for bowling. But at the beginning the children had to make do with unimproved nature, the sand and waves of the Irish Sea.

The house at Black Rock was ready for occupation in the summer of 1766. Emily called the house Frescati, perhaps after the town of Frascati outside Rome where fashionable villas clustered along the shores of the Tyrrhenian Sea. Just as it was finished Rousseau himself fled Paris and made for England. Nothing if not wholehearted when her mind was set on a project, Emily decided to offer him the post of tutor to Charles Fitzgerald and her younger children. She wrote to Rousseau, then holed up in Derbyshire in a state of advanced paranoia, and offered him 'an elegant retreat if he would educate her children'. Rousseau declined her offer, leaving England in May 1767, pursued as much by demons of his own making as by real foes of his ideas. The Duke then hurriedly hired another tutor who was installed at Black Rock in January 1767. Although Louisa reported that 'Charles has got a tutor who seems vastly good humoured and gentle with him', the arrangement was unsuccessful and the Duke began to look among the teachers in Dublin for a replacement.

A few months later a candidate emerged, as unknown as Rousseau was celebrated. His name was William Ogilvie. Ogilvie was a Scot who had been working for some years as a teacher in Dublin. Recommended to the Duke of Leinster as a good classical scholar, mathematician and French speaker, Ogilvie was hired for Charles Fitzgerald at first but on the understanding that he would teach the younger Fitzgerald children as they became old enough to move to Black Rock.

Emily's boys had had personal servants before, men to talk French and 'be about them', as she put it. But they had never had a tutor, and Emily was not sure what Ogilvie's status within the household should be. Should he be given tallow candles for his room, which would indicate that, like previous companions to her sons, he was first and foremost a servant? Or should he have wax candles, as befitted a gentleman employee or friend of the family? Emily was undecided, but her friend, Lady Leitrim, who was with her when Ogilvie was announced, declared, 'Oh moulds will do, till we see a little'.

At the beginning of 1768, Ogilvie and Lord Charles Fitzgerald were installed at Black Rock, pursuing a vigorous programme of Rousseauian exercise and less than Rousseauian book learning. In between digging in the garden, catching chickens, working in the stables and receiving visits from Louisa and his parents, Charles learned Latin grammar and read Latin verse (laboriously translating that story of forbidden love, Pyramus and Thisbe, from Ovid's *Metamorphoses*). He read French (that old Lennox favourite *Gil Blas*), English history and, for amusement, Fielding's *Tom Thumb*. Along with such school work Charles did drawing and sewing. He became so proficient at the latter that Emily said that he should become a master tailor.

As the brood at Carton and family confidence in Ogilvie grew, more and more children were taken over to Black Rock, and the girls were taught alongside the boys. By the end of the decade, Henry, Sophia, Edward and Robert were all there. A couple of years later Ogilvie also had Fanny, Lucy and Louisa.

The journey from Carton to Black Rock and back could easily be accomplished in a day with good horses, and Emily came over about once a week to check on her children's health and progress. In the summer she often stayed for days at a time, particularly after Louisa and Tom Conolly bought the house (or 'cottage' as they called it) next door. In her absence, Ogilvie was a meticulous correspondent, writing once or twice a week from the study where he kept his books. Ogilvie wrote about everything: every ache, pain, boil and scratch; the children's progress in learning or 'business' as he called it; their games and toys and the books he himself read in the evenings. Gradually his role expanded from that of tutor pure and simple. He became master of a whole household, running a dairy, laundry, stables and extensive gardens. He nursed the children when they were sick, and ran errands for Emily in Dublin, sending her books, clothing and advice about her health.

In between their visits, Ogilvie kept Emily and the Duke of Leinster informed about their children's progress with a constant stream of notes. He loved the children and referred to them as if they were his own, writing in 1769, 'Lord Charles and all my dear little folks are very well and business goes on uncommonly well. I have the honour to be, with greatest respect, your Grace's most humble servant.' Initially notes from Ogilvie only survived as postscripts to the children's letters. By 1771, however, Emily was carefully keeping everything that came from Black Rock.

There were two easy routes to Emily's attention, children and books. Ogilvie could and did write constantly about both. He read voraciously in the evenings, sitting in his study with his wig off and a bust of Cicero gazing down on him. Details of his reactions were thrown into his accounts of daily life at Black Rock. He read Sterne in the early 1770s but found it heavy going, in contrast with Diderot, which he read 'with more pleasure'. Fielding had his unqualified admiration and, although he thought Smollett pedantic and unpolished he enjoyed *Humphry Clinker* too. But it was upon Emily's children that Ogilvie lavished the bulk of his attention, both during the day and in his evening letters. 'Business goes on delightfully,' he reported in 1771, 'I shall say nothing of Latin, but they are improved much in their English and I give time and pains enough to French to expect they are the better for it. We likewise do geography and I make Henry draw every second day ... The other days we learn arithmetic.' Edward Fitzgerald, already at the age of eight a prolific letter writer and a favourite with his mother, added a few days later, 'Oh, about geography, I have learned the lakes and mountains and seas and [rivers] of Europe since you were last here.'

One evening in the summer of 1771, Ogilvie sat down in his study and described the daily timetable at Black Rock. In the morning the children swam in the sea and then did school work until nine o'clock when they went next door to Louisa Conolly's for breakfast. At ten or half past they came back and settled down to their school work until about one o'clock. Then they played croquet, bowls and other games, or dug in the garden until dinner time. On dull days they played chess while the little ones ran about. After dinner the children played and splashed in the sea until about five o'clock, when the older ones did a last hour or so of school work. At seven or half past seven they all trooped back to Louisa's for tea and supper and came back to bed at eight. For the rest of the evening, if he wasn't going out to see friends in Dublin, Ogilvie could 'settle to read' and write his letters.

Sometimes, while other tutors – Mr Warren the drawing master or Mr Luck who taught fencing, dancing and deportment – were with the children, Ogilvie, sitting near by, described the scene. 'Eddy is just eating a crust as long and thick as his arm. I stole a piece from him as he was drawing a square so he has laid down his pencil and says it is better to eat his bread first . . . He has begun his square again with a "now square, nobody'll eat your bread". Eddy is crying out, "O Monstrous O Monstrous; indeed I'll never draw, there's an end of it. Indeed Mr. Warren, I cannot draw it, there's the truth of the matter for you. I must try again, I must try again."'

Ogilvie did much more than preside over the children's education. He took the boys fishing in the bay and to Dublin for the theatre. All the children dug their gardens with him, obeying Rousseau's injunction to teach children the value of property by giving them land to till and make their own through cultivation. In summer they cut and made hay together. 'We had very favourable weather for our hay, which was made up Saturday night. Your Grace was very right in imagining that dear Lady Lucy had been a very happy being in the midst of it, for she was so indeed. From four o'clock till after seven she never rested but was as busy at work with her fork pitching as any of us, the happiest, busiest face I ever saw. We shall cut our other field next Friday and Saturday so that it will be in the best order for hay making this day se'enight, when we hope your Grace will enjoy the pleasure of seeing them all tumble in the midst of it . . . They all desire a thousand kisses to their dearest Mama.'

Ogilvie never stood on his dignity with the Fitzgerald children. Acting as their nurse in times of sickness did not compromise his sense of manliness. He performed the most motherly, or nursemaidly, of tasks cheerfully, carrying the toddlers to the beach in his arms, sitting beside them in the night if they had coughs or fevers and watching eagerly for the babies' first steps and words. 'We have been diverting ourselves with dear little Louisa attempting to walk in the nine pin alley. The wind throws her down poor little thing, and at every two or three steps she plumps down; but never hurts herself, for she is so *puissante par en bas* that her sitting part always comes first to the ground.'

Discipline accompanied jollity. Ogilvie was a consistent and careful disciplinarian, slow to intervene and moderate in his admonitions. If reason failed he sent naughty children to bed where they lay until dejection and boredom got the better of waywardness. If children apologised for their wrongdoing Ogilvie breathed a sigh of relief and allowed them up again.

Emily was far more capricious. Towards minor transgressions she was indulgent, allowing one of the toddlers to call her a 'hag . . . and all she can think of that is abusive,' adding, ''tis a dear thing and its naughtiness mighty pretty.' But she could quickly lose her temper and order a beating. The children adored and feared her. When he was twelve, Charles Fitzgerald sat down and wrote his mother an abject apology after he misbehaved. Emily kept it, noting on the back, 'Dr. little Charles' penitent letter wrote quite by himself, 1768'. 'My dear Mama,' the letter ran, 'I am very sorry that I have given you so much grief. I dun a great many things very improper and beneath a gentleman and below my rank. I am very sorry for my ill behaviour I have disobeyed you and Mr. Ogilvie Mama wich to be chure wass very improper. I own I am vastly distrest. I hope you will be so good as to forgive me. i give you my word and honour my dear Mama that I will never do such a thing again.'

By the time they were twelve the Black Rock children, as they quickly came to be called, could write their own apologies and endearments to their mother. Before they could write, Emily relied on Ogilvie to copy down requests for presents and expressions of love. Letters from Frescati were filled with tender messages. 'I asked [Lucy] if she would send a kiss to Mama and she said yes, yes, yes, dear Mama, where is Mama? Why don't she come, give Lucy raisins – Lucy want Mama.' 'Eddy will write Monday and bids me tell your Grace that he dotes on you and hopes you will take care of yourself. I asked Lucy what I should say to Mama for her and she told me, "Lucy good, Love her mama. Raisins and cakes, and for Louisa," and kisses me very pleasantly.'

Glimpses of plump, bare bottoms, sounds of kissing lips and pictures of tight hugs and squeezes rose off the pages of Ogilvie's letters. As he wrote out the children's thousands of kisses, was he adding his own desires to theirs, making of their messages an amatory code and conducting with Emily an epistolary romance every bit as illicit and delicious as that of Julie and Saint Preux in *La Nouvelle Héloïse*? His letters seemed to throb with double meanings. 'We received the asparagus and we told Lucy who sent them to her. She is very far from forgetting your Grace. She puts her little arms about my neck and squeezes and kisses me very often to show me how she will hug her dearest mama.' The most innocuous reports might be amorous messages. When, for instance, Ogilvie wrote about the children tumbling in the hay, he must have known that hay making (as comments about Sarah hay making in Holland House park had shown) not only had idyllic connotations but also sexual overtones. If Ogilvie's notes were love letters in disguise, their message could only mean one thing: that he passionately desired their recipient and he wanted her to know it.

Perhaps Emily made the first advance. Perhaps it was between the lines rather than between the sheets that the approach was made and the affair was for some time epistolary and not physical. But by 1771 Emily and her awkward tutor with the outdated wig and the despised Scottish accent were in love. For Emily romantic love was a newly defined and a newly felt emotion and one that was tumultuous and devastating, wreaking havoc with the way she perceived and organised her life. Instead of admitting the affair to her friends and sisters, as she might have done if it had been a flirtation with an Irish peer or an English earl, Emily hid her passion, nourishing it in secret with letters and notes. It was an epistolary passion worthy of *La Nouvelle Héloïse* itself. Deception, unnecessary for well managed flirtations, was at the heart of Emily's new feeling. Only Mrs Lynch the housekeeper and Rowley, Emily's maid, knew what was going on, and they were well rewarded for their connivance. Bound tightly together with paper, pens and sealing wax, Emily and Ogilvie deceived everyone, the Duke, the children and her sisters alike, and created for themselves a secret world where their romance flourished and grew unchecked.

PART THREE
'Are you not delighted with our dear
little Sally's thinking herself with child?'
Caroline to Emily, 14 June 1768.

'I am very glad you have bought that place at the Black Rock,' wrote Emily's seventeen-year-old son and heir, the Marquis of Kildare, in 1766. William was much too old to benefit from the Black Rock regime. By 1766 he had left Eton, a plump and hesitant young man whose lack of aptitudes and ambition were unfavourably compared with the shining talents of his cousin Charles Fox. While he remained the second son, Emily and the Duke regarded William's rotund simplicity as endearing. But when Ophaly died in 1765, William became his father's heir and something had to be done with him. His parents debated their son's future. In the summer of 1766 Emily consulted Caroline who recommended a foreign military academy. But the Duke despaired, writing from London where he had gone to consult William about his plans: 'Indeed my Emily, I am always glad to hear your opinion upon every subject and particularly about the children, who you

know are equally in our care. Of all the difficulties I was ever
under, what to do with William is the greatest I ever had, or I
hope shall ever have, and yet there is no harm in him . . . In
regard to geography, mathematics and what is called belles
letters, how is it possible to do more than advise him at his
age? . . . It is to be hoped, as parts break out at different ages,
his will some time or other.'

Eventually it was agreed that William would go to a military academy in France and from there would set out on the
Grand Tour, a journey which would, the Duke hoped, give
him a patina of learning and manners. For the first few
months of the Grand Tour William would have company
because the Fox family had decided to travel *en masse* to Italy
in the autumn of 1766.

After the success of her trips to Paris in 1764 and 1765,
Caroline was prepared to venture further afield. She had
many motives for her journey and its destination. Ste Fox,
recently married to Mary Fitzpatrick, a tiny, intelligent girl
much to Caroline's liking, wanted to resume his continental
peregrinations. Charles Fox was attracted by the literary and
amatory reputation of Italy, and Henry Fox was prepared to
spend a winter in the Mediterranean for his health. Caroline
wanted desperately to keep her husband interested enough in
life to pull himself out of his trough of boredom and morbidity and Italy excited her because she would, she hoped, see
her Roman history books come to life there. 'I love the notion
of seeing all the places one has read of in Roman history,
where great men have been and great things done,' she
explained to Emily.

Paris had prompted Caroline to new areas of reading and
study. After 1764 she supplemented her reading of novels and
histories with travel writings and maps, spending hours with
big maps spread out on her desk in a window seat in her
apartment. 'I wanted some new reading to be interested
about, having read so much in my lifetime, and story books
begin to tire me; besides they are read in a minute, and the

passion I have taken for maps and geography with this new kind of reading make it quite a business.' Now Caroline wanted to see some of the countries she read about although she worried about the length of the journey and especially about crossing the Alps, an ascent which few English women hazarded, despite the well publicised bravado of Lady Mary Wortley Montagu who had crossed Mont Cenis from France to Italy in September 1739.

Timorous as she was about travel, Caroline was in a buoyant enough mood that summer to lay the spectre of disaster at sea and discomfort on land. She was delighted with Ste's marriage and with her daughter-in-law. 'Ste is in such spirits its quite charming to see him,' she wrote in March. 'He talks so reasonably about his views with regard to marriage, and he has such delicacy and refinement, in a rational way not a romantic one, that I'm quite charmed with him.' 'I do think him lucky with his infirmities (for so one must call his deafness and his size) to get such a delightful girl that loves him. I am indeed vastly satisfied with this match.' Caroline was not possessive about Ste. She gave him up happily to Mary and, savouring the feeling of age that it brought her, looked forward to being a grandmother.

Lord Holland was cheerful too, calling his son 'a lucky dog'. Mary Fitzpatrick's arrival in the family meant another woman to tease with enquiries about sex and pregnancy and to embarrass with saucy couplets and stage whispers. He had had a bout of low spirits and poor health in the spring and Sarah often came over from Spring Gardens to cheer him up. Sometimes Bunbury came too, and Caroline worked hard at liking him. He 'mends upon acquaintance,' she told Emily, and ominously stressed how happy he made Sarah. By the summer Lord Holland had recovered and was amusing himself in Kent building follies in the grounds of his Kingsgate estate that, by their decrepitude, appealed to his mordant assessment of his own broken constitution.

Plans for Italy solidified. The group was to be Caroline and

Lord Holland, Charles and Harry Fox, Emily's William and his tutor Bolle, Ste and his wife Mary, Clotworthy Upton, an old hand at Continental travel, and Sarah, with their servants, carriages and baggage. In the end Sarah did not go, promising herself a Paris trip in the winter instead. The party met at Lyons in October and then divided for the journey to Italy; Charles, William, Bolle and Lord Holland embarked by boat for Marseilles and a sea journey to Naples. Upton, Caroline and Harry left to cross the Alps and descend to Turin and Florence. Mary and Ste went to visit his old haunts in Geneva, promising to meet Caroline's party before their Alpine crossing. 'William is very good humoured and agreeable and seems to like us all,' Caroline wrote to Emily before they set off.

The overland travellers went east from Lyons, followed the Val d'Isère, crossed the southern Alps by Mont Cenis and came down to Susa and Turin on the Italian side. It was not a hazardous journey provided the weather was good, but it was an unfamiliar one to English travellers. Amongst the Foxes' immediate circle, Horace Walpole had lived to tell the tale and Clotworthy Upton had been to Italy almost a dozen times. The ascent up Mont Cenis was spectacular. Travellers were carried in sedan chairs up a narrow mountain path bounded by rocks and vertiginous precipices by experienced Swiss guides who knew every inch of the terrain and made a living off the mountain's inhospitable slopes.

'As for the crossing of Mount Cenis itself,' Caroline wrote to Emily, 'I will not attempt to describe it, but refer you to some of your men acquaintances who have done it.' She admitted to being frightened and uncomfortable, troubled by her period but forced to continue the journey none the less: 'only think, sweet siss, I was unluckily out of order just the day I passed Mount Cenis.' When she did pluck up courage to look around her, 'the sight was indeed glorious', but scarcely susceptible to the kinds of moral reflections she was so fond of. Her response to the fog, the mountain and the vagaries of her own natural calendar was one of annoyance and fear.

Travelling through Savoy, with its pines, Scots firs, water-falls and high mountain views, was another matter. Caroline was at ease enough to philosophise and enjoy herself. 'What a number of reflections such a journey makes one make on the great and wonderful works of the Creator; and also how the love of gain causes us to break through all difficulties. One would imagine no human beings would ever have thought of passing the bounds nature seems there to have placed between France and Savoy; but the silk trade carried on between this place and Lyons has conquered those difficulties and mules loaded with that commodity and others continually pass and repass.'

Caroline looked about her and saw the civilising results of commerce everywhere. Unlike commentators who believed that trade brought nothing but grotesque luxury, debauchery and an abandonment of morals, Caroline believed, like many Whigs and most of her immediate circle, that industriousness improved man's lot. What happier people could there be than the busy Swiss she asked when she reached Geneva? 'Tis all bourgeois in this place; one sees everywhere industry, com-fort and excessive cleanliness ... There are no beggars here, no stealing, no murders or disorders happen; everyone is employed, everyone obliged to keep in their own station.' Despite her love of the past, Caroline believed that the modern world far surpassed the ancient in education, politics, hygiene, architecture and to crown its achievements had de-veloped the art of printing, in which the Romans had so signally failed.

From Turin Caroline travelled with Ste, Mary, Harry and Upton to Bologna, Florence and Rome, commenting all the way on habits of dress, manners of the Italians (the women she noted censoriously thought only of flirtation, 'they have no education at all'), landscape and trade. All the time her reading, especially in literature, moulded the way she saw, as she herself was well aware. 'I could not have imagined any-thing in the style of the country about Florence, it really resembles what one reads in story books and fairy tales. *The Traveller* justly observes of Italy "man is the only thing that dwindles there"; perhaps I don't say it right, but something to that purpose.'

Emily too saw through literature, despite the fact that she had never crossed the English Channel or the Alps. In her mind she saw the Rhône, down which William, Charles and Lord Holland travelled to Marseilles as 'terrible', because Madame de Sévigné had called it so. Caroline put her right. 'There is certainly no danger in that terrible Rhone described by Madame de Sévigné,' she wrote.

By the middle of November they were in Rome. Caroline was delighted to be there at last, proclaiming the city 'the heart of Empire, muse of heroes and delight of gods'. As the rest of the party trekked round the ruins, Mary Fox sat to Battoni for the Holland House gallery, wearing a travelling habit and holding a dog. Then they moved on to Naples, met up with the sea travellers and settled down to four months of assemblies, statue collecting and ogling remains. Caroline held a 'conversazione' of her own once a week, inviting ex-patriates and nobles from the Neapolitan court to talk (in French), play cards and keep up Lord Holland's spirits. As usual she denied any interest in being a hostess, saying simply, 'I own whether I like people or not I can't bear not returning civilities in a foreign country.'

Ostensibly Caroline had chosen Naples as their destination for Henry's sake. But she found plenty to do beyond her hostess's duties. Ruins were her speciality. Pompeii and Herculanium were close by, bountiful founts for speculation, moralising and imagining the past. In fact Caroline was a good deal more enthusiastic about Naples than her husband. At sixty-one, he was bored and tired of life, practising not the art of the connoisseur but the *ars morendi*, the art of dying in style. 'My distemper is incurable,' he wrote, 'it is, I find, old age.' 'I have no symptom of asthma, dropsy or distemper. I am in no pain, in no danger, but now and then very languid, and growing feeble, I think, in mind as well as body. I manage both extremely; sitting as now in the warm and clear sunshine and thinking of nothing that can (I won't say vex me) but even employ the understanding of a boy above ten years old.' Gradually, almost against his own wishes, Lord Holland revived. He began teasing his new daughter-in-law and jotting down verses. By the time he and Caroline went back over the Alps in April 1767, Henry was scribbling couplets all the way, one of which described his life as a retired statesman in Virgilian terms: 'resolved my life to spend / in idle cheerfulness the Muses' friend.'

Switzerland was the Foxes' last stop. Henry and Caroline paused there only to visit Voltaire at Ferney, and then hurried on to Paris, Calais, Kingsgate and home. Charles Fox and William Fitzgerald stayed on the Continent, the former to perfect Italian and his amatory strategy, the latter to continue the Grand Tour and his military training. William was an unenthusiastic tourist, seeing the sights, doing his lessons but always longing to go home. Emily complained that his letters were unintelligible and had to ask Caroline how he spent his time.

Before he left Naples, William bought several copies of Sir William Hamilton's book of etchings of Etruscan vases. One went to Castletown where Sarah and Louisa used it extensively in their decorative schemes for the long gallery. He also sent home the first of many Grand Tour consignments, a mixture of antiques, curios and junk, 'a box with some lava, snuff boxes and a bit of different sort of stuff that comes out of Vesuvius', whose contents were shared amongst the Black Rock and Carton children.

From Naples William and his tutor Bolle travelled to Rome, the epicentre of the Grand Tour, where he dutifully studied mathematics and dancing, hunted for antiquities and kissed the Pope's toe ('NB,' he wrote, 'it was very sweet'). But he felt as if he was suffering an exile rather than an education and in May 1767, when he had been abroad for nearly a year he wrote home, 'I must own Cecilia's letter makes me wish myself at Waterstone, but as people can't always have their wishes I am very happy as I am. You still make me more happy with the thoughts of your being content with my conduct.'

Pronouncing Rome 'rather a dull place' William and Bolle made for Florence. There William hired Conolly's old Italian tutor, attended 'conversazione' held by the British Minister Sir Horace Mann, bought vases and copies of Old Masters and amused himself with six or seven other Old Etonians who had converged on the city. Just as William was beginning to enjoy himself, Emily received a letter from Caroline saying that young men only went there for two things, art (or virtue, as it was called) and sex (or gallantry as she dubbed it). Since William's interests obviously lay with the latter rather than the former it might, she said, be time to move him to Germany before he became a *cicisbeo* to an Italian woman and stayed for ever.

Emily reacted swiftly. 'As to the voyage to Vienna, [it] came a little abruptly,' William wrote in the autumn of 1767. He did move on, but managed to spin out the journey, lingering in Turin and making a detour to Nice where Caroline and Henry were spending the winter. Not until November 1768 did he finally arrive on Teutonic soil, settling in Vienna for a winter's worth of military training. By then he felt he was on his way home. Dresden, with its famous picture collection and the china factory at Meissen, where William was surprised to see 'many girls painting', and Berlin ('swarming with soldiers') were followed by a quick swing through south Germany and Switzerland. The Grand Tour ended where it had begun, in France. In May 1769, almost three years after they set out, William and Bolle were back in Lyons, physically and financially exhausted.

While she was in Naples, Caroline received disturbing reports about Sarah, who was in Paris with Bunbury and Lord Carlisle. Caroline described Carlisle not only as Charles Fox's friend but as 'Sally's cicisbeo', adding, "tis a sweet youth'. Nobody, except himself, took Carlisle's passion for Sarah seriously. Much more worrying were the new alliances that she struck up in Paris. Caroline wrote to Emily, who had passed on Sarah's reports of a crowd of foppish young men, 'I am sorry dear Sal says I imposed on her un fagot de jeunes Français, because it makes me fear she has been flirting with some of them.' Sarah had been happy in Paris before. Now that Caroline was away and Holland House lent to the Duke of Richmond she was without her London base and she decided to return to Paris, eager to recapture such self-esteem as the admiration of the *saloniers* could give her.

Sarah went to Paris in a mood that combined 'low spirits' with reckless abandon. After four years of marriage her self-hatred was as biting as ever. She described herself as a 'pig', fat and brutish and, before she left, shut herself away in her rooms at Barton for four weeks with a 'nervous fever'. Rousing herself from this torpor, she sparkled and flirted in Parisian drawing-rooms, eclipsing her husband and earning the censure of Madame du Deffand. It was as if, having maintained for years the fiction of her happy marriage, Sarah now determined to make its failure quite clear, acting the part of bored wife and Parisian coquette to the hilt.

The group in which Sarah moved was made up of relatives and associates of Caroline's friends the Duc de Choiseul and the Prince de Conti. They were the court's radicals, many belonging to the Club à l'Anglaise, aping English manners and declaring their adherence to English liberties. Prominent among them was the Duc de Lauzun, a Parisian Casanova who prided himself on seducing the beauties of the day. Bored with his current mistress Madame de Cambise (who went on to become the mistress of the Duke of Richmond), Lauzun determined to practise his skills on Sarah, writing in his memoirs: 'she is tall; her figure is inclined to stoutness, her hair of the most elegant black and of a perfect growth; her bosom of dazzling whiteness and fresh as rose leaves. Eyes full of fire and character spoke the seductive and artless graces of her mind . . . Lady Sarah was kind, sensitive, frank, not to say impulsive, but unfortunately coquettish and fickle.' Lauzun described Sarah in terms as predictable as her behaviour was to become.

For two months Sarah flirted and lost at cards, attended by her husband, Lauzun and an increasingly desperate Lord Carlisle. Madame du Deffand, reporting to an eager Horace Walpole, concluded that Sarah had 'some secret motives' for her behaviour, adding shrewdly, 'she seeks diversion'. She was right: it was not that Sarah wanted a lover, it was that she no longer wanted her husband. Lauzun was baffled. Her flirtations led him on but gave him no reward. 'Lady Sarah loved me warmly and granted me nothing,' he wrote in his memoirs, claiming that Sarah told him, 'As we [English-women] choose our husbands, it is less permissible to us not to love them, and the crime of deceiving them is never forgiven us.' Underlying this remark was guilt that she no longer loved her husband and might deceive him.

Sarah was teetering on the edge of the precipice of adultery all through her Paris stay, half willing herself back, half throwing herself over. She had nothing and everything to lose: nothing of her husband's love or her own self-esteem, everything of society's approbation. Lacking the confidence that Caroline and Emily had to make their own rules, Sarah clung unhappily to rules that others made for her, already tormenting herself for breaking them. She wanted to be an irreproachable wife, to have children, love her husband and run her household. Even a discreet affair of the sort Emily and Caroline readily countenanced in their friends would shatter that illusion. And Sarah was not discreet. If she was going to have a lover she would conform to the most lurid pictures painted of adulteresses. For her there was no middle way, she was unable to flout the clichés of social relationships. She could either be the good wife or the flagrant whore.

As she flirted in Paris Sarah came to realise that she had already ceased to be the former. So it was only a matter of time before she was flamboyantly and disastrously unfaithful.

Letters and her sisters were her last lifeline. With their help she might avoid the precipice. When she came back to Barton in the spring of 1767, Sarah sent Louisa a string of letters that were replete with hints about her behaviour and emphasised her self-reproach and low spirits. Louisa and Emily failed to take these cries for help seriously. Just as they had deceived themselves about her marriage, so they now deceived themselves about its collapse, abandoning Sarah when she needed them most, hoping against hope for discretion and an affair which could be contained within the bounds of gallantry.

Sarah inferred that her behaviour in Paris had been balanced on a knife edge between flirtation and adultery. Louisa buried the revelation, replying 'low spirits proceed from the body's not being well, and in order to compose yourself, fix that in your mind and don't torment yourself with thinking you have done this thing or t'other thing wrong, or foolishly, in short don't take yourself to task when you feel low spirited.' Louisa concluded that in Paris Sarah was simply 'extremely diverted and was taken up with ... amusements and never had one bad thought about anybody or anything the whole time.'

Although Louisa's reply did not invite further confidences, Sarah continued to drop hints about her state of mind throughout the spring of 1767. They increased after Lauzun visited Barton in March and Bunbury left for Bath complaining of a bad stomach. In his memoirs Lauzun claimed that while Bunbury was away, Sarah had at last given in to him and they became lovers. Sarah did not admit it, but her letters to Castletown became so disquieting that Louisa put them to the flame. 'I burnt your note instantly,' she wrote to Sarah in March; and again in May, 'I have burnt your letter.' Meanwhile Louisa's admonitions to happiness continued, although by May a note of warning had crept into them, a suggestion that Sarah owed it to herself and to others to be happy. 'I hope you are cheerful, for indeed you must always be that, for it is wrong in a Dear heart like yours to be otherwise, for its showing oneself dissatisfied which I am sure you have no reason to be.' Thus another burden, that of failing to do her duty by those who loved her, was laid on Sarah's sinking heart.

Lauzun did not stay long at Barton. He claimed in his memoirs that Sarah became rapidly disenchanted with him. Bunbury came back from Bath, Lauzun returned to Paris. In June Sarah and Bunbury went to Spa in Belgium to take the waters. He still had a stomach complaint, she was 'wore to death with routing' as she put it to Susan and was, besides, still seeking distraction. 'My spirits are vastly lowered since you saw me,' she wrote to Susan in New York.

Spa continued the slide. Sarah danced, drank and gambled, easing herself into her new role as a woman of dubious reputation. She wrote to Selwyn of her cheerfulness, but she did not enjoy her own transgression and the more she flirted the more her self-hatred increased. Even Bunbury began to take a sardonic interest in his wife's activities. Dragging himself away from billiards, faro and quinze, Bunbury wrote a few lines to Selwyn. 'I cannot help . . . sending you two lines of the satire that has been made here, as a specimen of the poetical abilities of the author. Speaking of Lady Sarah's finery he says,

> For as for Shrewsbury's, and all such trumpery,
> To them she prefers her black-legged Bunbury.

The author very probably had lost money to me, and paid me thus.' No one, Bunbury implied, would suggest that Sarah loved her husband unless he had an ulterior and, probably, financial motive.

By the autumn of 1767, when they returned from Spa, Sarah's reputation had sunk low enough for gossip to spread both across the Atlantic and across the pages of London's scandal sheets. When Susan picked it up she acted with characteristic directness. Far from pretending as Sarah's sisters did that nothing was happening, Susan confronted Sarah with the stories. But it was by now too late for Sarah to grasp the lifeline. She wrote defensively, 'I have not at present any guess of what or how you have heard of me. I know what might be the foundation of many stories, but they must have been improved I fancy, before they could reach so far. I do not desire to hear any more particulars.' But she added sadly, 'that I have in every action of my life kept up the very good education I have had is, I fear, too much for me to say.' In the autumn and winter of 1767–68, Sarah was up in London often dining at Holland House and then going on to Richmond House for cards and chat. In October, Caroline, Henry and Charles Fox, with the disconsolate Carlisle in tow, left for Paris and Nice. After that Sarah went to Richmond House more frequently. Besides her brother and the Duchess there was often another man, Lord William Gordon, who quickly joined her circle of admirers.

Still the gossip about Sarah persisted. Rumours of a number of lovers, a story of an affair with an actor, another of an assignation in a Covent Garden *bagnio*: these were the stuff of gossip columns and stories in the sorts of monthly magazines Sarah herself used to read, the *Town and Country Magazine* and, going down a peg, the *Covent Garden Journal*. Sarah's life, or the rumours that swirled around it, eventually did become material for scandal sheets, and its plot line was remarkably similar to the 'true stories' found in fiction sections of magazines like the *Town and Country*, whose titles bore less than subtle witness to their subject matter: 'The Beauty Punished: A Moral Tale', 'The Dastardly Lover', 'The Wrong Sister', 'The Unfortunate Relapse: A Moral Tale'. Such stories, as Sarah knew well, had one, very simple plot. They told of innocence corrupted and pushed from disaster to destitution or death.

Sarah had played the part of tragic heroine often enough. She had been Jane Shore, the wronged queen, at Holland House theatricals in 1763 when she was eighteen, and she had played Cleopatra in Dryden's *All For Love* at Ste Fox's house in Wiltshire. But now, at twenty-two, she seemed bent on descending from heroically tragic parts to the sordidity of second-rate popular fiction, in which heroines died without the catharsis to which higher dramatic forms aspired.

In the spring of 1768, Louisa came to England and stayed at Barton with Sarah. Bunbury was away once more, but Lord William Gordon was staying. When Louisa left for Castletown in April he was still there and as spring turned to summer she was writing, 'pray always make my compliments to Lord William if he is still with you because you know what a favourite of mine he is.'

Eventually Lord William went back to London. At the end of May Sarah sat down in her closet at Barton and wrote two letters, one to Susan in New York, the other to Louisa at Castletown. Her first letter hit a note of frenetic chat. 'My dear Lady Susan ... I'm vastly glad to hear you don't know what low spirits are, 'tis a sign you are very well, but I hear you are grown very fat; do you know I'm not the least altered since you saw me, neither fatter nor thinner.' The second was very different, although it explained Sarah's preoccupation with her body's shape. It revealed that she was pregnant.

When Sarah announced her pregnancy the family reacted as if the rumours about her behaviour in the last two years had been just stories in the wind. Congratulations poured into Barton from Goodwood, from Stoke in Sussex where Lord George Lennox lived with his wife Louisa and the beginnings of a large family, from Carton and from Castletown. Only Caroline gave any hint of anxiety. She acknowledged that there might be some truth in the tales that still swirled around London, although she refused to make any connection between the rumours and the possible parentage of Sarah's child. 'Our dear sweet amiable Sally with the best of hearts, and the most delightful good qualities, which makes me love her as well as I do my own children, has, at least I fear she has, ... an imprudence in her conduct which makes our ill natured world abuse her most unmercifully.' This oblique statement was as far as Caroline would go. After that she followed Bunbury's lead in saying nothing and hoping that after six barren years the marriage had come to fruition.

Now and again Caroline had to dampen rumour and assure Emily that there was no truth in 'the ill-natured stories about [Sarah] that may have reached Ireland'. Emily and Louisa, responding to the hint, concentrated entirely on practical details and expressions of joy. Mingled with their delight was the hope that a child would domesticate Sarah. Louisa wrote at the beginning of July 1768: 'it is absolutely impossible for you to guess, my sweet Sally, at the pleasure I must feel in thinking of your situation.' Emily 'is as much delighted; she enjoys for you the thought of your home being made so delightful to you ... Not but that you were very happy before, but this will be such an addition, and we both agree in thinking of the comfort of it to you, so much more than in the worldly consideration of your having an heir for the estate, tho' that is pleasant too.'

In this way the act of collective self-deception that was Sarah's life ran on. Louisa dreamed of Sarah's child, 'a little girl just like yourself running about in a white frock and a long blue ribbon in its cap.' Contrary to conventional longing, no one seemed very eager for a boy, least of all Sarah herself, who had always loved the Carton boys more than their sisters. At the back of everyone's minds was the property law: if Sarah's child was not her husband's it was better that it should be a girl than a boy who would inherit the Bunbury lands and title without a genuine right.

Such fears were replaced by practical advice as the time of Sarah's lying-in approached. Louisa and Cecilia Lennox prepared to travel to London to be with Sarah during the birth and the confinement. Cecilia, now aged eighteen, had seen plenty of babies. They had been born constantly around her in Dublin and, she said, she understood them, 'better than anybody, and won't let it be swathed and pinned and rolled up tight like a bundle but let it be all loose like Mama's children and not allow one pin to be about it.' Sarah went to Brighton and Goodwood in the early months of her pregnancy, travelling up to London in October. She hired Mrs Moss, the nurse-keeper Emily used when she lay in in London, arranged a room for the birth, told her doctor to expect the baby sometime in November and, tired and very large, awaited its arrival.

18–19 December 1768

Sarah lay in a bath. Her belly rose like an island out of the warm water. She twisted and turned, trying to distract herself from the itching rash that covered her body. As she wallowed, exhausted by her weight and a succession of broken nights, the light in the room darkened. Maids brought candles and stoked up the fire. Soon afterwards her labour began.

She watched herself, as if from a great distance, travel up the hill of pain, dragged up to the top, exhaling and sliding trembling down the other side. People around her – the doctors, Louisa holding her hand – receded as she climbed away from them and came closer again when she reached the bottom. As the contractions came more quickly she stopped watching and the times of waiting on the plateau got shorter. Time stretched out into red seconds, refusing to move on. Hours seemed to pass and the doctors were still looking inside her, peering, consulting, feeling. When they said push, she began to push, sinking her mind into her abdomen, becoming a great muscle, forcing the burden out. Slithering and then rushing on a tide of blood the baby was born.

Sarah's milk came in quantity. But her nipples, sunk into the engorged breasts, refused to pop out. The baby, christened Louisa in the Holland House chapel, fed weakly, snatching at the breast, unable to hang on long enough to bring the milk down. Hurriedly, to Sarah's distress, a wet nurse was found. Soon little Louisa Bunbury nestled and grunted against a surrogate bosom. She sucked, slept and grew folds of fat and dimples. Sarah slept too. Lying among the pillows she was, to the casual observer, the image of contented motherhood. She adored her child and recovered well from labour. Caroline visited her sister constantly and reported to Emily that Sarah 'is grown vastly fat during her pregnancy; looks beautiful, the very picture of my poor mother.'

Belying the scene of contented nurturing was an air of frenetic concern. The house in Spring Gardens bulged with anxiety. Caroline admitted that she felt 'worried and uncomfortable'. Louisa Conolly was in a kind of trance, busy with practical details, scurrying about on the surface of life. Cecilia Lennox, who had come to take care of the baby, often found herself alone in the drawing-room while Sarah and her husband stayed in their apartments.

In the privacy of her chamber Sarah wept and confessed, tormenting herself with guilt and self-hatred. Charles Bunbury knew (and so it emerged did Caroline, Louisa, and most of London, from ladies-in-waiting to gutter journalists) that Lord William Gordon had been Sarah's lover for some time. He also knew that Louisa Bunbury was not his child. Something had always been wrong in his sexual relationship with Sarah. Whatever it was, it precluded conception. Bunbury was either impotent or uninterested or both. Gordon and Sarah were neither. Husband, wife and lover all knew that little Louisa was a cuckoo in the Bunbury nest.

Bunbury offered to bring Louisa up as his own child if Sarah would renounce Gordon and stay with him. He wanted to avoid public humiliation and besides, the baby, belching and blowing in the nursery above him, might be his only chance of a family. Sarah rejected the proposal and was unmoved by the entreaties of Caroline and Louisa, who grasped at this way of saving her from destitution and scandal. She was drunk with guilt. Guilt was Sarah's aphrodisiac and it was a perfect accessory to her self-hatred. She was determined upon her own downfall and all efforts to save her from herself were fruitless. When Bunbury offered her a lifeline, she produced a multitude of reasons for refusing it. 'To breed up another's child in Sir Charles' house, to be looked upon as a virtuous woman, she could not bear.' 'Self-reproach stung her to death,' she said. Besides, Gordon had a right to his own child and it would be better if she left her husband and went to him.

CHAPTER FOUR
DISASTER AND RENEWAL

Christmas came joylessly. In the house in Spring Gardens birth seemed little cause for celebration. Conolly arrived from Ireland and took Cecilia Lennox down to Goodwood. The Fox brothers left Caroline's house in Piccadilly and went to Ste's estate in Wiltshire to eat, drink, hunt and gamble away the holidays. Charles Bunbury left London to spend Christmas with his family at Barton. At the New Year Louisa left too, joining Conolly, Cecilia and her brothers at Goodwood. Only Caroline stayed on in London, nervously guarding Sarah against gossip and flight. She knew that Gordon was close at hand, but even her vigilance could not stop him walking back and forth in the Privy Garden in the hope of seeing Sarah and his child. Sarah saw him out of the window one day in early January, when Caroline was not with her. She called Gordon in to see the child and instantly fell back into what she called the 'delirium' of her passion for him.

Caroline thought she had done her job of chaperoning well enough to leave with Lord Holland for Wiltshire as soon as

Bunbury returned from Barton and Cecilia came up from Goodwood. At the end of January Sarah left her house in Spring Gardens and went with Cecilia, the baby and its nurse to Suffolk, where the Bunbury family was assembled to greet its newest member. Her husband stayed in London.

At Barton Sarah's moods swung wildly. The euphoria of the birth had worn off and she was often remote and distracted. Cecilia felt neglected, having to sit with Bunbury's sister Mrs Soames while Sarah stayed in her own rooms or trudged about the grounds by herself. The disaster came on Sunday 19 February, arriving slowly and then gathering other events and people into itself like a snowball picking up everything in its path. At first it was Sarah's disgrace, then Bunbury's, then a collapse which engulfed the whole extended Lennox family.

Sarah went out for a walk and never came back. Cecilia and the Soameses waited through the morning hours and on into dinner time, when a note finally arrived for Mr Soames from Sarah 'taking leave of them for ever', as Caroline put it later. Sarah had left not only tiny Louisa, but also Cecilia Lennox, stranded amongst strangers who were angry and distraught. In the grounds she had met Lord William and they had left Suffolk hurrying south. After crossing the Thames into Kent, they arrived in the afternoon at Knole, a rambling mansion lent to them by their friend the Duke of Dorset. Knole was big enough to hide the most conspicuous of runaways, but Sarah did not bother or even wish to conceal her whereabouts. She sent a note to Caroline in which she begged for her child, apologised for her deeds and explained where she was.

Sarah was bent on ruining her reputation in the most public way possible. Only a few days after her flight from Barton, newspapers which had collected evidence against her, disappointed of their expectations of a large fee to keep quiet, began to publicise her story. The *Chronicle*, a London scandal sheet, printed a summary of a letter purportedly written by Sarah to her husband. 'A very sensible and pathetic letter has been received from a lady lately absconded, in which she acknowledges great gratitude to the person to whom it was addressed; and that the step she has at present taken was in consequence of so strong an attachment to a certain Gentleman, that had she not pursued this measure it might have affected her life; that therefore, finding it impossible to be happy without the possession of that gentleman, she thought proper thus publicly to withdraw herself rather than clandestinely to raise to the name and fortune of the former person a number of illegitimate children; and this resolution still further led her to confess her suspicions respecting her last child.'

Once she had left her husband Sarah and her story entered the public world. She became not just a source of trouble to her family but also a juicy item of news. In coffee houses and taverns, in modest parlours and spacious libraries, men and women pored over the details of her life, sighed at or sympathised with her folly and recounted the story to their friends. Sarah had neither the money nor the desire to pay newspapers to keep silent; they were just one of the ways in which she was allowing herself to be punished. Scandal turned Sarah instantly into what she called herself at the nadir of her self-hatred, 'la peste publique'.

Any aristocratic scandal was valuable to newspapers at a time when many readers were openly hostile both to the idea of aristocratic government and to the idea of aristocratic sexual licence and saw the corruption of one reflected in the corruption of the other. But Sarah's story, as the *Town and Country Magazine* made clear in a detailed account of the affair published in April 1769, was especially good copy because of her own royal blood and her unfortunate connection with the reigning monarch. The *Town and Country* went so far as to hint that Sarah only married Bunbury 'through pique and disappointment' because she had failed to win a far bigger prize, and concluded with salacious piety, 'rank and beauty have been her ruin'. Sarah's life had become .

a source of half-envious ridicule for respectable readers, a text for the titillation of the prudish and a vehicle for anti-government commentators who were riding high after their champion John Wilkes's election for Middlesex the previous year. The *Town and Country* concluded its account with a moral which excused its own symbiotic relationship to the events it condemned: 'the world are now divided in their opinion whether B— deserves most pity or contempt. This we shall leave the reader to determine; only observing, that this history may serve as a lesson to deter the vainglorious part of mankind from choosing their helpmates for life from motives of false ambition or, having chosen them, to pay less attention to their wives than their horses.'

Caroline and Louisa were still hoping to avert complete disaster. After they received Sarah's note from Knole, they decided to try to prise Sarah and Gordon apart in the hope that she would go back to Bunbury with her name more or less intact. Louisa went down to Knole on 20 February 1769 and, after more tears and long conversations, brought Sarah back to Caroline's house in Piccadilly. Then Caroline sat down to write to Emily, knowing that if she did not, the newspapers would reach Carton before her letter could temper the bad news.

As long as there was hope that Sarah would maintain the unwritten rules of aristocratic gallantry, Caroline had kept her knowledge of the affair with Gordon to herself. But now that Sarah had lost everything – her good name, her husband, the protection of her family and her privacy – Caroline decided to tell Emily all she knew. She sat down in her parlour, dipped her pen into the well of grey-black ink and began to write the story in her familiar scrawl, using language as extravagant as that of a Grub Street hack. 'Piccadilly, Tuesday 21 February. Painful as it is to undertake the dreadful task of letting my dearest sister know what will almost distract you, yet you must know it, and I don't know who else could inform you, as hearing it by common report it might take you unprepared; and I enclose this to the Duke of Leinster to give you when he thinks proper. Poor dear unfortunate Sarah, miserable girl, notwithstanding all the kindness, fondness, tenderness and extreme perfect behaviour of Sir Charles to her, which she acknowledges and does justice to, left Barton last Sunday and went with Lord William Gordon to Knole, the house of his and my brother's *friend*, the Duke of Dorset. Guess the distraction of us all! That angel Louisa, whose goodness has long tried to save her fallen sister, went yesterday to Knole and by her entreaties fetched her back, only I fear to add to hers and our misery, as she is determined to return to him; says she knows its misery, but is distracted with her passion, with her sense of guilt, which she says has made her so very wretched for these many months past. She is in my house, so is Louisa. Ciss is at Barton with Mr. and Mrs. Soames; Conolly gone to Goodwood to fetch my brother. What can, what must be done? Sir Charles is distracted, but reasonable to a degree. Indeed my dear sister, his conduct since the suspicion of this sad affair has been unexceptionable and beyond anything one can have an idea of; she feels it most sensibly, it adds to her misery. Altogether 'tis a most strange, dreadful and horrid affair, must end in misery. Conolly is returned from Goodwood, my brother much shocked, as you may suppose. He is ill and cannot be here till tomorrow; he is calm but by what I can collect from Mr. Conolly will show great resentment to the Duke of Dorset.

'Poor Sarah left Barton at nine in the morning last Sunday. Ciss and Mrs. Soames waited long for her return, thinking her gone out walking, grew very uneasy when Mr. Soames received a note taking leave of them for ever. Good God, my sweet siss, what an event! My head is almost turned. Louisa bids me assure you she is well in health.'

The five days after Sarah came to the Foxes' house in Piccadilly passed in a welter of furtive preparation. Carriages, messengers and letters came and went, closely watched by the denizens of Grub Street and St James's. Cecilia arrived from

Barton with the baby and its nurse. Bunbury often walked from Spring Gardens along Pall Mall and up the gentle slope of the Haymarket to Piccadilly. But his conversations with Sarah were fruitless. She refused to return to him. Nor did she respond to the call of older affections and family duties; the Duke of Richmond, when he arrived, found her adamant in her objection. Gordon, everyone knew, waited beyond the pale of the family circle and it was to him, despite her denials, that she was going, accepting that once she left Piccadilly she would begin an exile from the family that might last forever.

Louisa spent the time before Sarah's departure dazed. Although she had known more than the rest of the family about Sarah's affair with Gordon, she 'would not understand how far matters had gone' as Caroline had put it, and now she seemed too full of misery to take anything in or give anything out. Cecilia told Emily that Louisa 'seemed to have lost all sense of love or feeling whatsoever, her voice sounded quite contracted so that she could scarcely bring out her words.' Louisa could not write and, for a few days, went deaf, as if she refused to hear any more bad news. Making arrangements for Sarah's journey and concealment was left first to Caroline and then, because she did not want to know where Sarah was going, to Charles James Fox.

On Sunday 26 February 1769 the family dispersed, uncertain when they would be together again. Charles Fox went with Sarah, the baby and her wet nurse to a boarding house in Redbridge near Southampton, where she registered as a Mrs Gore awaiting the arrival of her husband. The Duke of Richmond, with Louisa and Conolly in his carriage, left London for Goodwood. Caroline took Cecilia to Holland House because she seemed unwell. Sir Charles Bunbury and his brother Harry, a caricaturist whose gentle eye recorded the foibles of the rich in town parks and country pursuits, followed soon afterwards.

Caroline had encouraged Sarah's departure, but was desperate and overwrought after her sisters left, writing to Emily

Henry Fox, painted by Reynolds in 1764,
at the height of his political career.

Caroline, painted by Reynolds in 1758, when she
was 35, and called herself a 'woman of fashion'.

Caroline Lady Hol[land]
died 1774.
Ramsay. Pin[xt]

ABOVE: Caroline as she liked to think of herself in 1763 with her furs, letters and 'visage de quarante ans', painted by Ramsay for the Holland House gallery.

RIGHT: Ste Fox in the early 1760s by Reynolds: fat and adored.

Reynold's famous triple portrait of Fox with Susan Fox-Strangways
and Sarah leaning from a Holland House window, 1762–64.

RIGHT: Charles James Fox, aged 3, by Hoare, resplendent in silk dress and bandana.

BELOW LEFT: Fox in the 1780s, the 'champion of the people', dubbed by Gibbon 'the black collier'.

BELOW RIGHT: Fox in private, by Lawrence, called by Burke before they quarrelled 'a man made to be loved'.

LEFT: Cecilia Lennox, painted by Ramsay in 1768, a year before she died of consumption.

BELOW: The Duke of Leinster (centre) perhaps with William, his heir, seated on a rock, by Healy, for Castletown, 1768.

the next day: 'Indeed, my sweet sister, she is amiable to a degree, notwithstanding this horrid step she has taken. Her mind is not yet totally corrupted . . . She flatters us with a return and that she shall repent . . . My dear sister, what letters you receive from me – Good God! It makes a good mind shudder with horror to relate these fatal events.'

After a few days everyone was calmer. But nobody was happier. Those left behind speculated anxiously about the outcome of Sarah's flight and worried about its widening effects within the family circle. Caroline absolved Bunbury from blame but cast around for other victims in an effort to save Sarah herself. Her accusatory pen pointed at the Duchess of Richmond, friend of both Gordon and the egregious Duke of Dorset and she wrote splenetically 'I shall always hate her'. The Duke of Richmond was in a difficult position. He wanted to help Sarah – if possible by prising her away from Gordon and offering her the sanctuary of Goodwood – but such a gesture might appear to accept the Duchess's complicity in the affair. He beat a dignified retreat from the débâcle, announcing that he was going to his estate at Aubigny for an extended sojourn.

At Carton, Emily was full of anxiety and enquiry, writing daily to Piccadilly, Holland House and Goodwood. What had happened, she asked repeatedly, where was Sarah now, how were Louisa and Cecilia, who was Lord William Gordon? She got few replies. Two weeks after Sarah's departure, Louisa was still unable to pick up her pen; Cecilia was protected by her sisters from information that might compromise her reputation and chance in the marriage market. She could only write to Emily, 'You desire I will write more particulars about our poor unhappy sister. Why, my dear Mama, it is not in my power for I do not at all know where she is. It certainly was properer I should neither see nor have anything to do with her.' So it was left to Caroline to tell Emily the whole story, a task which she undertook with gloomy enjoyment and lawyerly accuracy, beginning, 'Lord

William and she it seems got acquainted last autumn twelve-month when I was at Nice,' and ending, 'I have wrote all this at your desire of knowing more particulars. Henceforward I shall seldom mention her. She wishes to be forgot, poor soul! To think of all her amiable qualities distracts one. Even this step, had she been a worse woman, she would not have taken.' Her verdict on Lord William Gordon was brief and unsparing: he was a 'beggar and mad'. Elsewhere she added, 'several of his family are shut up.'

Gordon was certainly poor, the second son of the third Duke of Gordon, an army officer by profession. He had just made himself even poorer by selling his commission, convinced that his affair with Sarah would ruin his chances of promotion. Madness was in the family too. Lord William's younger brother George who gave his name to the anti-Catholic riots of 1780, was subsequently confined in Bedlam for many years and ended his life rejecting the fervent Protestantism of his youth for Judaism. Lord William himself was regarded by the Lennox family as moody and unpredictable. Yet as a lover Gordon was, so the *Town and Country Magazine* declared, replete with attractions. 'He had many recommendations both personal and mental, which made him esteemed by all his acquaintance, and particularly by the ladies. His figure was tall and genteel, his features regular and expressive, his hair remarkably fine, and his whole person completely elegant: add to this, the happy art of pleasing in conversation and convincing in argument, founded on great natural parts, cultivated by a classical education.' Sarah saw in Gordon not only a man who could skilfully translate lust into passion but also a character quite unlike her husband's. Where Bunbury was predictable, fair and safe, Gordon was moody and odd, a man whose self-absorption, when enlarged to include his love for Sarah, could pass for absorption in another, so that solipsism and love became intertwined and indistinguishable. Sarah and Gordon came to one another looking at themselves; both found dissatisfaction within that was the driving force of their affair.

Gordon lopped off his title and his last syllable, tied back his red hair and attired himself as plain Mr Gore. Then he rode from Knole to Redbridge to be met by his putative wife. Once the family got word that Gordon and Sarah were together, they abandoned her, declaring in unison that she could not hope for forgiveness until she left him and showed remorse for her behaviour. Besides, another disaster was looming that engrossed everyone's attention as soon as Sarah had gone.

Sarah's abrupt flight from Barton had left Cecilia Lennox stranded there. According to the Duke of Leinster, her presence meant that she was open to suggestions of complicity in Sarah's immorality. In an abrupt letter to Caroline and Henry, the Duke demanded Cecilia's immediate return to Ireland. He hinted that although Sarah had gone, Cecilia was not perhaps in the best of hands. Caroline replied carefully to this outburst of propriety. Sending Cecilia back to Ireland precipitously without Louisa or Conolly, she said, would seem precisely as if they all had something to hide. 'To have her go off in such a hurry would look like doubting her conduct and as if we suspected her of being concerned in her unhappy sister's affair.' As a reply to any nascent rumours, Caroline recommended that Cecilia should go about in public as much as possible.

Thwarted and rebuffed by this decisiveness, the Duke scribbled back the sort of letter he sent more often to Carton servants than to members of his family. He wanted Cecilia back, he wrote; and then he suggested that the second Duke of Richmond had been quite right to entrust his younger children to Emily and himself. Caroline was 'indolent' and 'careless' about her sisters, and Holland House was no place for innocent young women to be. As proof he cited Sarah's marriage, contrasting it with Louisa's. One was the product of Holland House and its laxity. The other was arranged, carefully and so much more successfully, at Carton, under his own watchful eye.

The Duke's letter hit Caroline's age-old wound, the memory of her father's will of twenty years before. All the anger and pain of her own banishment from the family came surging back. It flooded over the anxiety of Sarah's departure and spilled into a feeling that now, as before, Henry Fox had been insulted unjustly. Long-forgotten fury and resentment burst out, joined now by an overwhelming feeling of injustice. No one, she felt, had been more solicitous about Sarah and Cecilia than she. If Louisa had fetched Sarah back from Knole, it was she who had tried to prevent her seeing Gordon after the birth of their child, she who had brought Sarah and Bunbury together to try to prevent a final split and she who had arranged for Sarah's retirement in the country. Moreover since those terrible days she had kept Cecilia close by her, carefully watching her health and reputation. Only a week or two before the débâcle she had suggested that Cecilia should go to France for the winter because she seemed unwell and offered not only to take her but also to make the journey on her behalf saying, 'its being right for her will determine us'.

Behind the Duke of Leinster's letter Caroline detected a disapproval of her husband that was more than political, a suggestion that the atheistical, free-thinking Fox ways had grafted immorality onto her own indolence. Since it was Fox around whom she had built her world, Caroline saw in the Duke's letter a blow to the sense of herself that she had so painstakingly built over the last twenty-five years, as sister to Emily, Louisa, Sarah and Cecilia, as mother to Ste, Charles and Harry and, above all, as wife to Henry Fox.

Caroline was too hurt by the Duke of Leinster's letter to defend herself or even demand an apology. But angry recriminations flew around embroiling the whole family. Both parties eventually appealed to the Duke of Richmond. The Duke of Leinster was 'very anxious to clear himself to you', as Louisa put it to her brother. Caroline demanded reassurance that she had not failed or shirked her duties. This she got. As discreetly as he could the Duke of Richmond supported his sister. But his approbation was not enough to restore Caroline's wounded self-esteem. She was determined to retaliate. Anger, pain, loyalty to her husband and a flaming sense of injustice combined to get the better of any urge to caution that she might have had. She lashed out furiously, determined to stave off an inner collapse with retaliation. No one at Carton escaped her fury. In a miserably angry moment she attacked Emily, accusing her of 'want of affection' and siding with her husband. Louisa tried to mediate, saying, 'the misfortune of my sister Holland's manner is, that she is warm, and if she says anything against anybody, she is apt to make use of the strongest expressions.' But the damage was done. Emily was hurt and drawn into the quarrel on her husband's behalf. In the stand-off between the Duke's mental rigidity and moral probity on the one hand, and Caroline's passionate and unbridled anger on the other, something of great importance was lost: twenty-five years of sisterly confidence, love and dependence.

After March 1769 no more letters passed between Holland House and Carton for a long time. When they began to arrive again it was death's messenger who brought them. In a matter of weeks the correspondence and trust of decades was stopped. Emily no longer saw Caroline's sprawling handwriting on the thick wads of paper sealed with busts of classical heroes, statesmen and writers. Caroline's pleasure at unfolding Emily's exquisitely written pages was gone. Everything that the letters implied was jeopardised. In the place of news, and confessions and gossip there was silence. Emily confided increasingly in William Ogilvie, Caroline turned her anxious eyes on to the troubles of her own family. Only occasionally was the gulf bridged by a message or report sent through Louisa.

The breach between Holland House and Carton, like Sarah's débâcle, reverberated through the family. The Duke of Richmond took Caroline's part and so relations between Goodwood and Carton became strained, even though those between Goodwood and Holland House were rocky. With

Sarah gone, the third Duke of Richmond remained close only to Louisa and his brother Lord George Lennox. Emily had been on cordial but not close terms with her brother but her husband's conduct meant that she could write only indirectly, through Louisa. Other relatives were drawn in. The Duke of Leinster's sister and her husband Lord Hillsborough, intimate at Holland House for some time, now cut it from their London itinerary.

Louisa, still only twenty-five years old, was in a responsible and difficult position. She was everyone's confidante, the only figure in the family to have kept the trust of all concerned. She was also the only person who could straddle the widening gaps between the parties. Maintaining impartiality was important for her because she needed to feel trusted and beloved. But this time even Louisa took sides, although she was careful to confide only in her brother. On 11 May 1769 she wrote to Richmond: 'It is most excessively vexatious to think of his behaviour to Lady Holland. I am more vexed at it now than ever, for I have so much reason to love him, yet cannot change my opinion with regard to that affair. I have great hopes that my two sisters will be as comfortable as ever, in loving one another as they used to do. My sister Leinster has never changed and is quite reasonable in not worrying at any anger of my sister Holland's and she hopes time will do something in her favour.' After a few months a pattern of communication between Caroline and Emily was established. Caroline wrote her news to Louisa, who passed on her letters to Emily. 'My sister Holland continues to write pleasant letters which I show to my sister L. and make her very happy,' Louisa told Sarah in 1771. Using her knowledge of the nature of family letters, Caroline thus managed to keep the channels of communication open and ready for a resumption of a direct and acknowledged correspondence.

By May 1769 the Lennox family party that had abruptly gathered in London in February was dispersed as well as shattered. At the end of March Conolly left for Ireland. After a

diversion via Goodwood Louisa picked up Cecilia from Holland House and followed him at the end of April. The Foxes
went to Kingsgate. Caroline did not much like the Kent
shore, where the plants battered by the wind grew twisted
and stunted. But now it suited her angry mood. 'I passed my
summer agreeably enough, though I had many things to vex
me,' she wrote in her journal. Bunbury, meanwhile, went between Newmarket, Barton and London, seeing relatives,
horse-dealers and, ominously for Sarah, lawyers.

Sarah had no idea that her affair had led to a breach between
Caroline and Emily. While the quarrel was boiling in London
and Carton, she and Gordon were in semi-seclusion at Redbridge, living as man and wife. Charles Bunbury, meanwhile,
was reaching a decision about his own future. While Sarah
stayed with him he was prepared to countenance her adultery.
It was her leaving that amounted to betrayal, exposing him to
ridicule and scandal. As soon as Sarah left Holland House,
Bunbury decided on a separation.

A separation was not necessarily or even usually a prelude
to divorce. Divorce was very expensive. Except in cases of
annulment (on the grounds of non-consummation, for instance), which were dealt with by the ecclesiastical courts,
divorce could only be secured by a private Act of Parliament,
and cost hundreds of pounds. Scores of thousands of couples
simply separated, formally or informally. 'Private' separations, as they were known, had dubious legal status, but were
a way of formalising a mutually agreeable split. A separation
deed was drawn up in which the husband agreed to provide
an annual maintenance allowance for his dependants, usually
balanced by an undertaking from the wife's trustees to
absolve him from any future responsibility for her debts.
There were clauses guaranteeing the wife the right to make
contracts and behave as if she were a single woman with regard to her financial affairs, her choice of abode and so on.

The whole settlement was drawn up by lawyers and guaranteed by trustees. Its legal status was dicey but the solemnity that surrounded its acceptance was supposed to ensure that all parties stuck by its provisions.

In a judicial separation case husband (or very occasionally the wife) had to justify his desire for a separation before the London Consistory Court, the Ecclesiastical Court that ruled on Canon Law. The Consistory Court was generally known as 'Doctors' Commons' after the building in which it sat. In ninety-nine cases out of a hundred (the exceptions were in cases of non-consummation or gross cruelty by husbands), justification took the form of proof of wifely adultery. Many separations involved affairs on both sides. But since a wife could not divorce her husband for adultery it was her behaviour that was offered in evidence, even if the desire to separate was mutual.

Before the case got to Doctors' Commons, a husband might take civil action for damages by filing what was known as a suit for 'criminal conversation' against his wife's lover. A 'crim. con.' suit was decided according to Common Law and held in the King's Bench Court. It could, by means of witnesses, statements and a jury verdict, establish a wife's guilt and the husband's right to compensation from her lover. Often however, crim. con. suits were used, not so much to punish the lover financially as to lay the groundwork for a judicial separation or divorce. Charles Bunbury, knowing that Gordon was penniless and in no position to pay damages, and desirous of as little publicity as possible, went through the motions of a crim. con. suit, but reserved most of his energies for the case in the Consistory Court at Doctors' Commons.

After a judicial separation in Doctors' Commons, a parliamentary divorce might follow. Initially used by aristocrats who wanted to secure their estates to legitimate heirs, after the mid-century parliamentary divorce became available to anyone with determination and several hundred pounds.

Even so, there were only a few more than a hundred parliamentary divorces in the eighteenth century: unless the parties (or more usually the husbands) wanted to marry again, separation and cohabitation were cheaper and less spectacular. Divorcees (like Caroline's friend Lady Di Beauclerk who was divorced in 1768) often remarried again immediately. Long-term divorcees were thin on the ground and the social limbo in which divorced women existed was partly the result of their extreme rarity. Nobody knew how to treat them or whether, once remarried, the stain of their adultery was wiped away.

Bunbury eventually initiated and got a parliamentary divorce. (It went through in 1776.) But at the beginning he asked for nothing more than a judicial separation in Doctors' Commons. The case of *Bunbury v. Bunbury* had three stages. First, on 22 April 1769, Bunbury's lawyers filed a 'libel' which laid down the grounds (in this case adultery) upon which he wanted a separation. Second, various witnesses, all called by Bunbury's lawyers, made depositions to the court between 22 April and 22 May. Sarah could have offered a defence at this point, with witnesses of her own, but she was too far away in Scotland and too far gone in self-abasement to attempt one. Third, the court pronounced sentence.

Roger Rush, Bunbury's valet, Charles Brown, a servant at Barton and John Swale, Bunbury's lawyer, all testified to the truth of the libel: that Bunbury and Sarah had not met or had sexual intercourse since Sarah left London to go to Barton (something necessary to prove for legal reasons), and that Gordon and Sarah had committed adultery. Margaret Frost, another Barton servant (and sister to Sarah's maid who stayed with her) and Martha Bissell, the owner of the Redbridge boarding house, eagerly supplied corroborative details, which they could repeat outside the courtroom for the benefit of the press and a fat fee. Mrs Bissell, speaking in well schooled legalese, stated that Gordon and Sarah had 'carnal knowledge of each other and thereby committed adultery together'. Margaret Frost declared that the miscreant couple 'lived and cohabited together as man and wife, and went by the name of Mr. and Mrs. Gore and lay in the same apartment in which there was but one bed.' Her deposition continued, 'in the morning before she went away the deponent went into the said Lady Sarah Bunbury's bed chamber in order to ask her ladyship if she had any commands to London and the deponent then and there saw the said Lady Sarah Bunbury and William Gordon Esquire, commonly called Lord William Gordon, naked and in bed together.'

On 17 June the court, faced with this uncontested evidence, pronounced Bunbury's libel to be correct and authorised a judicial separation. The libel, now the verdict, declared that 'Lady Sarah Bunbury, being of a loose and abandoned disposition and being wholly unmindful of her conjugal vow etc did carry on a lewd and adulterous conversation with Lord William Gordon.'

A separation made Sarah's position even more public. It nullified her marriage contract and called for a separate maintenance agreement in which the couple's finances would be reordered. It also protected Bunbury's estate from claims by any further children born to Sarah and her lover. Little Louisa Bunbury was still legally Bunbury's child, but *de facto* she was now a bastard with an uncertain future and fortune.

By the time Mrs Bissell had given her testimony to Bunbury's lawyers, Sarah and Gordon had left her house, driven north to Scotland by the winds of scandal. They took refuge in Carolside, a house near Relstone in Berwickshire lent to them by a friend of Gordon's. But rumour quickly found them. In its August 1769 issue, the *Town and Country* conjured up for its readers a meeting in a lowly retreat modelled on storybooks whose plots turned on concealed identities and coincidental meetings. Under the heading 'Amorous Intelligence' its writer, 'T L', reported, 'knocking at the door of a cottage to obtain information'. Lord William Gordon opened the door and offered him hospitality in the house where to his 'infinite surprise' he found 'the charming and accomplished LSB'. 'TL' concluded, with an eye to the following month's copy, 'I was greatly astonished to find that a mutual satisfaction seemed to reign in their countenances, that they dwelt with pleasure on their reciprocal passion, which was still visibly glowing in its primitive ardour. Nay, the very step that had in some measure banished them from the world and driven them to their present retreat afforded them a solace for any little temporary wants – and they glorified in having risked ALL FOR LOVE.'

Was Sarah's behaviour the result of a grand passion? Was she indeed, as the *Town and Country* suggested, playing Cleopatra to Gordon's Antony, overcome by love and ready to jeopardise everything for it? Sarah left Bunbury and Barton from choice rather than necessity. She could have stayed with her husband, kept her slightly tarnished reputation and her social position. She could even, after a decent interval, have resumed her affair with Gordon. Bunbury demanded an end to it more because it had begun to hurt his public stature than because it trampled on his private feelings. He had after all let the affair, or flirtation, with Lauzun run its course and rumour had it that Sarah's lovers were legion. Sarah's refusal to give Gordon up, her public renunciation of respectability and the blame she loaded on to herself spoke of other imperatives. As her family and her social circle cast her off Sarah reconciled two warring parts of herself. She was no longer a woman whose low opinion of herself was at odds with the beautiful and intelligent woman others saw. Others now estimated her as she estimated herself, as worthless, as the 'pig' with the 'hoggy paws', 'abandoned and undeserving'. Sarah came to rest on the bottom and her sinking explained her self-hatred so well that she welcomed and even gloried in her fall. Sarah loved Gordon because he was the vehicle of her self-chastisement. But once he had helped her to her nadir Gordon had little more to offer, and Sarah could now begin

to climb very slowly out of the pit. She had kept her lifelines –
pen, ink and paper – and she began to write, cautiously at first
and then in reams, to Louisa.

Initially Sarah's letters from Scotland consisted entirely of
confessions of guilt and declarations of hopelessness. Then, as
she began to build up a new sense of herself and find faults in
her lover, they became enquiries about help and requests for
reinstatement in the family. Her sisters put a price on read-
mission. Caroline had always been prepared to have Sarah
back, but her condition was, as she put it, 'a life of penitence'.
Louisa, unaware that she was making Sarah the scapegoat for
family misfortune, demanded misery too. 'She is very unhappy,' Louisa wrote to the Duke of Richmond in July 1769,
'and we who love her cannot wish her otherwise.'

Sarah stayed with Gordon in Scotland all through the summer and autumn of 1769, writing long letters to Louisa,
searching for forgiveness. The terms of her rehabilitation
gradually became clear. She had to renounce Gordon, put
herself at the disposal of her family and constantly display a
penitent countenance and mind. She could have her child with
her but no friends and no company other than family and servants. In return the family would undertake to look after her
and little Louisa and would forgive her aberrant behaviour.

While Sarah was pondering these harsh terms the rest of the
family were once again caught up in tragedy and dispute.
Cecilia Lennox was ill with a dry cough and wasting disease.
Bristol waters were prescribed by Dublin doctors and Cecilia
set off for England, accompanied by William Ogilvie, in July
1769, 'much grieved at leaving Ireland so soon again'. At the
end of Cecilia's course of waters, Caroline paid the bills and
took her back to Kingsgate 'very ill indeed'. Cecilia was
frailer than ever and a warm dry climate seemed the only
hope. Caroline arranged the trip. They would travel from
Kingsgate to Paris and from Paris to Nice. Ostensibly, it was
a family party; in fact it was for Cecilia. Charles, Harry and
Lord Holland went only to keep Caroline company and to

make it seem as if the journey was determined by pleasure rather than the desperate state of Cecilia's health. Before they left Kingsgate Lord Holland wrote to a friend: 'I am not going abroad on account of my own health. But I am going because Lady Holland's good nature will not let her amiable sister, who is dying, go only with a servant. The worst of it is, there are no hopes, but it would be cruel to tell her so, and never was more melancholy journey undertaken.'

By the time the party reached Paris at the end of October, Caroline's anger had burst out from under her dejection. She felt deserted by her siblings. The Duke of Richmond was hunting at Aubigny, Louisa and Emily stayed put in Ireland and Sarah was still lost to the family. She, derided by the Duke of Leinster as being careless of her sisters, was left to accompany Cecilia on a hopeless journey and watch her die. To her daughter-in-law Mary Caroline wrote on 1 November, 'when I think of the trouble, plague and distress my own family have brought me into . . . [I] determine fully to have done with them when this sad event is over and trouble myself no more about anyone but my own children and yours.' At the same time she wrote to Louisa asking why nobody had helped with the expenses of Bristol and the Paris journey, adding angrily that the family had 'imposed a hard task upon her'.

Caroline's task did not last much longer. Cecilia died quietly, 'without a pang or a fight' in the afternoon of 13 November 1769 as Caroline watched over her. Her departure from the world was as muted as her life in it. At the end her only regret was that Emily was not with her.

Grief and anger mixed together drove Caroline to her writing-table. Unwilling to reopen any communication with Carton, she wrote to the Duke of Richmond, to Louisa and, repeatedly, to Ste and Mary. 'These are melancholy times my dear Ste,' she wrote a few hours after Cecilia's death, adding, 'many, many things I have had to vex me of late.' Paris failed to distract her. 'Nothing here amuses me that I used to like,' she said, so the party left soon afterwards for the south.

Better news for the family arrived at Carton and Nice at the beginning of December. Sarah had left Lord William Gordon and was going to Goodwood with little Louisa Bunbury. She promised not to return to Gordon and to live a penitent and retired life under her brother's protection. Even so, Caroline kept her distance, calling herself Sarah's friend rather than sister and raising immediate doubts about the plan's success. 'I am as glad as any of her friends at the step she has taken, but should be more glad had I much dependence on the steadiness of her reputation. However, one must hope for the future and be pleased with the present.' Of all the family, Caroline was the most tolerant of moral frailty. If her verdict on Sarah's re-habilitation was so lukewarm, the attitudes of Louisa and the Duke of Leinster would be much more stringent and Sarah's course of penitence would be a long one.

Sarah arrived at Goodwood in early December 1769. She stayed in the main house for a few weeks and then moved, with her child, maid and nurse, to Halnaker, a small manor house on the estate. Halnaker was an old-fashioned house, stone on the ground floor, half timbering above with mullioned windows and deep embrasures; a house lacking all the comforts of modernity. Sarah was immediately lonely there. Gordon returned to his family in Scotland. Neither parted unwillingly, but both had regrets, Sarah for her child, Lord William for himself. Although she was sensitive to the mention of Gordon's name for years to come, Sarah's remorse saw off the best part of lust, leaving only regret and memory. Once installed at Goodwood she did not want Lord William back.

What Sarah did want and what her future offered was a problem that engrossed the whole family. She was only twenty-four and her beauty and vivacity would soon return.

It seemed unlikely that she would spend the rest of her life in complete retirement. But she was ostracised from society. Respectable men and women, her erstwhile friends and acquaintances, would not or could not see and receive her. When there were guests at Goodwood she had to stay out of sight. Even her relatives were careful. Conolly was nervous about having her at Castletown and Louisa nursed his wishes to the point of excess. The Duke of Leinster barred her categorically from visiting or even writing to Emily. Holland House was Sarah's best hope of a respite from Sussex, but until Caroline's anger against the family died down even its doors were closed to her.

After their early anger had subsided Emily and Caroline both expressed their wish that Bunbury would divorce Sarah and that eventually she might marry again, even if she refused to marry Gordon. Louisa and the Duke of Richmond, on the other hand, strongly urged that Sarah should return to Bunbury and live a life of humble contrition. Still full of guilt and desperate for the family's forgiveness, Sarah agreed, saying that going back to Barton was the only restitution she could make for her crime.

While the family waited for Bunbury to decide Sarah's fate, the Duke and Louisa urged on Sarah the necessity of behaviour that reflected her situation. Just as before Sarah had studied how to please the King now she practised the display of penitence. At first her demeanour of settled sadness was everything that Louisa and the Duke of Richmond demanded, and she was careful that her behaviour and dress showed an equal desire for atonement. Louisa, arriving at Goodwood in the New Year, described Sarah's manner to Emily with satisfaction. 'She likes this quiet life of all things, and seems to have attention to the most trifling things. One thing is her dress. She means to study whatever is cheapest and plainest. And she does dress quite plain, no conceits of any sort.' And when Louisa suggested that a local painter come and give them lessons in oils, Sarah, unpowdered and sombrely dressed, asked on cue, 'was he a neat, fine gentleman, because if he was she thought it would not be so proper for her to see him.'

Louisa Bunbury softened Louisa's heart by calling her 'Aunt', 'quite plainly'. But Sarah came in for frequent chastisement. 'She tells my brother and I everything she thinks, and is so desirous of being set right where she is wrong and very ready to accuse herself of doing wrong,' Louisa reported to Emily. Sarah pleased Louisa by saying that 'her situation' was 'the best that she could have wished for herself at present'.

Louisa and, to a lesser extent the Duke of Richmond, wanted Sarah to suffer for the havoc she had unwittingly unleashed in the family. Louisa was bearing a heavy burden, carrying the confidences of all her siblings and entrusted by them with the task of gluing the broken vessel of family happiness back together again. Some of this anxiety she passed on to Sarah as a need to share out the misery. To herself Louisa explained her pleasure at Sarah's misery a different way. It was, as she told Emily, a happiness at recognising Sarah's underlying goodness of heart. 'From her own account of herself, moments of cheerfulness was the most she could brag of, for happiness she had not, and the idea of wrong was so constantly present to her thoughts that she could never drive it away. I own I feel great pleasure when she relates all she suffered, for I have the happiness of discovering such a perfect good mind throughout it all.'

Louisa also had other reasons for wanting Sarah to plumb the full depths of remorse. In the first place, Sarah's affair threatened to undermine one of the foundations of Louisa's life. Louisa had always believed that doing good and being good brought happiness and, above all, love. Virtue secured her place in the family. If Sarah's crime went not only unpunished, but swiftly forgiven, and if Sarah was just as loved as an adulteress as a wife, then Louisa's life, based on goodness and service, was devalued. Louisa needed Sarah to feel miserable to confirm her own sense of worth.

In the second place, part of Louisa (and a part that, unlike Caroline, she had never managed to work into the fabric of her life) was fascinated by misdemeanour. Back in London in February 1770, Louisa went to a masquerade in Soho. At first she said she would not dress up but simply disguise herself with a mask of white trimmed with gold. But at the last minute she changed her mind and went dressed as an abbess in a white-corded gown, beads, gauze, black veil and 'scarlet knot to tie the diamond cross'. As everyone knew, an abbess was not so much a figure of goodness as a symbol of depravity, the common name for a Covent Garden procuress, a keeper of prostitutes and doyen of brothels. So Louisa saw herself as both protectress and procuress, an ambiguous figure who had not only tried to save Sarah from her fate but had also connived at it, turning a blind eye to her sister's affair. She enjoyed the evening enormously, writing to Emily, 'I was never more diverted than at the masquerade; it was one of the prettiest sights I ever saw.' But Louisa could only play at being bad. As soon as her costume came off she tried to shed her guilty delight in transgression and frowned even more strongly upon it in everyday life. Sarah embodied sinfulness and she must regret her behaviour.

But Sarah's regret could not be everlasting. Another, more mundane life had to take the place of grandiloquent sorrow, especially since Bunbury showed no sign of wanting her back. Gradually her spirits improved and she started to want more than family approbation for her remorse. By the summer of 1770, she was often cheerful for days at a time. She loved her precocious daughter, carefully recording her first babbles, syllables and words, and she was happy at Goodwood if there was a family party she could join. In the spring of 1771 Sarah visited Louisa, Caroline and Lord Holland in Bath, a place where a woman ostracised from London society could go with impunity. Caroline was delighted to see her and noted in her journal, 'Miss Bunbury a charming child'. After this reconciliation with Caroline, Sarah eased her way back into the family circle. She saw Ste and Charles James Fox and she visited her aunt Lady Albemarle. The O'Briens arrived back from New York in 1770 and Sarah soon became intimate with Susan again. Sarah's transgression meant it was now hard to decide whose morality was the more compromised, the lady turned adulteress or the heiress who had married the actor: they were equally degraded and outcast.

Louisa was anxious about Sarah's rehabilitation. She wrote and counselled caution and deception. No one must think that Sarah was too cheerful. 'You have so little disguise that when you feel in spirits you allow your natural vitality to appear. I dislike disguise as much as anybody can do, and yet I think in your case a little is absolutely necessary . . . I would have you use disguise enough to look grave.' As late as 1772, nearly four years after Louisa Bunbury's birth, Louisa was still watching Sarah for signs that she might slip back into frivolity and immorality. She told her sister not to be too cheerful in public and warned her against the company of men, especially men who might lead her astray. Charles James Fox, who combined free thought with charm, was an especial risk, in Louisa's view, not just to Sarah but to every woman. 'Dear Charles,' she wrote, 'it seems so odd to talk of him as if of a dangerous person, but indeed he is to you or to any young woman with whom he converses freely . . . His free notions with respect to religion and women are his greatest faults.' Army officers, too, were the object of Louisa's censure; they joined glamour to immorality.

Louisa reluctantly recognised that her sister deserved small, rationed rewards for good behaviour. By the early 1770s Sarah was allowed to go to Kingsgate and to London, although she rarely went beyond the confines of Holland House Park and Whitehall. Even public spaces opened up to her although some, like the Court, would be closed for ever. After a few years of penance Sarah could venture again to pleasure gardens, theatres and the painter's studio – places where morality was sufficiently compromised every day to let a fallen woman go without comment. In the mid-1770s Sarah described a foray to London to Emily. 'The Duchess [of Richmond] was going to town for a short time. The town was remarkably empty as it always is in September because of the shooting, so I thought it would be wiser to take the opportunity, as I knew I could not go without a fuss till next September . . . I one day went with the Duchess to see a new ballroom that's prettily fitted up, and to look at Sir Joshua's pictures; and, that one jaunt excepted, I never went out of Whitehall walls or saw a single creature, for I told nobody that I was in town so nobody thought about me.' Confined in Richmond House, Sarah contented herself with armchair shopping, 'making the shopkeepers bring me all sorts of pretty things to look at, as I wanted to see all that was to be seen and yet not go out.'

At Holland House Sarah was soon back in Lord Holland's heart and Caroline quickly forgave her. Chastisement held few attractions for Caroline. Besides, welcoming Sarah back was one way Caroline could demonstrate to the Duke of Leinster that she did indeed care for her sisters. Louisa thought that Sarah's visits to Holland House would give her 'the reputation of living in the world again', but Sarah did not stop going. She was loved and needed there. Indeed, very soon it was not so much Caroline who was offering succour to Sarah as the other way round. Caroline was distressed about her sons, miserable about Henry and seemed to be in failing health.

PART TWO
'That miserable sickness in
her stomach still continues'.
Louisa to Sarah, 23 April 1774.

Caroline had looked forward to old age. 'I flatter myself I shall go gently down the hill to a better place,' she wrote to

Emily in 1768 when she was forty-five. She had also happily contemplated a retirement from politics that would be made serene and comfortable by the love of her husband, sons and sisters. But when her fiftieth birthday came round at the end of March 1773, Caroline surveyed her world and found it wanting. Lord Holland was making no attempt to stop life drifting away from him. He had, as Charles James Fox put it later, 'given up', lost interest in the pursuits of the living and fixed his sights on oblivion. The quarrel between the Hollands and the Leinsters was still stuck on the rock of mutual obstinacy and she seemed to be in the throes of the menopause, bleeding painfully, sometimes for weeks on end. To cap it all, her sons' extravagant gambling was enthralling the press and taxing even the vast Fox fortune.

In 1768, Lord Holland, by now sixty-three and feeling his years, had written to a friend: 'I cannot help feeling, even in the midst of so amiable a family, the truth of what Bishop Hough said, that the length of days is not a desirable thing. I often cry out Oh! wearisome condition of mortality.' Nothing changed his mind in the years that followed despite his sons beginning their parliamentary careers. Both Charles and Ste entered Parliament in 1768, Ste to make brief appearances, Charles to take the House by storm, dazzling everyone with his brilliant oratory. But Lord Holland did not regard Charles's triumphs as sufficient compensation for the ill treatment he believed himself to have suffered from the monarch (who had refused him an earldom), from his political allies (who had deserted him) and from the press and City aldermen (who were now questioning his accounts as Paymaster). 'Honesty is not the best policy' and 'good nature does not meet with the return it ought to do' were his new political truths.

In the summer of 1770, when he and Caroline returned from Nice, Lord Holland took to a wheelchair, a sturdy machine built with wood and iron to support his growing weight. He was pushed about the green lawns of Holland

House, winked at by its mullioned windows and shaded by cedar trees whose age mocked at his infirmities. On wet days he was stationed by the fireside in the drawing-room. Both he and Caroline avoided the picture gallery, occupied by those they never saw now. Emily, reading a folio volume with the Duke of Leinster near by; Sarah, leaning out of a window with Charles and Susan; the Duke of Richmond and his Duchess; Sir Charles Bunbury wearing frilled cuffs and a gleaming white cravat: the gallery's optimistic display of family unity and happiness was another mockery and another cause for bitterness.

Thinking about her sons' affairs, Caroline needed a calmness which she had rarely had even in more cheerful times. Ste and Charles had become notorious at Newmarket and all along St James's for the magnitude both of their bets and of their losses. Night after night Ste and Charles met at Almack's, sometimes riding down from Newmarket for the purpose. Inside the gaming room of the club they exchanged coins and promissory notes for rouleaux or tokens of fifty pounds each, stacked them on the green-baize table tops and began to play. Their embroidered frock-coats were turned inside out for luck, or replaced by plain great-coats. Over their lace cuffs they pulled pieces of leather, like those worn by the Holland House footmen when they cleaned the plate. To crown this costume gamblers wore high hats with broad brims covered in flowers and ribbons, claiming that they prevented carefully arranged curls from disorder and sensitive eyes from the light. This attire failed to bring the Fox brothers any luck. They were notorious and insouciant losers: hundreds and then thousands of pounds disappeared in a night's sitting.

Lord Holland hated to see his sons dissipate money accrued in order to lend muscle to their political ambitions. It was Charles's losses that hurt him most because it was Charles he had groomed for political success from the time twenty years before when he had sat him on top of the side of beef at Holland House. In 1772 and 1773 relations between loving father and errant son frayed. 'Never let Charles know how excessively he afflicts me,' Henry wrote to Ste in the summer of 1772. Caroline reacted with much less detachment, regarding her sons' indulgence as an unfavourable verdict on her motherhood. Because Ste was her favourite son it was he who distressed her most. In the summer of 1773, Lord Holland tried to stave off disaster by paying off some of his eldest son's creditors in return for a promise from Ste that the profligacy would stop. Ste signed the agreement but carried on gambling, and Caroline wrote angrily to him a few days later, 'you have played again, lost 3000 pounds, God knows how much more perhaps, for after this what dependence can be had upon your resolution? You will, you must inevitably be ruined. I'm hurt, I'm angry and will trust myself to say no more.' But she did, scribbling through her tears, 'remember your promise. Let your name be scratched out of every club in London if you expect ever to be received by your afflicted mother. Lord Holland knows nothing of this. I wish to keep it from him, but cannot answer for myself. Oh Ste, what misery you bring on and will do to all you love.' Caroline told Henry everything. He was still her fountainhead, the source of her self-esteem and, she felt, the only confidant she had left. Ste gambled again and his creditors, alerted by Lord Holland's earlier payments, closed in for the kill.

When Ste's finances collapsed in the autumn of 1773, Lord Holland decided to clear all his son's debts completely, freeing his own income and estates for his grandchildren. Puffing and wheezing, overweight and distraught, Lord Holland sat with his chair rolled up to a table and signed paper after paper. He sold stock and annuities, spare bundles of land and unwanted effects. In the middle of the task, on 5 October, he had a stroke.

It was a mild stroke, mainly affecting his vision, making him see objects doubled and distorted. But to Caroline it presaged his end and with it the end of her world. She was in no doubt who should carry responsibility for her husband's illness and death: all those whom he had loved and trusted and who had betrayed him. 'Oh Ste, this last attack, whatever it was, I'm confident has been owing to the disagreeable business he has of late been engaged in on your account. Lord Holland's ill state of health, I'm persuaded, is solely owing to the vexations of his mind, which have been too powerful for a benevolent, friendly-feeling heart like his. Rigby, Calcraft etc, etc, began; the Duke of Leinster, Lord Hillsborough, Sarah greatly contributed; and Charles and you have put the finishing touch. How painful this idea must be to you I know. Charles does not feel it, but he will sorely one day; so he ought. And indeed Ste, fondly as I once loved you both, I do not scruple distressing you by telling you how much you are in the wrong. Indeed, indeed, you ought to feel it and let it be deeply imprinted on your mind.'

Caroline wrote on and on, as if the act of writing down her feelings could expunge them, hoping against hope that anger might get the better of her love for her sons and leave her uncaring and unburdened. In her heart she knew that she could neither forget nor cease to love them and the knowledge only added to her pain. 'As for myself, perhaps you have done me no harm, only contributed to wean me from the afflictions of this life and make me look more comfortably towards a better where ... happiness was intended for us. As for Charles, I must endeavour to drive him from my thoughts entirely; happy shall I be if I can accomplish it.'

Lord Holland did recover. He was well enough to take pleasure in the birth of his grandson Henry at the end of November and to discharge debts accrued by Charles Fox to the tune of £140,000. Sometimes he was alert and even cheerful, as if after a wait longer than he had wished, the end of the journey raised his spirits. But his memory was patchy and his powerful constitution gradually failing. Nobody expected him to last the winter, but he did. Caroline took him to Bath and to Ste's house in Wiltshire, where he sat in his chair, heavy and immobile, rousing himself now and again when his grandson was brought to him or his grand-daughter Caroline clambered on to his knees. As the weeks passed he stopped fretting about his sons and, sloughing off the world, wanted only to be with them and to feel their love.

Friends noticed that while Lord Holland seemed to be sliding painlessly out of life, Caroline was often in agony. Pain in her back sometimes made her unable to walk upstairs. She had lost her plumpness, a 'falling away' friends ascribed to family troubles, and she bled continually, a sign, she thought, of the menopause. The doctors in Bath and London, in whom she had for so long placed money and faith, assured her that she would soon get well and she believed them. 'Please God to restore my health, I do not despair of being a tolerable comfortable old woman.'

About the time of Lord Holland's stroke, Caroline's round about enquiries about the Carton family brought news which she received with a mixture of emotions: anxiety, then a sense of satisfaction mixed with guilt. Louisa reported that the Duke of Leinster was unwell. He had for some time suffered from asthma, but he was now troubled by a new complaint, diagnosed as gout. His feet had swollen and the swelling travelled quickly up to his knees, filling his legs with fluid. Emily was 'vastly vexed', as Louisa put it, because her husband was a difficult patient, an active man who chafed at idleness. But Emily had no fears that her husband's life was in danger.

The Duke of Leinster's doctors – Quin in the country and Smyth in town – had another opinion. They pronounced the gout dropsical, the sort of disorder that presaged a lingering death as the kidneys failed and the body gradually became saturated with fluid. The Duke sat in Leinster House with his legs out on a stool. While he grumbled at his inertia, Dr Quin took William Ogilvie aside and told him that the Duke was going to die. He was entrusting the knowledge and the task of telling the Duchess the news to Ogilvie because he occupied a special position within the family.

Ogilvie immediately told Louisa the doctor's conclusion, and they shared the secret until Louisa told Sarah who told Caroline and the rest of the family. By 7 November water had filled the Duke's legs as high as his thighs. He lay in his bed now, free of pain, in good spirits, stoically waiting to die. Everyone knew that once the fluid reached his lungs, death would follow quickly. Emily, Louisa wrote, 'is unhappy about it, and I believe has very little hope in her own mind.' But Emily did not confide in Louisa, who stayed at Castletown. She poured out her heart to Ogilvie, who came up to Dublin from Black Rock every day during the last stages of the Duke's illness.

Caroline heard of the Duke's imminent death in mid-November 1773. Although she had come to hate him, she never wanted death to be the means of settling the quarrel between them. She thought of Emily's misery and of her own need for a confidante. The love she felt for her sister came welling up and overwhelmed her. Picking up her pen she wrote: 'My dearest sister. Ill as I am and little able to write, I cannot resist sending you these few lines to express my concern to you for the present anxiety you suffer. God knows how much I should wish to be able to relieve it, and how sincerely I wish all may go better than your present fears allow you to think. Adieu, my dearest, best beloved sister; for that must ever be the case, notwithstanding all that has passed. I'm going soon to Bath. Yours most affectionately, C. Holland.' With these words the quarrel of four and a half years was ended. Much later Emily turned the letter over and inscribed it in her tiny neat hand, 'My sister Holland, after a long silence, November 23rd 1773'.

When Caroline wrote her note, the Duke had been dead for four days. By the time Emily received it, he had been buried in Christ Church Cathedral and she, dressed and veiled in black silk and lace, sat in the cheerless expanse of Leinster House receiving calls and answering letters of condolence. She wrote back thanking Caroline for her note and quickly received a reply. 'I cannot resist the pleasure of thanking my dear sister for her kind letter, so great a balm to my mind is the renewal of our long interrupted correspondence; every trace of the occasion of it is long wore out of my mind. I had the beginning of this winter burnt every paper that could record it, and should sooner have wrote to you but that I did not know whether in the anxious state of your mind it would be proper.'

Emily grieved for her husband. Despite the clouds of its later years – her growing love for Ogilvie, the Duke's refusal to compromise in the quarrel with Caroline – it had been a successful marriage. For twenty-five years the Duke had loved his wife passionately. He had pandered to her pride, encouraged her extravagance and satisfied her vanity; and if, after Ophaly's death and Ogilvie's arrival, Emily had become dissatisfied with the terms of her marriage, widowhood offered no solution.

Soon to be Dowager Duchess of Leinster (although she refused to don the title except in the most public of circumstances, insisting that she was still simply the Duchess), Emily was living on a jointure and without the almost unlimited credit the Duke's name and lands had secured. The Duke of Leinster's will, however, was extremely generous, a recognition of Emily's expensive habits. To the jointure of £3,000 a year agreed in their marriage settlement of 1747 he added another thousand pounds. Provision was made for younger sons and daughters (the boys were given land, the girls marriage portions) and while they were still in their mother's care they were each given a yearly allowance. Emily had Carton and all its furnishings for life, provided she did not remarry or go to live in England. So she was not in straitened circumstances. It was her son William, who now assumed the title of second Duke, who would have to bear the burden. He still had to pay old Lady Kildare £3,000 a year. His mother's £4,000 and the allowances for his siblings, along with the interest on debts of almost £150,000 virtually wiped out his income, and he did not even have Carton to retreat to.

Despite her prosperity, Emily was in a difficult position. The Duke's death exposed her affair with Ogilvie. As long as he lived, his social standing and political influence protected her from Dublin gossip; only muted rumours about the Duchess and the tutor had so far crept about. Now nobody stood between Emily and exposure. Moreover, the Duke's fertility had covered Emily's infidelity: Lord George Simon Fitzgerald, born on 16 April 1773, was probably not the Duke's son, but an Ogilvie, every bit as illegitimate as Louisa Bunbury.

Emily was not overcome with guilt about her affair as Sarah had been. She had had every intention of keeping her husband, her lover and her good name. Pushing the rules of aristocratic gallantry to the limit she managed her affair with great aplomb and discretion. But she was not prepared to give Ogilvie up – as rumour and convention demanded – when her husband died. Emily might borrow the form of Rousseau's *La Nouvelle Héloïse*, but she spurned the conclusion. She was no Julie, to die with her passionate impulses thwarted. In a gesture of defiance she left Dublin and, summoning Ogilvie and the children from Black Rock, she took them all to Carton.

Louisa had mentioned Ogilvie only rarely in her letters to England. But on 21 January 1774 she wrote to Sarah: 'I quite dote upon Mr. Ogilvie. He is such a good sort of man, and very pleasant to us, from entering into all our ways, and if I can't be with my sister, I frequently leave my directions with him to make my sister do what is good for her and he does it. Only think what a blessing it is to have such a man take care of the boys. In her present situation, what a distress it would be to her to know what to do with her sons. But she may be perfectly easy while they are in his care.' Ogilvie was filling Louisa's thoughts and she decided the time had come to introduce him to the rest of the family. Louisa had watched Emily and Ogilvie fall in love at Black Rock from the vantage point of her cottage next door. She may even have known that they were having an affair. But she did not know about Lord

George Simon's possible parentage and she refused to recognise the depths of Emily's involvement. Mr Ogilvie as an embodiment of Saint Preux, as Rousseau come to life, was romantic and just about tolerable. But Louisa was unable to countenance anything more. Emily's open flouting of convention after the Duke's death stunned her.

In the winter and spring of 1773–74 Emily, Ogilvie and the children moved between Carton and Black Rock depending upon whim and weather. Emily had always been determined and she had always got what she wanted. None the less the gossip immediately began. The Earl of Bellamont, who was engaged to Emily's eldest daughter, began to make trouble about the marriage settlement and delayed the wedding, so banking up the fires of speculation about a troop of bastards and a secret marriage between the Duchess and the tutor.

Emily was not immune to gossip, but she allowed others to fight for her reputation and, while they did so, she resolutely went her own way. Once she was settled with Ogilvie and the children, Emily grew 'better' as Louisa put it to Sarah. Her most pressing worry was not the dark undercurrent of scandal but the indomitable and obvious performance of her own body. If, or when, she got pregnant again, her child would have no ducal covering for its illegitimacy.

By mid-January 1774, Emily had decided to go abroad, taking Ogilvie with her and offering her children's health as an explanation. She wrote to Caroline describing the plan, but missing out any mention of Ogilvie. Caroline replied to her sister's letter with a short sad note dated 29 January 1774. 'Pray go sweet siss, and God Almighty send you success in an undertaking so worthy of your good sense. . . . Lord Holland bids me tell you he loves you dearly and approves your scheme; I'm sure, dearest sister I'm totally disinterested in so doing, for my gloomy situation of mind makes me think we shall never meet again.' 'Adieu dear sister,' Caroline added, as if she knew that these were the last words she would ever send to Emily, 'Adieu. I'm tired with writing. Yours ever. C. H.'

*

At Castletown Louisa had received 'a terrible account' of Caroline's health from the Duke of Richmond. This and Caroline's own letter convinced Emily that if she went abroad immediately she would never see her sister alive again. So instead of starting out on a new life herself, Emily decided to go to London with Louisa and to be with Caroline on the last lonely journey from life into death.

The Duke of Richmond had given few hopes for Caroline's life. She was emaciated and shrunken, racked with pain that shuddered down her back. She retched and vomited continually, unable to keep down any nourishment. The doctors who plied the wings and galleries of Holland House were divided in their diagnoses. Some thought she had cancer, others not; some said she could recover, others that she could not last long. Caroline confused the doctors she had once placed so much trust in because she fought and controlled her pain, concentrating on her illness all the obstinacy she had shown towards those who had fallen foul of her sense of justice or her wishes. She had much to live for; her ailing husband and sisters, her sons and grandchildren, books and friends, the towers and gardens of Holland House and the happy retirement she had promised herself there.

Forgetting the anger and the quarrels of earlier years, Caroline directed her will inwards. When she heard of her sisters' departure from Ireland she began to rally. Louisa and Emily arrived in London at the end of February and were surprised to find Caroline 'better' and talk of cure in the air. But Caroline's animation was spasmodic. Emily and Louisa could see that the eyes that filled with tears on their arrival, and again and again in the days that followed, glittered too fiercely, that Caroline's cheeks were hollow, and that, for all her nimbleness, she stood still for long seconds, fighting the pain that surged through her body. None the less, Louisa told Sarah, 'her spirits are wonderfully good when she is tolerably easy.' Holland House was full of visitors and Caroline was still playing the role of hostess. Dinner passed without her, but after dinner she roused herself and stayed with her guests as long as she could. In the evenings after visitors had gone, Louisa and Emily sat with her gossiping and distracting her from pain with 'chit-chat' as Louisa described it in one of her daily bulletins to Sarah.

Louisa was surprised that Holland House was functioning in its time-honoured way and astonished that Caroline still dressed and walked about. She had expected to find her sister resigned to death and she imagined a swift and dignified departure with solemn leave-takings and uplifting sermons. But Caroline was spurning death. Her face was turned towards the living; she eagerly drank in stories of love affairs, drawing-room news, political hubbub. After a lifetime decrying politics and the world, they were now what she wanted. Gossip was a sign of an involvement in life, and Caroline still wanted to live. She rejected any religious disquisitions: God, she seemed to imply, was for the dying. 'She has never at any time talked to either my sister or me upon any serious subject whatever,' Louisa told Sarah, bewildered that Caroline dismissed any thought of the afterlife.

Caroline was comforted by her sisters' presence, by the sense of physical unity and the reminder of past happiness that they brought. She asked little of them, happy just to have them by her. But she could soon no longer disguise her pain. In the second week of April her nausea and vomiting became worse and the pain in her back and abdomen grew incessant. Grains of opium, carefully measured by the score, numbed the agony and Caroline fought on. In mid-April Harry Fox arrived from Paris, *en route* for Boston, where the regiment he was joining was stationed. He stayed a week saying goodbye, but Caroline seemed in too much pain to regret his departure.

Still she clung on to life. The doctors, unused to such tenacity, began to doubt their earlier diagnosis of cancer. Hunter, the famous surgeon, carefully hedged his bets, saying that Caroline's pulse was not 'that of a dying person' and concluded that 'the progress of her disorder', whatever it was, would be 'slow'. After two months in London Emily decided to go back to Ireland. She was exhausted and worried by her separation from Ogilvie and the children. Caroline was saddened by the news, but buoyed up by Louisa's promise to stay another fortnight.

Before Emily set off, Louisa changed her mind, suddenly anxious about being away from Conolly any longer. Caroline was too fragile to accept Louisa's change of heart easily but she had strength enough to let her sister know it, as Louisa told Sarah. 'It seemed a disappointment to her, she said it would have been such a comfort to her and wanted to contrive my not going, but ended with saying I had been very good to her and she was only sorry I had hinted it as she had thought a great deal about it.'

Louisa and Emily left for Ireland at the beginning of May 1774. After their departure both Caroline and Lord Holland continued on their inexorable journey, he with something like melancholy enjoyment, she trying furiously to grip and hold the things and people she held dear as she passed them one by one on the descent. Lord Holland's slide was gradual, but sometime in the spring he slipped into a kind of unconsciousness. Lying in his chamber, almost insensible to his surroundings, he seemed sunk within himself, inhabiting an underground inner world, unruffled by medicines, bedpans and the heaving servants who lifted and turned him in his bed. His swarthy cheeks were drooping and slack. The energy that had tightened his body and driven his ambitions had drained away and his hands lay gently flattened on the counterpane.

Lord Holland was dying a good death. Somewhere, deep down, cynicism, and the mischievousness that had tempered it, still simmered. Instead of fighting death, Lord Holland sneered and mocked at it, hoarding his wit for one last display. One day, George Selwyn left his card. The footman, hardly expecting a reply from his almost unconscious master, but nervous in the circumstances about Selwyn's reputation for necrophilia, asked if he should send Selwyn up next time he called. From the depths of himself, as if he had been keeping the words for a suitable moment, Holland unexpectedly spoke up. 'If I am alive,' he said, 'I will be delighted to see him; and if I am dead, he would like to see me.'

In the weeks that followed, Lord Holland said little more. He was reconciled with his sons, forgetting the dissipation of his fortune, happy that each evening they came and sat with him. Ste Fox's wife, Mary, lived at Holland House, moving between its sick inhabitants with patience and composure. By the end of June Lord Holland had sunk deeper into death. He seemed to be unaware of his family and his breathing slowed to loud snores. He died as he wanted, without struggling, on 1 July.

Louisa arrived back at Holland House on the day Lord Holland died, summoned from Ireland once again by desperate reports of Caroline's health. This time Conolly was with her and she was determined to stay to the end. Almost as soon as she arrived Louisa had to go with Mary Fox to Caroline's room and tell her that her husband was dead. They broke the news in stages, making it easier for everyone to manage. Caroline did not mourn Henry. Her emotions were concentrated on herself. Besides, the wit, energy and sensuality – all the things she had loved in him – had died already. Louisa told Sarah, 'she says she can't feel as if it had happened now, but as if it had happened a great while ago.' In spite of her acceptance of his death, Caroline could not imagine life without her husband. She asked Louisa over and over again what would become of her, begging her sister to do her business and take care of her.

Caroline's refusal to accept death called for constant delicacy. Louisa wrote to Emily on 4 July: 'she distressed me vastly last night by asking me if they thought her case hopeless. I was obliged to deceive her, which grieved me, as I should take it so excessively ill to be treated in the same manner. But having always heard it was her wish to be deceived, I did it.' Louisa was particularly worried because Lord Holland

had left so much in Caroline's power in his will that she had
to make a will of her own if his was to be properly executed.
Caroline was very disturbed by Louisa's gentle suggestion
that she make a will, rightly understanding it as a verdict on
her own situation. Although she said nothing to her sister,
Caroline knew then that she was dying, and told her maids
that she would not live for many days. Even after her will was
drawn up and signed she kept silent speaking her mind only
obliquely in the 'dreadful nervous horrors' that accompanied
her bouts of pain, when her tormented mind wandered between the past and the future and looked forward with terror
to extinction. In spite of her pain and Henry's death, Caroline
still did not give up. She was frightened and angry but unre-
conciled to death.

Caroline's body finally failed her spirit. By 8 July it began
to swell, feet first and then her hands and face. Her mind,
though, was still clear and still rebellious. On the night of
the tenth of July, as Louisa and Mary were leaning over her,
wondering if she were still breathing, Caroline said quite
audibly, 'I am very sorry that I must go and leave you all, but
I find it must be. However, I will hope to the last, because
people are sometimes so ill in my disorder.' The next day she
lay down at last, overcome by nausea and pain, giving in to
the anguish. Louisa noticed that her sister was like a woman
in labour, 'dozing between the pains'. The dosage of laudanum was increased drop by drop, and when it failed to dent
the pain the doctors mixed hemlock with it, which acted as a
powerful sedative. By 16 July Caroline's body had given out.
The stench of faeces was added to the aroma of hemlock in
her room. Relatives and friends had all said goodbye. Only
Louisa and Mary stayed, watching Caroline fight her way
out of life as she had been born, on convulsions of agony.
But when the end came Caroline needed neither God nor
guidance. She met death angrily, head on, only giving up her
life when it was snatched from her, awake and in agony until
her last hours. On 19 July Caroline developed a hiccup; her

breathing failed slowly over the next few days and on 24 July, with Louisa by her bedside, she died.

Louisa arrived back in Ireland at the end of July 1774. She found Emily at Black Rock with Ogilvie and the children. William, now second Duke, was installed at Carton. Carton had been left to Emily for life, provided she remained a widow and stayed in Ireland. But by the time Louisa returned, Emily and Ogilvie had bartered the great house away, swapping it for the unfinished cluster of buildings at Black Rock, the promise of some money (which rumour put at £40,000) and, most important, a sense of obligation. William was grateful to his mother: as the new Duke he needed Carton to sustain his pre-eminent position amongst the aristocracy and to offer any bride of his own a suitable country house. Gossips in Dublin saw the transaction in a different light. Glossed by the terms of the Duke's will, Emily's willingness in handing Carton over was seen as proof of her marriage. Lord Bellamont, who had grandiose ambitions and was anxious for advancement within the Protestant élite, began to regret his engagement to Emily Fitzgerald. Instead of social standing and political influence he seemed to be getting an alliance with a family who countenanced and concealed a connection with a schoolmaster. Bellamont tried to withdraw from the marriage contract. He strode up and down the Dublin streets denouncing Ogilvie and Emily to all his acquaintances. Finally he sat down and wrote a letter to William at Carton, renouncing Emily Fitzgerald and demanding to know the truth behind the persistent rumours.

Allowing Bellamont to renege on his marriage contract would have seemed confirmation of his charges. The second Duke of Leinster, who did not want anyone to know that he had been fooled into striking a bargain for Carton when it might have come to him by law, was as anxious as Emily and Ogilvie to push through the wedding and confirm their version of events. Despite the blow to his pride, the young Duke wrote Bellamont an open refutation of the rumours about his mother. 'My Lord. I showed your Lordship's letter to my mother and she declared to me that she was not married to Mr. Ogilvie and she was sorry to find that from his connection with the family by having the care and education of her children that report should have spread of there being a greater intimacy. I am your Lordship's most obedient humble servant, Leinster.' Emily had answered her son's question with a careful sophistry. She denied that she was married, but she only regretted rumours of an affair. William did not notice. He was, as Sarah later noted, 'terrified' of his mother and felt compelled to stand by her. Armed with her statement he demanded that Bellamont marry his sister. Bellamont agreed with great reluctance, arriving at Carton on 20 August. Then, at the last moment, he refused to marry Emily Fitzgerald, lost his temper, reasserted his belief in the secret marriage and, in a fit of rage, denounced Emily as a 'whore'. A general fracas followed. Bellamont claimed Emily Fitzgerald as his source of information and stuck by his story. Louisa, leaping to her sister's defence, questioned Bellamont's moral probity, saying that he had ruined the reputation of a Miss McDermot. There was talk of a duel; but after a day of arguments, claims and counterclaims, a day which Louisa looked back to as one of the worst in her life, Bellamont was harried and cajoled towards the minister and, amidst his protests, he and Emily Fitzgerald were married.

Emily allowed her sister and her sons to fight for her reputation in the dispute with Lord Bellamont. But the Duke of Leinster and, probably, Louisa knew that Bellamont was not far from the truth. It is more or less certain that some time in August, Ogilvie and Emily were married in Dublin, whether before or after Emily Fitzgerald's marriage to Bellamont, no one revealed. Secrecy was sworn and the secret was kept safely. William, Louisa and Emily's friend Lady Barrymore agreed to tell everyone that it looked as if Emily and Ogilvie might be married in the future. Only once in the years to come did the Duke of Leinster let his mother's secret slip out. Writing to his mother in May 1776, he apologised profusely for his error and in so doing confirmed that his mother had indeed married Ogilvie before they left Ireland. 'I am sorry you should think that I either desired or ordered Mr. Lyster to say your marriage was in August; nor, I am sure, did he mean to do so. Therefore I hope you'll excuse us both; for me it was inadvertency, and him, not knowing.'

Leaving their secrets behind, Emily and Ogilvie left Waterford for Bordeaux on 8 September 1774. Apart from William, Duke of Leinster, Emily Bellamont and Lord Charles Fitzgerald, who was now in the navy, they took the whole Fitzgerald brood with them. Charlotte, now sixteen, was the eldest child still at home. She was old enough to be married but was regarded as plain, bad tempered and a family liability. Behind her came the children of the 1760s: Henry, aged thirteen; Sophia, twelve; Edward, eleven; Robert, nine; and Gerald who was eight. Finally there came what Caroline had called Emily's 'little, little family', Fanny, aged four; Lucy, three; Louisa, two; and George Simon who was only a year old.

Emily, embarking for France and a new life, was nearly forty-three. She complained to Louisa of rheumatism and low spirits, but these were ways of describing the mixture of anxiety and joy that filled her. By defying both convention and rumour she had gathered everything she needed for her adventure, and she was determined to do in her own life what Rousseau, with his contradictory urges to subversion and sobriety, had been unable to do in *La Nouvelle Héloïse*. Not only was she keeping her lover, she was also going to live in style. Besides her jointure of £4,000 a year, they had allowances for the children and the extra money from William for Carton: plenty to live on in France where goods were cheap. Emily and Ogilvie would live in comfort if not in ducal style. Ogilvie was a shrewd investor. Emily was never without a carriage, and although she sometimes made do with last years' fashions, she still read books straight off the press. When they eventually came back to Ireland, as Emily planned, Black Rock, enlarged and ennobled, would be waiting for them. All the time they were in France, Black Rock was Emily's place of happy memories and dreams, the 'dear place' where she and Ogilvie had 'spent so many happy hours in *conversation sweet*, as Milton says'.

Gazing over the prow of the *Nelly* as she bounced towards France in an early autumn storm, Ogilvie and Emily saw obstacles as well as delight ahead. Their return to Black Rock depended on Louisa's skills in persuading their friends and relations to treat Mr Ogilvie as a gentleman and to accept Emily as an honourable woman. But their own future depended on creating a way to live. Emily's first marriage had been governed by a set of conventions which she accepted and enjoyed. For this new life there were no rules. There had been unions between peers and actresses, earls and courtesans, but there were few precedents for the marriage of a duchess and family servant. Not only the pattern of day-to-day living, but the very framework of the relationship had to be forged. The money was almost all Emily's, but the ability to manage it belonged exclusively to Ogilvie. The children were hers, but had been in his charge for six years. She had the social cachet, but the social distance between them was narrowing, despite her refusal to call herself anything other than the Duchess of Leinster. The old relationship of command and obedience was in disarray. She could no longer give her husband orders, he no longer need obey. Indeed, if Emily had turned for help to advice manuals written for women of more humble origins than herself, she would have found that society sanctioned a reversal of their old roles, he commanding, she complying. But their earlier relationship made even a notional compact of simple dominance and dependence impossible now. Wants, needs, duties and demands had all to be apportioned and worked out in the months to come; and, as Emily was to find, the strategies she had used to control her first husband were useless with her second. This time it was she rather than her husband who was jealous and sexually infatuated. Much in this new partnership was undecided and at risk.

Three people had been left the uneasy possessors of Emily's secret when she sailed away: Louisa, William and Lady Barrymore. William found the burden too heavy to bear and left Ireland soon after his mother, planning to keep out of the way in London for a few weeks. Inevitably, though, he met family friends who wanted to know the truth about his mother's relationship with Ogilvie and he was soon scurrying back to Ireland to lie low at Carton. Lady Barrymore dropped judicious hints in Dublin drawing-rooms suggesting a wedding sometime in the future, while Louisa wrote to and visited family and friends by turns, 'setting things right' as she put it, with the Jocelyns, Rodens, the Clements, old Lady Clanbrassil, Mrs Crosbie, the two Mrs Nicholsons, Mrs Vesey, Lord Russborough, Mrs Greville and various Macartneys: all Emily's particular friends. Together Louisa and William tackled old Lady Kildare, worried that she might object to Emily's marriage more on her late son's than her grandson's behalf. William dutifully reported their conversation to his mother, saying, 'we reasoned with her much on the subject, and I think we parted with her more reconciled.' As usual the old Countess rose to the occasion. She wrote to Emily applauding her choice and decrying her haste; then she moved swiftly on to a recipe for eye drops.

Louisa's approaches to the Lennox side of the family were cautious and gradual. Her first letter to Sarah, written two days after the emotional scenes at Emily Fitzgerald's wedding, was evasive and contained. 'The new married couple are to set out today for Bellamont Forest. They were married at Carton and all came here yesterday. She looks so happy its pleasant to see her and I hope he will be sensible of her merit, but he is so odd that he frightens one.' But Louisa could not withhold her news for long. Lady Barrymore had already dropped a hint about Emily's intention to marry Ogilvie to Lady Ailesbury, who had passed it on to her daughter the Duchess of Richmond, and now everyone at Goodwood was agog to know the truth of what had already happened and what might happen in the future. On 25 August Louisa declared that the Earl of Bellamont was 'a *bad man*'; on 4 September she admitted she felt uneasy and 'unsettled'. By this time Sarah had guessed the cause of Louisa's anxiety and asked point blank for confirmation or denial of Emily's marriage to Ogilvie. Noting on the letter front 'read this to yourself', Louisa replied carefully to Sarah's request, following the plan she had agreed with William and Lady Barrymore and which she thus described to Emily: 'I say we *suspect* that things may be in time ... This we tell in confidence as our own opinions, but positively assert that things are not yet concluded.'

To Sarah, Louisa wrote: 'These reports about her being married are at present quite without foundation. But there is so great a partiality that I would not answer for its being always the case; and to say the truth, I should fear that these reports were likely to determine an event of that sort, as nothing but parting with *him* will prevent people saying *worse* if it should not end in marriage, and that step of parting with *him* would be the most cruel thing she could do by her children.' Louisa offered two separate explanations for the marriage. The first was that marriage was forced on Emily by rumours; indeed that scandal had determined Emily upon a course by no means inevitable. The second, which Louisa threw in for good measure, was that the children needed Ogilvie and that the wedding was thus for their sake.

Both reasons rang hollow because the Goodwood household knew as well as Louisa that Emily would never be manoeuvred into a position of disadvantage. Louisa herself knew, but was unable to admit, that Emily's affair with Ogilvie was not a sudden romance born from grief and vulnerability, but a long-standing liaison based on shared interests and an active, mutual passion. At Goodwood, Sarah and the Duchess of Richmond easily saw through Louisa's queasy reasoning. The Duchess said that if Emily had no feelings for Ogilvie then there was absolutely nothing wrong with keeping him on as an employee. Sarah wrote to Louisa saying that she suspected that Ogilvie had been in love with Emily for some time. The Duke of Richmond added that he thought that Emily returned Ogilvie's feelings. Louisa was astonished at Sarah's perspicacity, writing to Emily six weeks after the *Nelly* sailed: '[Sarah's] loving you is not extraordinary, but her knowledge of the human heart is a little so I do think. Do you know that from what she picked up from me some years ago, and from you, when you were in England, the thought of *his* being in love with you had come into her head more than once, and when she told me the last time I saw her that we should *spoil him*, she meant it for a hint ... She knows the exact progress your heart made and understands how this attachment came about as well as if she had read your mind ... She says that Mr. Ogilvie could not but fall in love with you when he saw your character in the brightest light, which he had an opportunity of doing more than anybody, as you talked to him about your children.' After a few weeks the red herrings about Bellamont's scandalmongering and the welfare of the children were quietly dropped.

With varying degrees of amazement and reluctance members of the family came to understand that Emily and Ogilvie were in love and that their marriage was either concluded or inevitable. While her siblings shifted, turned and became reconciled, Emily herself waited, using Louisa as a conduit to family approbation, allowing her daughter Charlotte to give news of the party's progress through France and leaving Ogilvie the difficult task of putting his relationship with Louisa on to a footing of familial friendship. The second Duke of Leinster was shocked by his mother's insouciance but he was far too much in awe of her to do anything other than accept her marriage and eventual return to Ireland, contenting himself with writing on 11 September 1774: 'I confess my pride will be hurt and I feel sorry for it, and though I shall never feel pleasant at the sight of Mr. O. – from the idea – yet if properly managed we may live in friendship, though not in that degree of intimacy that perhaps you might wish or require us, yet a line must be drawn. Let what will happen, I shall not divulge your secret, nor will I give you up.'

The Duke and Duchess of Richmond, older and more knowing than the young Duke of Leinster, discounted their own pride and concentrated on the difficulties Emily might encounter by marrying someone who was not only her social inferior but had also been, until recently, receiving wages from her husband. They were accustomed to thinking of Ogilvie – if they thought of him at all – as a man who took orders and they had no idea how to receive him as one of the family; and this was especially true for Louisa who had known Ogilvie for six years as a tutor. But Louisa needed her sister's love and wanted to be generous towards Ogilvie. On 13 September she sat down and confessed to Emily both her anxieties and her determination to overcome them. 'My feelings about it have just been these. Two or three days at most, I believe, my pride was a little hurt. I am not sure it was my own pride; I rather think it was the prejudice of the world which one imbibes insensibly more than one thinks. But the more I consider it, the less I have to say about it. I agree with Sally, who says that one thinks it more desirable for you not to change your situation at all, but if you do I am clear in my opinion that it is the best match you can make ... Give my affectionate sisterly love to Mr. Ogilvie, for whom I feel it ... God bless you, my dearest, dearest, sister; I do love you with all my heart and soul.'

Once Emily's wedding was announced as certain, Sarah was her sister's most vociferous supporter. Love and revere Emily as she did, Sarah also saw advantages for herself in her sister's marriage. She relished both the drama of the event and the feeling that Emily's effrontery threw her own misdemeanours into the past and she was delighted that there were now two scapegraces in the family. Sarah was also shrewd enough to recognise Ogilvie's importance to Emily and she lavished upon him her most grandiloquent sentences. 'Though I am not known to Mr. Ogilvie by sight, yet I flatter myself I am enough known to him by my affection for you as to give me a right to begin my acquaintance with him now more personally ... I flatter myself that he will one day come among us and take as a *right* that regard, affection and esteem which everybody who knows you ought to be already inclined to give him from his being your choice.' Sarah wrote on, happy to have a crisis to relieve the boredom of Halnaker and complete her reconciliation with her sister. Ogilvie was in no position to cavil at Sarah's degradation. So Sarah's happiness was genuine and untrammelled: she had nothing to lose and much to gain. From her isolation in Sussex she looked joyfully forward to weeks at Black Rock chatting to her sister while little Louisa played with her Leinster cousins.

As Emily's entourage travelled slowly from Bordeaux, where the *Nelly* had docked in the middle of September, and up the valley of the Garonne river to Toulouse, Charlotte Fitzgerald coyly recorded its progress in fictionalised form. She kept a diary in which Emily was called 'Stella', that most literary of heroines, and Mr. Ogilvie was 'Davy'. At first the entries were commonplace. There was little to report from Bordeaux or on the road except for the minutiae of health, weather and travel. But on 26 October 1774 Charlotte recorded, as if it were the final chapter of a novel, a more important event. 'After breakfast Stella, Davy and Charlotte had a very interesting conversation on a subject which Davy and Charlotte had been conversing on before breakfast and which determined Stella upon a certain point ... Returned to dinner to the Inn where the Reverend Mr. Ellison, a Fellow of Trinity

◆

College, Dublin, was waiting for them. As dearest Stella had been engaged for some time to marry Davy, she was prevailed upon by his entreaties to embrace this favourable opportunity of an English clergyman, and condescended to make Davy the happiest of men by fulfilling that engagement on which the happiness of life depended. The marriage ceremony was performed by Mr. Ellison after dinner in the presence of Charlotte and Mrs. Rowley, the lovely Stella's woman. Stella was as beautiful as an angel. Mr. Ellison went away soon after that. Charlotte wrote letters and the lovely and adorable Stella and Davy spent a happy, dear evening.'

Mr Ellison the clergyman was the excuse rather than the reason for this ceremony. Perhaps the real cause lay dividing in Emily's womb: she was or soon would be pregnant again. Though she might have an affair with Mr Ogilvie and even travel through France with him, she could not, after the announcement of their engagement, have his child without publicly becoming his wife.

The family had been warned to expect Emily's announcement. But they did not know why Emily had hurried into matrimony so soon and they were surprised that she risked extra censure by marrying Ogilvie while she was conspicuously a widow, draped in black and still in mourning for her first husband. To marry so soon after the Duke of Leinster's death suggested a lack of reverence for his memory, an immoderate passion for his successor, a sudden need for legitimacy, or all three. Despite her support for her sister, Sarah could not resist reporting, on 11 December, that the Duke of Richmond and Lord George Lennox 'think it will hurt you vastly in the world to have married within even a year after your mourning; and they are vastly hurt at its being before the mourning was out.' But in the wider world, talk of Emily's haste was drowned out in wonder at the fact of the wedding itself. Mrs Delany, the famous conchologist, gossip and creator of cutouts, wrote to a friend: 'I mentioned the Duchess of Leinster's marriage to her son's tutor. People wonder at her marriage, as she is reckoned one of the proudest and most expensive women in the world. But perhaps she thought it incumbent (as Lady Brown says of Her Grace) "to marry and make an honest man of him".'

Emily's response to this sort of gossip was silence; to her brother's disapproval it was a disarming letter in which she accepted some of his criticisms, deflected others and won everybody round. 'I am content that you should call me a fool, and an *old fool*, that you should blame me and say you did not think me capable of such a folly; talk me over, say what you please, but remember that all I ask of you is your affection and tenderness.' Sarah was amazed and impressed. Describing Emily's letter to Susan O'Brien, Sarah wrote: 'My brother says there is no resisting her owning herself in the wrong and begging so hard to be loved . . . I assure you, my sister *gains* friends instead of losing any by her manner.'

Three months after the marriage ceremony in Toulouse Emily and Ogilvie seemed to have swept away all the major obstacles to the family's acceptance of their unorthodox union. Louisa had busied herself creating a pedigree for Ogilvie. 'I don't exactly know Mr. Ogilvie's age, he is related to Lord Finletta, and was disappointed by the late Lord of that name, of being provided for, as he had promised to do something for him; but having some dispute with him on that account, he came to Ireland where he had some friends, who assisted him in setting up a school, I believe the very first in Dublin . . . This is his history, which does not in any shape contradict what we heard about his being of a good gentleman's family.' But a genealogy was not really necessary; everyone knew that Ogilvie was a man of obscure origins and a good education and everyone knew that Emily was infatuated with him. She had managed the transition from adulteress to wife with magnificent aplomb, picking up a house and some extra cash on the way. But now she and Ogilvie faced a much greater, more mundane challenge. They had to forge a set of rules to live by and work out ways to manage their emotions, their children, their friends, finances and everyday life.

PART THREE
'Joy of my heart, charm of my
life, comfort of my soul'.
Emily to Ogilvie, 5 July 1777.

From the very beginning of their married life it was obvious
that Emily and Ogilvie would not adhere to the friendly,
courteous, frequently distant model of aristocratic unions.
Both of them saw passion and emotional entanglement as the
driving force in their relationship. When she fell in love with
Ogilvie the central features of Emily's life were transformed
and marriage to him fixed this change irrevocably. Emily's
children and sisters had previously taken pride of place in her
heart. Now Ogilvie emphatically came first; and if Louisa and
Sarah accepted the change as they accepted everything that
Emily dealt out to them, many of the Fitzgerald children did
not. Lucy and Sophia, in particular, resented their stepfather's
dominance and their mother's love for him. They battled
against Ogilvie all their lives, trying hopelessly to win their
mother back.

For a decade after her marriage, Emily was enfolded in the
drama of her passion for Ogilvie, calling her feeling 'the madness of love' and luxuriating in its extremity. When Ogilvie
went away, Emily described herself as 'whimpering like a
fool', bereft of his body and his conversation. None the less,
this was no one-sided dependence. On the strength both of
their previous relationship, her passion and fashionable conventions of marital fidelity, Emily made demands on her
husband that she had never made upon the Duke of Leinster.
She wanted Ogilvie by her side every day and she asked for
absolute fidelity from him. Even a glance at another woman
was tantamount to a betrayal. In 1778, Emily became convinced that Ogilvie was attracted to one of their servants; a
common occurrence at Carton, but now something that
aroused suspicion and torment. 'I own to you, I fret constantly,' she wrote to Ogilvie, after nursing her jealousy for

weeks. 'Why should I conceal it? Your manner and looks with that girl Marianne . . . have haunted me, and your wanting so precipitously to get her out of the house seems to confirm to me that my fears are not without foundation. You see by this how high an opinion I have of your heart, honour, humanity and sentiments towards me, since the same circumstances could be looked upon in direct opposite light. But I know you so well, my dear William, that I am certain you would wish to remove any object that you thought likely to cause me any inconvenience, but, at the same time I have the strongest dependence on your never acting contrary to the love you have shown me. I cannot help being jealous of what your intentions may sometimes be.'

Emily's obsessional jealousy climbed to extravagant heights whenever Ogilvie went away. In 1777 he was briefly in London, and Emily convinced herself that every woman in the drawing-rooms was plotting to snatch her humble balding husband from her arms. She wrote to him in a fever of imagined disaster. 'God knows, my angel, if the beauties of the age will but spare me one dear heart on which depends my all, I would willingly let them enjoy the triumph of beauty. But when I think that by their allurements and to gratify the vanity of a moment they may rob me of all my heart holds dear, I feel to hate them.'

Emily's fears, her 'nervous horrors' and 'sinkings' were real enough, despite being unfounded. But her jealousy was not purely self-destructive. She felt with Ogilvie, as she had never felt with the Duke, that she had a right to feel jealous and a right to make demands upon her husband. So her outbursts, however abject, were founded on a new kind of confidence: that the needs and rights in this marriage were finely balanced. Although she may have doubted it temporarily Emily also knew that Ogilvie was, as he told Sarah, a 'fool' about her and that he needed her as much as she needed him.

Ogilvie was every bit as committed as Emily to the romance of their marriage. He deferred to his wife in matters of taste, offered her companionship and always loved her body. In 1783, when Emily was fifty-one and he a decade younger, he wrote to her from London: 'I am really dying with impatience to see your beautiful face again and to hug your lovely person in my fond loving arms – to meet your warm tender embraces and to hang on your sweet balmy lips. I am dying to call you mine again, to feel you such and to assure you of my unalterable love and affection.'

Despite such declarations, Ogilvie never gave way to jealousy and never doubted that his love was returned. Because of his self-control and confidence he maintained an emotional dominance in the relationship. Emily would always have the social distinction and most of the money, but Ogilvie's control of her heart more than balanced any advantage birth and her jointure gave her. At times Ogilvie was ruthless in his control, using Emily's love for him to extract gestures of submission. When they were parted in 1777, Emily, desperate to have him back, wrote abjectly, 'believe there is nothing I will not do that you wish which I *can* do. I'll drink no tea, eat no butter, I'll ride.' She even gloried in her submissiveness, writing a few days later, 'dearest love, how I do long to have you scold me.' But although she was eager to cede her emotional independence to her husband, Emily never abandoned her emotional rights. Ogilvie might control her feelings but she demanded a good price for them. So a finely balanced relationship developed, a fragile house of cards that stayed standing because each partner had the means to bring it crashing down.

Inside this self-made mansion of love Ogilvie and Emily roamed freely. They were well aware that their situation was, as Emily put it, 'an uncommon one' and 'uncommonly happy'. 'Let me tell you ten thousand million of times that I love you to distraction,' Emily wrote in 1777. She called her husband 'joy of my heart, charm of my life, comfort of my soul' and made much of their married state. 'Come to my heart my dear husband, love, friend, all that is dear,' she

wrote in 1777, signing herself 'ever your tender and affectionate wife,' adding, 'how pleasant to write those words!'
Ogilvie was her 'sweet William', her 'dearest angel'. She was
his 'adorable angel' and his 'dearest rogue'.

They had much in common besides love. Emily described
Ogilvie as 'one of us', a man in the Lennox mould who united
strong feeling with a dependence on reason. Like the Lennoxes, Ogilvie loved books, children and conversation. He
was a committed Whig and a supporter of the rights of colonists. Like Louisa, Emily and Sarah he vehemently defended
the rights of the Irish Parliament against encroachment from
Westminster, and like all the Lennoxes he was a Francophile
and a good French speaker (although as Sarah was quick to
point out, his French emerged strongly salted with a 'Scotch'
accent). Within this union of views there were differences.
Ogilvie was less worldly and more religious than Emily. He
condemned drawing-rooms and theatres as harmful to youthful minds and he insisted on daily religious observance.
About the theatre Emily demurred. It never lost its allure for
her; she continued to go whenever she could and she encouraged her children in amateur theatricals and their cult of
Mrs Siddons. But she did go to church, if there was an Anglican service to be had, and read soothing psalms and sermons
in troubled times. In the 1790s when family life and national
politics came together with disastrous results, Emily read and
re-read Blair and Prior, the most popular sermonisers of the
day, comforted as much by their familiarity and 'pretty expressions' as by their sentiments.

After their wedding in Toulouse, Emily, Ogilvie and their entourage continued south, stopping briefly at Montpellier
before settling at Marseilles for the next eighteen months.
Emily sat through the winter and spring at Marseilles, grumbling about the wind and growing larger. The children
continued the pattern of their Black Rock life, mixing sea
bathing with gardening and book learning. It was a tranquil

life, but Emily was moody, swinging from joy to misery and back again in the space of a few days. Her equanimity was often upset by the arrival of the post from London and Dublin. Louisa's weekly letters recorded the reactions of Emily's friends to her wedding and her new life. Sarah wrote at length about her daughter and the families at Goodwood, Stoke and Holland House. In October 1774, Sarah wrote with news that Ste Fox, now Lord Holland, was ill. He died of dropsy in November leaving his year-old son Henry with a title he had held for less than six months. Still in mourning for Caroline and the first Lord Holland, the family was dismayed. Lady Mary Coke, who lived next to the Holland House estate, noted with gloomy enjoyment in her diary that above the great door of Holland House there were now three escutcheons emblazoned with the Holland crest, one for each death.

Ste's widow, Mary, decided to let Holland House until her son came of age and to auction off, for the sake of economy, all its contents except for family portraits and a few treasured objects. For twelve days in the middle of November 1775, friends, enemies and relatives who wanted to salvage a memory or just browse amongst the family's possessions, crowded into the house and moved with the auctioneer from room to room, through the out-houses and stables to the orangery where even the trees in their tubs were sold off. Laid out to view were Henry's well thumbed volumes of Catullus and Horace, Livy and Martial, Caroline's poems, novels and plays, the furniture and porcelain they had amassed together in Paris and even the inkstand and pens she had used to write her letters. Beds, window curtains, commodes, carpets, grates and tongs, prints and statues, vestments and cassocks in the chapel, kettles, cooking stoves, egg spoons and hair brushes: everything was sold off. The material accumulation of Caroline's life was dissolved. Her knicknacks and collections of Sèvres, her cheap novels and luxurious carpets were dispersed. The 'high varnished French grey chariot' in which she had gone visiting and to Court, 'the crane neck post chariot' she had used for longer journeys and the 'neat phaeton' for jaunts to town and in the park were no longer needed. All that remained were the portraits she had accumulated, stowed away to wait for Lord Holland's majority, her sons Charles and Harry, and her letters, bundles tied in other people's chests and drawers.

Buyers at the Holland House sale were unsentimental. Mary, now Lady Holland, bought a few things from her infant son's estate for common use. Sir Charles Bunbury, who in 1770 had given Henry Fox a bust of Democritus, the laughing philosopher, now saw it knocked down to the highest bidder. He strolled round and, at the end of the sale, took away a catalogue in which all the prices were scrupulously recorded and added up. The effects in Holland House, accumulated by Henry and Caroline layer by layer over thirty years, fetched £4499 7s. 1d., from which Mr Christie, the auctioneer, carefully deducted his commission of £449 2s. 4d.

News like this was not conducive to the calm Emily had promised herself when she embarked for France. She was often low and nervous and looked back at her time in Marseilles with mixed emotions. Despite her happiness she was oppressed with a 'disorder' which she attributed to 'the dreadful scenes I had gone through the last two to three years'. In the spring of 1775, five-year-old Fanny Fitzgerald fell ill and died. Six weeks later another child was born. Still in a nervous state, overcome with memories of death, Emily called her daughter Cecilia in memory of her sister Cecilia Lennox.

Cecilia Ogilvie, like her putative brother, was dark and good looking. 'The most beautiful little creature it was possible to see,' Charlotte wrote in her diary. Ogilvie was delighted that he could now acknowledge a child of his own; the older Fitzgeralds treated Cecilia as a precious toy. Gradually Emily's spirits lifted. 'Did we not dote upon one another?' she later wrote to Ogilvie, remembering their time in Marseilles.

Marseilles was hot and uncomfortable, despite the sea bathing. Even though friends passed through and the town was big enough to have a social season of its own, it never seemed to Emily more than a temporary home. During the winter of 1775, the Duke of Richmond, reconciled to his sister's marriage and as eager as ever to support the interests of the family, offered Emily the use of the château at Aubigny where Louise de Kéroualle had spent her last years. The château was gaunt and splendid, built of stone with round, bulging towers, steep roofs and small mullioned windows. It stood in forested hunting country west of the Loire in the middle of a large estate.

The château at Aubigny had been uninhabited since Louise de Kéroualle's death forty years before, and it was still full of her paintings and furniture. It was the sort of old-fashioned house that Caroline had loved, but which to Emily, with her taste for comfort and modernity, was full of defects. Its thick stone walls kept it cool in summer but, as she pointed out, no amount of wood from the forests could warm its chilly expanses in the winter. None the less, Emily gratefully accepted her brother's offer. She and Ogilvie, with Charlotte, Sophia, Edward, Robert, Gerald, Lucy, Louisa, George, Cecilia, Mrs Lynch the housekeeper and Rowley, Emily's maid, arrived there in May 1776, to be greeted by the Duke of Richmond himself. The household was soon supplemented by two footmen, a tutor, and several local menservants and maids. Soon after the family had settled in, the Duke persuaded Emily and Ogilvie to go with him to Paris and float themselves into French society. Emily went to Court and together she and Ogilvie went to salons and drawing-rooms, favouring Walpole's friend Madame du Deffand over Caroline's favourite Madame Geoffrin.

From the time he went to Paris with the Duke of Richmond, Ogilvie was welcomed into the family circle, although the Duke never allowed him to pass beyond the barriers of politeness into friendship. Henceforth, when Emily and Ogilvie went to England, they stayed at Goodwood and

Richmond House. But on the few occasions that Ogilvie went alone to London, he stayed at a hotel, only going to Richmond House to dine. The women of the family rapidly succumbed to Ogilvie's self-confidence and sexual charm, although Louisa was initially hesitant about how to behave towards him and Sarah thought him insufficiently handsome for her sister. But the men – Conolly, Lord George Lennox and the Duke of Richmond – for whom Emily was not a mother, but simply a close relation, had less to lose by her disapproval. They were intimidated by Ogilvie's intelligence and lack of polish, pronouncing him rough and ill at ease. Ogilvie was always an anomaly in the family circle. For Emily's sake, nobody, particularly Louisa and Sarah, wanted to offend him. But only Louisa was on an intimate footing with him; everyone else was, to varying degrees, ill at ease in his company.

Once they were settled at Aubigny, Emily and Ogilvie lived a life of domesticity that was disturbed only by occasional trips to Paris and England. They hired a tutor for the children and Ogilvie retired to a gentleman's life. He attended to family business, hunted in the forest during the winter and read in what Emily called his 'dear little closet'. Emily was ambitious for her husband, anxious to display his intelligence to the world and keen that worldly success should paper over the obscurity of his origins. But for Ogilvie this life was enough. 'I hate going anywhere at night and dislike being by myself,' he wrote to Emily when he was away on a trip in 1782, 'so that, upon the whole, I am not sure but a wife and a parcel of brats, though troublesome, is as good a way of spending one's time as another.'

Children and the prospect of children dominated life at Aubigny. There were young ones to educate, older ones to launch into the world and, just as she had been for the last thirty years, Emily was constantly announcing pregnancies. The children, Charlotte excepted, were cheerful enough. The older boys, Henry, Robert and Edward, studied with the tutor, Mr Thompson, walked in the château's formal gardens and played in the grounds with the children of Aubigny's more prosperous inhabitants. They grew up bilingual and as Francophile as their mother. Charlotte and Sophia read, sewed, practised music, drawing and dancing and waited on their mother, living in a kind of limbo between childhood and coming out into the world as marriageable young women. The youngest children ran and toddled in and out of Ogilvie's closet and Emily's apartment. After dinner, when Mrs Lynch had put the babies to bed, the older children read with their mother and stepfather and, if Ogilvie was in indulgent mood, might play a few hands of 'commerce' or other games of cards.

Emily's health cast a cloud over this domestic routine. By the mid-1770s she was well past forty and, although she continued to have periods into her late fifties, her body's cycle had become a source of misery to her. Her period now 'often affects me some days before, particularly my spirits,' and was 'a time when I can enjoy nothing and feel myself a plague to everybody.' She had repeated miscarriages which made her weak and tearful, compounded her natural indolence and confined her to the château for weeks on end.

In 1777, after Emily had another child, Charlotte, (who did not survive infancy), and three miscarriages, Ogilvie insisted they part for several months, saying they could not risk another pregnancy and that he could only resist passion's call if they put at least one sea between them. He left in mid-June for Paris, London and Dublin. Almost as soon as she had lost sight of his carriage on the Paris road, Emily was writing to him. 'But a few hours are past, my dearest, kindest, best of angels, and already it seems as if we had been separated for an age! Let me tell you ten thousand million of times that I love you. Yes, my dear angel, if ever human creature adored another I do you ... You are gone, but you love me, this fills my heart with thankfulness to the supreme being.' A few days later she collapsed, desperate for Ogilvie, enmired in 'distressing thoughts', imagining him unfaithful and then dead.

On 20 June she wrote to him: 'in short my love, it is plain we cannot bear this separation; our hearts are torn to pieces by it.' Despite her weak state she planned to set off for Paris immediately, dismissing the advice of Charlotte and Mrs Lynch as the counsel of 'cold, prudent advisers'. In Paris, Ogilvie contemplated returning. But he had a variety of motives for his journey. Besides Emily's health there was the need to settle a good deal of business at Black Rock and the need, too, to assert his emotional dominance. On the back of Emily's letter announcing her wish to join him, Ogilvie noted that he left for Dieppe immediately after receiving it, 'being now convinced that it was not possible to continue so near my dearest love as Paris without forgetting every other consideration to fly to her.'

Ogilvie got the subjection he wanted. Emily wept, cowered and hinted at suicide. 'My mind is all distraction, my heart is broke. Oh William, William it is past. Nothing can now recall you to give me comfort. I must suffer this dreadful torment, it is the will of God ... Don't think I have not called reason and religion to my aid. I have indeed ... When Rowley said he is gone, when she brought me that dreadful cruel letter, Oh William it was too much for me; no agitation you ever saw in me ever equalled it. I can neither sleep nor eat – My dear children, nothing gives me comfort; all, all is misery ... and now, my William, see me at your feet, plunged in the deepest distress. I beg and implore you, return ... for pity's sake save a wretch from misery. There are times when I am capable of anything ... Oh my William, you know too well the dreadful violence of my passions.' Mrs Lynch the housekeeper also wrote to Ogilvie, unable to bear Emily's wild unhappiness any longer. 'I cannot disguise to you that I never saw her Grace worse nor indeed so bad as at present; the agitation on her nerves is very great and her health and spirits both much affected.' Ogilvie landed in Ireland only to read this abject parcel of letters. Then he got back on the boat again. By the time he got home, Emily was calmer. She had recovered from her miscarriage; her period had come and gone and she was cheered by the knowledge that Ogilvie was on the way. But Ogilvie had made his dominance and her need for him quite clear. Henceforth he had only to threaten departure to bring Emily to his feet. As late as 1792, when she was sixty-one, Emily was still conceding emotional ground to her implacable husband, still worried about his anger and her response. 'I can bear anything better than your being cross,' she wrote.

Despite the fact that Ogilvie's journey in 1777 was purportedly undertaken to stop Emily getting pregnant too soon after her last miscarriage, she announced only a few weeks after his return that she was pregnant again. This time the pregnancy prospered and in May 1778, when Emily was nearly forty-seven, Mimi Ogilvie was born, her twenty-second child. With Mimi's birth, Emily ended half a lifetime of childbearing. Her first child George, Lord Ophaly, was born in January 1748, thirty years before. By the time Mimi Ogilvie was born, George had been dead for thirteen years and Emily was already a grandmother.

After Mimi Ogilvie's birth in Paris in May 1778, life at Aubigny settled into a routine around the hunting and shooting season, trips to Paris and abroad and emotional partings with children who left to marry or begin their lives in the professions. Charles Fitzgerald, always one of Emily's favourite sons, had been the first, after William, her heir, to leave the family. He joined the navy before the family moved to France, serving in the Caribbean during the American war and eventually rising to the rank of Rear Admiral. Next it was Henry's turn. He left Aubigny for Paris in 1777 and after studying at a military academy there he went to England and joined the army. Edward also bought an army commission. He trained in the Sussex Militia under the Duke of Richmond's eye and then progressed to service in Ireland and America with the 96th and 19th Regiments of Foot.

When her sons left home Emily kept their hearts. She was still their lodestar and confidante; many of them married late, as if they were unable to share her place in their hearts with another woman. Lord Edward Fitzgerald, in particular, was extravagantly fond of his mother. His letters after he left home were full of devotion and charm; they were, indeed, love letters. After reading the first volume of Rousseau's *Confessions* in 1783 he wrote to her: 'Dearest mother, what would I give that Jean Jacques had had a mother such as you are to me! What a happiness it would have been to him to have [had] such a heart to open himself to. By a few *peeps* into the second volume, I see he wants such a person; for, *entre nous*, your best *male* friend will not do. One is afraid to open all one's weaknesses to a man. Let him be ever so closely united to you, one is afraid of his sense or of his advice, and I own I do not perfectly understand friendship with a woman without *un petit brin d'amour*, or *jealousy*, which I think is one of the passions attending love.'

But it wasn't just Edward who confided in his mother. Charles, Henry and Robert told her all their secrets long after they were grown up. Charles's letters were vain and literary, Edward's loving (and eventually lovingly deceitful), Henry's self-effacing and Robert's discursive and explanatory. Charles Fitzgerald's letters home set a tone of frankness that all his brothers followed and they, like him, were to see the world through books and rhetorical flourishes. 'Going through Somersetshire always reminds me of Tom Jones,' Charles wrote in 1770. 'I imagine I see Allworthy's and Western's houses in every vale; as to Sophias they are scarce, for I think the western part of England is remarkable for ugly women.'

Emily encouraged in her sons a morality closely akin to that which had operated at Carton. Her sons' amours were a compliment rather than a betrayal, an indication that no serious attachment had displaced her in their hearts. Charles Fitzgerald recognised very soon that sexual banter was the currency of filial devotion and he filled his letters with it. In 1775 he wrote from Spanish Town, Jamaica, 'the jet black ladies of Africa's burning sands have made me forget the pale unripened beauties of the north,' and he added a few months later, 'among the number of your grand children you'll soon have one of a copper colour.' In return for their confidence Emily gave her sons love without censure and their self-esteem flourished in the confidence of her devotion.

The filial duties of Emily's daughters were much more arduous. From them Emily demanded companionship as well as frankness and love. Charlotte's position at Aubigny was especially difficult. Emily acknowledged that Charlotte was old enough to be married, but she was reluctant to relinquish a companion who read to her and helped with the children. 'The sweet babes, though lovely at times, are often too much for me, particularly the sweet Ciss, unless I have somebody to manage her, lift her up and down and supply all her number-less wants; now to have a servant always in the room is tiresome, I think. This Charlotte supplies often.' Charlotte did get away briefly to Ireland in the summer of 1777, but her visit was not a success. She quarrelled with the young Duchess of Leinster, failed to find a husband and fell dis-astrously in love. Soon she was back in Aubigny, angrily fetching and carrying for her mother, censured by everyone for her plainness and petulance. 'Pray has she no desire to overcome her temper?' Sarah asked in 1776. It was not until 1789, when she was thirty-one, that Charlotte married and left home. After that Sophia took over her duties, and although she eventually had a house of her own, Sophia never married.

Beyond expecting devotion, however, Emily was not demanding of her children. She rapidly abandoned any hope that William would cut a figure in the Irish Parliament and any worldly ambitions she had for her other sons were lost in her sense that they existed to serve her. Her children, both girls and boys, she said, 'have shown me on all occasions how much they prefer being with me to anything else.' The most expressive children became the most loved. 'I get bored of everything and want to have you to go and talk to; you are, after all, what I love best in the world,' Edward wrote in 1787, when he was twenty-four. She loved him back and accepted his devotion as her due, noting, 'In Edward, nothing surprises me, Dear Angel; he has always loved me in an uncommon degree from childhood.'

In the summer of 1779, Emily and Ogilvie returned to England together for the first time, running the gauntlet of both the Court and family opinion. Sarah cavilled at Ogilvie's looks and manner but was in no position to criticise her sister. Since Emily's departure for France five years earlier, Sarah's world had contracted, making her feel her isolation in Sussex more than ever. The deaths of Caroline and Henry and then of Ste ended visits to Holland House and Kingsgate. Harry Fox was in America and Charles Fox, busy with politics, gambling and women, rarely visited his family. If she went up to London after 1775, Sarah had either to stay at Richmond House or with her old aunt Lady Albemarle. Most of the time she remained in Sussex and spent her time with her brothers' wives, Louisa Lennox at Stoke and the Duchess of Richmond at Goodwood.

In Ireland, Sarah's prospects were brighter. The first Duke of Leinster's death had removed the main obstacle to her rehabilitation there. When Louisa was able to persuade Tom Conolly to receive her at Castletown, a few of her old friends followed suit. Sarah went back to Ireland in the summer of 1775, fifteen years after her disastrous launch into the London marriage market. She was happy to be with Louisa, planning the decorations for the long gallery at Castletown, visiting Carton and helping to supervise the alterations to Black Rock. After a few weeks she wrote to Susan O'Brien: 'I pass my time here very pleasantly; I live almost all the day long with my sister; Mr. Conolly seems to like my being here and shows me so much kindness that I hope it is not disagreeable to him; and I'm sure it makes Louisa happy for she scarce passes a day without telling me that having me with her is one of the greatest pleasures she has; there is something so pleasant in being so sincerely loved and welcome that it is not wonderful I should be perfectly content and happy here. We have a good deal of company . . . They come in a very pleasant way, dropping in at dinner time and going away soon after, so that they never interfere with any employment we have . . . Some of my old acquaintance among the ladies have been *more* than civil to me, quite kind indeed, and some of Louisa's acquaintance have been very civil, but great part of both sorts have taken no notice of me.'

Despite her forgiveness by Louisa and her partial social rehabilitation, Sarah was far from cheerful. Nothing could disguise the fact, especially after her divorce from Bunbury was finalised in 1776, that there was a vacuum at the centre of her existence. She tried to fill it with long letters to her sisters and a vicarious emotional life which centred around the inhabitants of Goodwood and Stoke, Susan O'Brien's attempts to become reconciled with her mother, Emily's troubles with William and the builders at Black Rock. Throwing herself into the lives of others gave her a sense of drama that was lacking in the dry, comfortless desert of her own inner life. The recipients of Sarah's long letters of advice and disquisition were not always grateful for her efforts. Sarah's dislike of herself rubbed off on her views of others, spicing her letters with a commentary that unwittingly raised the ire of their recipients. In August 1777 the Duke of Richmond reproached her for her indiscretion and she wrote sadly to Emily: 'he says, what is very true, that one has no business to speak of other people's affairs . . . poor *peste publique* is forever saying things they think wrong, and which I cannot for the life of me see the necessity of keeping secret; but in time I hope to mend my practice.' 'She is not one of those that drives away disagreeable thoughts, but indulges them,' Emily wrote sharply, recognising that Sarah's gloomy letters served a greater purpose for their sender than for those to whom they were addressed.

But no letter could last for ever. Sarah always had to return from the paper world she had created to the damp Halnaker manor house, her winsome, untutored daughter and the routines of her dependent life. There were small improvements in her situation. The Duke of Richmond was building her a new house on the Goodwood estate and Sarah spent a good deal of time planning and supervising its construction. At other times she walked and sewed, read novels and the papers and made intermittent attempts to teach Louisa Bunbury French. Much of her time was spent with Lady Louisa Lennox and the officers of the 25th Regiment of Foot which Lord George Lennox commanded. Sarah was warming to soldiers, catching their turn of phrase, their belief in military glory and their sense of manliness. Military life, with its uniforms, musters, parades, advances, repulses and defeats satisfied her taste for drama and emotional extremity. Telling stories of military endeavour used all her talent for rhetoric and verbal extravagance.

The dramatic events in the American colonies in the mid-1770s gave Sarah a focus for her unused emotions. She eagerly read news of the conflict and then the war and, after initial wavering, she was, like the rest of her siblings, firmly on the colonists' side. The Duke of Richmond set the standard for the family's opposition to the war, sailing through the British fleet in the Solent with an American flag tied firmly to his masthead. Louisa bought a bust of Washington and displayed it prominently at Castletown, despite her reservations about full independence for the colonists.

Sarah's attitude towards the American war was coloured both by her brush with the King and her prejudice against settlers from the north of Ireland. At first her dislike of the monarch and the Massachusetts Bay colonists was evenly divided. 'In short,' she wrote to Susan O'Brien, 'I think there is no deciding who is precisely wrong and who is precisely right. Only two things, I think, won't bear dispute; 1st, that those who cause most lives to be lost are the worst people;

secondly, that the Bostonians, being chiefly Presbyterians and from the north of Ireland, are daily proved to be very, very bad people, being quarrelsome, discontented, hypocritical, enthusiastical, lying people.' By 1777, after the Declaration of Independence and the entry of France into the war, Sarah declared, 'I grow a greater rebel every day upon principle' and laid the blame for the war at the King's door. But her attitude towards military conflict was changing. While she condemned this war, she had begun to find allure and glamour in soldiers and militarism. When Harry Fox returned from America in 1779, she took note of his opposition to the war, but dwelt lovingly on his qualities as a soldier, writing to Susan: 'his looks, his manners are all delightful; he has the most true, *good*, military air ... I think I can't give you a better account of a young officer.' A year later, after Admiral Rodney had destroyed the Spanish fleet off Gibraltar she wrote, 'how splendid was our great and glorious success in Spain.'

Behind Sarah's orotund phrases lay a series of events that Louisa and the Duke of Richmond watched unfolding with foreboding. In 1776 Sarah met an officer of the 25th Regiment called George Napier. Napier, an impoverished younger son of a Scottish baron, the fifth Lord Napier, was partly Irish. His mother had Dublin connections, and he joined Lord George Lennox's 25th Regiment with introductions from Tom and Louisa Conolly. Described as 'the most perfect made man possible' and 'the most active and handsome officer in the British Army in America', Napier was six foot two inches tall, Roman nosed and short sighted. Although he had received a gentleman's education under David Hume, Napier was a career officer with little time for classical learning. Despite his looks he was conscientious rather than dashing, scrupulous rather than showy, a methodical and careful man, at home with muster rolls and account books as well as uniforms and swords.

Napier quickly made his way into the inner circle at Stoke

where Lord George Lennox frequently entertained his officers. His good looks and dedication to the military profession equally quickly impressed Sarah. By the autumn of 1776, their friendship, carried on under the gaze of Napier's wife, had an evidently sexual element and Sarah had fallen into the familiar pattern of confession and self-recrimination in her letters to Louisa.

Louisa responded in the old way too, with cryptic caution. At first it was Napier's interest in Sarah rather than the other way round that gave her grounds for disquiet. Sarah disguised her feelings for Napier and told Louisa that he had fallen in love with her. In August 1776, Louisa replied: 'I am now come to that part of your letter about yourself and your friend. I do believe, as you say, e'er long, all things will be forgot, at the same time that I believe it will be severely felt at the moment, and to show you how free I am from *rancour* on their account, I formed a most hearty and sincere wish, that those feelings might turn out to his advantage and be the means of regulating his conduct in the future.'

In the months that followed, Sarah continued to see the Napiers at Stoke and to maintain that her own heart was not involved. Gradually both Louisa Conolly and Louisa Lennox realised that she was deceiving them and that her 'assurances of not having that *sort* of liking' for Napier were false. Sarah was immediately under a cloud, banned from Stoke and in danger of losing all the credit she had so laboriously built up over the years of dull days and good behaviour. 'I am sadly out of favour at Stoke, partly by my own fault,' she confessed to Emily. Louisa's letters took on their old admonitory tone. On 23 December 1778, she wrote: '*oh* my dear, dear sister, if you could but know the satisfaction it would be to us all, to feel secure of you, I am sure you would never distress us again. Let your good nature from henceforth be appropriated to our use, and shut up all the avenues to vanity, which betrayed you into distress.'

Sufficient pressure was put on Napier to make him transfer

his commission from the 25th to the 80th Regiment, which was due to see active service in America. He left Sussex with his wife and children in the spring of 1779, going to Leith in Scotland and the Channel Islands before finally leaving for New York in a convoy of merchant and transport ships, accompanied by two fleets of warships, at the end of May. They arrived in Brooklyn at the end of August and stayed for the rest of the year. 'I am happy to think you have so much reason to be satisfied with the Napiers as I find you are,' Louisa told Sarah. 'I pity you very much for having been obliged to refuse seeing him before he went. But it was certainly right, for it is impossible (I think) to keep the right medium upon such occasions.' Once the Napiers had left, Louisa slackened her vigilance, reasonably certain that Sarah would not attempt a clandestine correspondence and would soon forget the affair.

But if Napier did not write, Sarah followed his movements carefully. 'I've had accounts that some friends of mine are safely arrived in New York,' she wrote cheerfully to Emily on 15 December 1779. She also became uncharacteristically circumspect, saying nothing about Napier to Susan O'Brien and revealing little to Louisa. Early in 1780, Sarah learned that Napier had been ill in New York but had eventually recovered and gone down to Charlestown where his regiment was besieging the town. A few weeks later she had some more news. Mrs Napier, left in New York, had succumbed to the same fever, and died.

Some time during the next year, Napier proposed to Sarah and she accepted. Louisa and Emily acquiesced in her choice, although the Duke of Richmond, unwilling to forfeit his role as protector, demurred. Only after all the arrangements for her wedding were complete did Sarah write to Susan, giving a highly selective version of the progress of her affair and going on to say: 'he says he has known me long enough to judge of my character, that he has a peculiar turn of mind which prevents him being mortified about my character, that he don't marry me out of vanity to brag of my merits, but because he is convinced that my character and disposition, such as it is, suits his, and that if I love him he has not the least doubt of our being happy. He knows I do love him, and being certain of that he laughs at every objection that is started for he says that loving me to the degree he does, he is quite sure never to repent marrying me.'

At the age of thirty-six, Sarah came to her own decision. She was not swayed by her brother's disapproval or Susan's dismay and she and Napier were married in Goodwood parish church, with Lady Albemarle as their witness, on 27 August 1781. After the wedding she told everyone of her happiness and confidence in the future. Much later she said simply that Napier 'made me like this world'.

Napier reconciled Sarah to life. Through his eyes she saw herself and the world about her transformed. His temperament and career allowed her to inhabit the role of wife so completely that she ceased to live an inner and an outer life, one of fantasy, the other of day-to-day grind. She was an officer's wife, living out dreams of her husband's valour and glory; she was a household economist, managing their small income and modest quarters; and she was a mother, producing, year after year, children whom she bred up to revere their father and follow in his footsteps. Their first child, Charles James Napier was born on 10 August 1782; his arrival was open and joyful, very different from the birth of Louisa Bunbury fourteen years before. With a characteristic Gallic flourish, Sarah told Susan, 'je suis enchantée de mon fils'.

8 November 1792

In White's Hotel near the Petit Palais preparations for a grand dinner were almost complete. Swags of bunting in red, white and blue ran round the hall, fastened to panelling and picture rails with swirling rosettes. Tiny *tricolores* were arranged on the tables like bunches of flowers. Flags of the French Republic and banners of regiments in the Republican armies hung suspended from the ceiling swaying gently in the heat that rose from fireplaces and sconces. A military band tuned up in one corner of the room, strident piccolos and cornets celebrating French victories in the Low Countries in the first year of the Republic.

The band struck up triumphal music – the Marseillaise, marching songs. A crowd of men and women poured into the hall: French, English, American, Prussian, Dutch, Austrian, Italian. They called themselves Friends of the Rights of Man, in honour of Tom Paine. Servants came in with food and wine; glasses clinked, laughter and conversation filled the room.

Out of the noise, somebody called for silence. Toasts were shouted out from different tables, half heard in the applause. 'Tom Paine and the new way of making good books known by royal proclamation and King's Bench prosecution!' 'The English patriots, Priestley, Fox, Sheridan, Christie, Cooper, Tooke and Mackintosh!' 'The Lady Defenders of the Revolution, especially Mrs. Charlotte Smith, Mrs. Williams and Mrs. Barbauld!' Cheering and stamping. 'To the coming Convention of Great Britain and Ireland!' 'To the speedy abolition of hereditary titles and feudal distinctions in England!' 'To the people of Ireland; and may government profit by the example of France, and reform prevent revolution!' Shouts, more cheers and a toast for the band: 'May the patriotic airs of the German Legion (Ça Ira, Marseillaise, etc.) soon become the favourite music of every army, and may the soldier and citizen join in the chorus!'

In the uproar several men stood up, amongst them Lord Edward Fitzgerald, solid and small, with closely cropped hair and a pock-marked face. Silence fell and one by one they solemnly renounced their hereditary titles. Glasses were raised and Republican wine replaced the holy water of baptism. Edward Fitzgerald was renamed le Citoyen Edouard Fitzgerald, Sir Robert Smythe the plain Robert Smythe. For one heady moment, casting privilege aside, they believed in their new identities, reborn into a new life.

CHAPTER
FIVE

OLD
AGE

PART ONE

'Nothing can ever diminish my domestic comfort
and happiness but illness and death'.
Sarah to Susan, 25 February 1783.

The Napier family grew fast. Emily, George, William,
Richard, Henry, Caroline and Cecilia, named either for
sisters or for kings, had joined Charles James by 1791. The
family income did not increase in the same way. By Sarah's
old standards it was very small. She had five hundred a year,
the interest on her fortune which she was allowed as part of
her divorce settlement with Sir Charles Bunbury. Napier,
having sold his commission in the 80th Regiment of Foot, had
nothing. Napier's poverty allowed Sarah to campaign for preferment on his behalf. In between confinements she devoted
herself to her husband's cause, haranguing relatives and
friends who might have commissions, sinecures or salaried
employment at their disposal.

Napier did not stay without a salary for long. In March
1782, Lord North's government, weakened by years of battering from the opposition over the American war, finally
collapsed. In the new administration, Charles Fox was Secretary of State and the Duke of Richmond Master of the

Ordnance. General Conway, the Duke of Richmond's step-father-in-law was Commander-in-Chief of the army and Charles Keppel, Sarah's cousin, was made 1st Lord of the Admiralty. With relatives so thick on the government benches, Sarah hoped for a juicy sinecure. Indeed, Richmond quickly found Napier a job, Superintendent of the Woolwich Laboratory, in charge of gunpowder production for the nation. Equally quickly, Sarah identified its defects: hard work, low pay and the need to live in London. 'His place will never exceed £300 a year, which being a most uncertain income and requiring such close attendance that he must not quit London for one week even, makes it *pas grande chose*,' she grumbled to Susan. Comparing Napier's salary with her brother's easy income of £20,000 a year she became daily less grateful for his patronage. Very soon she was writing round her relatives in search of a better place for him. But her blunt approaches were misplaced anyway: the King so hated the coalition that took office after Rockingham's death in July 1782 that he refused every appeal for patronage. All Sarah could expect was an office directly under the control of one of her relatives and these Napier sought only as a last resort.

Before long Sarah was putting together a new philosophy of life to go with her lack of funds. Now that she was remarried and newly respectable once more, Sarah could expect to re-enter some (if not all) of the drawing-rooms that had been closed to her for so long and there she might talk her way into a place for her husband. But Napier refused to play the game of favours given and received upon which preferment depended. Poverty for him was a matter of pride. So Sarah, too, began to turn against using her connections for profit. As doors slowly opened to her she declined to step through them, scorning those who had cut her off when she left Sir Charles Bunbury. She rejected aristocratic, drawing-room life, except within her immediate family, and set up, in justification, two contrasts. One was between '*degenerating* or rather *bending to the times*' as she put it, and upright and unflinching probity. The other was between the world of the drawing-room, and what she called her own 'domestic comfort and happiness'. By the mid-1780s these two contrasts had bcome partly fused. The first fusion produced a cliché: aristocratic culture, with its dependence on sinecures and places, was 'degenerate'; the family, 'domestic happiness' offered a far more secure foundation for happiness. The second produced a new definition of manliness. The honest man, devoted equally to his family and his country, who lived to serve rather than to profit, became Sarah's new ideal. Gone were the 'foppish' aristocrats she had admired in her youth. Gone too the wild imprudence of men like Lord William Gordon, whom she now saw as unprincipled and a wasted talent. In their place was Napier, six feet tall, active in the service of his country; a man who wore his poverty as a badge of virtue. 'Mr. Napier would not take anything on the score of perquisites,' she explained to Susan in 1782, adding in a later letter, 'Mr. N. has the *esprit* and *rage du service* beyond imagination ... He has served near 20 years, is a deserving officer.' Napier had inscribed one of his journals with the motto '*acti laboris jocundi sunt!*' (*sic*) and this determination to find joy in work was eagerly seconded by Sarah, who saw herself as Napier's partner, a soldier's wife prepared to share every exigency demanded in the nation's service.

In the early 1780s, these connections were tenuous. But Charles James Fox added for Sarah a political dimension to her views and helped to translate them from a set of ideas into a way of life. From the mid-1780s onwards, Fox came to represent, for his family and for thousands of others, some kind of political equivalent to Sarah's new ideal of disinterested service to the nation. Already, by July 1782, when Fox dramatically resigned from the government, citing undue royal influence, Sarah was writing, 'I am so far from thinking he seeks greatness, that I am sure greatness pursues him into gaming houses.' After Fox's Bill for the reform of the East India Company was defeated in December 1783 she declared him to be 'a great man', saying, ''tis the cause of humanity he supported'. As the decades passed, Sarah saw an ever-closer connection between the honourable, impoverished Napier family and the disinterested popular politics of Fox.

Sarah was not alone in advancing her husband's claim to patronage. When Fox and Richmond came into office in July 1782, Emily lost no time in putting pen to paper on Ogilvie's behalf. Since their visit to England in 1779, Ogilvie and Emily had been restless. They wanted to leave Aubigny but were unsure where to settle. Emily favoured Ireland. She wanted to enjoy her late motherhood at Frescati and to make 'Black Rock children' of her young brood – ten-year-old Lucy, eight-year-old George and little Cecilia and Mimi Ogilvie. But Ogilvie was worried about his return to a country he had left as a humble tutor, anxious enough about his new role as a gentleman to feel that his identity might slip if he was confronted in the Dublin streets by former pupils.

Emily got her way. The family moved to Black Rock in the spring of 1781 and Ogilvie began gingerly doing the rounds of Dublin drawing-rooms. By now he was carefully dressed and could behave as gentlemen thought he should. But he remained guarded and suspicious with those he did not know well. Stupidity or inattention seemed to him to be deliberate neglect and he saw contempt for his origins and old life in the eyes of those he met. Many men, especially in Ireland, had made their way to dizzy heights from beginnings they wished to forget. But hardly any had done it solely by marriage.

Emily thought that gossip about Ogilvie's origins would be silenced by a successful entry into both the Irish House of Commons and Dublin's best drawing-rooms. She had high hopes of Ogilvie's entry into Dublin society. Like Sarah she had developed a new ideal of manliness. Hers was a cult, not of birth or service, but of ability. Ogilvie, she repeated over and over, was a man of 'sense', and she was determined that her choice should be vindicated in the only arena she knew, the world of politics and government. She wanted his intelligence to be rewarded with enough social and political influence to restore her to something like her former glory in Dublin. This time, though, she would be the wife not of the first man of birth but of the first man in ability.

The family was also important. Emily wanted her sons to acknowledge Ogilvie as a man of influence and intelligence and it annoyed her that her older sons enjoyed political influence as a birthright. Ogilvie himself had little interest in politics. He was a canny investor and a good businessman. But Emily was determined that he should have a political career. So, to please his mother, the Duke of Leinster brought Ogilvie into the Irish House of Commons as Member for one of the Boroughs under his control.

Once in Parliament, Ogilvie joined Charles, Henry and Edward Fitzgerald as one of the Duke of Leinster's members. In the dying days of the North administration they were nominally in opposition, but the position changed radically when Charles Fox and the Duke of Richmond came into office in the Marquis of Rockingham's administration. While Irish 'patriots' like Leinster and Conolly could not be seen to be in open alliance with Dublin Castle, they sensed that there could be tremendous advantages to working with an administration that was both personally and politically sympathetic. Emily saw opportunities for Ogilvie. She despised both Conolly and her own son as 'très médiocre' and hoped that Ogilvie could step in and command the MPs returned by her son and brother-in-law. She also hoped that he could get a lucrative office out of the London government.

Emily's eye settled on the vacant office of head of the Registry of Deeds in Ireland, a fat sinecure of £1,500 a year. Almost as soon as Richmond and Fox came into government in the new administration in March 1782, Ogilvie was enquiring about the place. Failing to extract it from the Lord Lieutenant, Lord Portland, he set off for London at the beginning of July.

*

Ogilvie could not have arrived in London at a less propitious moment. Rockingham's death on 1 July sparked off eighteen months of turmoil that completely changed not only the political life of the nation but also the lives and loyalties of the extended Richmond–Fox–Leinster family. Political differences caused nearly irreparable schisms between brothers and sisters, and parents and children. As the 1780s wore on into the 1790s, the gulf widened. The Regency crisis of 1788, followed by the French Revolution which began the next year, broke up for ever the fifty-year-old alliance which had been set up with Emily's marriage to the Duke of Leinster and Caroline's elopement with Henry Fox.

The Marquis of Rockingham's death brought Lord Shelburne to power. Ogilvie expected to arrive in London and find that, in Shelburne's new administration, Charles Fox was Foreign Secretary and the Duke of Richmond was Master of the Ordnance with a Cabinet place. But Fox refused to serve under Shelburne. He suspected Shelburne of answering first to the King and only second to the Cabinet. But he had not forgotten his parents' belief in Shelburne's treachery twenty years before, so he also hated him on their behalf. Fox resigned. Richmond stayed with Shelburne's government. Relations between them, lukewarm for some time, cooled rapidly as Fox mercilessly attacked the government from the back benches.

The split between Richmond and Fox determined the line along which family loyalties would divide in the next decade. Richmond believed that loyalty from his sisters was due to the family as an institution. But he also quickly came to see any affection for Fox, or any sympathy with Fox's escalating hostility to the Crown, as a personal betrayal, reasoning that he gave his sisters sanctuary in difficult times and that in return they should offer him loyalty of both heart and mind. Emily agreed, saying that taking opposite sides from her brother seemed 'unnatural'; she wished she could have supported him, both as her brother and as head of the family. But she did not. Politics was a matter of belief as well as of family alliances. If the family had ever taken precedence over principle, it could no longer do so by the 1780s, when divisions centred on such fundamental issues as the King's relationship to Lords and Commons and the rights and wrongs of the French Revolution. Many families were torn apart by differences on these issues; women and many others who had no franchise were just as vociferous about their beliefs as those directly involved in the political process. Besides, Emily had never allowed her husbands or brothers to speak for her on political matters.

Louisa and Sarah were initially cautious in deciding between Richmond and Fox. 'I cannot submit my faith implicitly to the forecast of either my brother or nephew, each being liable to err in judgement,' Sarah wrote. 'I have at least the pleasure to think both act right in following their ideas of right.' Louisa, as usual, took her brother's side more eagerly, saying: 'in regard to his present politics, I hear various opinions regarding them and am very sure I am no judge of them, but I have a *feel* that he is right.' When Ogilvie came to London he was initially even-handed, waiting (without success) on Charles Fox, visiting Richmond House and presenting himself to Emily's old aunt, Lady Albemarle. But when he had no success in his quest for a sinecure it was to Fox that he turned for help.

Only a few years before Fox had transfixed the drawing-rooms with a Francophile outfit of red-heeled shoes and a wig of cascading blue curls. In opposition he still gambled, whored and drank, but he was gradually reshaping his persona from that of salon wit to that of 'champion of the people', a man who stood against Crown and Court. He abandoned salon dress for 'undress', a simple frock-coat and breeches, usually in the buff and blue of Washington's army, and exposed his thinning curls to the wind. Gradually, as he lurched from indebtedness to bankruptcy, this outfit became more tattered. Yet Fox's deliberate slovenliness made him seem like Dr Johnson, not so much an ordinary man of the people but an extraordinary, even saintly being. People marvelled at Fox's honesty and simplicity and politely turned the other way when he indulged his habit of clearing his throat and spitting on the carpet.

Ogilvie, just learning to feel at ease with court dress and manners, was nonplussed by the mixture of manufactured disorder and unselfconscious eccentricity that Fox displayed. He grumbled to Emily that he waited in vain for hours to see him. But when he eventually had his audience, Ogilvie was completely charmed. Fox became Emily's 'dear nephew'. Soon he was more: a sinner-saint, a way of life, almost a religion. This kind of conversion – which the Duke of Richmond watched with growing frustration – was only partly political. People loved Fox because he made his friends and followers feel desired and benevolent. He was a shy man, Emily said, and one who wanted always to think the best of his friends. People mistook shyness for modesty, attention for affection. Arriving indifferent, they went away infatuated: Ogilvie, despite his capacity for reserve and domination, was no different. He went back to Ireland without the office he came for but with a new love, Charles James Fox.

Sarah knew Fox's charms of old. But in deference to Napier's career she kept her distance from her nephew throughout the autumn and winter of 1782. In March of the following year she received a small reward. 'Mr. Conway has *at my request* (not my brother's) given Mr. N. a Captain's commission in the 100th Regiment,' which was stationed in the East Indies. 'I confess I shall consider it a little hard,' she concluded bitterly to Susan, 'that having such connections in the last 2 ministries it ends, after one year, in sending my husband to the East Indies a Captain.'

Before Sarah could ask for the major's commission, Richmond was out of office and Fox, in alliance with his old enemy, North, was back in. The King, hostile from the start to the new regime, was determined not 'to grant a single peerage or mark of favour' as he put it. The 100th Regiment was

◆

disbanded and Napier, having given up his place at the Woolwich Laboratory, remained a captain on half pay. Louisa worried about him, writing to Ogilvie in 1783: 'Mr. Napier hangs upon my mind. I wish very much that something was settled about him, for I see that they will have millions of children – and yet he is so army mad that I think one should run a great risk of making him uncomfortable by desiring him to give it up.'

The general election of 1784 that followed the defeat of the East India Bill, and thus of the Fox/North coalition, ended any lingering hopes that Emily and Sarah had about preferment for their husbands. It also completed the first stage in what Emily's son Charles Fitzgerald called 'the revolution in our family politics'. Charles Fitzgerald was still a Foxite in the 1780s and he filled his letters during the election campaign with praise of Fox and denigration of the Duke of Richmond, secure in the knowledge that Emily took Fox's side. Louisa warned Sarah to be on her guard if she met any Conolly relatives who were not Foxites and told her not to let out her true 'sentiments'.

Fox himself scraped back into Parliament in the election. But many of his supporters, including Sarah's ex-husband Sir Charles Bunbury, did not. The Fox/North coalition was roundly defeated, and when William Pitt formed a new administration, the Duke of Richmond was rewarded for his support with his old office, the Ordnance. Emily and Sarah remained on Fox's side. Emily was anxious to avoid disagreement with her brothers. So she shut up her new house in Harley Street, where she had frequently entertained Fox and his associates (including the 'dear Duchess' of Devonshire) during the election campaign, and went to Ireland for the summer. In June, Louisa offered the Napiers, who were still drifting without any home or prospect of augmenting their income, the use of Stretton Hall in Staffordshire. Stretton was not far from the road which took Dublin travellers to and from the packets at Park Gate. Conolly kept the house 'as a place to retire to, in case of an unpleasant situation in this country, which is an idea that has possessed his mind these five or six years past.' For forty years Stretton had been occupied by a few servants, a symbol of Conolly's refusal to countenance an Irishness that, in English eyes, he could never lose. The Napiers moved into the Hall in August 1784, planning to stay until their campaign for a commission was successful. Despite her growing family, Sarah was bored in the country. 'We are still here,' she wrote to Susan sometime that winter, 'and I fancy shall not stir, unless the dearness of the country shall drive us into Wales.' A few months later they moved out, travelling to Castletown in search of even cheaper living and a cure for Louisa Bunbury, who had developed consumption.

The Napiers' arrival at Castletown signalled a new phase not just in Sarah's life but in those of Louisa and Emily too. For the first time in many years the sisters were together; 'we three' Sarah called them, as if they were Macbeth's witches, sitting over the fire concocting plans. They all had similar preoccupations. Emily and Ogilvie were at Frescati with Sophia, Lucy, Cecilia and Mimi (but without Lord George Simon, who had died in 1783). Edward Fitzgerald, on leave from the army since the end of the American war, was often there. Until the summer of 1786, Ogilvie wrote later, 'he was with us, indeed, wherever we went, and those were the happiest years of our lives.' Louisa was happy too. When Sarah had given birth to a girl in 1783, Louisa had asked to adopt her, saying that Sarah was far more interested in boys than girls. Sarah refused at first but then repented, telling Susan O'Brien that consideration of the child's prospects if Louisa adopted her had changed her mind.

Emily Napier arrived at Castletown in December 1784, 'given away' as she bitterly described it later. Louisa became everything but her legal mother to her. Children had lived at Castletown before: Louisa had given a home to two of her nieces, Conolly's sister's children, whose mother had died.

But Emily Napier was different. She was Sarah's child, a blood relation. Two weeks after she arrived, Louisa wrote delightedly to Sarah: 'Mr. Conolly says she will be the prettiest Lennox that ever was seen, and I really do see a likeness to my sister Leinster. The first look struck me to be that of Cecilia's but now I think it is my sister Leinster.' Louisa felt guilty taking Sarah's child, knowing that Emmy came as much for money as for love. But she washed away her guilt with an outpouring of love that, she hoped, would make up for Sarah's sacrifice. 'The moment I awake I long to see her and dote on her to a ridiculous degree.' 'I beg you will kiss the blot on the word immediately three lines back because it is her dear little finger that made it.' Emily was 'the pretty Emmy, the blessed lovely Emmy.' 'She loves dancing . . . and has a notion of turning her little arms over her head as I have taught her. You would laugh at seeing what an old fool I am when by ourselves, dancing with her till I'm out of breath.'

Emily Napier gave Louisa a new emotional focus. She felt, at the age of forty-one, like a first-time mother and wanted both her sisters to see her with her 'treasure' as she called Emmy. 'I quite long that my sister Leinster should see her,' she wrote to Sarah soon after Emmy arrived, and when the rest of the Napier family accepted her invitation to come to Castletown she was overjoyed.

So began a short, relatively settled period of domestic concerns. Emily and Sarah, bringing up their second families, shared with Louisa a late motherhood. At ages when their contemporaries were saying goodbye to children who were leaving for matrimony or a separate life, they were worrying together over new teeth and inoculation. Emily settled back happily into her old position as the Lennox matriarch. If not queen of Ireland she was still queen of her own family. When Sarah arrived at Castletown in 1785, Emily was nearly fifty-four. She was a grandmother many times over, of both legitimate and illegitimate children. In the eyes of her husband and family she was still a beautiful woman. The soft fashions of the 1780s, with their plain gowns, bright sashes and billowing neckerchiefs, suited her ample form. Sore eyes (alleviated by the application of leeches) bothered her, she complained of a rheumatic leg and her periods were now troublesome. But she had, as she said later, a constitution of iron and, despite her aversion to exercise, she had fewer ailments than Sarah, who was fourteen years her junior. She was passionately in love with her husband. When Ogilvie went to London in 1782, she wrote to him, 'Dr Mimi was in bed an hour with me this morning and so like you! Guess if I kissed and mumbled her, dear little thing.'

Emily still regarded herself as a woman of fashion. She retained her love of novelty in literature and dress and she kept her cosmopolitan outlook. As the 1780s wore on and especially after the beginning of the French Revolution in 1789, anti-Gallic chauvinism swept the British Isles, even creeping into Emily's family. The Duke of Leinster might just as well not have gone on his long and expensive Grand Tour in the 1760s. Since inheriting he had stayed put in Ireland and now confessed to his mother 'I hate *Monsieur*'. But Emily kept her Francophilia. She was more likely to go to Nice than Brighton for a dose of sea air, she filled Frescati with French furniture and fireplaces and when Rousseau's *Confessions* appeared from 1781 she reverently put each volume beside his other works on her library shelves.

While Emily maintained the demeanour and establishment of a metropolitan hostess, Louisa cultivated a determined eccentricity in dress, manner and acquaintance. Castletown was very much a country house. Dogs trotted about and lolled in the long gallery with the family in the evenings, 'perfuming the air not a little' as Louisa put it. The Conollys entertained on Sundays, which Sarah called 'a kind of public day' at Castletown. Louisa rarely went out except to occasional official functions, to Carton and to Black Rock. Friends came to stay at Christmas when there was still a round of entertainments and parties. Louisa spent most of the day, weather permitting, outside, wearing sturdy boots and a riding habit. After Emily Napier arrived, Louisa carried her around in her arms, accompanied by a footman who took turns with the plump little burden.

As time went on Louisa began to look beyond the Castletown gates and to take an interest in the 'middling sort' and the poor. She started to visit the labourers and their families who lived in Celbridge, on the edge of her estate. On journeys away from Castletown she studied the lives of others with anthropological fervour. In September 1782 she sent Sarah a report of one such field trip in the north of Ireland, dinner with a family 'in the middling rank of life'. 'They played on the flute, guitar, musical glasses and sung, and seemed so happy that it was a pleasure to see them. "So," thinks I, in my own mind, "here are a sort of people totally unknown, but just in their small neighbourhood, and of course not sought after, and whom probably in the great world, would not only pass unnoticed but would be reckoned vulgar (and which I believe they are) that to me are very pleasant people and at a venture (if I must decide) I should prefer to *Lady Melbourne*, *Lady Jersey*, the *Duchess of Devonshire* etc, etc, etc . . ." In short, my dear Sal, merit is *the* thing to admire, and whatever station we find it in we must like it, approve of the possessors of it.' Louisa also went about incognito using her reading as a guidebook to help her place people she met from other walks of life. In 1783 she and Conolly dined at the Ordinary Inn at Matlock in Derbyshire, 'where the company was completely mixed. Some *rich* looking traders from Sheffield, some housekeepers, some second rank fine people, a quiet lawyer and his wife, and us. We arrived at the Inn before suppertime, . . . [and] for the fun of it joined the company. I saw some of the company very curious to know who we were, a prating lady attacked Mr. Conolly and gave *her* opinion about all the beauties in London. She was exactly the character of the witty ladies in a vulgar story book.' Louisa stood the company at her end of the long table a bottle of wine and 'quite enjoyed seeing the good people so comfortable'. But eventually a servant revealed that Louisa was connected to the Duke of Richmond and their secret was out. 'The prating Miss immediately held her tongue, my Sheffield friend looked at me with respect, and the fun ended. So I went to bed, but had been much entertained first.'

Such adventures were exciting exploits rather than part of everyday life. Louisa did not develop a politics to go with her cult of the ordinary. Rank had to stay, she believed, because through it God allowed men to exercise charity and loving kindness. But poverty could, and should, be alleviated. Louisa insisted that the material gap between rich and poor was too wide, leading to excess on the one hand and thieving on the other.

Like Emily, Louisa stayed plump as the years went by, and her complexion, roughened by hours out of doors, kept its rubicund glow. A pastel drawn in the 1780s shows her hair falling in big curls round her neck, still showing brown through the powder. Her chin filled out as she grew older and her nose sharpened. A white gauze neckerchief encircles her shoulders and with an informality that she insisted upon for all but the grandest occasions, she wears a soft white 'dormeuse' cap trimmed with lace.

Sarah cultivated an even more matronly air, dressing with selfconscious modesty. When she was drawn in the late 1780s or early 1790s she wore her hair simply drawn back, topped by a mob cap with a dark velvet trimming, which was held on by a handkerchief tied under the chin. A white gauze handkerchief chastely covered her shoulder and chest, tucking carefully into the front of her gown. For good measure she added a lace mantilla or shawl. This modest portrait was a far cry from the voluptuousness of her portrait by Reynolds of 1764–5 in which she was scantily clad, with her hair uncovered, her neck, chest and even her foot almost bare. Sacrificing to the Graces in 1764, Sarah was herself the sacrificial centre of the painting, offering her body to the world. Her later portrait was drawn to fit a much smaller pocket, of course. But

Sarah's aims were different too. Contentment, serenity and modesty were the qualities she now wanted to show the world.

Nobody doubted Sarah's happiness. On her birthday in 1783 she wrote to Susan, 'Feby 25th, 1783 . . . this is my birthday. I am 38 and I see nothing "new under the sun" except that till I was past 36 I find I never knew what *real happiness* was, which from my marriage with Mr. Napier till now is much greater than I had any idea of as existing in human life . . . indeed, if I am to judge from the *present* of the *future*, nothing can ever diminish my domestic comfort and happiness but illness or death, for you know I mind poverty as little as anybody.' Louisa had sealed Sarah's happiness with sisterly approval, writing the year before: 'I know *full well*, my dearest Sally, what that love is, and that nothing can ever equal it. I am going perhaps to surprise you by saying, that I don't believe you ever experienced what I call *real love* before, and you never *knew* what the first of all happiness was, till now. I have perceived by several of your letters that you understand that point *much better* than you did, at least *my* vanity makes me think so, because your ideas correspond so much more to my own.'

Sarah basked in her sister's approbation. Her remarriage which, by mutual agreement, was described as a union of love in marked contrast to the mad passion of her affair with Gordon, rehabilitated her at Castletown and with many of Louisa's friends. Napier astutely befriended Conolly, and their friendship swept away Conolly's lingering doubts about having Sarah in his house. Sarah could never undo all the social damage of her adultery and separation. But, paradoxically, the increasingly conservative temper of the times came to her aid. Louisa and her friends pointed to Sarah's handsome, ever-growing family as a justification of her actions. Without the separation and divorce, they could hint, Sarah would never have become the model of motherhood and domestic felicity that she now was.

To begin with Sarah and Napier, who was waiting eagerly for the resumption of war, were only visitors at Castletown. but as the peace lengthened, they settled down and joined in the round of visits that was at the heart of family life. Between Dublin, Castletown, Black Rock and Carton there were constant journeys. At Black Rock, Edward Fitzgerald toyed with the idea of becoming a lawyer. But he confessed to finding the Irish Parliament more exciting than Mansfield and Rousseau easier than Blackstone. Emily's girls read French with her and travelled to Dublin to learn drawing and deportment.

In 1787 Sarah and Napier decided to settle in Ireland for good. With Conolly's help they bought a house in Celbridge a few hundred yards from Louisa's gates. It was solid and unadorned, three storeys high and seven windows wide, set on a slope above the main street in a small park of its own. By her old standards it was modest – a house for a merchant with an income of a thousand pounds a year, redolent of prosperity rather than aristocracy. Sarah's few acres hardly kept the town at bay; the local board school, which her boys attended, was just down the street.

Looking back, the second half of the 1780s seemed to all the sisters a golden time of fecundity and tranquillity. 'The happiest years of any of our lives,' was how Ogilvie described them. But that happiness was remembered through the disasters that came afterwards. At the time, anxiety, grief and anger sometimes broke through into quotidian pleasures, blotting happiness out completely.

Soon after Sarah arrived at Castletown in the summer of 1785, Louisa Bunbury's consumptive symptoms got worse. By the autumn Sarah had given up hope. Louisa died at the end of the year. Sarah grieved openly and well; after three months the needs of other lives brought her back into the world. 'My 4 little children have *all* had different illnesses and kept my mind much employed, and of course their recovery gives a new spring to my spirits, which has been very useful to me,' she wrote in March.

By May, Louisa Bunbury's memory was less insistent. 'In

the same half hour I can laugh and in a few minutes feel *un serrement de coeur*, as if all nature was darkened before my eyes and I had no further business on this earth. I reproach myself for having, only for one hour, forgot my loss, and I revive it with all the strength of my imagination.' Soon Louisa was an intermittent and less disturbing ghost, casting shade but not darkness, almost crowded out of memory by Sarah's new family.

Louisa Bunbury's death closed the saga of Sarah's adultery and separation. But in doing so it revived her memory of her first marriage, the affair with Gordon and the changes in her life since Napier's proposal. It reminded her, too, of her brother's dislike of her marriage and the fact that he, the primary trustee of her divorce settlement, had control of her income. Sarah decided that she wanted Napier to have control of her annuity of £500 a year. The Duke of Richmond refused to cede it. A rancorous quarrel ensued, ostensibly about money, but really about Sarah's new sense of herself.

Sarah's brother had provided for her from the time she left Gordon in the winter of 1769 until, and beyond, her divorce. Although she had an annuity (wrested with some difficulty from Bunbury), the Duke still housed her and gave her the protection of his good name. Sarah could not control her annuity herself, but she wanted Napier to have that role. She no longer saw herself as a ne'er-do-well aristocrat, but as a military wife and respectable mother. Richmond, well aware that Sarah was challenging his familial authority by her demands, refused to budge.

Sarah lost her attempt to wrest her annuity from her brother's control. Afterwards her dislike of him increased. She seized every opportunity of making him feel isolated and uncomfortable. As usual, Charles Fox and national politics were her chosen weapons. Events of the late 1780s gave her plenty of opportunities for fights.

In late October 1788 George III went mad, so mad that 'he called Mr. Pitt a rascal and Mr. Fox his friend'. The King became unable to carry out his constitutional duties and a

Regency, which would put the Prince of Wales at the head of government, seemed likely. Charles Fox and his supporters, who had sided with the Prince in his oedipal struggle with his father, sensed that they might be able to seize the government from Pitt. The horizon seemed especially bright for the opposition in Ireland. If the Prince of Wales were appointed Regent he would be able to bring his supporters to power there, even if he failed to dislodge Pitt from Westminster, because the Irish government was directly under Crown control.

In December 1788, while the King struggled and raved at Kew, Emily sent Ogilvie to London in the hope that he might become a go-between in negotiations between the English and Irish opposition. Emily called the Prince of Wales 'tiresome', although she sympathised with his extravagance and thought he had been badly treated by the refusal of both Parliament and the King to pay his debts. She expressed concern for the King's sufferings, but she longed for a Regency that might bring Fox to power, explaining to her daughter Charlotte, 'I am sure the Prince has been as unhappy as any of [the King's] children, for he has an excellent heart. His situation is a very delicate one; we expect with impatience to hear that he is declared Regent.' Ogilvie was nervous that Conolly and the Duke of Leinster might resent his unofficial mission. But Emily brushed his worries aside. 'They forget, dear souls, both of them, that they have not given reason by their conduct in politics to make it safe for people to trust them, and also that their abilities being esteemed with reason *très médiocre*, men of sense will always be applied to first, notwithstanding their greatness.' Emily hoped that when the Prince became Regent and Charles Fox assumed power in London her choice of husband would be justified and that Ogilvie would, by virtue of his intelligence, take his rightful place in Irish government.

Instead the opposite happened. In March 1789 the King recovered and the Foxites were execrated anew. The Fitzgerald family emerged from the crisis split by different loyalties, spreading the quarrel among the Lennox children down into the next generation. Sarah, fervently Foxite, described the politics of Emily's sons soon after the King's recovery. 'The Duke of Leinster is stout ... Charles Fitzgerald is a Pittite and is to have a good place, we hear. Henry is a valiant knight and scorns to change his buff and blue. Robert is a Pittite and chargé d'affaires, secrétaire et plénipotentiaire à Paris; ... as he never was in Parliament, was a Pittite from choice, got this place from his uncle ... I own I do not *regret* his being on that side; but I am provoked at Charles who does it only for a dirty thousand a year, a sinecure! Dear Edward is also a thorough Foxite.'

Sarah did not write about Emily's daughters. This was partly because she had what Louisa termed 'a preference for boys', which meant that, whatever the context, she was more likely to write about boys, her own or anyone else's, than girls. But it was also because, despite her consuming interest in politics, Sarah professed to believe that women's political views had no bearing on the political process. This was more a gesture to received opinion than a belief that she acted upon. Sarah herself had campaigned on behalf of her first husband, and she wrote sympathetically about the Duchess of Devonshire's contributions to Fox's campaigns in Westminster in the 1780s. None the less she did not write much about the political opinions of her nieces.

In fact, Emily's daughters had political opinions every bit as strong as those of her sons. Lucy and Sophia sided with Fox; Charlotte, who had recently married a Pittite MP, Joseph Strutt, took her husband's part. By the early 1790s the rift between Lucy and Charlotte was wide. Charlotte was 'Mr. Strutt in petticoats and he is Charlotte in trousers and both old Maids,' Lucy wrote in 1793, furious that neither were proud of 'the dear Cousin and his love of Liberty'.

Try as she might, Emily could neither ignore her children's political beliefs nor hide her own. Politics got everywhere:

into the boudoir, onto the dinner table and between the pages of the most motherly letters. Politics altered love itself; and although at times of national and familial calm it dropped into the background, it was always there. After 1789, Emily's relations with her children were subtly altered. She increasingly avoided political discussions in letters and concentrated on family matters; what to eat after an attack of gout; the sorrows of weaning a child from the breast; births, deaths, weddings. But still politics crept in. Reporting on a forthcoming christening at Carton in 1791, she could not help noting with approval, 'the whole family is to be dressed in buff and blue', the colours of Foxite opposition.

After the Regency crisis, Sarah and Emily finally gave up hope of preferment for their husbands. Sarah settled down at Celbridge in her 'new, dear, cheerful, comfortable, pretty house' with her 'very pretty little flock of brats'. She still thought of herself as impoverished but said that Conolly's help and her annuity made them 'quite easy, for we can feed, clothe, and keep (at a common school in the village) our boys, though we can neither have carriages, dress, company or many luxuries.'

As Sarah bedded down, Emily prepared to leave. At the end of the 1780s she shifted her base to London ('Dr Papa does not love Ireland,' she confessed to her daughter Lucy). Then she set about finding husbands for her remaining daughters, Lucy, Sophia, Cecilia and Mimi. Harley Street was soon filled with visitors and she especially welcomed young Foxite politicians like Lord Foley and Charles Grey. Emily would happily have married her daughters to any young men of fortune, but she selected men who clustered around Fox. Their presence in Harley Street gave a good indication of her own political opinions. Prominent amongst her visitors was Lord Grey, later prime minister and architect of the Reform Bill. Grey was an outspoken supporter of the French Revolution and he continued to support it even after the fall of the monarchy in 1792, when many early enthusiasts turned cold.

In April 1792 he founded the Society of the Friends of the People, to press for parliamentary reform. Grey opposed the war with France that started in 1793 and remained Francophile and Foxite right through the dark days of 1794, when the tumbrils rolled through Parisian streets and Fox was widely regarded and caricatured as a regicidal *sans culotte* wielding a dagger and wearing the revolutionists' 'bonnet rouge'. Emily, meanwhile seems to have been scheming to marry him to one of her daughters. In September 1794 she wrote to Lucy, 'you will say I am *persuading* you to marry Lord Grey, for that is the way you dear girls exaggerate. I am only talking reason to you, which you won't listen to.'

Emily's partiality towards Grey may have been based partly on his association with Fox (although the two men did not see eye to eye on the question of parliamentary reform). But she could not have been unaware that Grey's radical sympathies were, by 1794, regarded by many as dangerously democratic and probably Republican.

Attitudes towards France and the French Revolution had shifted markedly between 1789 and 1793. By 1793, to be openly Francophile, as Emily was, was seen by some as an aberrant and almost seditious stance. In 1789 the Whig opposition had welcomed the revolution as a new 1688, a new Glorious Revolution that could plant English liberties in French soil. Radicals – many non-conformist, a few aristocratic – saw events in France as a progression of the American Revolution, and hoped that the removal of privilege, political equality and parliamentary reform would now spread across the Channel. The years just before and just after 1789 saw the most sustained radical and reformist activity since the English Civil War nearly a hundred and fifty years earlier.

By 1792 this early euphoria had given way to polarisation and hardening of attitudes, and the government and conservatives had seized the political initiative from the opposition and the reformers. The Paris Insurrection and the September Massacres, the subsequent Edict of Fraternity, execution of the King and Queen, abolition of the monarchy and advent of the Terror changed the opinion that many held of the character of the revolution. Many now saw it not so much as 1688 but as 1642, not as a Glorious Revolution but as another regicidal tyranny. The Whig opposition fell into disarray and Pitt's government mobilised political support to begin stamping out radical activity in Britain. By 1793 supporters of the revolution were already a minority and by 1794 politicians like Fox and Grey who denounced the war with France could only count on the support of 30 or 40 of their fellow MPs, 200 less than a few years before.

Yet Grey's politics may have seemed to Emily mild in comparison with the republican enthusiasms of her son, Lord Edward Fitzgerald. When Edward returned from his visit to Paris in 1792 she wrote: 'he is mad about French affairs – the levelling principle, and indeed seems entirely engrossed by these subjects, upon which he converses in a charming pleasant way. Though I fear he has made out a system to himself too perfect for this world, and which to bring about would be the cause of much disorder, and much blood would be spilt. This he denies . . . One must not say the mob before him, but the people. I think it charming to hear talked of, but I fear they will never realise it.'

Edward's conversion to Republicanism had a sudden birth in Paris at the end of 1792, but its gestation had been slow, nourished by a tradition of political opposition (both Irish and Foxite), a sojourn in North America and a long immersion in the works of Rousseau, Voltaire and English radicals like Priestley and Paine.

Edward joined the British army in 1780, at the age of seventeen, and soon afterwards embarked for America, where he fought in North Carolina 'against the cause of Liberty', as he later described it. At the end of the American wars in 1783 he was put on half pay and desultorily studied fortifications in between attending the Irish Parliament as one of his brother's members. In 1788 he went to North America again, to Nova

Scotia in Canada. By this time his Foxite commitment to generalised notions of liberty was romanticised with a strong dose of French noble savagery. He applauded in Canada both the 'equality' of the white settlers, amongst whom 'there are no gentlemen' and the unencumbered life of the Indian 'savages', who had none of 'our fictitious, ridiculous wants' and were 'what nature intended we should be'. Edward was enchanted with the Indians' way of life, writing to Emily, 'My dearest mother, if it was not for you, I believe I should never go home', and transposing, for her amusement, life in Harley Street with Indian life in Halifax, Nova Scotia. If they had all been savages, he wrote, 'there would be then no cases of looking forward to the fortune for children – of thinking how you are to live; no separations in families, one in Ireland, one in England: no devilish politics, no fashions, customs, duties or appearances to the world to interfere with one's happiness. Instead of being served and supported by servants, everything here is done by one's relations – by the people one loves; and the mutual obligations you must be under increase your love for each other, . . . Now the dear Ciss and Mimi, instead of being with Mrs. Lynch, would be carrying wood and fetching water, while ladies Lucy and Sophia were collecting and drying fish. As for you dear mother, you would be smoking your pipe. Ogilvie and us boys, after having brought in our game, would be lying about the fire while our squaws were helping the ladies to cook, or taking care of our papouses: all this in a fine wood, beside some beautiful lake, which when you are tired of, you could in ten minutes, without any baggage, get into your canoes and off with you elsewhere.'

Edward returned to England in 1790, in time to celebrate what Fox called 'the noblest cause that ever was in the hand of Man', the French Revolution, which had begun a year earlier. He celebrated his Foxite connections by an affair with Richard Brinsley Sheridan's wife (who died giving birth to his child), and went to Paris in 1792, where he stayed with Paine and renounced his title. Finally he proved his radical sympathies by marrying Pamela Sims, the illegitimate daughter of Philippe 'Égalité', the Duc d'Orléans. In 1792, after early French military success, he saw in the Parisians a cameraderie that made them like the Indians of Nova Scotia and a greatness which made them citizens of the world. 'All their pamphlets, all their pieces, all their songs extol their achievements but as the effect of the principle they are contending for, and rejoice at their success as the triumph of humanity. All the defeats of their enemies they impute to their disgust at the cause for which they fight. In the coffee-houses and play-houses, every man calls the other *camerade*, *frère*, and with a stranger immediately begins, "Ah! nous sommes tous frères, tous hommes, nos victoires sont pour vous, pour tout le monde."'

Even in his revolutionary enthusiasm, Edward never forgot Emily. He wrote constant vivid accounts of his devotion to her, like this one sent from Ireland in 1793: 'I dote on being with you anywhere, but particularly in the country, as I think we always enjoy each other's company more here than in town. I long for a little talk with you, sitting out in some pretty spot, of a fine day, with your long cane in your hand, working at some little weed at your feet, and looking down, talking all the time.'

Lord Edward was confident that his mother shared a good many of his views (although he was equally certain that Ogilvie did not). Writing from Paris a couple of months after the Republic was declared and just after the French had scored resounding military victories in the Low Countries, he said, 'I am glad Ogilvie warms up a little. I knew he would', as if he was certain that his mother for one was cheered by the success of the Republican armies. Emily's love for her favourite son predisposed her to like what he liked. But she was no cipher and, as if in proof, she consoled herself after his departure to Paris and then to Ireland with the writings of the radical chemist Joseph Priestley. No hint of this reading emerged in Emily's letters. She had always been good at keeping her own counsel. For years she had kept her affair with Ogilvie a secret. The date of her marriage was still mysteriously imprecise and she had kept the probable secret of George Fitzgerald's parentage from everyone, only referring to him once in her correspondence with Ogilvie as 'your boy'. Now her political opinions – a desire for parliamentary reform, a dislike of a strong monarch, even an urge towards her son's 'democratic' Utopia – were all concealed. Up to the middle of 1794 she seems to have supported Edward's political stance, and even perhaps gone along with his wish to see the example of France repeated in Ireland, where he established himself in 1792, and quickly made contact with the radical United Irishmen. But as she realised the implications of his Republicanism – that after 1794 it meant rebellion and violence – and as it was made clear that he was a target for government spies, her enthusiasm waned. She began to long for him to stop his secret activities in Ireland. She became more circumspect than ever, and he, perhaps suspecting that his letters were read by government censors, wrote in 1794, 'I won't bore you with any more politics, dear mother, as I know you don't like them.'

Sarah's volubility made up for Emily's reserve. She staunchly supported Fox, calling him 'more glorious than ever' in 1793. She felt sympathy for the aims but abhorrence for the methods of the revolution as the Terror progressed. 'I pity the deluded multitude and wish them success *at home* but *ruin* if they go one step out of France.' Taking her cue from Fox she regarded war against France as a trumped-up excuse by European monarchs to extend their despotisms at home. But as a military wife she wanted victory. 'I think our war the King's war, very wrong and very foolish, but still I wish it success.' Sarah welcomed war because war offered Napier hope of active service, after years as a half-pay captain.

Early in 1794 Napier became a major and was appointed Deputy Quarter-Master General to Lord Moira's army in Holland. Sarah's new principles of duty and honour thus saw active service for the first time. They came through with colours flying. Sarah played her role as an impoverished major's wife to the hilt, relishing its indignities and the contrast with the well-serviced comforts of Castletown and Celbridge. Leaving all her children behind except Napier's daughter, who insisted on being with her father, and her son Charles, who was in training for his own enlistment, Sarah travelled down to Southampton, 'like a poor Captain's wife as I ought to do, in a chaise and pair, three of us (no maid) and one man on horseback.'

At Southampton the army was assembling. Napier was recruiting troops and planning the move of men and matériel from England to the Continent. Officers in artillery regiments, sergeants in charge of men and arms, clerks who tried frantically to record the movements of supplies, wagoneers who wanted work and payment: all crowded into Napier's rented quarters. Sarah described the scene in biblical language, as one of Babylonian chaos. 'Various and constant are the occupations of Major Napier, and constant and unremitting is his attention. Ceremony don't belong to his character and poverty makes us confine ourselves to cheap lodging with three small bedrooms and one parlour, into which are introduced about 20, 30 or more people of various denominations from 8 in the morning till 11 at night ... All march in at all hours on business. To this must be added "les dames de la ville", now and then wives of officers, officers themselves sometimes on duty, sometimes as visitors, half a dozen very young men, who, belonging to the departments, call in and run in and out like children for a hat or a paper forgot.' 'I have no place to be but in this *coffee-room* of his,' she added cheerfully.

Sarah's description of the army at Southampton made it clear why soldiers were viewed with such alarm by those who strove to uphold propriety. The scene in Napier's lodgings violated several of the hierarchies by which the household, the nation and the state were conventionally supposed to be ordered. In the first place, social distinction was cast aside.

Officers (including aristocrats like Napier), conscripted soldiers, craftsmen and casual labourers from the lowest ranks of society mixed together without the 'ceremonies', as Sarah called them, that accompanied and helped define class relations. Secondly, women of all sorts were crowded together. In Napier's cramped hot rooms, officers' wives and young unmarried girls like Louisa Napier, who were supposed to be protected from any open expression of sexuality, rubbed shoulders with 'women of the town' who had come to recruit officers for amorous intrigue. Finally, this sort of scene was a violation of the conventional ordering of space within a dwelling. Aristocratic houses like Castletown had carefully planned gradations of space. Business visitors, labourers and servants went round to the offices through a side entrance. Personal callers waited in the chilly expanse of the entrance hall and were then led to drawing-room, long gallery or parlour depending on their state of intimacy with the Conollys. Even in humble households these divisions applied: visitors were received in the front room, but the family lived mainly in the back. Napier's lodgings jumbled together everybody everywhere. On occasions Sarah received friends and even officers in her bedroom. Small wonder, then, that soldiers epitomised danger for those anxious to maintain hierarchies of all sorts, and epitomised glamour for those who were allured by the breaking of taboos.

Sarah enjoyed this blurring of boundaries, and she seized the opportunity it offered to take on some of Napier's work herself. While he made decisions about movements of troops and supplies in one room, in another she organised and paid recruiting officers who were raising a company, claiming in justification that Madame de Sévigné's daughter had done the same thing more than a century before. When she had raised 30 out of the 100 men Napier needed she wrote triumphantly to Susan, 'None of these would have been got but for *me*.'

Even when the army left Sarah maintained her good spirits, buoyed up by a sense of achievement and a string of notes from her husband. Tender letters arrived from Ostend, Flushing and from Camp Wairloos in Flanders. 'I consider every hour which I am without you as so much lost in my life.' 'For heaven's sake, Sally, think that on your care of yourself depends my hope of future happiness: whilst you are well I am comfortable in any situation.' 'I am very well and yours soul and body.'

Lord Moira's army had a less than glorious sojourn in the Low Countries. Napier was back in England in July, one of many thousands of soldiers who retreated from the Continent in the face of French advances. Both he and Sarah reached Ireland a few weeks later, Napier to recruit in the north, Sarah to re-establish herself at Celbridge to supervise the education of her children.

The Napier boys went to a religiously mixed local school where they learned good Latin, a smattering of mathematics and a tolerance for their schoolfellows, the sons of Celbridge's prosperous families. It was a different education from that of their cousins or father. They learned no French, which was increasingly seen as a feminine accomplishment rather than a language of civility and cosmopolitan, aristocratic conversation. Teaching of Latin expanded to fill the place left by this shift.

But Latin's associations were very different from those of French. For a long time Latin had been associated with statesmanship. Young men read reams of satires, poetry and speeches and polished their oratory to the curves of Latin cadences. At the peak of their careers they had themselves carved, senatorially, in togas, so that the beer bellies of John Bull were enfolded in the drapery of Cicero. Latin meant things Roman, too. From Stowe to Chiswick and Kingsgate, gentlemen built houses for retirement, in self-consciously 'Roman', often specifically 'Virgilian' designs.

But this was changing. Latin was increasingly seen as the language of empire and of war, Caesar on the march rather than Virgil at rest. With the expansion of the ambit of Latin came a new sense of self for the boys who learned it. The Napiers defined themselves not so much as members of a European aristocracy, as their aunts and uncles had done, but as servants of empire cast in the mould of classical heroes: literary still, but with a different literature.

The Napiers' destinies were never in doubt. George Napier kept a portrait of Frederick the Great in his study to remind himself and his sons of the man he regarded as the greatest modern soldier before Napoleon. Their politics would be radical but monarchist: a cult of Fox and a demonology of Pitt held sway in the Napier household. Their private lives were to be governed by propriety and domesticity, free from the expense of illegitimate children and the bouts of venereal disease that dogged Emily's sons.

Much of what Sarah and Napier demanded of their sons they achieved. Her five boys turned into three generals, one captain in the navy and only one barrister. In her old age, Sarah liked to spurn any credit for their success. She gave the laurels to her husband, saying, 'as they rose out of infancy I left them to their father's management and studied to become the friend not the tutoress of my sons.' But she was disingenuous. Napier taught his sons military engineering, swordsmanship and a sense of duty and honour; Sarah watched over everything else. First and foremost she gave them a sense of life as literature, and a storehouse of literary references by which they interpreted their own feelings and actions. Her favourite texts, particularly Pope's Homer, became their touchstones. William Napier whiled away time in quarters on the Spanish Peninsula by reciting chunks of the *Iliad* and astonished his fellow officers by his memory of ancient history, romances and chivalrous poetry. Before battles, Charles James Napier comforted himself with tales of the heroism of ancient heroes and he loved to describe his situation by quoting theirs. Literature served militarism. It cauterised the pain, squalor and boredom of the battlefield and dignified butchery with glorious precedents. William

Napier absorbed his mother's love of literature so well that he transcribed war into words, writing in several volumes and rolling prose a history of the Peninsular Campaign that, for his readers, elevated war into a work of art.

When her sons left home Sarah wrote to them constantly, alert to any slip in their standards of behaviour or even any slump in their deportment. They tried hard to be the sons she wanted. As they worked their way up the army hierarchies her image was never far from their minds. Charles James Napier who, as a young man had longed to leave the army, calling it a 'trade in blood', dreamed of his 'beloved mother' before he blew up the fort of Imamghar, in his campaign to capture the Indian province of Sind, a mission that earned him temporary opprobrium but secured his place in the heart of the nation and the history of empire. Much earlier he wrote to her saying simply, 'we are what you have made us.'

The Napiers exaggerated to please their mother. Politics and social experience as well as family imperatives helped to shape their attitudes. All the Napier brothers felt themselves to be outsiders, not rich enough to hobnob with their social equals and not English enough to feel comfortable at Court or in Westminster. They were one step further away from money and the sources of political power than their parents, without substantial legacies or landed property. Moreover, their politics, learned on their parents' laps and on visits to Fox at St Anne's Hill, were made active and practical by their experience of the atrocities of the Irish Rebellion of 1798.

PART TWO
1798, 'fatal year'.
Emily's note on a letter from Edward Fitzgerald.

The Napiers had not been back in Ireland long before Sarah began to notice that the people of middle rank and the poor who laboured in the fields around Celbridge were openly expressing disaffection with London and Dublin. Some justified their opposition by talking of Irish nationalism, others used the language of universal rights laid out so popularly by Tom Paine in *The Rights of Man*. Proselytizers in the north were successfully popularising, among Roman Catholics and Protestants alike, a radicalism that looked to Paine for ideas and France for their expression. Radical enthusiasm in Ireland had the same origins and engines as that on the mainland, but the mixture of a Protestant administration and a largely Catholic population gave nationalism and republicanism an added twist. When Napier returned from Londonderry at the end of 1794, he reported that dissension was rife in Belfast and the surrounding counties.

Everywhere the situation was confusing. Opposition to Dublin and Westminster was fractured; alliances were volatile. By 1795 people began to sense enemies all around, and individuals began to lead double lives. The respectable Belfast printer by day was a United Irishman at night, meeting with others in secret after 1794 and committed increasingly to armed rebellion. A Catholic silk merchant and United Irishman had yet another identity, that of government informer. A servant might bring his master a glass of wine on a silver tray and then, after hours, become a 'Defender' cutting down trees to make pike handles, forswearing allegiance to state and Protestants alike.

Enmities hardened in a worsening economic climate of rising taxes, falling land revenues and a decline in manufacturing. Reactionary Protestants disliked anyone who promised emancipation for Dissenters and Catholics and pledged themselves to Westminster as long as Westminster upheld Protestant dominance. Republican Protestants, both Dissenters and aristocrats, spoke of universal rights, secular republicanism and, eventually, freedom from Westminster. Forward-looking Roman Catholics hoped for emancipation: while denouncing Dublin they remained loyal to Westminster, believing that emancipation could emanate only from

LEFT: *La Belle Cuisinière* after Boucher, typical of the moralising domestic scenes in Louisa's print room.

BELOW LEFT: William Kent's card for Fourdrinier, who produced paper for the Foxes' circle, and a print of Holland House in 1751.

BELOW RIGHT: Horner's trade card. Emily sent Louisa to his shop in 1759 to look for India Paper for Carton.

LEFT: Charles Bunbury with a wild and haunted look in the year his marriage collapsed: a print after Reynolds.

BELOW LEFT: The châteaux at Aubigny to which Emily and Ogilvie retreated from the fray in 1776.

BELOW RIGHT: William Ogilvie in his mid fifties, stern and unbending, sketched by his son-in-law, Charles Lock about 1795.

RIGHT: Emily, painted by Reynolds about the time of her second marriage.

HOTEL DE VILLE

ABOVE: 'Til I was past 36 I never knew what *real happiness* was': Sarah in the 1780s.

RIGHT: Sarah's plans of houses; Celbridge which she and Napier bought in 1787 and Moldcomb on the Goodwood estate.

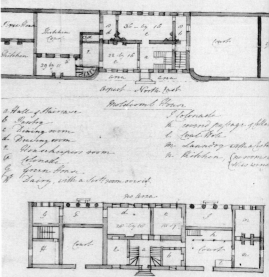

ABOVE: George Napier, short sighted but 'the most perfect made man'.

RIGHT: The third Duke of Richmond by Romney in 1777: political differences (and with Sarah, money) were beginning to strain family relations.

LEFT: An entry from Caroline's journal of 1768: her sons teased her about her illegible handwriting.

BELOW: Emily's hand remained exquisite all her life. This note was written to her great niece, Ste's daughter Caroline Fox.

RIGHT: Louisa's open unpretentious hand from a letter written when she was 74, also to Caroline Fox.

BELOW: Sarah's 'blind' hand, written on 'carbonic' paper using a special machine that kept the lines straight.

Fox, a Jacobin Macbeth is refusing to take responsibility for corrupting the Irish rebels.

England. Other Catholics wanted a Roman Catholic state free from Protestants, and created for their pedigree a Gaelic past of Catholic kings, Gaelic songs and Irish jigs. They styled themselves 'Defenders' and formed a large underground network.

Even these identities were fluid. After 1794 the Catholic Defenders, who were nationalist and 'Gaelic', merged with the secular, republican, United Irishmen. Hybrids began to appear: Catholics who mistrusted Protestants but spoke the language of universal rights found in *The Rights of Man*; Protestants who subscribed to Paine but talked of Irish nationalism. United Irish leaders upheld cosmopolitan values and Gaelic trappings simultaneously. Arthur O'Connor was a secular Protestant barrister who, with ludicrous self aggrandisement and an eye to his Catholic followers, called himself 'King of Connaught'. Edward Fitzgerald, Paine worshipper and Francophile, danced Irish jigs to the music of pipers, sang patriotic songs and celebrated St Patrick's day. Concealed in a chest he kept a uniform to be worn on the first day of the Irish Republic. It was a crazy amalgam of the Gaelic and the French. The green suit was decorated with red braid. It had rose-coloured cuffs and a cape. Rounding off the ensemble was a giant red cap of liberty with a green rim and a large silk tassel bobbing at the top.

So as the political and economic crisis deepened, the fanciful and the macabre jostled side by side. Ordinary life went on but the sense of impending doom grew. Men and women, in streets and shops, taverns and fields, became worried about soldiers in billets and garrisons. The army and the militia, always a source of grievance, were increasingly objects of fear. Many of the elements of Pitt's 'Reign of Terror', begun in 1794 to suppress radical activity throughout the kingdom, were soon apparent: the imprisonment of printers and journalists, the development of spy networks and loyalist informers and, eventually, the imprisonment of radicals for the utterance of so called 'seditious words' and the suspension of *habeas corpus*. Looking back, people identified 1795 as the point of no return, the year in which the prologue to the rebellion began.

Between 1795 and 1796, Defender and United Irish networks merged into one United Irish movement. Reactionary Protestants formed so called 'Orange lodges', groups pledged to uphold what they thought of as the Williamite settlement, which were largely impervious to United Irish revolutionary politics. Reports of 'Orange' atrocities spread. Some Dublin Protestants threw in their lot with Westminster, others with more militant (but usually anti-Catholic) Protestants in Dublin Castle. Still others, like Thomas Conolly, vacillated, siding first with Westminster, then against it, clinging to the language of paternalism and economic justice, eschewing discussion of rights and earning nobody's respect. 'Patriot' politicians like the Duke of Leinster were outpaced by events. Their opposition to Westminster now looked so pale as to seem like support, and they retreated from the fray disowned by former friends and enemies alike.

Relentlessly the nation pulled itself into the vortex. Government actions – making oath-taking a capital offence, pardoning repressive magistrates, and partially suspending *habeas corpus* at the end of 1796 – enraged radicals but were denounced by fierce loyalists as too weak. Opposition and sectarianism grew. There were rumours of French invasion plans and a gradual mobilisation of volunteers and militias. Rumour prompted action which fuelled rumour and prompted fear and interrogation. Was the secret-society member a government spy? Was the housekeeper loyal to her mistress, and was the mistress of the same mind as the master? Was the master the tool of Dublin Castle and was the Castle frustrating or co-operating with Westminster? Was Westminster a friend to loyal Catholics or secretly committed to Protestant ascendancy? In the maelstrom of fear and speculation, some individuals panicked; others took a hard line, stuck to it and lost their heads. As rebellion began the endless

remaking that constituted the nation's sense of itself was re-
morselessly speeded up. By the time the Act of Union was
signed, a new nation had emerged, not only constitutionally
but narratively as well, and it had a new martyrology to add
to its myths of itself.

From 1795 onwards opposition groups began arming themselves. Pikes were the simplest weapons. Smiths forged the
heads and parties of men went out at night to fell young trees
for the handles. Other arms were commandeered by insurgents and piled in secret caches. In July, a hundred and fifty
Defenders marched up to Sarah's house in Celbridge. Their
leaders fired shots at the upper windows and then demanded
arms. Sarah was away and her housekeeper, armed with one
of Napier's pistols, refused them entry. The whole band then
trudged disconsolately away. Louisa feared that Castletown,
where Napier's weapons were hurriedly secreted, would be
the next target of the 'rioters' as she called them. Conolly and
Napier, like Sarah, were away. Left alone, Louisa ruminated
upon and then panicked about an attack on the house. She
ordered every gun in Castletown to be primed and loaded and
put the house into a 'state of defence'. Then she went into
Celbridge, driving the length of the main street from Castletown's gates to Sarah's house at the other end. She went down
side streets and alleys and knocked on many doors. 'I went
myself to every house,' she explained to her brother, 'spoke
to every poor person to explain the nature of this mischievous
manner of proceeding, entreated them to desist and repose
some confidence in two such friends as Mr. Conolly and
myself, who never had nor would ever deceive them.' But
Louisa was already far from neutral. She wanted the people of
Celbridge to commit themselves to her and as she went she
made a list of those prepared to do so. 'I have all their names
down and of course shall be more likely to find out our
strength if anything happens. The housekeepers seemed
vastly pleased at this sort of association that I have set on foot

and I think it can't do any harm and may do good.' Louisa's list was bound to arouse the suspicion of those who already saw her in a double light, as both the apotheosis of liberal paternalism and a symbol of the repressive regime. Besides, a list compiled while Defenders melted away down the town's alleys was meaningless. Those who might be loyal to the Conollys or the government feared reprisals if the Defenders knew it. Those who had no intention of staying loyal might sign for cover or refuse to sign in case they were accused of double-dealing by their colleagues.

In the end Louisa had no need to use her list. The Defenders disappeared with their rifles and pikes and hid themselves in their daily occupations. Sarah's sons, who had enjoyed the military spectacle on their front lawn, returned to their schooling. At Castletown, Louisa put the arms away, prepared for the harvest and celebrated Emily Napier's birthday. Beyond Carton, on his small estate of Kilrush, Lord Edward Fitzgerald settled down for the summer with his young wife Pamela. By this time, Lord Edward had left the Irish Parliament. He defiantly hung a portrait of Tom Paine over the mantelpiece in his sitting-room at Kilrush and began to associate with aristocratic radicals like Arthur O'Connor and United Irishmen like the Sheares brothers, all of whom had been in Paris in 1792.

As long as the United Irish was a legal organisation, Lord Edward could associate with United Irishmen without formally belonging to the movement. But the organisation was forced underground in 1794 and Lord Edward eventually followed, dampening family anxiety as best he could. He joined at the beginning of 1796 and by that summer was in Hamburg and Switzerland with O'Connor, pressing the French to send an invasion force to Ireland that would begin an Irish revolution.

From Hamburg and Switzerland Edward sent Emily in London a series of letters which concentrated on the old themes of their correspondence: his love for her, hers for him, and their enjoyment of literature and the natural world. But his description of Switzerland was vague, more a sop to government censors than to his mother, who knew her son's views and probably the purpose of his mission too. 'I had a very pleasant tour, am in raptures with Switzerland. I left my friend O'Connor in Switzerland taking another tour. There never were two persons who more thoroughly admired Switzerland than we did. He saw it with the Rousseau enthusiasm. He is as fond of Rousseau as I am, so you may conceive how we enjoyed our journey.'

This concoction, with its repetitions and flat descriptions was not enough to set Emily's mind at rest. Lord Edward's references to Rousseau, who had written a constitution for the republican Swiss, were a broad hint that he was deep in political activities. She began to expect bad news. Worry spoiled the pleasure of Lord Edward's return from Hamburg and the company of his son 'little Eddy' whom Edward had given to his mother to look after. 'My poor anxious mind is ever looking forward to some distress,' Emily wrote to her daughter Lucy on 8 October 1796. After Lord Edward's return from the Continent, Emily rarely wrote about Ireland to anyone, and referred to her son's politics as 'a certain subject', something it was too painful, and unwise, to name. From 1792, Lord Edward must have known his letters would be opened by government officials and checked for seditious content. By the mid-1790s Emily and Sarah, too, suspected that they had a circle of readers wider than the family. Sarah continued to be hopelessly indiscreet, making no concessions to the officials reading her scribbled letters in the central Dublin Post Office. But she reminded Lucy Fitzgerald that opinions expressed in letters were not private matters; on the contrary, they were brought into the public domain by the zealous action of government censors.

Now that Lord Edward was committing treason by plotting the downfall of the government, Emily's enjoyment of her son's republicanism was at an end. She tried without success to talk him out of it. On 12 November she wrote to her daughter, who had joined Lord Edward at Kilrush (again without explicitly mentioning politics), 'and so my sweet Lucy, you have had conversations with that angel Edward! I can easily believe you might say many things that might have an effect and do good, as it is a subject you have read a good deal about, considered well, and your own good strong judgment would assist you. I too have seen the dear precious drop fall down that dear cheek, but that is when the heart feels the distresses of others. To work upon those feelings only makes him feel wretched, but it does not remove the prejudice.'

Emily saw disaster ahead. Even as she hoped against hope that her son would abandon his revolutionary plans, she began to create a heroic version of him in her own mind, an image of her son that would withstand any battering it might receive if he were caught and unmasked. Creating a hero of her son prepared her for cataclysm. 'I find my mind much less weak than I thought it would be,' she wrote to Lucy a few weeks later, adding, 'please tell Eddy so and press him to your heart for me.'

Throughout 1796 Lord Edward put a lighthearted face on to his radicalism, content that it should appear as patriotic posturing that would annoy rather than threaten the authorities. Lucy Fitzgerald, who described his capers in her diary, found meetings with radicals a source of sexual excitement and 'democracy' itself an aphrodisiac. While the United leaders planned rebellion, she nurtured an infatuation for Arthur O'Connor. 'Dec 13. We had a dance in the evening. Our company was Cummins and the butcher's daughters. I danced with Arthur [O'Connor]. We danced a great many Irish jigs. Ed. is a great hand at them.' 'Mar 23 [1797]. We had a visit from Mr. Henry and Mr. Leeson. They are both Democrats. I gave Mr. Henry a green cravat and Pamela Mr. Leeson, and we made them ride home in them.' 'Apl. 18. We went to town for a ball at Lady Clare's I had my hair turned close up, was reckoned democratic, and was not danced with.'

As the months passed, political events dwarfed such gestures.

After an abortive French naval expedition in December 1796 and outbreaks of violence across the country, Camden, the Lord Lieutenant, moved against the United Irish leadership. By June 1797 most of the Ulster leaders were behind bars. Papers stolen by informers in Ulster incriminated other leading radicals, Lord Edward Fitzgerald amongst them. Emily learned of this in London at the end of January 1797. The embarrassed government offered Lord Edward a discreet and safe passage out of the country soon afterwards, but he refused to take it.

Like many mothers, sisters and wives caught up in the rebellion, Emily could now only wait, scan the newspapers and long for her son's safety. Despite having a brother in the British Cabinet and a son prominent in the Irish peerage, Emily was far away in London, cut off from Ireland both by distance and the censor's pencil. Her helplessness made her fatalistic; after January 1797 she gave up hoping for the best and prepared to think of Edward as a martyr. She cherished little Eddy, who had stayed with her in London, as an image of his father, and she began a collection of relics. 'Yes, that dear lock so lately growing on Eddy's precious head is a very acceptable present,' she wrote to her daughter Lucy. 'I put it in my bosom, after dear little Eddy had kissed it a thousand times. "Papa's hair, Eddy's own Papa's hair!" I really believe he understands it all, pretty love.'

In May 1797 the harbingers of rebellion were discovered at Castletown and Celbridge: servants suspected of being United Irishmen and members of a party who had been breaking into houses in the neighbourhood and seizing arms. '*Our* footman and twelve Castletown servants and workmen have been taken up as housebreakers and United Irishmen,' Sarah told Susan. Sarah, unlike Emily, was on the spot. She could see that for the moment these ramshackle revolutionaries posed no threat to the political order and she responded to the news with a detachment that continued throughout the rebellion. Her anger was reserved for the Dublin administration whose '*real* and *manifest* cruelties and oppressions' she saw as the cause of disaster. Disaffection was the government's fault, she said. The mass of the population turned to a few Republicans for help only because neither the government nor the 'supine' opposition had offered any hope of emancipation and reform of the penal laws. Rebellion was wrong, she concluded, but explicable; yet Republicanism was abhorrent. Despite their cults of Napoleon and Caesar the Napiers described themselves as staunch adherents to the settlement of 1688 and advocated government by a compact between King, Lords and Commons. However much they demanded a limited role for the monarch and however much they railed against George III, they remained monarchists, opposed to 'democratic' or Republican movements.

Sarah's coolness in the face of rebellion came partly from her political assessment, partly from her sense of being an outsider. She believed that the population was overwhelmingly loyal and that the 'great weight of Monarchists' would mean that rebellion was localised and insignificant. She had little to fear she said. She and Napier had little to lose either: no income from Irish land, no government offices or estates. Sarah waited for the rebellion with a clear conscience and the *sangfroid* she believed appropriate in a military wife.

Louisa reacted to the arrests of the Castletown workmen with anything but detachment. She had developed a Manichaean attitude towards the local people, believing that those who were not with her were against her and persistently confusing disaffection towards Dublin and Westminster with disloyalty towards herself. Moreover, she asserted that because she had consistently set politics and religion aside in her dealings with her tenants, so they should now do the same and see her as an individual rather than a representative of a government she did not support. She explained later why the arrests upset her. 'My feeling so much as I did arose from the very great mortification I felt in having spent near 40 years (in what I considered a laudable pursuit) in vain. After having shown the greatest goodwill to the different classes around me, without ever once having been conscious of a moment's pride or severity towards them, and not even suffering my amusements to be independent of their advantages, I had flattered myself with the hope of possessing their friendship and confidence and then when ill advisers came to them with new proposals, that they would at least have consulted me before they engaged in so deep a business.'

When the contract of paternalism was shattered, Louisa had no way to describe her servants except as hostile or faithful. Equally, she had no other way to frame her own position, reasoning that hostility to the government meant sympathy for the rebels. So with fractured logic, Louisa put herself in the government camp, 'against' the disaffected, preferring not to see shades of loyalty or alliances of expediency. For the previous forty years she had thought of herself as Irish – 'we Paddy's' she used to say, or 'we Irish'. Her failure to understand or stand aside from definition by opposition meant that by 1798 she had pushed herself into saying 'we' and meaning the Irish government.

So for Louisa, 1798 represented a crisis of self-definition. She was temperamentally unable to write, as the Napiers did, 'we have never in word, thought or deed, contributed to the misfortune of this ill-fated country and sympathising in the distress of others is our only misfortune individually.' In other ways, too, Louisa was connected to the existing social hierarchy. Conolly's enormous income came mostly from Irish lands (lands which, rumour hinted, might be passed to Catholics or Frenchmen in a successful revolution); and there was Castletown, its park and comforts. 'I am obliged to say us now,' Louisa wrote to her brother in June 1798, 'for although Mr. Conolly has ever opposed the votes of the government, he will stand by any existing government rather than none.' Louisa recognised the inadequacy of her own taxonomy; she was reluctant to stand by the government. But she could not think in any other way. After the rebellion she wanted desperately to forget what had happened and clung to paternalism as her only refuge. She redoubled her charitable efforts and insisted upon displays of harmony between Catholics and Protestants, and rich and poor.

After the arrests of 1797 Louisa lived in unhappiness, clinging to those servants and tenants who professed their loyalty, but expecting betrayal. 'We all suffer much from the misery it has given my sister, finding *ingratitude* in so many and such old servants,' Sarah wrote with mixed asperity and sympathy. 'That is what cuts one to the heart, for it damps all *her* pleasure, which consisted in doing good to all around her.'

In the spring of 1798, amidst reports that the French were preparing another invasion fleet for Ireland, and rumours that the United Irishmen were organising an underground army and stirring disaffection amongst the Celbridge poor, Napier began to garrison Castletown and his own house. In the fields of loyal tenants who farmed the land around, Napier had ditches dug in parallel lines of defence, and earthworks thrown up at the peripheries where sentries could watch for an attack. Preparations for defence seemed to confirm the imminence of attack. But reports of a coherent plan of rebellion and well organised army of rebels were only partially true. Napier's preparations for war were far more practical than those of the United Irish leadership.

Responsibility for rebellion lay with the United Irish leaders in Dublin. Despite the presence of a large underground army (put at about 280,000 men in some membership returns), the United leaders were divided about the timing and course of any uprising. There was supposed to be a plan co-ordinated with a possible French attack. But communications with exiles in Paris were confused: Wolfe Tone, Napper Tandy and Edward Lewins all claimed to speak for the United Irish there. Some of the Dublin executive wanted a definite French commitment, others wanted to rise without French support. While they dithered and argued, support for rebellion in the counties reached a pitch in February 1798 and then sank rapidly when no word came from Dublin to rise.

At the end of February, before any decisions were taken, Arthur O'Connor was arrested in England on his way to France. On 12 March the government decimated the Dublin leadership of the United Irishmen by arresting almost all of them as they gathered to discuss strategy at the house of a wool-merchant, Oliver Bond. Only three members of the Dublin Executive, as the Dublin leadership was called, escaped. Of these, only Lord Edward Fitzgerald, who had avoided arrest because he had turned up at Bond's so late, was in Dublin.

Lord Edward went into hiding and, with a new executive, the Dublin United leaders tried to continue preparation for a rising. As they did so, support in the countryside was ebbing away. On 30 March 1798 martial law was proclaimed throughout the country; disarming, arrests and terror followed. Everywhere, and often amongst the yeomanry and militia quartered on the population, Orange emblems fluttered, symbols of Protestantism and loyalty that damned all Catholics as traitors. Martial law bred reprisals. Fears on the Catholic side of massacres by Orangemen within the militia and yeomanry and on the loyalist side of rebel seizures of property polarised loyalties. By late spring of 1798 the heterogeneity of the United Irish movement was gone. It had become an organisation Catholic at the core, with secular Protestants at the top. Even in Ulster, where Dissenters had played such an important part, most Protestants, fearful for their lives and property, put themselves under Orange protection.

In Dublin and surrounding counties, terrified United Irishmen looked to Lord Edward Fitzgerald for an announcement that he was to lead an immediate rebellion. But as the rump of the United Irish leadership contemplated the impoverishment and demoralisation of the movement, their belief grew in the necessity of French help. Hoping for a French invasion in May, they tried to keep their followers calm. Lord Edward, moving between safe houses in Dublin and preoccupied with avoiding arrest, was no longer aware of the fears of United Irishmen in the countryside. He and the other Dublin leaders drifted into a half-farcical limbo. They discussed military strategy for a French-led rebellion even while some, including Lord Edward, argued for a rising without French help. They made plans for a National Assembly for the new Irish Republic. Lord Edward, in a crazy reprise of his days as a youthful amateur at Holland House, disguised himself as a woman and visited his wife Pamela. Moving between hideouts he put on a pig-tailed wig and a countryman's great-coat. Once, safely installed in new lodgings, he left his boots outside the door with his name carefully written around the inside.

Lord Edward had none of his mother's capacity for secrecy and decisive action. Plans were made but no one in Dublin could take the decision either to halt or to call the rebellion. While in the countryside terror slipped into terrorism, followed by arrests, reprisals and panic, Lord Edward took walks at night along Dublin's canals, jumping from the towpath into half-submerged barges by the bank. One day, in a bathetic echo of his carefree life at Frescati, he did some digging in the garden of the house where he was hiding.

The Irish Chancellor, Lord Clare, had given Ogilvie assurances that the government would connive at Lord Edward's escape even before he went into hiding. When he refused to go, the family realised the depth of his involvement. Sarah expressed little surprise when she heard that he had narrowly escaped arrest at Bond's. Publicly in letters that the censors read, she might maintain his innocence. But privately she wrote, 'my mind sank within me'. A week later Sarah's suspicions were confirmed by an acquaintance with government contacts. In a diary she was keeping to read to Napier, who had a serious fever, she wrote, 'Mr. Henry says ... *entre nous*, there was a committee, and that government say they knew of it a month ago; that delegates of each province send their delegates to Dublin and that Edward was to order for Leinster how they were to proceed.' Lord Edward was in fact commander for the whole of the United Irish forces under Dublin control. Apart from this misconception Sarah's information was correct.

Sarah's immediate worries were for Pamela, Lord Edward's wife, and for Emily. 'We know nothing yet of how my poor sister will take it – I fear very badly,' Sarah wrote on 15 March, three days after the arrests in Dublin. But Emily had already decided how to present herself in misfortune. In the letter to her sisters that she wrote after hearing the news, she reasserted her earliest role, that of mother, figurehead and refuge, declining to give the censors confirmation of her misery. '22nd March. I know my dearest sisters will wish to have a line from myself. I know their dear hearts suffer on my account; thank God I have nothing to fear for my beloved Eddy. I am not in the least nervous, my health very good, and you know my dear sisters how mercifully I have ever been supported in trying occasions. Try, my dear Louisa not to abandon your dear mind to despair about the times. Let us cherish hope. You, my dear Sarah, have had the severest of all trials in your fears for your husband's life from a *fever* . . . I rejoice to hear he is better . . . God bless you all.' With this magnificent display of stoicism, Emily reaffirmed her matriarchal authority. The 'we three' of the last decade, the sense that Sarah had had of an equal sisterhood, was overlaid once more with a knowledge of Emily's pre-eminence. 'We three' they were, but also two and one.

But even as this old hierarchy was being restored, the relationship between Louisa and Sarah, in which Sarah played the part first of renegade then of impoverished supplicant, was changing. Sarah had always castigated herself for weakness and contrasted her own wickedness with Louisa's goodness and strength. Now the position seemed to be reversed. Louisa became more terrified as the rebellion came closer. At the end of March 1798 she allowed the army to search Castletown for concealed weapons, an act tantamount in Sarah's eyes to throwing in her hand with the government.

And when some Catholic prisoners were set free from nearby Naas gaol she expressed fear rather than pleasure. 'She was *not* glad the prisoners were released,' Sarah wrote in her running diary. After years of emotional subservience and in the midst of worries about her husband, the rebellion and Lord Edward's safety, Sarah took a modest, written revenge. 'What perversion in the noblest nature may be compassed by cunning, by nerves and by habits of hearing terror rung in her ears for years! I had neither time nor thoughts to answer, argue or try to convince her.' When Emily's letter of the 22nd arrived Sarah wrote, 'I am charmed with her elevated spirit and character, and trust it will save her from many hours of misery which poor Louisa passes so unnecessarily for want of using her reason.' Finding herself stronger than Louisa lessened Sarah's sense of dependence by creating for the first time in their relationship an equality of failure.

The rebellion also confirmed Sarah's identity as a military wife who shared her husband's duties. 'I fight a good battle with myself and keep very equal in my attendance and manner to you,' she wrote to Napier when he was sick, relishing the chance to use the military language that could transform her inner struggles from a drama into a battle. When an officer called at Celbridge and wanted to search the house she refused him. 'I am your representative in this instance,' she noted for her husband. Throughout the summer of 1798 Sarah's prose kept its zest; anxiety and excitement ran hand in hand as she wrote. No matter how miserable the family became nor how close the rebellion, Sarah was conscious that she was living up fully to the standards of courage and honour Napier asked of her.

In April 1798 the government began a ferocious campaign of disarming using the dispensations of martial law. Disarming started in the adjoining counties of Kildare, King's, Queen's and Tipperary to the south and west of Dublin, and by the middle of May had reached Celbridge and the neighbouring towns of Leixlip, Maynooth and Kilcock. A Scottish regiment, divided between the towns, plundered at will and threatened to burn houses. Still clinging on to her tattered paternalism, Louisa went from house to house in Celbridge, trying to persuade the angry and frightened inhabitants to give up their arms, effectively acting on behalf of the government. 'I have spent days in entreaties and threats, to give up the horrid pikes. Some houses burnt at Kilcock yesterday produced the effect. Maynooth held out yesterday, though some houses were burnt and some people punished. This morning the people of Leixlip are bringing in their arms. Celbridge as yet holds out, though five houses are burning. Whether obstinacy or that they have them not, I cannot say. But you may imagine what Mr. Conolly and I suffer. He goes about entreating to the last – spent all yesterday out among them, and today is gone again. He goes from Maynooth to Leixlip and Celbridge and begins again and again to go round them.'

Atrocities led to reprisals. Rebels who had not given up their arms waited in vain for word from Dublin. On the 17 May the remnants of the United Irish Executive, which now consisted of, among others, Lord Edward, Samuel Nielson and Francis Magan, who were respectively a fugitive, a drunkard and an informer, met in Lord Edward's hiding place in Thomas Street. Letters were read out from United Irish committees in Dublin county remonstrating about their leaders' vacillations. Still no decisions were taken.

Lord Edward moved from house to house in Thomas St, ending up at the house of a feather merchant named Murphy. It was here, on 19 May, that the Dublin authorities caught up with him. The party sent to arrest him consisted of Major Sirr (the Chief of the Dublin police), a Major Swan with a party of half a dozen soldiers, and a Dublin editor and yeomanry officer called Ryan. They found Lord Edward in bed. He was nursing a heavy cold, propped up on pillows, and reading *Gil Blas*, a favourite book from his Black Rock years. When the men burst into the room, Lord Edward threw the book aside and leapt out of bed. He fought arrest violently and was wounded in the shoulder before he was bundled out of the house, put into a sedan chair and driven to Dublin Castle.

To be captured reading rather than intriguing was a fitting end to a career which seemed to his family to have been lived from a story or a play. *Gil Blas*, too, was an entirely appropriate book for a man whose life had all the elements of a picaresque romance. It was a comedy about a Spanish soldier's son who impersonated his social betters, made and lost fortunes, fell in and out of love, was arrested, imprisoned, freed and, at the end, allowed to retire to the country with a modest fortune and a chastened spirit. Edward, however, could look forward to no such happy ending. After his arrest he was sent, with his shoulder wound festering in the heat, to Dublin's gaol. Nobody had the courage to write directly to Emily and tell her that the government had arrested Edward and had enough evidence to send him to the gallows. For a long time nobody had the courage either to tell her that Edward was seriously wounded. It was not until 28 May that she was given an accurate version of her son's arrest. 'Mama was last night told of his being wounded,' Lucy Fitzgerald recorded in her diary, adding, 'why was it kept so long from her?' Emily responded with decision. If her son was ill she must go to him, she said. Before she did she must try to get his trial delayed. Lord Henry Fitzgerald had already left. Emily said simply that she would follow as soon as possible.

In Dublin, Sarah and Louisa put Pamela on a boat for England, in compliance with government orders. They were refused permission to see Lord Edward, and had to be content with ambivalent reports from the surgeon that filtered out from Newgate Gaol in Green Street.

More arrests followed Lord Edward's capture, persuading what was left of the United Irish leadership that the rebellion must begin immediately. Signals to rise were sent to local organisations weakened by arrests and the disarmament campaign. From 24 May groups of rebels six or eight hundred strong, many armed only with pikes forged in village smith-ies, began to assemble in valleys, woods and quiet village streets. Loyalists watched the enemy emerge from the mists; not a revolutionary force but bands of poorly armed men moving down roads in search of a main army. On 26 May, after risings in Carlow and at Naas, Clare and Prosperous in Kildare county, Louisa looked out of her bedroom window and saw a party of 200 rebels armed with pikes make their way across the lawn in front of her house. It was three in the morning. The air was warm and still, heated by days of unusually hot weather. Apart from rustles and clinks, the men were silent. They locked the gates at either side of the park, left word that they would harm none of the inhabitants of the house and lodges and moved off into the night to join a rebel army. Louisa, staring out from her bedroom bedecked with purple ribbons, was terrified. Although she admitted that 'they marched in great order and quietness and did not molest me,' she added that, 'it was not a *pleasant* sight.' She decided to put Castletown into a state of defence and had doors blocked, windows shuttered and servants armed. Then she took up her pen. Writing might provide her with a defence against fear. 'I will endeavour to keep a journal of what passes here,' she wrote to Ogilvie.

As the rebellion spread from Kildare to Wicklow and Wex-ford, Lord Henry Fitzgerald was making his way towards Dublin, determined to see his brother. Lord Edward's con-dition was getting worse. The balls were still in his shoulder, the wound was discharging pus and the heat prevented doc-tors operating. The Dublin government had already refused Louisa permission to see her nephew. Now he refused Lord Henry too. 'Has he got fruit?' 'Does he want linen?' Lord Henry wrote in his notebook. On 30 May Ryan, whom Lord Edward had stabbed repeatedly during his arrest, died, adding a charge of manslaughter to the charge of sedition. 'How will the death of Ryan affect him? What informers are supposed to be against him?' Lord Henry wrote anxiously.

Captured rebels and rumours came into Dublin while Lord Henry waited; different reports that flowed into one story. The risings in Carlow and Kildare had been local and unconnected. There were burnings, killings and horrific torture, but no apparent plan. But in the south an army of 20,000 had marched into Wexford town and proclaimed a republic. While groups of victorious rebels roamed the streets and householders hurriedly hung green flags out of their windows, a mixed bunch of leaders, including two Protestant landlords sympathetic to the United Irish cause, tried to impose some sort of order. Only one garrison, at New Ross, stood between the United army camped outside Wexford and county Waterford. If New Ross fell, government supply lines to the military base at Waterford would be severed and the rebels might open up the sparsely garrisoned counties to the south and west. As news of the rebel success at Wexford and of atrocities on both sides reached Dublin and Castletown, Louisa's confidence faltered and gave way. She abandoned her short journal, writing on it, 'too full of misery to continue'.

In London, Emily feverishly attempted to gather support for her son. She went to the Prince of Wales and to his brother the Duke of York, and asked them to intercede with the King on Lord Edward's behalf. She sent notes to Fox and her brother asking for help, but she had few useful allies. Fox and the Prince of Wales were liabilities, the latter seen as a wastrel, the former as a regicide. Only Richmond could be of any use. Seizing his chance to assert himself within the family, Richmond hurried to see Pitt and asked for a postponement of Lord Edward's trial. With Pitt's permission, Richmond wrote to Lord Camden, 'in whose justice and moderation I have too much confidence not to believe but that they will have weight.' Fortified by her brother's optimism, Emily set off for Ireland on 1 June. Her youngest daughter, Mimi, went with her. Ogilvie stayed in London with Pamela and Lord Edward's three children.

At Leinster House, Lord Henry Fitzgerald had become desperate. On 1 June and again on the 3rd, Lord Clare refused him permission to see his brother, although in his second letter he admitted that Lord Edward's condition was serious. The same day Lord Henry received a smuggled letter from an acquaintance who had been picked up and confined in Newgate. 'My Lord . . . I take the liberty of writing to inform you that your brother, Lord Edward, is most dangerously ill – in fact dying – he was delirious some time last night. Surely, my Lord, some attention ought to be paid him. I know you'll pardon this application. I am yours, with respect and regard, Matt. Dowling. Past Two. Seeing you or any friend he has confidence in, would, I think, be more conducive to his recovery than 50 surgeons. I saw him a few moments last night – but he did not know me. We'll watch over him as well as is in our power.'

Lord Edward was dying from septicaemia, wild with pain. On 2 June his jaws locked and closed on his tongue in a spasm that lasted half an hour. That evening his mind began to wander. He paced up and down his cell, saying that he did not want to live and that 'God would receive him for having contributed to the freedom of his country'. Dr Garnett, the surgeon attending him, was alarmed at the ferocity of his desire for death and martyrdom. 'No remonstrance could restrain him; he raved most impetuously and exerted a wonderful degree of strength even with his wounded arm; I said everything I could think of to dissuade him from agitating himself. He cried out, "Dear Ireland! I die for you! My country, *You will be free*," And then "Damn You! Why don't you let me die! I want to die. You are a tyrant. If I had a knife I would kill myself".'

Lord Edward's shouting caused a commotion in the goal. Prisoners who were free to walk about, Matthew Dowling among them, gathered on the stairs leading to his room. People in the street heard Lord Edward shrieking. Dowling was called into Lord Edward's cell and entreated to calm him down. Lord Edward seemed not to recognise him, shouting 'damn you, damn you' loudly and indiscriminately to everyone who came near him.

Eventually he was exhausted. Forty drops of laudanum pacified him and stopped his jaw dropping open. But he slept little during the night and his pulse became rapid and irregular. At eleven o'clock the next morning, 3 June, Dr Garnett went into Lord Edward's room again. 'While I sat by his bedside he observed to me "I have a brother Henry that I dote on; I wish greatly to see him, but I suppose that cannot be allowed." After a short pause he said, "I have a brother Leinster for whom I have a high respect. He might depend on everything I did."' This pathetic plea did no good: Garnett had instructions to allow no visitors.

Unbeknown to the doctor, however, the authorities, realising that Lord Edward was dying, had allowed a message to reach Louisa at Castletown which hinted that Lord Edward had little time to live. Louisa immediately set off for Phoenix Park with Emily Napier. There, Louisa left Emily in the carriage, went into the Vice Regal Lodge and asked for Lord Camden. A few minutes later she came back, Emily Napier reported, 'in a most dreadful state of agitation, saying as she leant back in the carriage, "order them to drive home. I have knelt at his feet and the brute has refused to let me see my dying Edward."' Instead of going back to Castletown, however, they decided on one last effort and drove round to Ely Place where Lord Clare, the Lord Chancellor, lived.

Lord Clare had already decided upon clemency. When Louisa and Emily arrived, he ordered his own carriage, bundled them into it, drove to Leinster House, where they picked up Lord Henry, and went on to the prison. There he was the only one of the party to break down, weeping openly in an adjoining room while Louisa and Henry sat by Edward's bed.

Later Louisa wrote Ogilvie an account of their visit. 'I first approached his bed; he looked at me, knew me, kissed me, and said (what will never depart my ears), "it is heaven to see you!" and shortly after, turning to the other side of his bed, he said, "I can't see you!" I went round and he soon after kissed my face, and smiled at me, which I shall never forget, though I saw death in his dear face at the time. I then told him that Henry was come. He said nothing that marked surprise at his being in Ireland, but expressed joy at hearing it and said, "where is he, dear fellow?" Henry then took my place, and the two dear brothers frequently embraced each other, to the melting of a heart of stone, and yet God enabled both Henry and myself to remain quite composed. As everyone left the room, we told him we only were with him. He said, "that is very pleasant." However, he remained silent, and then I brought up the subject of Lady Edward, and told him that I had not left her until I saw her on board, and Henry told him of having met her on the road well. He said, "And the children too? – She is a charming woman" and then became silent again. That expression about Lady Edward proved to me that his senses were much lulled, and that he did not feel his situation to be what it was; but thank God they were enough alive to receive pleasure from his brother and me. Dear Henry, in particular, he looked at continually with expressions of pleasure ... When we left him, we told him that, as he appeared inclined to sleep, we would wish him a good night and return in the morning. He said, "Do, do," but did not express any uneasiness at our leaving him. We accordingly tore ourselves away ... He sometimes said, "I knew it must come to this, and we must all go," and rambled on about militia and numbers; but upon my saying to him "It agitates you to talk upon these subjects," he said, "well, I won't.'"

Three hours after Louisa and Henry left, Dr Garnett wrote the last entry in his notes. 'Two O'clock – After a violent struggle that commenced a little after twelve o'clock, this ill-fated young man has *just* drawn his last breath. *J. Armstrong Garnett. June 4 1798.*'

Dr Garnett's account of Louisa's visit was very different from her own. He noted that Lord Edward had scarcely recognised his aunt and brother. His body was occupied with death and his mind with rebellion. Garnett told him that Louisa and Henry were in the room. He named and kissed them affectionately but soon his attention wandered. 'He raved while they were with him of battles between the insurgents in the north and some regiments of militia. He talked of the Fermanagh militia and talked of a battle in Armagh that lasted for two days.'

Louisa said nothing to Ogilvie about Lord Edward's dementia. Her letter had two functions. The first was to give Ogilvie the news of Edward's death in such a way that when he caught up with Emily on the road he could put Louisa's letter into her hand. The second was to offer Emily a picture of her son's last hours that she could carry through her grief. In Dr Garnett's notes Lord Edward was a revolutionary in the last stages of dementia. In Louisa's letter he was a loving brother, nephew and father, rambling a little, but beatific and, at last, at peace. Emily never gave any sign that she suspected that it was a fabrication and all the family connived at the deception.

Ogilvie set off after Emily and Mimi as soon as Louisa's letter reached him, first dispatching a messenger who overtook the party at Towcester and prepared Emily to hear the worst. He took Sophia and Lucy Fitzgerald with him to comfort their mother. At the same time, Pamela left Harley Street for Richmond House and the protection of the Duke of Richmond. Ogilvie's party caught up with Emily at Coleshill in Warwickshire. For a few days they all stayed where they were and then turned round and sadly made their way back to London.

Members of the family consoled themselves in different ways. Louisa found refuge in practical details. She arranged Lord Edward's funeral (a botched affair that took place in St Werbergh's Church at the dead of night) and collected relics. 'I have got the watch and chain that hung constantly round his neck, with a locket of hair which I send you,' she wrote to

Lord Henry. 'I have also been with Hamilton the painter. There are two pictures of him, one for your mother and one for you.' She hung on to the belief that Edward was not really guilty of treason. 'The friends that he was entangled with pushed his destruction forward, screening themselves behind his valuable character.' Lord Henry and Sarah, who never doubted Edward's guilt, dissipated grief in anger. Lord Henry dispatched a furious letter to Camden, the Lord Lieutenant, accusing the government of murder. 'Now, my Lord, shall I scruple to declare to the world – I wish I could to the four corners of it – that amongst you, your ill-treatment has murdered my brother, as much as if you had put a pistol to his head.' Sarah also blamed the government and trusted to time to restore Lord Edward's good name. Lucy Fitzgerald sat down as soon as she got back to Harley Street and dashed off a letter entitled 'To the Irish nation', that exhorted the Irish people to fight for 'happiness, freedom, glory': 'One noble struggle and you will gain, you will enjoy them for ever.' This letter was never sent, but Lucy did dispatch a letter to Thomas Paine, sending him a picture of Lord Edward: 'Citizen, In those happy days when I dwelt under the humble roof of my beloved brother Edward, your picture ornamented his chimney. As the small circle drew round the fire, their eyes rested on the resemblance of the Author of The Rights of Man. Citizen, although he was unsuccessful in the glorious attempt of liberating his country from slavery, still he was not unworthy of the lessons you taught him. Accept then his picture from his unhappy sister.'

Emily wrote nothing about her dead son. Indeed, a month after Edward's death she wrote to Henry, 'Goodwood July 1798. Fatal year! We are neither of us in a state at present, my beloved Henry, to touch on a subject so heart rending and distracting as all that has passed within these last three months of wretchedness; but I am sure you will be glad to know from myself that I am much better.' The Duke of Richmond described Emily as 'quiet and composed'. Knowing that Emily was unwilling to write about her son, Louisa and Sarah felt that they could not do so either. The subject became a barrier between them. Louisa admitted later that 'all the misery that I had endured on my sister Leinster's account had worked me up into such a dread of seeing her that I almost wished never to see her again.' Sarah left Louisa to make the first move, taking refuge herself in what she called her 'inferiority'. Eventually, however, she wrote a long letter to Emily which she regretted as soon as it had left her hands. She followed it with a contrite note to Lucy Fitzgerald, asking how she should approach the task of writing, 'for till I have resumed the habit of corresponding with her, I must feel the common lot of separation which commonly ends in a degree of coolness which would make me wretched to be sensible of from her whom I love much more like a mother than a sister.'

It was Emily, three months after Edward's death, who broke the silence. In the middle of September Louisa received a letter which began 'My beloved sister, I live to say my Eddy is no more!' She begged Louisa to visit her. 'You, my Louisa,' Emily wrote, 'have ever been my comforter. You share it all and yet have the power of soothing, you have ever been the companion of my sorrow.' Louisa wrote back straight away: 'My beloved, my adored sister. My heart still beating with the agitation that the sight of your dear handwriting gave me this morning . . . I sit down without delay to thank you. I longed to have the ice broke, that numbed my correspondence, but have never felt courage to do it myself.'

Although she did not write to her sisters for three months after Edward's death, Emily had not been inactive. She curbed her grief by devoting herself to little Eddy who became a surrogate for his father. She went through Edward's last letters and labelled them. 'Six precious letters I received at Ealing and Tonbridge,' she wrote on the back of the letters Edward sent from Hamburg and Ireland in 1796 and 1797. On the cover sheet that bound the bundle she wrote 'precious remains'. She also copied out a passage from Joseph Priestley, which she entitled, 'Dr. Priestley, applicable to my beloved and adored Edward', noting on the back, 'private paper for myself only'. Then she put the note aside, an open invitation to anyone who found it to discover and disclose its contents.

The passage Emily transcribed was a justification of rebellion. Using Priestley as her authority, as she had always used texts to make sense of her life, Emily determinedly memorialised her son as a martyr whom time would vindicate. Priestley said that rebellion was justified if government was oppressive, because a government was made for the happiness of its subjects. So an oppressive government was unconstitutional and should not be protected 'from the generous attack of the noble and daring patriot'. Priestley went on and Emily added her own underlinings: 'if the bold attempt be precipitate and unsuccessful the government will be sure to term it rebellion, but the censure cannot make the thing itself less glorious. The memory of such brave tho' unfortunate friends of liberty and of the rights of Mankind as that of Harmodius and Aristogiton among the Athenians and Russell and Sidney in our own country, will be held in everlasting honour by their grateful fellow citizens, and History will speak another language than laws.'

This passage came from a fairly obscure pamphlet by Priestley put out in 1768 by a triumvirate of radical publishers during the height of Wilkes's attack on parliamentary prerogative, entitled *An Essay on the First Principles of Government; and on the Nature of Political, Civil and Religious Liberty*. There was no collected edition of Priestley's works in which Emily might have found it in the 1790s. She may have read it when it came out. The Duke of Leinster, interested like Wilkes in attacking Westminster (though not for the same reasons), may have bought it and put it in the Carton library. Edward Fitzgerald may have brought it to his mother's attention. But however she got the pamphlet it was rare and radical stuff for a duchess to be reading and suggests that her researches in radical politics went far further than she ever suggested in her letters.

Between 4 June, when Edward Fitzgerald died, and 9 September, when Emily finally wrote to Louisa, the rebellion had been brutally crushed, resulting in heavy casualties which reflected the relative strength of government and insurgents. About 30,000 rebels died – some in pitched battles, many more in reprisals and indiscriminate murders – while 2,000 troops and loyalists were killed.

For Ireland the outcome of the rebellion was Union with Great Britain. For the Lennox family it was reunion and reconciliation. When the rebellion broke out the family had never been more divided. They disagreed about the war in Europe, about the French Revolution, about the monarch and the British government. None of this changed, and the old alliance between Lennoxes, Foxes and Leinsters was never re-forged. But the horrors of the rebellion made everyone – Sarah and the Duke of Richmond, in particular – determined to paper over the cracks. Sarah went on grumbling, of course; she grumbled that Louisa too easily forgave a government that first allowed Edward Fitzgerald to die and then took his estate from his widow and children, and she grumbled that Conolly had lost his nerve after the rebellion and become an abject supporter of government reprisals. But after the end of 1798, when Napier took a government post – Controller of Army Accounts in Ireland – these criticisms lost their sting, and Sarah tried to abide by a tacit agreement to leave politics out of family relations.

This injunction was easiest for Emily, who had been practising secrecy for some time. It was attractive to Louisa who wanted to forget the way in which she had acted during the rebellion. It was hardest for Sarah who had made politics the basis for good or bad relations with the male members of her family. She violated the new apolitical spirit all the time. Politics was still the air she breathed. But she did try to put politics aside, particularly in relations with her brother.

The Duke of Richmond and Lord George Lennox were the main beneficiaries of this truce. Richmond had offered a temporary refuge at Goodwood to Lord Edward's wife Pamela, and his sisters were impressed by his kindness. After Edward's death Richmond arranged for Pamela to travel to her relations in Hamburg (with the promise of a pension from the family which was hardly ever paid). 'My brother's conduct on this occasion has made a deep impression on me,' Sarah wrote. Emily was grateful to her brother as well. Letters of thanks and visits to Goodwood restored the conventional hierarchy among the Lennox siblings and allowed them to enter the nineteenth century publicly united.

PART THREE
'What a day I have lived to see, when
my heart strings were torn from me'.
Louisa to the 3rd Duke of Richmond, 3 May 1803.

Emily, Louisa and Sarah began the new century with a sense of having seen too much and endured too many deaths. Emily observed that, contrary to what she had read and thought, old age did nothing to blunt her ability to feel. Thinking about Lord Edward's death brought all her other dead children back to her: George Fitzgerald, her last son who died when he was ten; her first George, Lord Ophaly who had died in 1765; Gerald Fitzgerald who had disappeared in 1788; Louisa Fitzgerald, nursed so tenderly by Ogilvie at Black Rock; and all her other dead infants, a Charlotte, two Carolines, Fanny, Augustus, Henrietta and another Louisa. By 1800, 12 of Emily's 22 children were already dead, all victims of childhood illness except Gerald, who had gone down with the ship in which he was serving.

Outward events mirrored the sisters' inner weariness. Revolution, war in Europe and a realisation that the old century had ended in destruction rather than hope all combined to give them a feeling of approaching ends. Louisa said in 1801 that at fifty-eight she could not expect to live long, and decided then and there that she was entering her old age.

Sarah was fifty-five in 1800. Her eyes bothered her but she was full of energy still. She worried less for herself than for Napier, cooped up in a Dublin office 'like the black hole at Calcutta', working through an immense backlog of army accounts.

Emily was sixty-nine. She still grieved for Edward and at times now saw her life as a tragedy. In 1803, on the anniversary of Edward's death, a day she always passed in mourning, she wrote to her daughter Lucy, 'the loss of my child is always one of those melancholy thoughts that return almost as often as at first and depress my spirits often and are not entirely absorb'd in the great misery and calamity of my life.' None the less, she was still vigorous. She gave assemblies at her house in Harley Street, wrote letters, read and demanded the unceasing attention of her husband and children.

For the first few years of the nineteenth century tid-bits of family news went back and forth across the Irish sea; Conolly's asthma, Napier's sore gums and weak chest, news of children's marriages and old people's deaths. Sometimes the correspondents travelled too. In July 1801, Louisa spent a few weeks with Emily and then went with Ogilvie and the youngest members of Emily's household to Brighton for bathing and sea air. The next year she and Conolly were in England again, going to London, Goodwood and then Harrogate. Emily Napier, now almost twenty, accompanied Louisa everywhere. Louisa made half-hearted attempts to introduce Emily to prospective husbands, but both accepted that she was to sacrifice her future to her aunt's old age and that filial devotion must make up for married love. In her dreams Louisa transformed herself from aunt to lover in a guilty effort at recompense. 'I certainly never cease thinking of you, and dreamt of you the whole night,' Louisa wrote to Emily in 1807. 'In short, my love, my attachment to you is such, that it is like a lover's. I have not words to express all that passes in my heart and thoughts about you.'

In 1803 the news from Ireland became more sombre. Conolly's asthma attacks got worse and he succumbed to what the doctors called 'influenza'. After a week's illness, on 27 April 1803 he died in Louisa's arms. To the last he was self-deprecating. 'The last articulate words that he uttered (holding my hand) were, "I have left you all I could, knowing that you will make better use of it than I ever should",' Louisa reported to the Duke of Richmond.

In the months that followed Conolly's death Louisa clung to these words. They gave her a reason for going on; Conolly had left everything in her hands and she had to carry out his wishes. To begin with, however, she could do nothing. For a week she lay in her closet at Castletown with Emily Napier constantly by her side. Sarah was at Castletown too. She made sure that Louisa was never alone and tried, as she put it, to 'bring her about by slow degrees to *use herself* to misery, for misery was in every room, in every face, in every thing around her'. Sarah believed that grief should be extracted from the sufferer as a disease was drawn out of the body and consequently took every opportunity to remind Louisa of her loss. Louisa had always taken the opposite view. She hid her strongest feelings, believing that their exposure would be damaging and foolish. Emily complained that Sarah was making Louisa worse, 'foreseeing nothing for dear Louisa but endless misery' and the Duke of Richmond, asserting his newly rediscovered authority wrote to Napier hinting that Sarah should leave Louisa alone to grieve in her own way. Sarah went back to her house in Celbridge and Emily reported that when she did return to Castletown, 'she was astonished at the change she found in Louisa for the better.'

Louisa coped with the transition from wife to widow by working through Conolly's papers. 'A great deal is left for me to do and the fulfilling all his benevolent intentions will become an object for the remainder of my life, when it shall please God to permit our reunion.' Conolly had left Louisa Castletown for life, with a jointure of £2,500 a year, the sum agreed in their marriage settlement. There were legacies for servants and £10,000 to be divided amongst Sarah's children. There were also huge liabilities: personal debts, arrears of income tax, loans and interest on loans left unpaid for many years. In law these debts all passed to the heir to the estate, Admiral Pakenham, who had married Conolly's niece and would inherit Castletown when Louisa died. But Louisa felt that Conolly had given her the duty of discharging the debts and she began working slowly through them with the same care that she had always given to her household accounts.

Emily knew that buried in Tom Conolly's accounts was a secret that the family had kept for many years. She waited apprehensively as Louisa went through her husband's scribbled and haphazard records. It took Louisa 13 months to find what Emily feared was there; payments for lodging, for gifts, an unexplained annuity perhaps. When she found these accounts she believed that her siblings were completely in ignorance and explained to her brother: 'I met with a blow which almost overcame me. That of a mistress having been in question for many years back. You know enough of the mould in which I am cast to comprehend what such a discovery cost me, but I am determined on behaving towards his memory as I would have endeavoured (at least) to have done towards himself. Resignation, patience and no complaint are the way to shut the door against one's worst enemy, one's own passions; and jealousy having always been a strong ingredient in my composition, I resolved on giving it no admittance, for women cannot be judges of men's sentiment upon that subject. It would be the height of ingratitude in me to doubt his love for me after the unremitting proofs he gave me of it, tho' I cannot judge the mixture that attended it.'

Emily had for years hidden her knowledge of Conolly's mistress from Louisa, conniving in his deception both because she did not want to see her sister wounded, and because she had been largely responsible for bringing about the marriage. So for her own sake and for Louisa's Emily stayed silent. Louisa had always proclaimed her marriage to be the bedrock upon which she had built a happy life. She knew very well that Conolly had little intelligence or political *savoir-faire*. But she had come to feel that he offered her trust and fidelity instead.

From the very first, Louisa had put enormous store by her husband's faithfulness. Her position was an unusual one. Despite the increasing fashionableness of domestic felicity towards the end of the century, aristocratic women were given little expectation, upon marriage, that their husbands would be faithful. Before her marriage to Napier, Sarah subscribed cheerfully to the view that male adultery was no worse, and just as commonplace as gambling and drunkenness. Louisa did not agree. In a letter written some time in the early 1770s she explained why. 'I cannot undertake to answer that part of your letter at length, where you condemn me for saying that my heart would be broke by the inconstancy of my husband, because it would take up more time than I have at present at my disposal. But as shortly as I can, I will. In *primis*, I am *sure* that you are perfectly *right*, and recommend the only good and wise conduct, and the only one to bring back a husband, and it is certainly what I should try at. But I fear I could not do it. I own to you that I feel myself in the wrong, for I don't find in myself the least disposition towards making an allowance for my husband being a human creature, and like all other men. I have let myself go too far, expecting him to be all perfection in that *one* particular, and have allowed myself to place my greatest happiness in consequence of it; and 'tho 'tis my firm belief that as yet it has been the case, and that in all human probability 'tis likely now to continue, yet I do mean to take myself to task about it, for I feel I am wrong. I know myself to be [of] a most jealous disposition, and my natural violence would add to it, so that I have always dreaded the least spark of it, for fear that it should lead me wrong ... In the case of another I can make allowances and see the human creature in the action can be very miserable without being unreasonable and hard. Now with my husband I fear I should be both, and all things put together makes me think that if one's heart can be broke by vexation, such a situation would have that effect upon me; and I should feel I was doing wrong at the same time, which would be an additional vexation. I don't quite agree with you that drunkenness or gaming is as bad to the wife as inconstancy. I am sure its worse for the men, as its hurting an amiable character, which love does not. But a wife, I think, can make more allowances for these faults than for one which wounds her love so deeply. I don't know how it is, but I can never dwell a moment on the thought of losing my husband's love, without feeling it is the worst misfortune that can happen to me.'

Given the strength of Louisa's belief in the value of fidelity and the degree of trust she had placed in Conolly, Emily was justifiably anxious about Louisa's ability to recast the way in which she understood and described her marriage. How could she cope when she discovered that her adored husband had for years kept a mistress? But Louisa was consistent. She preferred to push aside the revelation rather than change her mind about her husband. 'My rooted affection for him remains unshaken,' she wrote, 'and I cherish the hope that when Death ... shall again unite us, I shall not be disappointed of that pure love, that with me, had begun this side of the grave. The worth and excellence of his character I can contemplate with pleasure, and venerate the same, making his opinions ... my chief guide.' So she went on as she had always done, feeling that Conolly in heaven was scarcely further than the next room and sure that the explanation that he would eventually give her would vindicate her trust.

If Louisa did not change, Castletown quickly did. Louisa had a substantial income of her own now. She could decide upon the size of her household, the use to which the buildings were put and the number and scope of her philanthropic activities. She immediately began to economise, citing Conolly's debts as the reason. But her shrinking household reflected her own intentions and careful personality. She had never been interested in display or grandeur; she loved to economise and hated waste. She also wanted to put as much money and time as possible into charitable activities.

Sarah watched the Castletown household diminish in size and opulence. She was horrified, unable to understand that Louisa derived pleasure from economy. Sarah had always regarded Louisa as first and foremost a munificent hostess who spread largesse in her immediate family circle and used her pin money alone for charity. The devoted philanthropist she saw emerging from the silken cocoon of aristocratic marriage was less to her liking. 'Her family is to be on the 4th of June thus reordered,' Sarah wrote to her son Charles after Conolly's death, 'from about 60 in the hall and 12 in the steward's room and never less than 10 in parlour, her whole family, herself and company will never exceed 20. Three quarters of the house to be shut up as the rest will do. The farms to be let. The two lawns, wood are kept only. Thus, my love, you will arrive to see the *close* of a great, a noble, a generous, benevolent, charitable and hospitable establishment.'

A year after Conolly's death, Napier's health, which had been worrying Sarah for years, became much worse. Napier's slenderness became emaciation and the soreness in his gums became a debilitating pain that spread down his throat. Sarah told Susan, 'long sufferings have wasted him almost to an *atrophy*.' Napier thought he was going to die in February 1804. But he continued his work and recovered slightly in the spring. In the summer he relapsed and Sarah decided to take him to Bristol. The melancholy party set off in June; Napier exhausted and coughing, Sarah, whose sight was already failing, and the three girls, Louisa, Caroline and Cecilia. Napier rallied briefly in Bristol and Sarah, convinced by optimistic doctors, believed he would recover. 'Those who pretend to know assure me that I am almost a convalescent,' Napier wrote at the end of July, adding mordantly, 'I can't say that my own sensations are in union with theirs.' He was right. On 13 October, aged fifty-three, he died.

Napier had given Sarah a reason for living, and after his death she could at times see no point in carrying on. Everything she had done had been for him, she thought. 'I have lost him who made me like this world. It is now a dreary expanse, where I see thinly scattered a few beloved objects whose welfare and prosperity have still such strong hold on my heart as to keep it alive to whatever concerns them. But its *pleasant prospects* are all vanished! . . . While he lived I saw all objects through the medium of my own happiness. Even the joy occasioned by advantages falling to the share of any of my children was doubled because I shared it *with him* . . . To endeavour to be worthy of his love gave animation to my existence. From his precepts and example I was taught to bear adversity, to make any sacrifice to duty with cheerfulness, not to value life *too* much and never to cease being grateful for the many blessings which it had pleased God to bestow on us.'

Despite her misery Sarah did not slip back into the corrosive self-hatred of the days before her marriage. Devotion to Napier had indeed made the world seem a better place. In so doing it had changed Sarah too, giving her an envelope of self-esteem and a feeling of being loved that made grief bearable.

Sarah cried with her children and with Louisa and Susan O'Brien, who both came hurriedly to Bristol when they learned that Napier was dying. Expressing grief and anger at her loss was a help. But none the less, she was dazed that in the face of annihilation, ordinary life went on. She felt paralysed, stunned by the enormity of the contrast between the quotidian and the eternal. 'My mind *feels in prison*, it brings to me those sensations which I ever supposed were felt by the Royal Family of France in the Temple. Here *we are*, but it *must end*!'

Napier left Sarah everything and made her responsible for all his affairs. To his sons he bequeathed his weapons, 'the example of my long and faithful services to my King and country' and a warning against Republican ideas. His daughters got no mention in his will and no inheritance. Just before he died Napier also sent his son William a long letter about 'the duties of an officer and a gentleman' which ended, 'keep this letter and show it to your elder brothers that they may remind you of its contents should pleasure or passion ever tempt you to swerve from the principles it is intended to inculcate.' He also charged his sons to prove their piety to God and their affection towards their parents by serving King and country with honour. For the rest of their lives Sarah's sons strove to live up to his injunctions and his example; their father, they believed, had told them what they should do and their mother had given them the means to do it.

Sarah was completing the first letter of her widowhood to Susan when a messenger arrived. 'Just as I had finished writing new misfortune comes on me! The poor Duke of Leinster is no more! ... Ah me! What havoc does death make in a circle where I enjoyed all happiness. Death comes remorseless and sinks them in the tomb.'

In destroying some bonds death reminded everyone of the importance of others. Sarah and Louisa turned to Emily in their distress and she turned to them for comfort when the Duke of Leinster died. Their old relationship, at once sisterly and maternal, was reaffirmed. In November 1804 they all met in London and used the comfort of old certainties to alleviate new distress. 'I passed three hours yesterday with my two dear sisters,' Emily wrote to her daughter Lucy. 'All hearts opened to each other's griefs. Our sorrows and our comforts all passed in review before us from their early childhood. Oh what a heartfelt satisfaction to hear them say as they both held me in their arms that the precepts I had early instilled had been of such use to them and been the comfort and support of their lives, that they owed more to me than to any human being ... I found both these dear hearts in perfect unison with my own. Griefs have this effect!'

Sarah inherited all Napier's debts. They were small compared with Conolly's, but so were his assets. Sarah economised by moving in with Louisa; on the one hand she made light of her poverty, on the other she listed all the calls upon her income. 'I have *no* right to complain, for nobody need *starve* with £500 pr. anm; tho' I certainly cannot do justice to my six unprovided children, nor can I assist in the smallest degree my three eldest . . . In short, *I want help very much*.' Very soon she was looking around for a way of increasing her income. Believing firmly that Napier had died in the King's service just as surely as if he had fallen in battle, Sarah decided to lobby the Crown for a pension as a reward for his exertions. She wrote a long memorial to the King extoling Napier's virtues and had, for some time, high hopes of success. But as 1805 wore on without any reply, she decided that a more personal approach might yield dividends and planned to appeal to George III as a fellow sufferer from failing sight. 'Do you think,' she asked Susan in July, 'that if I S.N. wrote you S. O'B. a letter full of details of my situation with *some* remarks on the sympathetic feelings of one blind person for another . . . do you think you could with natural propriety send it to Lady Ilchester as an interesting letter to you and without a word more? Do you think she would *talk of it* (I desire no more) before the King?' Sarah was careful to insist that she must be talked of before the Queen as a fat old lady down on her luck. Her friend Lady Charleville was instructed to tell the Queen that Sarah was 'still well looking and pleasing – but she has quite given up figure and appearance and dresses in all respects as an old woman.' This pathetic picture was painted to disguise the real nature of Sarah's supplication, a blatant attempt to reap a reward for the humiliations she had suffered at the King's hands forty years before. Her appeal to sentiment worked. The King granted her £800 a year, a sum she always insisted was in recognition of Napier's services, but which was none the less granted directly to herself and her children.

Just over £100 of Sarah's pension went to Emily Napier, the portions for Louisa, Cecilia and Caroline Napier who all lived with her were added to Sarah's own share, and brought her income up to a grand total of something like £1,200 a year. Some of this was invested to provide money for the Napier girls after Sarah's death. Some went to pay off debts. Celbridge was sold, and although she was never paid in full for it, the house was no longer a drain on Sarah's income. So with Louisa Napier in charge of domestic economy and household accounts, Sarah and her daughters could live in comfort, if not splendour. None the less she often borrowed money. Charles Napier lent, or gave, his mother £475 in 1808, £136 in 1814 and small sums thereafter.

After the pensions were announced, Sarah was in good spirits. 'My dear sister and I pass our present time between preparations for going to England for a year and the pleasant prospect we have of the excellent situations of our nine children (for she calls them hers too),' she told Susan in the spring of 1806. By May Louisa and Sarah were established at Hans Place off Sloane Street in Kensington. Sarah decided to stay on in London and bought a house round the corner in Cadogan Place for £1,600. This purchase fixed a pattern of life that changed little in the years to come. Sarah stayed in London, visited and cared for by her children. Louisa lived with Emily Napier at Castletown. Charitable activities took more and more of Louisa's time, but she came to England occasionally. Emily spent her winters in London and her summers in Wimbledon, where Ogilvie had bought a cottage a few years before. 'Quite a little thing,' Emily told Lucy in 1799. 'Can't be called a place for it is merely a little bit of kitchen garden surrounded with roses and honeysuckles and one little field; ... It is not at all the sort of thing you would like, nor should I some years ago; but it exactly suits me now, for I really cannot walk without feeling so much inconvenience afterwards from it that it takes off from all the pleasure in it.' Ogilvie insisted that winters were spent in their new house, 44 Grosvenor Place. 'In this I don't entirely agree with him,' Emily confided to Lucy. 'For with the help of a good map and a story book, the evenings, I think, in winter go off very well. But certainly being in the way of seeing my friends, which one always is in London, is pleasant too; so perhaps he is right.' She still kept to the timetable of the London season. 'My sister Leinster is a *point de reunion* to many, and *so* well,' Sarah noted in 1806. 'She went to Mrs. Fox's ball and she herself gives assemblies.'

Old age brought new anxieties and rhythms. Instead of slowing down, as convention had it, life seemed to speed up. Atrophy of bodies, loss of friends and a concomitant sense of the past disappearing combined to heighten a sense of change. Not only family and friends were lost: surroundings changed and, as they did so, brought memory rushing back. Anything might bring the past out of forgotten experiences. In 1807, Louisa stayed a night in a Dublin hotel, Lennon's, which had been constructed out of houses that she remembered from her youth. 'I remember the rooms so well where we used to dance,' she wrote to Emily. 'It is so odd to look back at those distant times and the variety of *feels* are very very much missed. So many that we loved are gone and so many that we now know not *then* in existence.'

For Sarah and Emily it was books rather than places which brought the past back. Sarah was being read Marmontel's *Memoirs* in 1806. They reminded her not simply of her sojourns in Paris in the 1760s when 'I knew the man a little', but that her life, as she now thought of it, had not yet then begun. For her part, Emily read the letters of Lady Mary Wortley Montagu. They made her think of her long dead mother and of changing manners. Lady Mary, Emily noted in a letter to her niece Caroline Fox, had been 'very gallant' in her heyday of the 1730s and 1740s, and her conversation was blunt and direct. 'I am apt to think that want of delicacy was very much the fashion in those days,' although by the 1750s and 1760s it was 'going off', 'but I still remember it was retained by all those who were reckoned *wits* among the old ones, and there was always a fan held up to the face when their jokes were repeated before any young people by those of middle age.'

Emily was not sentimental; she did not find a golden age of aristocratic licence in past behaviour and she was inclined by temperament and principle to see a correlation between change and amelioration. But she did notice a difference in the way in which women of her class chose and were allowed to behave. She herself had been a convert to some of the changes brought about by notions of sensibility, particularly the idea of marriage as a union of love, and she had reaped the benefits of these ideas being taken up by men. But looking back to the days when Mrs Greville lay on a *chaise-longue* in 'undress' at Holland House and Lady Townshend paraded her command of ribald innuendo made her aware that she had lived to see the inner worlds of women of her class transformed.

Occasionally and paradoxically however, change could emphasise continuity. Several of Emily's and Sarah's children married within the family or within the family circle and with marriage came a sense of time coming round again. Lord Henry Fitzgerald married Charlotte, Baroness de Ros, the grand-daughter of Henry Fox's friend, Charles Hanbury Williams. Looking round the sumptuous de Ros estate at Thames Ditton in Surrey gave Sarah what she called 'Holland House feels'. Mimi Ogilvie also married into the Holland House circle. Her husband was Charles Beauclerk, son of the notorious Topham Beauclerk and his saintly wife, Lady Di. Sarah's fifth son, Henry, married Caroline Bennett, one of the Duke of Richmond's illegitimate daughters. William Napier married Caroline Amelia Fox, daughter of General Henry Fox, Caroline's 'little Harry'. Richard Napier married into the extended Conolly family. The most unlikely circle was completed several years after Sarah's death when her daughter Emily married Sir Henry Bunbury, the nephew and heir of her first husband, Sir Charles Bunbury.

As family matters like these became more important,

politics loosened its hold on Sarah's imagination. 'I have no opinion on political subjects now,' she told Susan in May 1806. This was an exaggeration, of course. She was excited when Charles Fox at last came back into government in 1806, but her high hopes of the new ministry were dashed by Fox's death that September. When the Duke of Richmond died in December of the same year, one chapter in the family history was finally closed: political disagreement would no longer be so blatantly personalised within the family. Henceforth, for Sarah, international affairs became far more interesting than goings on at Westminster. It was war that held her attention now. Her new heroes were General Moore (under whose command her sons were enlisted) and Napoleon. All her anxieties were centred on her sons who left, one by one, for the Continent and the fighting.

Louisa let politics slip more completely than Sarah. After Conolly's death she stopped following Westminster affairs unless they dealt with Ireland. Her life had always had a religious rather than a political foundation and after the rebellion she had every reason to think about her relations with others (especially her tenants and labourers) in religious rather than political terms. Many of those Louisa lived amongst saw life in the same way, even those who had had great hopes of the rebellion, and many came to regard her philanthropic activities with admiration.

Louisa had been known in the Castletown neighbourhood as a modest woman who carefully fulfilled the customary (if not customarily observed) duties as mistress of a great house. But now she began to give her life to these activities. Castletown's public rooms were largely shut up. Louisa, Emily and their guests lived in the long gallery and its anterooms. Louisa entertained very little and dressed more severely than ever. An old Castletown servant wrote, 'I remember often seeing her pass out of the garden to the house, dressed in her usual long, light-grey cloth pelisse, or surtout, having huge side pockets, and those pockets stuck full of the largest parsnips and carrots, their small ends appearing; these being doubtless for the poor, who were permitted to come to the house two or three times a week for food.'

Louisa's first charitable exercise was to build a church by the Celbridge gates at Castletown. 'She is quite a child about building a church here and persuades herself it is a kind of duty in her to give up her time and thought to it as well as her money,' Sarah wrote in 1805. The church, intended for Celbridge's Protestants, was built by Castletown labourers with local stone. Before it was finally finished in 1813, Louisa had moved on to a much bigger project, a school for Celbridge's children. 'We have got quite a creditable school of 45 children held (as it was first thought) for Protestant children, but I have had the satisfaction of seeing many Catholics among them. I asked no questions, but examined their writing and spelling equally, and pleased myself with the thought that I had Catholics and Protestants all mixed up as they should be . . . and growing together in their childhood, in all probability will make them grow up with cordiality towards each other.' In this way an educational project became a religious one, something that could, to Louisa's mind, heal the rifts which the rebellion had brought so starkly into the open.

At first the children were taught only reading, writing and arithmetic. But after 1814 the school began to expand. Two lodges were converted into quarters for cooks and teachers, and Louisa reroofed Conolly's old kennels and began an 'industrial school' there. Boys were taught trades like carpentry, shoemaking, tailoring and basket making, while girls learned domestic husbandry and economy. All were encouraged to read, write and learn to keep simple accounts. Thrift, self-sufficiency and ecumenical religious observance were Louisa's priorities. She spent a good deal of time and money on the school. She designed the buildings, engaged the masters, judged the children's work and wrote rules and prayers for them all.

By May 1820, 300 children were coming to the schools, staggered through the day in batches of 75. Louisa was surprised at these numbers, which proved, she said, 'the necessity of these day schools, for we cannot say that Celbridge is a remarkably populous place.' The cardinal lessons she wanted the pupils to learn were, she said, 'the necessity of justice against the hardship of injustice, the necessity of truth against the mischief of lies' and 'the necessity of loving one another against that careless indifference about the happiness of others, which has been known to produce the sufferings of oppression, tyranny and even cruelty.'

Louisa stressed that learning had two linked effects. It could produce individual prosperity and happiness and it could also make for an increase in general trade and thus bring about what Caroline Fox had called 'the civilising effects of commerce'. Religious tolerance was what Louisa wanted most of all. One poem that she wrote ended, 'no disrespectful word touching religion shall be spoke by Protestants to Catholics or from Catholics to Protestants.'

Castletown, contrary to Sarah's gloomy prognostications, was still a busy place, just as full of people as it had ever been. But now less was consumed inside the house and more distributed to those beyond the gates. Instead of decorating indoors or building gazebos and temples for herself, Louisa constructed workshops and built a giant press for extracting oil from beech nuts, almonds and walnuts. When hard times hit during and after the Napoleonic wars she employed as many labourers as she could. Not everyone was interested in joining in her schemes for greater industry and prosperity. She berated Celbridge's labouring women for their 'idleness' because, she said, they did not want to weave or spin to earn cash. But many of Celbridge's inhabitants felt gratitude and even love for Louisa as they watched Castletown become, year by year, less of a centre for sport and entertainment and more of a monument to philanthropy.

Louisa's schools were her main occupation late in life. But they did not stop her travelling. She was in England in 1806, arriving too late for Charles Fox's death, but just in time to be there when the Duke of Richmond died at Goodwood at the end of the year. Sarah thereafter claimed most of her attention when she came to England.

Sarah's increasing blindness made day-to-day life difficult and dull. She relied more and more on Louisa Napier and visitors to entertain her. But she endured her blindness stoically and described it almost as if it afflicted someone else. 'Phipps tells me of a most charming cataract, which he is to rid me of when I am quite blind, so I wait with patience and no confidence,' she told Susan in March 1807. She had already lost the sight of her right eye and with the left could only see in one blurred circle. She could write, word by word, but she could not read and needed a constant companion. In 1810 an oculist performed a gruelling and painful operation on the defunct right eye, working on the principle that organs responded sympathetically and that he might thus induce the left eye to work. The operation was a failure. Sarah insisted that her lack of sight was providential because it meant that she could not see the sufferings of her younger daughters, both of whom developed consumption. Cecilia Napier died in 1808 and Caroline in 1810. 'Time and death rob me each day of the use I might put my eyes to and lessen their loss,' Sarah said.

Sarah did not mind being read to, but she hated not being able to write. In 1808 Louisa devised a writing-table for her which was made, Emily told Lucy Fitzgerald, 'very ingeniously and cleverly from Louisa's directions and plans' by a local carpenter. 'By means of springs, grooves etc she can write; a scrawl as you may guess, but perfectly legible. And this is a very great pleasure to her and employs her hours. She hates it seems to dictate and it used to worry her and make her nervous. Now she writes all herself in her scrawly way and Caroline copies it afterwards into a fair hand.' Soon special paper was added to the machine and Sarah's letters were sent as they were written, the large words constrained to regularity by being written between pieces of wood which were moved, line by line, down the page. 'By a most delightful invention of your aunt' and Richard's I am enabled to write this with my own hand upon carbonic paper, invented by Wedg-wood for taking copies,' Sarah explained to William Napier.

After her sons left for the Continent in 1808, Richard Napier, who was the only one not in the armed forces, made Sarah a relief map of the Peninsula. Spain and Portugal were described by raised pieces of cardboard and, Emily said, 'he has contrived by little pebbles to mark out the different places by feeling, very cleverly; the rivers by bits of twist. In short I find I can't describe it well but the result is that she feels out any place she wants to find in a minute and diverts herself for hours with it.' Emily was amazed at Sarah's dedication to the ideals of militarism. 'She is full of military ideas and Glory is what she principally looks for in her sons.' In 1809 Emily noted that Sarah 'is all anxiety for news from Spain, hopes the English army will not retreat and dreadful as it may appear to look to, she actually wishes a battle.' The Peninsula campaign was a victory for the Napier cult of disinterested service and for the rarefied, literary militarism with which Sarah had inculcated her sons. George Napier lost an arm in the Battle of Cuidad Rodrigo; William Napier was badly wounded when a bullet lodged near his spine; both these injuries were worn with pride as evidence of their bravery. The laurels went to Charles James Napier, who was captured by the French at Corunna and presumed dead for three months. Sending word to his mother to tell her he was alive he quoted, 'Hudibras, you lie. For I have been in battle slain/And yet I live to fight again.'

Sarah sunned herself unashamedly in the warm rays of her sons' glory. She received letters of praise on their behalf from Wellington and they themselves seconded his approbation. 'Such as your children are,' Charles Napier told her, 'they are *your* work.' Soon she began to be credited with unusual wisdom, like the blind seers of legend. She became an early example of the revered widow, a type that Queen Victoria would turn into a cult. It helped, of course, that her sons, William Napier in particular, were thought to be almost inhumanly handsome, figures of Mars personified. The novelist

Amelia Opie said of William Napier, 'I never saw a handsomer man! I could not help looking at him. He is very black, with black moustachios.'

As something of a type, representative of suffering but glorious widowhood, Sarah was a repository for others' imaginings. But she was never a cipher. She retained both her acuity and her Foxite beliefs. But from about 1808 onwards, Sarah's commentary on the Crown became progressively less acerbic: a diffuse patriotism and an increasingly sentimental loyalty to the royal family were added to her social and political shrewdness. She began to think of George III as a figurehead rather than a fool and ruminating on the King's possible death in 1809 she wrote that 'the decease of a good old King who certainly is altogether beloved by his subjects will leave a deep impression of sorrow.' Susan O'Brien, visiting Sarah in 1817, noted with surprise that her earlier hostility both to the monarch and the Crown had dwindled. Sarah was moving with the times, sharing in a general softening of attitudes towards the monarch and the monarchy and in a national mood of greater insularity and more strident militarism.

Emily was bewildered by Sarah's dedication to the abstractions of military life and astonished at her declaration that she could not 'be a mother when glory was in question'. But Emily had not changed with the times. She remained true to the way of life and patterns of thought which she had established in the 1760s. She was still a believer in reason, a disciple of Rousseau and Voltaire, cosmopolitan, hostile to a vaguely defined militarism and Francophile to the core. She never, in her voluminous correspondence, praised the Hanoverian monarchy and she looked on the war as a horror which prevented her going to France. Age did not change her. She lost none of her extravagance or any of her faculties. In the summer of 1809, when she was seventy-seven, Emily sat for her portrait to Sir Martin Archer Shee. She sat firmly upright and gazed away from the viewer, much as she had done when she sat to Reynolds half a century before. The vulnerability of that earlier portrait had gone. In the place of the beautiful countess sat an old woman with a cap of black lace, determined and somewhat distant. 'It will not be what you were at 20 or 40,' Ogilvie wrote, 'but it will be the most beautiful woman of your age in the kingdom.'

Ogilvie nurtured their love through the winter of Emily's old age, coaxing it gently as if they were still young and she would never die. He still sent her love letters when he went away; in August 1812 he wrote from Dublin, 'I last night after dinner received your letter of the 6th written as beautifully and with as steady a hand as the first letter I had the happiness of receiving from you about forty five years ago. How can I ever be sufficiently thankful to Providence for continuing the blessing of my life to me, and with a degree of health and strength that enable you to bear up against the infirmities of old age and to enjoy the different objects that attach you to life, or how can I ever be sufficiently grateful to you dearest Emily for the steadiness and warmth of your attachment to me. Be assured, my beloved Emily that I am thoroughly sensible of and properly grateful for the one and the other . . . I can truly assure you that from the first moment of our attachment to this instant you have been the first and reigning object of my thought and feeling and that you will continue to be so till the last hour of my life and that no other object has ever engaged my affections or interfered with my attachment to you.'

Ogilvie, at seventy, still acted like a young man, planning, investing, travelling and building. He assumed that Emily could maintain her youthfulness too. For a long time she did. In 1811 Sarah described her as 'in wonderful health for 80'. She still dined out, visited her children and went to nursery garden for plants ('to the detriment of my pocket'). Her grandson 'little Eddy' who had lived with her since Lord Edward Fitzgerald's death, absorbed much of her attention when he arrived home from Eton in the holidays. Emily watched her grandchildren's political development carefully. While Fox was alive she had taken 'little Eddy' on ritual visits to St Anne's Hill. After Fox's death, when his mantle passed to the third Lord Holland, Emily looked to Holland House for guidance. In 1808 she asked Lord Holland for help in sending the young Duke of Leinster, just out of Eton, some suitable Foxite reading. 'You would I trust, help to form, steady and fix his principles in the political way particularly; you can't imagine how much I have this at heart!'

Gradually time took its toll. In 1813 Emily suddenly grew old. 'Little Eddy' embarked for the Peninsula in February and his departure left her low and 'not well'. She revived in the summer. Ogilvie thought her well enough for him to go to Ireland for several weeks, from where he sent a last, loving note on 16 July. It ended, 'God bless you, I am your most tenderly affectionate husband WO.' But from then on, Emily's 'constitution of iron', as she called it, steadily failed. In the spring of 1814 she had a bout of pneumonia, from which she seemed to recover. 'Thank God the attack is over,' wrote her daughter Cecilia. 'She has thrown off an illness which would have killed anyone but herself. When I came yesterday they thought she had not two hours to live, but today she is well. Pulse calm, head quiet, heat gone.' But Emily's invincibility was only imagined by a family which she had dominated majestically for so long. In the third week of March illness returned, and on the 27 March she died. She was eighty-two years old, a woman who had had two husbands, twenty-two children and many secrets.

Emily's death made Louisa feel she was next in line. 'At 70 one has a right to expect that death may carry one off any day,' she told Sarah, as if she looked forward to the event. None the less Louisa was still active and well. In the spring of 1814, immediately after Emily's funeral, she set off with Emily Napier on a trip to Holland and Brussels. 'Here I am at the age of 70 able to please all the young people about me, and could do more, if prudence did not stop me,' she said. The party toured museums and manufactures, and hobnobbed with the English diplomatic corps and the Dutch royal family. Louisa visited charitable institutions to garner hints for her Castletown projects. On the way back to Ireland they visited Napiers, assorted Fitzgeralds scattered up the course of the Thames and the new generation of Lennoxes installed at Goodwood. The year 1815 was spent at Castletown, but in the following year Louisa and Emily Napier joined Sarah at Brighton, and in 1817 Louisa went back to Brussels.

Sarah was much less mobile than her sister, although her conversation, Susan O'Brien noted in 1817, was 'just as free and wide ranging as it had ever been'. Sarah was 'altered in appearance' Susan wrote, 'but not in intellect or in her usual style of conversation. She is happy in her family's attention and affection.' Sarah was contented, as far as her blindness and dependence on others would allow. After the peace of 1815 she paid visits to her sons in turn, accompanied by Louisa Napier. Sarah's days, when she was at home in Cadogan Place, followed an unvarying pattern. After a family breakfast she went to her own room, where she received visitors and wrote letters. At about five o'clock she dined and then sat in the drawing-room, the sightless cynosure of all eyes. Adored by her sons and attended by Louisa and her daughters-in-law, Sarah sat, like a rock in the sea, blind and immobile but determining what happened in the space around her. She had a happy old age, although Louisa Napier, visitors noticed, seemed bitter and often angry, particularly as Sarah, like the old actress that she was, always stole the limelight.

In 1818 the darkness before Sarah's eyes began to spread slowly over her mind. When Louisa arrived in London that year she was shocked at her sister's deterioration. 'She is very weak and her appetite is bad. Her mind appears to be quite composed and at times she converses as usual. But her general state is that of sleepiness over her faculties and she does not say that she suffers.' Sarah drifted in and out of contact with the world, sometimes chatting with animation, sometimes nodding into purgatorial sleep. More and more she sat and allowed others to do things for her. She made the long journey to Castletown in 1819 and stayed for several months. Although she seemed happy there with Louisa, Emily Napier reported that her mother was difficult and demanding.

Abandoning first sight and then memory, Sarah's body seemed to be taking her, faculty by faculty, out of life. But in the end it was Louisa who fell ill first. In 1821 she succumbed to a painful wasting disease, diagnosed by her doctors as an abscess of the hip. Louisa expected death. For two months, in the spring of 1821, she settled her affairs and tried to prepare Emily Napier for life without her. She ordered a tent to be erected on the Castletown lawn in front of the house and she often sat in it, gazing not into the empyrean where her dead husband awaited her, but at a worldly creation, the house she had cherished with fierce obsessiveness for sixty-five years. Louisa made no secret of her approaching death and she parted from her worldly interests in turn, bidding farewell to her house, with its cottages, woods and lake; to the Liffey that tumbled over the rocks she had put on its bottom in a half-hearted attempt at the picturesque; to her family of servants; to the masters and pupils in her school; to the inhabitants of Celbridge and to her beloved Emily Napier.

Louisa looked forward to heaven. A few weeks before her death she said to Emily Napier, 'the idea of those that I shall meet again, my dear brothers and sisters, my beloved husband, Oh how impatient I feel when I think the time is drawing near when we are to meet again.' Before that reunion, she thought (as many theologians and believers did) that there would be a period of chastisement when she could right all her wrongs, and when her guilts, especially about her wealth and her conduct during the rebellion, would be washed away for ever. She would, she said, 'be happy to be allowed to make expiation for all the faults I have committed before I am allowed to partake of the fullness of eternal happiness, and I like to think that all the poor people whom I might have assisted, and that in my prosperity I neglected, will be witness to the justice of the punishment I receive and will forgive me.'

After a long and debilitating attack of pain and fever, Louisa's doctor, Crampton, told her she would soon die. She calmly sent for the minister who was to conduct her funeral and told him that she wanted her coffin to be placed alongside Thomas Conolly's in the family vault. She asked that her workers and servants attend her burial. Then she made her will and waited for the end. A few days later she died in Emily Napier's arms.

After Louisa's death, a delegation from Celbridge asked George Napier if the inhabitants of the town could see her body before it was put into the coffin. George Napier agreed, and made arrangements for local people to go up and see her body as it lay, dressed and prepared for burial, in her bed-chamber. He watched from a recess as people filed past the body and years later, when the Victorian cult of death had given him prose suitable to the emotional intensity of the occasion, he recorded their reactions in his memoirs. One white-haired old man fell to his knees beside Louisa's bed, kissed her cold hand and sobbed out, 'Oh my dear, sweet lady, my long tried, my only friend, why have you left this poor creature to die alone? You who used to come to his bed-side when he was sick, and cheer him up with your good word, and give him the drop of soup and the bit of meat, and tell him to have comfort, and now you've gone before me after all. But I'll not stay long, I'll follow you, for you'll clear the way for a poor sinner like myself and God will receive me from you.' Then he crossed himself, laid her hand gently down and, his face streaming with tears, tottered out of the room. A younger man knelt by the bed, kissed Louisa's hand and exclaimed, 'Protestant, Catholic, what is it but a name? But look at her, look at the tears of the poor, the old, the young, the infirm, the helpless and tell me ye priests, if these are not her passports to heaven? No, no, if the soul of our sweet Lady Louisa, the poor man's friend and comforter is not gone to heaven, then there is no God, no mercy for the human race. Protestant, Catholic, what is it but a name?' A few weeks later the Roman Catholic men of Celbridge sent Emily and George Napier an address, signed by 17 men on behalf of the whole parish. It contained a paean to Louisa's religious tolerance and worldly liberality. 'In her,' it said, 'the poor have lost a comforter and protector, the middle class a patroness and adviser and the higher orders an amiable lady and inestimable friend.'

As soon as the sun rose on the morning of Louisa's funeral people began to collect in the park in front of the house. By the time everything was ready, hundreds (George Napier said thousands) were assembled; people from all over the county and beyond. They waited in front of the wide steps to Castletown's front door and watched as the coffin came out, carried by Louisa's labourers. When the coffin appeared everyone in the crowd took their hats off and knelt down. An eerie silence settled over the scene.

The funeral procession formed. The coffin was carried high up by Louisa's workmen, surrounded by mourners from all the local gentry families, led by the Duke of Leinster. On the word for the procession to move forward, the crowd rose from its knees and silently closed round the coffin. With the uncanny quiet punctuated by wails from the women, the crowd moved off to the church Louisa had built by the Celbridge gate. While the minister read the funeral service the Catholics waited, hats off, outside the church. After the service the bearers lifted the coffin up again and carried it down the length of Celbridge main street to the family vault in the old Protestant church. There Louisa's mortal remains were lowered slowly down beside her husband's bone-filled coffin. A way had to be cleared in the crowd for Emily Napier to reach the entrance to the vault. The sea of people parted and she walked in, threw herself on Louisa's coffin and sobbed. 'After some time,' George Napier recorded, 'I gently took her away and ascending the stairs she again passed through the people, who had not moved, but waited her return, and as she moved along leaning on my arm, her heart almost ready to burst with convulsive sobs, they tried to soothe and cheer her with every endearing expression of affection and love and gratitude, calling on her to remain with them and not leave Castletown.'

Emily and George stayed three months. They transferred the Schools of Industry to a board of trustees, handed over Castletown to Thomas Pakenham and then left for England. Emily probably carried out Louisa's instructions about her private papers, burning them all. Then she had to decide about her own future. Emily had never felt close to Sarah. She nursed a bitterness about her mother's guiltless handing over of her to Louisa, despite the fact that she loved her aunt with an intensity that bordered on worship. She did not want to live by herself. So she set up home with George Napier and looked after his house and children. A decade after Louisa's death, Emily Napier married, becoming Mrs Henry Bunbury, a proud and successful mistress of Barton House.

Sarah had mind enough to know that Louisa was dead and feeling enough to mourn. Soon afterwards she began to fade. A friend noted that 'since Lady Louisa's death Lady Sarah has had no enjoyment in life.' Her memory flickered intermittently, then gave out, leaving her mind and body immobile. Susan O'Brien went to visit Sarah in London in 1825 and came away horrified. Sarah was blind and mumbling. The memory that had sustained a friendship of 65 years was gone. Susan talked, and conjured up their past together. But Sarah had no recollections now. The disaster of her first marriage and the triumph of her second were equally laid waste in the empty places in her mind. She had forgotten the King's proposal just as surely as she had forgotten the birth of her son Charles James Napier and her anxiety that, if she stopped looking at him, he would stop breathing. 'I went to see my poor decayed friend S.N.,' Susan wrote in her diary, 'and a greater decay of nature cannot be! Alas what a lesson!' But Sarah offered no lessons; her sightless eyes and vacant head had become only the subjects for others' imaginings. She had only to sit life out; and sit and wait she did until she died a year later in October 1826.

Epilogue

When all the Lennoxes were dead, Ogilvie remained, the last survivor of his generation. He was still a man interested in conquest, determined to tame what seemed beyond his control. He was seventy-four when he became a widower, eighty-six when Sarah died. He called himself a recluse, someone no longer interested in human hearts. Instead he turned to the elements. As befitted a man from the margins who had reached the firm ground of financial probity and polite society, he concerned himself with barriers and boundaries, in particular with harbours and shore lines. For years he studied sea defences and harbour building and dreamed up ways to make safe places away from the destructive sea. Sea walls, secure anchorages and life-boats became his obsessions.

Ogilvie lived at Ardglass on the dark north-eastern shores of Ireland, a hundred miles from Dublin, alone in his castle with a small family of servants and a head full of schemes to tame the sea. He was still a man of enormous vitality, who seemed to defy nature (and 'throw off the years' as Louisa had put it) by becoming more youthful as he aged. Only a few wisps of hair remained on his wind-browned head, but he was as wiry as ever. The forbidding manner was still there too, reinforced by austere dress and months of solitude. As he strode along the shore he seemed to be pulled along as much by his own preternatural energy as by the wind that tugged at his black hat and thick frock-coat. To one side of him the sea crashed in and withdrew; to the other sheep with cunning eyes nibbled the spongy grass. Between them Ogilvie walked with undeviating purpose, a man who had always made other men afraid.

Ardglass Castle had come from Lord Charles Fitzgerald, Ogilvie's first pupil at Black Rock. Lord Charles had been estranged from the family since he voted for the Act of Union and accepted a government post. When he died in 1810, Ogilvie had paid off his creditors and taken over the estate. The humble teacher who had turned stepfather now became inheritor.

Ogilvie was no longer interested in estate management. He wanted to be a master of the water not the earth. After he took on the estate he turned his attention to the harbour at Ardglass, designing and building a long retaining wall out into the sea. This pier, as he called it, was a massive structure over half a mile long and fifty feet in height. It made Ardglass harbour into a safe haven where wandering ships and navy patrols could find shelter from the murderous waters of the Irish Sea. The sea roared against the pier's walls in storms, black and frothing grey at the surface. Within the pier's protective arm was the harbour, where battered vessels rested.

Ardglass pier was a structure of the mind as well as a massive physical presence. The maniacal fervour that Ogilvie put into its building belonged to the new, Victorian, age. Curling 3,000 feet out into the sea, and rising many feet above it, the pier was eloquent of the desire for domination and control. Ogilvie, and many who came after him, no longer saw the sea as something sublime and terrible, beyond man's mastery. It had become an unconquered place, an element that impeded trade, separated man from man and offered resistance to those who sought to control it. So it must be surveyed, mapped, civilised and brought into harbour. As stone after stone was lowered to the seabed beyond Ardglass, it was not just a retaining wall that was being constructed, it was a way of see-ing the world. Yet the sea was resistant, chafing at the restraint, fighting back and remaining, for all man's best efforts, dangerous and estranging.

Ardglass was Ogilvie's monument to himself, a confident and even aggressive testimony to his will to succeed in a hos-tile environment, against all the odds, and on his own terms. 'I am sorry that I undertook it at so late a period in my life,' he grumbled. But he went on, and after the harbour was finished he built a life-boat station as well, with a life-boat to save those who could not make it to the harbour's safety.

Like his pier, Ogilvie endured, living almost until the dawn of the new age. He died at the age of ninety-two, five years before Victoria came to the throne, and crossed over to another shore from which no human ingenuity could find re-turn.

Sources and Bibliography

MANUSCRIPT SOURCES

Some of the following archives are extremely large. I have noted only the parts of the archives which have been of use to me.

Bodleian Library
Napier Papers
General Correspondence of George and Sarah Napier: Includes drafts of letters, including letters from Sarah to Charles James Fox and her brother the third Duke of Richmond, and some of their replies. Correspondents include Louisa Conolly (a series from 1814–20, mostly about travelling on the Continent and setting up her school at Castletown) and Lord and Lady Moira. There are a few letters from Emily, Duchess of Leinster, Pamela Fitzgerald and Susan O'Brien. Hon. George Napier's will. Misc. accounts, inventories relating to Sarah's widowhood and old age.

British Library
Add. MS. 30.990
A bundle of miscellaneous letters to Emily, Duchess of Leinster mostly concerning the events of 1798, with a series of letters from Lord Edward Fitzgerald from 1796–7.
Holland House Papers
Correspondence of Lady Susan Fox-Strangways and her parents, 1749–69. Correspondence of Lady Sarah Lennox and Lady Susan Fox-Strangways, 1761–1817. Correspondence of William O'Brien and Lady Susan Fox-Strangways, 1763–1805. Correspondence of Lady

Susan Fox-Strangways and Caroline and Henry Fox, Baroness and First Lord Holland, 1763–66.

General correspondence of William O'Brien, including an autobiographical fragment which confirms that his family was Catholic.

Journal of Lady Susan O'Brien (née Fox-Strangways).

Correspondence of Henry Fox and Lady Caroline Fox, 1744–69.

Correspondence of Henry and Caroline Fox and the second Duke and Duchess of Richmond, 1743–50, including autopsies of the Duke and Duchess of 1750 and 1751 respectively.

Correspondence of the third Duke of Richmond and Henry Fox, 1750–65.

Correspondence of Emily, Countess of Kildare and James, Earl of Kildare, subsequently first Duke and Duchess of Leinster with Henry and Caroline Fox, 1748–66.

Correspondence of Charles James Fox with his parents, 1763–65.

Correspondence of Stephen Fox, second Lord Holland with his parents, 1756–73.

Correspondence of Henry Fox and his brother and sister-in-law, first Lord and Lady Ilchester, 1742–70.

Correspondence of the second Lord Holland and his wife, 1774.

Travel Journals of Lady Caroline Fox, 1763–70.

Account book of Lady Caroline Fox, 1773.

Misc. papers relating to leases and purchases of land by Henry Fox, 1749–67.

Misc. verses in various hands, collected and written by Henry Fox.

Correspondence of Sir William Bunbury and Henry Fox, 1762.

Correspondence of Lady Hervey and Henry Fox, 1750–53.

Correspondence of Alison Cooper to Henry Fox about his illegitimate children by her, 1765.

Correspondence of Emily, Duchess of Leinster and William Ogilvie with the third Lord and Lady Holland, 1798–1808.

General correspondence of Hon. Caroline Fox, including letters from her great-aunts, Emily, Duchess of Leinster, Lady Louisa Conolly and Lady Sarah Napier (née Lennox).

NOTE The letters between Sarah Lennox and Susan Fox-Strangways were almost all published in 1902 as *The Life and Letters of Lady Sarah Lennox*, edited by the Countess of Ilchester and

Lord Stavordale. The edition also included the 'Memoir on the Events Attending the Death of George 3 by Henry Fox, first Lord Holland', and 'Captain Henry Napier's Memoir of Lady Sarah's Early Life', taken from the manuscript version now in the Napier Papers in the Bodleian Library. I have followed this edition in matters of naming (Caroline Fox's notoriously difficult handwriting often allows for several different readings of words and names), punctuation (upon which it rarely follows its largely unpunctuated originals) and so on.

The Holland House archive is vast. The logic of its assembly seems to have been dictated by an urge to document the life of Charles James Fox. Because of this almost every letter of any political significance has survived. So have letters between Charles James Fox's relatives (the often 'trivial' correspondence between his parents, for instance) that his survivors thought might have some bearing upon his life. But, by the same token, much has disappeared. Although we know from internal evidence that she wrote at least once a fortnight to her sister, the only letters from Emily to

Caroline that survive are those sent jointly with her husband or those addressed to Henry Fox. Similarly, there are no letters from Louisa or Sarah to Caroline. Letters from the Lennox sisters do crop up in some numbers addressed to later Holland generations – the third Lord Holland and Caroline Fox, in particular.

Napier Papers
General correspondence of George and Lady Sarah Napier, mainly drafts of letters to Lord and Lady Moira, Lady Ailesbury and General Conway.
Correspondence between George and Lady Sarah Napier and their son Charles James Napier, 1801–1809.
Accounts relating to the sale of the Napiers' house in Celbridge, Co. Kildare.
Correspondence between George and Charles James Napier, mostly after 1826.
Correspondence between Emily Napier and Charles James Napier, mostly after 1821.
Journal of Hon. George Napier, 1779.

Greater London Record Office
Records of the Consistory Court of the Bishops of London, 1769.

Irish Georgian Society

Correspondence between Lady Louisa Conolly and Lady Sarah Lennox, 1759–1820.

NOTE These letters are the originals from which the Bunbury Letter Books in the West Suffolk Record Office were copied. Besides the main correspondence, they include many letters from Louisa Conolly to her brother the third Duke of Richmond, letters from Louisa Conolly to Emily Napier and miscellaneous papers written by members of the Napier family about Louisa Conolly's death. Absent from the collection is any material relating to the events of 1798. This was extracted by the original buyer from the Bunbury family, Mr McPeake, before he gave the collection to Hubert Butler, who passed it to the Irish Georgian Society. These Irish Georgian Society Manuscripts have now gone missing. But by good fortune they were meticulously copied by Mrs Eleanor Burgess in the 1960s and she generously allowed me to use them.

National Library of Ireland

Leinster Papers
Correspondence of Emily, first Duchess of Leinster, consisting of:

Letters between Emily, Duchess of Leinster and James, Duke of Leinster, 1759–62.

Letters between Emily, Duchess of Leinster and William Ogilvie, 1771–1813.

Letters from Lady Caroline Fox to Emily, Duchess of Leinster, 1756–74.

Letters from Lady Sarah Lennox to Emily, Duchess of Leinster, 1759–94.

Letters from Lady Cecilia Lennox to Emily, Duchess of Leinster, 1769.

Letters from Lord Edward Fitzgerald to Emily, Duchess of Leinster, 1771–92.

Letters from William, Lord Offaly to his mother Emily, Duchess of Leinster, 1765–94.

Letters from other Fitzgerald children, Charles, Henry, Robert, Charlotte, Sophia and Lucy to their mother Emily, Duchess of Leinster, 1768–94.

General correspondence of Emily, Duchess of Leinster, including letters from the Countess of Kildare, Lady Barrymore and Lady Clanbrassil.

NOTE This collection of 1,770 letters contains few letters sent after 1794, with the exception of the correspondence between Emily and William Ogilvie. Apart from letters sent by

Emily to her husbands it consists entirely of correspondence received.

A carefully selected part of the collection was edited by Brian Fitzgerald and published as *Correspondence of Emily, Duchess of Leinster*, as follows:

Vol. 1, 1949: Letters of Emily, Duchess of Leinster; James, First Duke of Leinster; Caroline Fox, Lady Holland.

Vol. 2, 1953: Letters of Lord Edward Fitzgerald and Lady Sarah Napier (née Lennox).

Vol. 3, 1957: Letters of Lady Louisa Conolly and William, Marquis of Kildare (second Duke of Leinster). NB. This later volume contains no letters written by William after 1769 and thus no reference to Emily's second marriage.

Public Record Office of Northern Ireland

de Ros Papers

Uncatalogued letters from the de Ros family papers, mainly letters which came into the archive via Lord Henry Fitzgerald, who married Charlotte de Ros in 1791, all dated post-1789.

Downshire Papers

Bundle of letters from William Ogilvie to Lord Downshire, 1815–25.

Leinster Papers

Letters of William, Lord Offaly to Emily, Duchess of Leinster, 1756–60s.

General correspondence of William, second Duke of Leinster.

Letters and papers relating to the affairs of 1798.

Correspondence and papers of the third Duke of Leinster.

McPeake Papers

Photocopies of material mostly relating to the events of 1798 but covering the years 1783–1815. Includes the selections from the papers now in the possession of the Irish Georgian Society.

Terling, Essex

Strutt Papers

Bundle of letters from James, first Duke of Leinster to Emily, Duchess of Leinster, 1766.

Letters from Emily, Duchess of Leinster to her daughter, Lady Lucy Foley (née Fitzgerald), 1791–1810.

General correspondence of Lady Lucy Foley, including letters from her Fitzgerald siblings, William Ogilvie and Lady Louisa Conolly.

General correspondence between Lady Lucy Foley and members of the Strutt family.

Letters from Emily, Duchess of Leinster to her daughter Lady Charlotte Strutt (née Fitzgerald), 1793–1804.

Trinity College Dublin
Conolly Papers
Castletown Accounts, which include:
Tradesmen's receipt books, 1777–1806.
Servants' wages receipts, 1763–70, 1785–96.
Land agents' account books of lands in counties Dublin and Kildare.
Prices of groceries, 1782–5, 1790–95.
Memoranda of the consumption of different foods tabulated, 1783–87.
Monthly and quarterly accounts of house bills, servants' bills, tradesmen's bills, 1758–78.
Servants and household accounts, 1791–1803.
Expenses of hounds in food and wages, 1787–88.
Castletown expenses and tradesmen's bills, 1792–97.
Personal account books of Thomas Conolly, 1766, 1767–70, 1775–84.
Accounts of the servants, windows and hearths at Castletown for tax purposes.
Dairy accounts, 1798–99.
Alphabetical list of the library at Castletown, c.1780.

West Suffolk Record Office
Bunbury Papers
Bunbury letter books: 36 volumes, in copy books, of letters from Lady Louisa Conolly to Lady Sarah Lennox, 1761–1821, together with misc. other papers relating to Louisa's life, all in the hands of Emily Bunbury (née Napier).
Catalogue of the library at Holland House, 1775.
Inventory of Furniture and Effects at Holland House, 1775.
Papers of Sir Charles Bunbury, relating to the affairs of Henry Fox, first Lord Holland at his death, including 1771 rent book for Holland House, letter book with details of money owed to Fox as Paymaster of the Forces, other papers related to Fox's tenure at the Pay Office.

West Sussex Record Office
Goodwood Papers
Correspondence of the second Duke of Richmond and his wife, mainly from the late 1730s.
Letters from the Earl of Kildare about his marriage to Lady Emily Lennox, 1746–7.
Letters from Emily, Countess of Kildare, to her parents, 1748–50.

BIBLIOGRAPHY

Chapter One
Prologue and Part One
Ruth K. McClure's *Coram's Children. The London Foundling Hospital in the Eighteenth Century*, 1981, gives details (taken from the charity's minute books) of the opening of the Foundling Hospital. Phillis Cunnington and Catherine Lewis, *Charity Costumes*, 1978, the same authors' *Costumes for Births, Marriages and Deaths*, 1972, and Anne Buck, *Dress in Eighteenth-Century England*, 1979, provide information on the clothes of foundling children, and details of the century's costumes and fashions: I have used them throughout the book. *Images of London. Views by Travellers and Emigrés 1550–1920*, describes the second Duke of Richmond's commission from Canaletto of the two views from Richmond House. Ronald Paulson, *Hogarth: his Life, Art and Times*, 1971, also contains information about the Foundling Hospital as well as a description and analysis of 'The Indian Emperor', his painting of amateur theatricals which shows Caroline Lennox, aged nine, on the stage, her parents in the audience and a bust of Newton surveying the proceedings. The Earl of March, *A Duke and His Friends. The Life and Letters of the Second Duke of Richmond*, 1911, contains information about the career of the second Duke of Richmond, together with excerpts from his letters. Robert Halsband's, *Lord Hervey, an Eighteenth Century Courtier*, 1973, tells the story of Hervey's friendship with Stephen and Henry Fox, describes the marriage of Stephen Fox to the thirteen-year-old Elizabeth Strangways-Horner and gives details of Hervey's relations with the second Duke of Richmond at the Court of George II. The Earl of Ilchester's *Henry Fox, First Lord Holland, his Family and Relations*, 2 vols., 1920, is a sympathetic account of Fox's political career. Its account of Fox's friendships and its use of the vast Holland House archive cut several corners for me.

Part Two Peter Clark, ed., *The Transformation of English Provincial Towns*, 1984, Sir John Summerson, *Architecture in Britain 1530–1830*, 1953, and R. S. Neale, *Bath 1680–1850: a Social History*, 1981, were all useful in constructing my picture of

Bath. John Brooke's *The House of Commons*, 1968, together with the DNB have been invaluable in tracing the political fortunes of the male figures in my narrative. John B. Owen, *The Eighteenth Century 1714–1815*, 1974, Stanley Ayling, *The Elder Pitt, Earl of Chatham*, 1976, Paul Langford, *A Polite and Commercial People*, 1989, have similarly helped my understanding of the ideological and political underpinnings of the Whig élite in the mid-eighteenth century.

Part Three Four books provided sumptuous accounts of Dublin's architecture and of the building of Irish country houses, Carton and Castletown prominent among them: Desmond Guinness, *Georgian Dublin*, 1979; Dan Cruickshank, *Georgian Buildings in Great Britain and Ireland*, 1985; Maurice Craig, *Architecture of Ireland from the Earliest Times to 1800*, 1982; and Jacqueline O'Brien and Desmond Guinness, *Great Irish Houses and Castles*, 1992. Without the work of Roy Foster, Marianne Elliott and other Irish historians I could have provided no account of the waves of colonisation in Ireland and the heterogeneous society they created. Roy

Foster's *Modern Ireland 1600–1972*, 1988, and J. C. Beckett's, *A Short History of Ireland*, 1952, were both invaluable. A. P. W. Malcolmson described the marriage settlement of Emily Lennox and James, Earl of Kildare and put it into the context of other Anglo-Irish marriages in *The Pursuit of the Heiress. Aristocratic Marriage in Ireland 1750– 1820*, 1982. Brian Fitzgerald's *Emily, Duchess of Leinster 1731–1814. A Study of her Life and Times*, 1949, is an early, impressionistic but loving life of Emily which concentrates on her first marriage and life at Carton. Emily's description of the English landscape she admired has a parallel in contemporary landscape painting which has been admirably explored by John Barrell in *The Dark Side of the Landscape: The Rural Poor in English Paintings 1730–1840*, 1980. The implications of the poses of Reynolds's portraits of Emily and Kildare have been discussed in Michael Fried's classic, *Absorption and Theatricality: Painting and the Beholder in the Age of Diderot*, 1980.

Two books helped me reconstruct Fox's career at the War Office and in Parliament in the late 1740s: A. J. Guy,

Oeconomy and Discipline, Officership and Administration in the British Army 1714–63, 1985, and *The Political Journal of George Bubb Dodington*, ed. John Carswell and C. A. Duelle, 1965. The Earl of Ilchester's *Home of the Hollands 1605–1820*, 1937, Leslie Mitchell's *Holland House*, 1980, and *Holland House*, 1875, by Princess Marie Liechtenstein, all contained useful information about the Foxes' acquisition of and improvements to Holland House. Details of the first Duke of Richmond's fireworks are found in Horace Walpole's correspondence and Christopher Hogwood, *Handel*, 1984.

Chapter Two

Part One For the life and career of the third Duke of Richmond (whose personal papers all appear to have been burned after his death), see Alison Gilbert Olson, *The Radical Duke. Career and Correspondence of Charles Lennox, third Duke of Richmond*, 1961, and M. M. Reese, *Goodwood's Oak. The Life and Times of the third Duke of Richmond, Lennox and Aubigny*, 1987. Hardwicke's Marriage Act is described in J. H. Baker, *An Introduction to English Legal History*, 1979, and changing attitudes to marriage in Lawrence Stone, *The Family, Sex and Marriage in England, 1500–1800*, 1977. The most accessible edition of Madame de Sévigné's letters is edited by Leonard Tancock, 1982. There is an extensive literature about letter writing, which includes Bruce Redford, *The Converse of the Pen. Acts of Intimacy in the Eighteenth Century Familiar Letter*, 1986, Janet Gurkin Altman, *Epistolarity. Approaches to a Form*, 1982, and Elizabeth C. Goldsmith ed., *Writing in the Female Voice. Essays on Epistolary Literature*, 1989.

Part Two Brief histories of the Conolly family are found in Lena Boylan, *The Conollys of Castletown. Bulletin of the Irish Georgian Society*, 1968, and Brian Fitzgerald, *Lady Louisa Conolly 1743–1821. An Anglo-Irish Biography*, 1950.

Part Three Biographies of George III include Stanley Ayling, *George the Third*, 1972, and John Brooke, *King George III*, 1972. Nesta Pain, *George III at Home*, 1975, gives details of the monarch's obsessive domesticity after his marriage and *The Diaries of Colonel the Hon. Robert Fulke Greville*, 1930, describe his madness. The

Correspondence of George III contains his letters to Lord Bute. Sir Lewis Namier's *Crossroads of Power. Essays on Eighteenth Century England*, 1962, discusses the political turmoil in the years after George's accession, as does J. Brewer, 'The Misfortunes of Lord Bute', *Historical Journal*, 1973. The 1662 version of the *Book of Common Prayer* contains the service of matrimony in use when Sarah married Bunbury.

Chapter Three
Part One Alec Clifton-Taylor's *Six English Towns*, 1978, gives a picture of Bury St Edmunds in the eighteenth century. Caroline's furnishings at Holland House are deduced from the inventory of 1775 printed for the sale of that year as *Catalogue of Furniture and Effects in Holland House*, 1775. For the Foxes' patronage of Reynolds and Ramsay, see Nicholas Penny ed., *Reynolds*, 1986, and Alistair Smart, *Ramsay*, 1992. Richard Wendorf discusses Reynolds's portrait of Sarah in *The Elements of Life: Biography and Portrait Painting in Stuart and Georgian England*, 1990, as does Malcolm Warner in 'The Sources and Meanings of

Reynolds's "Lady Sarah Bunbury Sacrificing to the Graces"', *Art Institute of Chicago Museum Studies*, vol. 15. The Foxes' friends are almost all to be found in the DNB and in the four volumes of J. H. Jesse, *Selwyn and his Contemporaries*, 1843–44. Roger Lonsdale's *Eighteenth Century Women Poets*, 1989, prints Mrs Greville's poem on sensibility and a summary of her career. The very different world of blue stockings is described in Sylvia Myers's *The Blue Stocking Circle: Women, Friendship and the Life of the Mind in Eighteenth Century England*, 1990. Early feminist thought is discussed in Katharine Rodgers's *Feminism in the Eighteenth Century*, 1982, while Vivien Jones's anthology of writing about women, *Women in the Eighteenth Century. Constructions of Femininity*, 1990, sets feminism in the context of other writing about women.

Two books helped my understanding of women's salons in Paris in the mid-century, La Duchesse d'Abrantès, *Une Soirée Chez Madame Geoffrin*, 1831, and Janet Aldis, *Madame Geoffrin, her Salon and her Times 1750–1777*, 1905. From a plethora of books on

London, I should mention two, Mary Cathcart Borer's *An Illustrated Guide to London in 1800*, 1988, and W. Roth, *The London Pleasure Gardens of the Eighteenth Century*, 1896. Ronald Paulson discusses the literary use of metaphors of the stage in *Popular and Polite Art in the Age of Hogarth and Fielding*, 1979. Highfill, Bunnin and Langhans's *Biographical Dictionary of the London Stage 1660–1880*, 1987, describes playhouses, productions and actors' careers, including that of William O'Brien.

A good discussion of theories of gambling in France is found in John Dunkley, *Gambling, A Social and Moral Problem in France 1685–1792*, 1985. John Ashton's *The History of Gambling in England*, 1898, describes what games were played where, when and how. Sir George Otto Trevelyan's leisurely and orotund *The Early History of Charles James Fox*, 1880, describes the Fox brothers' gambling and Charles James Fox's conduct in Parliament in the early 1770s, while C. W. and P. Cunnington's *Handbook of English Costume in the Eighteenth Century*, 1972, gives details of his sartorial habits.

Part Two Trevor Lummis and Jan Marsh's *The Woman's Domain. Women and the English Country House*, 1990, discusses women's role in estate management over four hundred years. *The Guide to Castletown House* by Paul Caffrey, and Margaret Ann Keller's *The Long Gallery of Castletown House, Bulletin of the Irish Georgian Society*, 1979, both describe Louisa's work on the Castletown interior. Fiona Hunt, 'The Print Room at Castletown House' (BA Thesis, Trinity College, Dublin), has identified many of the prints in the print-room. The room is also described by Christopher Moore in Fenlon, Figgis and Marshall eds., *New Perspectives; Studies in Art History in Honour of Anne Crookshank*, 1987.

Attitudes to childbirth are discussed in J. S. Lewis, *In the Family Way. Childbirth in the British Aristocracy 1760–1860*, 1988. Wet nursing is described in George D. Sussman, *Selling Mother's Milk. The Wet Nursing Business in France, 1715–1914*, 1982. The *Catalogue of the Library of Holland House*, 1775, lists the different medical textbooks there. Children's education in the round is the subject of John Lawson and Harold Silver, *A Social History of Education in England*, 1973, while the education of aristocratic boys is described in George C. Brauer jr, *The Education of a Gentleman. Theories of Gentlemanly Education in England 1660–1775*, 1959. Rousseau's *Émile or On Education* was published in 1762 while *Eloisa or a Series of Original Letters Collected and Published by J. J. Rousseau* appeared a year earlier. Rousseau's attitudes towards women and his brief sojourn in England are described in Joel Swartz, *The Sexual Politics of Jean-Jacques Rousseau*, 1984, and Sir Gavin de Beer, *Jean-Jacques Rousseau and his World*, 1972, respectively. Changing attitudes towards marriage are discussed in Lawrence Stone *The Family, Sex and Marriage in England, 1500–1800*, 1977 and John R. Gillis, *For Better, For Worse. British Marriages 1600 to the Present*, 1985. The reciprocal relationships between love in life and literature is the subject of Joseph Boone's *Tradition Counter Tradition. Love and the Form of Fiction*, 1987, while John Mullan considers fiction and theories of feeling and sensibility in *Sentiment and Sociability*.

The Language of Feeling in the Eighteenth Century, 1988. **Part Three** Travellers' impressions of Naples and Sir William Hamilton are described in Flora Fraser, *Beloved Emma, The Life of Emma Lady Hamilton*, 1986. The Duc de Lauzun's claims to have been Sarah's lover are made in *Memoirs of the Duc de Lauzun*, trans. C. K. Scott-Moncrieff, 1928.

Chapter Four

Part One *Town and Country Magazine*, April and August 1769, and the *London Chronicle* both carried details of Sarah's elopement. E. R. Curtis deals with the affair in great detail in *Lady Sarah Lennox. An Irrepressible Stuart 1745–1826*, 1947. The testimonies of Bunbury's servants are quoted from the records of the Consistory Court of the Bishops of London Depositions books. Laurence Stone's *Road to Divorce. England 1530–1987*, 1990, describes the relationships between suits for criminal conversation, separations and parliamentary divorce. The *Journal of the House of Lords* prints the evidence against Sarah and the Act granting Bunbury a divorce in the journals for 1776. Lady Mary Coke's

gossip is from *The Letters and Journals of Lady Mary Coke*, 4 vol., 1889–96.
Part Two Mrs Delany's letter about the marriage of Ogilvie and Emily is from Lady Llanover ed., *Autobiography and Correspondence of Mary Granville, Mrs Delany*, 6 vol., 1861–2. Gossip about Ogilvie's antecedents and early career is found twice in *The Farington Diary, by Joseph Farington, R. A.*, ed. James Greig, 1922–28. Charlotte Fitzgerald's diary is quoted in Hon. Charles P. Strutt, *The Strutt Family of Terling 1650–1873*, 1939.

Chapter Five
Part One The White's Hotel dinner and Tom Paine's sojourn in Paris were written up in the following newspapers: *Dublin Evening Post*, 6 Dec 1792, *The Annual Register* for 1792, *London Chronicle*, Dec 1792, *The World*, Dec 1792. For Paine and other English *émigrés* in Paris see Audrey Williamson, *Thomas Paine; his Life, Work and Times*, 1973; Eric Foner, *Tom Paine and Revolutionary America*, 1976; J. G. Alger, *Englishmen in the French Revolution*, 1889.

Amongst the corpus of literature devoted to the

Napier brothers I have made particular use of the following: Stephen Gwynn, *A Brotherhood of Heroes. Being Memorials of Charles, George and William Napier*, 1910; General W. E. Napier ed., *Passages in the Early Military Life of General Sir George T. Napier KCB, written by Himself*, 1884; Lieutenant-General Sir William Napier, KCB, *The Life and Opinions of Sir Charles James Napier*, 4 vol., 1857; H. A. Bruce, MP, *The Life of Sir William Napier*, 2 vol., 1864; C. J. Napier, *An Essay on the Present State of Ireland*, 1839; Rosamund Lawrence, *Charles Napier, Friend and Fighter 1782–1853*, 1952. Priscilla Napier's *The Sword Dance. Lady Sarah Lennox and the Napiers*, 1971, tells Sarah's story as part of the Napier family history.

Charles James Fox's brief period in office is described in John Cannon, *The Fox-North Coalition: Crisis of the Constitution, 1782–4*, 1969. Leslie Mitchell's *Charles James Fox*, 1992, discusses Fox's attitudes to the French Revolution and Republic. Fox's marriage and death are related in I. M. Davis, *The Harlot and the Statesman*, c.1986.
Part Two No account of the Irish Rebellion could be told

without Thomas Pakenham's classic *The Year of Liberty. The Story of the Great Irish Rebellion of 1798*, 1969. Marianne Elliott's *Wolfe Tone, Prophet of Irish Independence*, 1989, and *Partners in Revolution: the United Irishmen and France*, 1982, was similarly indispensable in clearing a way through the Irish underground of the 1790s. David Dickson's *New Foundations: Ireland 1600–1800*, 1987, takes the story up to the point of Union. Anthony Malcolmson brought to my attention an anonymous pamphlet, *Protestant Ascendancy and Catholic Emancipation Reconciled by a Legislative Union*, published by a radical London printer in 1800 and rumoured to be by William Ogilvie. The pamphlet argues that the Union is in the best interests of Catholics because they will only achieve emancipation with the help of radicals at Westminster. There is no reference to the pamphlet in any family correspondence, nothing to confirm or deny that Ogilvie was its author. Its view is consistent with that taken by the Napiers and some English Whigs.

Several lives of Lord Edward Fitzgerald print letters and extracts from diaries that have since been lost. The earliest is Thomas Moore's *The Life and Death of Lord Edward Fitzgerald*, 2 vol., 1831. Moore seems to have been given free access to letters and papers in the hands of Mimi Beauclerk, which are now lost. These seem to have included many letters from Edward to Emily, letters from Emily to Mimi and perhaps to other friends, and a good deal of misc. material. Gerald Campbell's *Edward and Pamela Fitzgerald*, 1904, prints extracts from diaries and letters written by Lucy Fitzgerald that I have been unable to trace.

Part Three *The Marlay Letters, 1718–1820*, 1937, ed. R. Warwick Bond, a selection of correspondence to members of the Charleville family, includes letters from Louisa and Sarah about the deaths of both Napier and Conolly, as well as letters from Sarah about the monarch and her efforts to get a pension. Linda Colley's *Britons: Forging the Nation, 1707–1837*, 1992, points up the increasingly conservative and militaristic views held by many in the two decades after the French Revolution. Finally, Marmontel's *Memoirs* were published in 1805.

Note on the Leinster Papers, National Library of Ireland

At first sight this huge collection looks like a coherent archive, an 'autobiography' of sorts, put together and frequently annotated by Emily as a record of her life. There are gaps, most notably in the years between 1769 and 1774. But these are easily explicable; Emily, like Caroline, could have destroyed all the papers that referred to the Fox–Leinster quarrels of 1769 and with them all reference to Sarah's elopement and the death of the first Duke of Leinster. The collection, with the exception of the series between Emily and William Ogilvie, more or less comes to a halt in 1794, and thus appears to have been separated from what must have been an equally bulky second part, covering the years between 1794 and Emily's death in 1814.

When we consider what is *not* in the collection, however, doubts begin to surface about its shape being determined by either Emily's own 'editing' or by simple loss. We know that the second half of the collection (or at least some of it) survived until the 1830s; Thomas Moore, biographer of Edward Fitzgerald, printed in his biography of 1831 both letters that are now in the NLI and letters from post-1794 that are now lost. Thus neither Emily nor Ogilvie (who left the family papers to his daughter Mimi Beauclerk) separated the parts.

Two other doubts arise. The first is that there are no letters in the archive from any male members of the Fox–Lennox family: Henry Fox, the third Duke of Richmond, Lord George Lennox, and most surprisingly, Charles James Fox. Indeed, there is no specifically 'political' correspondence at all. In their insistence on sisters, husbands and children the Leinster Papers seem the mirror image of the Holland House Papers.

Secondly, 1794 as a cut-off date for the collection could be seen, in the light of the above, to be anything but arbitrary. With the Terror reaching its bloody conclusion in Paris and Foxites like Emily and Lord Edward Fitzgerald who had walked an ideological tightrope between Francophilia and loyalty to the British Crown under great pressure, the family correspondence must have been tense and anxious and can only have become more so as Edward Fitzgerald went underground and the rebellion in Ireland approached.

Taking all this into account, it is possible that the letters post-1794, together with other political material, were removed. A collector interested in politics might have taken out this material and abandoned the rest, discarding all the letters now in the NLI as domestic and trivial. Alternatively a family member may, after 1830, have sifted through the whole collection and produced a new version of Emily's life, eliminating everything politically or morally compromising. At any rate it seems fairly clear that after the deaths of Emily and Ogilvie the collection shrank. Although both hand and motive remain obscure, its shrinkage seems too considered to be simple 'natural wastage'.

Index

THE LENNOX FAMILY

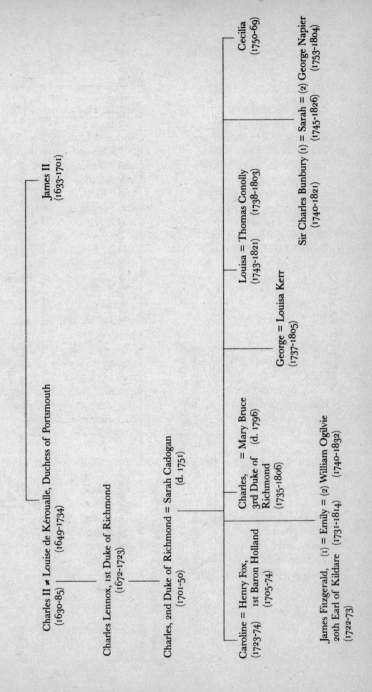

James II
(1633-1701)

Charles II = Louise de Kéroualle, Duchess of Portsmouth
(1630-85) (1649-1734)

Charles Lennox, 1st Duke of Richmond
(1672-1723)

Charles, 2nd Duke of Richmond = Sarah Cadogan
(1701-50) (d. 1751)

Caroline = Henry Fox,
(1723-74) 1st Baron Holland
  (1705-74)

James Fitzgerald, (1) = Emily = (2) William Ogilvie
20th Earl of Kildare (1731-1814) (1740-1832)
(1722-73)

Charles, = Mary Bruce
3rd Duke of (d. 1796)
Richmond
(1735-1806)

George = Louisa Kerr
(1737-1805)

Louisa = Thomas Conolly
(1743-1821) (1738-1803)

Sir Charles Bunbury (1) = Sarah = (2) George Napier
(1740-1821) (1745-1826) (1753-1804)

Cecilia
(1750-69)

THE FOX FAMILY

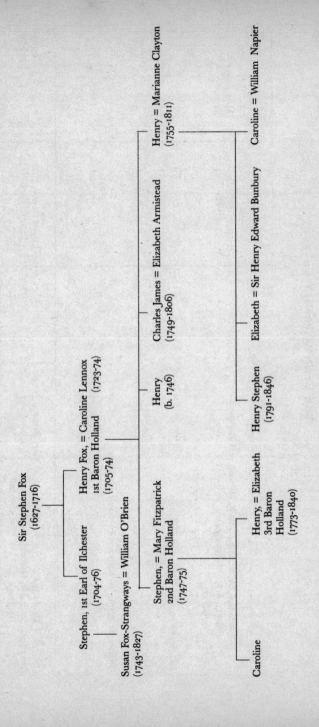

THE FITZGERALD AND OGILVIE FAMILIES

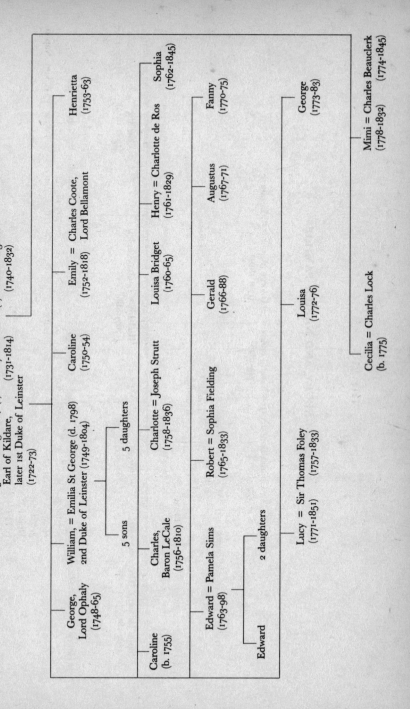

James Fitzgerald, (1) = Emily Lennox = (2) William Ogilvie
Earl of Kildare,   (1731-1814)   (1740-1832)
later 1st Duke of Leinster
(1722-73)

George, Lord Ophaly (1748-65)

William, = Emilia St George (d. 1798)
2nd Duke of Leinster (1749-1804)
5 sons   5 daughters

Caroline (1750-54)

Emily = Charles Coote, Lord Bellamont (1752-1818)

Henrietta (1753-63)

Caroline (b. 1755)

Charles, Baron LeCale (1756-1810)

Charlotte = Joseph Strutt (1758-1836)

Louisa Bridget (1760-65)

Henry = Charlotte de Ros (1761-1829)

Sophia (1762-1845)

Edward = Pamela Sims (1763-98)
Edward   2 daughters

Robert = Sophia Fielding (1765-1833)

Gerald (1766-88)

Augustus (1767-71)

Fanny (1770-75)

Lucy = Sir Thomas Foley (1771-1851)   (1757-1833)

Louisa (1772-76)

George (1773-83)

Cecilia = Charles Lock (b. 1775)

Mimi = Charles Beauclerk (1778-1832)   (1774-1845)

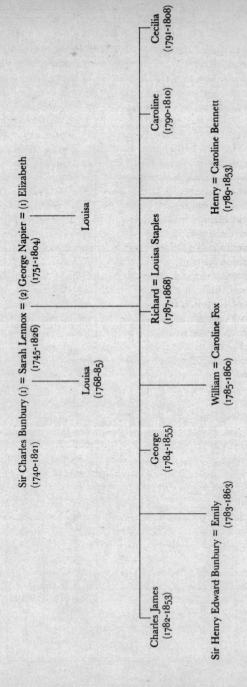

THE BUNBURY AND NAPIER FAMILIES

Sir Charles Bunbury (1) = Sarah Lennox = (2) George Napier = (1) Elizabeth
(1740-1821)   (1745-1826)   (1751-1804)

Louisa
(1768-85)

Louisa

Charles James
(1782-1853)

Sir Henry Edward Bunbury = Emily
(1783-1863)

George
(1784-1855)

William = Caroline Fox
(1785-1860)

Richard = Louisa Staples
(1787-1868)

Henry = Caroline Bennett
(1789-1853)

Caroline
(1790-1810)

Cecilia
(1791-1808)